JUST DESSERTS

"Indispensable. . . . Put this on your Christmas list; it's marvelous reading, fine cookery."
—*Publishers Weekly*

"Dessert should be a joy. This book definitely makes it so. . . . Exceptionally fine and accurate recipes . . . easily prepared."
—*Chicago Sun-Times*

"You'll get a year's worth of different dessert ideas from this book."
—*Philadelphia Daily News*

"If you want to add a classic dessert cookbook to your kitchen library, this is it."
—*The Jersey Journal*

"Foolproof. . . . Good value."
—*Booklist*

Books by Anita Borghese:

The Great Sandwich Book
The Down to Earth Cookbook
The Complete Book of Indonesian Cooking
The International Cookie Jar Cookbook
Foods from Harvest Festivals and Folk Fairs
Just Desserts
The Great Year-Round Turkey Cookbook

JUST DESSERTS

The Complete Dessert Cookbook

Anita Borghese

5B A SCARBOROUGH BOOK
STEIN AND DAY/*Publishers*/New York

FIRST SCARBOROUGH BOOKS EDITION 1979
Just Desserts was originally published in
hardcover by STEIN AND DAY/*Publishers* in 1977

Designed by Leo McRee

Printed in the United States of America
Stein and Day/*Publishers*/Scarborough House,
Briarcliff Manor, N.Y. 10510

Library of Congress Cataloging in Publication Data

Borghese, Anita.
    Just desserts.

    Includes index.
    1. Desserts. I. Title.
TX773.B636   641.8′6   77–8596
ISBN 0–8128–6033–0

To Mary,
dear friend and peerless dessert devotee

Special thanks to Michael Goldstein of
The Art of Wines, Pleasantville, New York.

Contents

CHAPTER 1

Past Delights

There was cakes and apples in all the Chapels,
With fine polonies, and rich mellow pears.
—Reverend Richard Harris Barham, "Barney
Maguire's Account of the Coronation "

Whether or not the famous apple proffered by Eve in the Garden of Eden could be construed as the world's first dessert is a matter for conjecture. But that people have been craving fruits and sweets since the beginning of recorded time seems a certainty.

The ancient Egyptians doted on marzipan made of crushed almonds, gathered lotus blossoms to make into jam, and nibbled on dates, figs, pomegranates, and melons. They had flourishing vineyards and orchards bearing every kind of fruit imaginable. Bakers, highly skilled in their art, turned out myriads of pastries and honey-laden sweetmeats. The backbone of their desserts, honey, was mixed with flour and oil to produce a simple, if heavy, cake. For more exotic bakery specialties, fruits and flavorings of saffron, cinnamon, or ambergris were mixed in. What these early unleavened cakes lacked in texture was made up for in charm when they were baked in the form of birds, animals, and obelisks.

All around the Mediterranean, people from earliest times planted fruit trees and vineyards, among them the Greeks. These dining sophisticates ate their fruits both fresh and dried for dessert, along with almonds, roasted chestnuts, and all kinds of sweetmeats made with the ubiquitous honey. Having insatiable appetites for cheesecake, they made this treat in endless variety and left a wealth of cheesecake recipes behind. Gingerbread had its birth on the island of Rhodes, Athens became famous for its honey biscuits, and cities all over Greece vied with one another for producing the best sesame honey cake, which was baked in all sorts of shapes and with all kinds of flavor variations.

The Romans, who go down in history unmatched in the supersaturation of food served at their banquets, gorged themselves on every conceivable delicacy, many of which they learned about directly from the Greeks. Not only did they borrow the concept of fine dining from their Hellenic neighbors, but also their chefs and bakers, and even the idea of having a special room set aside for the sole purpose of preparing food —the kitchen. While the Romans spared no expense in providing themselves with such exotic entrées as parrots from Africa, venison from Gaul, oysters from Britain, and flamingos from Persia, their desserts were profuse but comparatively simple. They had candied dates stuffed with nuts, honeyed sweetmeats, tarts, cheesecakes, fried bread with honey, fruitcake made with raisins, pomegranate seeds, and pine nuts, and fruits in great variety which they dried, preserved, made into compotes, or ate raw as part or all of a meal. Their food was often served on jewel-encrusted plates set upon tables made of ivory or bronze and draped with gold-embroidered cloths, so it probably went unnoticed that desserts were unpretentious.

With the fall of the Roman Empire, knowledge of the culinary arts nearly disappeared into oblivion, but some recipes were kept and used in the monasteries, the only places where relatively decent cooking was done for hundreds of years to come. So little progress was made in culture in general and cooking in particular that a Latin cookbook written in the first century A.D., presumably by the Roman epicure Marcus Gabius Apicius, was still being used in the abbeys in the fifteenth century. As they safeguarded the Apicius cookbook, so did the monks preserve species of plants, shrubs, and fruit trees by growing them behind monastery walls while the outside world was being ravaged intermittently by plagues, famines, and wars. Without the brothers' interest in agriculture, some of the strains of fruits we take for granted at dessert time today might have vanished forever.

Annual fairs held in European cities during the Dark Ages began to introduce people to fruits and other foods from different areas of Europe and the East. Chestnuts, plums, and Gorgonzola cheese from Italy, apples and Roquefort cheese from France, ginger, lemons, figs, and cultivated strawberries from Spain, could now be had by many. Crusaders returned home from the East with remembrances of sherbets and exotic fruits, and samples of sugarcane, dates, almonds, and spices. Most of these foods eventually found their way into European menus.

While cooking and dining were for the most part characterized by crudeness during the Middle Ages, toward the end of that period lavish feasting emerged among royalty, the aristocracy, and the clergy. Dozens of elaborate and contrived dishes were served on great occasions, and interspersed throughout such meals were "sotelties," or subtleties, symbolic devices made of pastry or sugar formed into various representations, figures, scenes, or happenings. They were usually made to depict mythological persons or events, or an event in the life of the guest of honor, before whom they were set. Sotelties became more elaborate in relation to the importance of the feast at which they were presented, and the subjects ranged from Saint George slaying the dragon to a crowned eagle served at a coronation feast. Sometimes soteltie subjects were more lascivious than subtle.

Entertainment, as well as sotelties, was provided between courses of a meal, and was known as *entremets*. It meant literally "between courses or dishes" and was provided at intermissions throughout the meal to divert the high-spirited guests and keep them from getting into brawls and fistfights during the long hours of feasting. There were musicians, mimes, minstrels, wrestlers, jugglers, sword swallowers, jousters, acrobats, and dancers to keep the company amused.

Desserts were often cakes, junkets, rice with almonds and cinnamon, and figs served in endless forms. The latter, during one fourteenth-century English feast, were combined with raisins to make puddings, fried in pastry, roasted on the spit, served with almonds, and made into fritters. Fine white flour for cakes and pastries was available to those of means, and cheese pies, curd pies, custards, tarts, and fritters took preference over fruits. But for those who chose to have fruit, even rose hips could be had. The Spanish, who had lush orchards of fruits in great variety, carved their freshly picked apples, pears, and oranges round and round with scrolls, loops, and zigzags before bringing them to the table.

As time passed, it became less popular to offer extravagances of entertainment during a dinner, and instead sweets such as pastries, blancmanges, custards, and so forth would be served after a meat course. Then another meat course would be served, followed again by sweets. These sweet courses gradually assumed the name of the former entertainment, *entremets*, and the final course of the meal ended with more sweets and fruit and sometimes cheese.

Dessert as the actual end of a meal didn't exist until fairly recent times. It was during the reign of Louis XIV that the serving of dishes separately, one after the other, began. Shortly before, sweets and fruits had appeared at various times during the meal, and courses had no particular order, were served in helter-skelter fashion, and each person ate whatever he could reach from where he sat. Meals were divided into courses, but each of these courses contained the elements of an entire meal from meats to sweets, and each course landed on the table in its entirety. Spicecakes and pastries were served alongside tongue, baked songbirds, and mustard. Roast goat, almond soup, and rabbits would all be on the table with a custard cream pie, and cabbage soup might well find itself sitting next to the custard, or pickled cucumbers next to apple tarts.

When a sequence of courses finally evolved from this hodgepodge of serving, the last to come to the table was called *entremets,* or "dessert." The word *dessert* itself comes from the French *desservir,* literally "to disserve," or clear the table, since it became the custom to clear the table before the sweet course appeared.

During the Renaissance, sophistication came to dessert and the entire table. In Italy, and particularly in Florence, not only did painting, sculpture, poetry, literature, and architecture flourish, but there was a distinct change in food preparation and eating habits. Cooking became refined, table manners became elegant, the fork was invented, and a blossoming of the decorative arts brought to the table Venetian glassware, porcelain and glazed earthenware, dishes and serving pieces of gold, embroidered cloths, and silver flatware. Catherine de Medici took this Florentine heritage to France when she became betrothed to Prince Henry, and ushered in a new era of cooking and culture in her adopted land. Her retinue of chefs and cooks brought along recipes for sherbets, ices, and ice creams in flavors and colors enough to dazzle a Howard Johnson, almond custard called frangipane, marzipan, dainty cakes with custard fillings and gay, intricate decorations, and zabaglione, among the sweets. These dishes, which gradually became known in other parts of the Continent and in England, were the beginnings of desserts as we know them today.

In time, royalty began to develop a sophisticated interest in foods and the culinary arts, and sometimes donned aprons to experiment in their own kitchens. Many famous dishes, including desserts, were devised by or for regal personages of the day. The first petits fours, for example, were made at Versailles by a pastry chef to amuse Louis XIV and his court during their dalliance in the countryside. Louis, although not considered a gourmet, nevertheless had a lively interest in eating and regularly looked for new treats to arrive from his kitchens. Fine fruits were among his favorite foods, with emphasis on peaches, pears, and oranges, and he had a collection of over a thousand orange trees planted on the grounds of Versailles as well as indoors in silver tubs to create a luxurious *orangerie.*

Madame du Barry on one occasion prepared a dinner for Louis XV that included a dessert of strawberries in cherry liqueur, and on another occasion made a handsome peach cake. She was rewarded for these efforts when Louis presented her with the *cordon bleu.* Madame Pompadour, not to be outdone, had her chef prepare elegant little suppers for the monarch, and let the most outstanding dishes be named after herself.

To the east, King Stanislaus of Poland was busy creating the baba au rhum, and sometime later and farther east, Alexander I nibbled on a Russian cheesecake creation called Paska, and later introduced it to France, where it became coeur à la crème.

Marie Antoinette sometimes brightened the days of her somewhat dull husband, Louis XVI, by assuming the role of milkmaid and churning up some butter for the royal table—in a silver churn, of course—and at other times by making beautifully conceived meringue cakes called vacherins.

In England, Henry VIII was so interested in his gastronomic well-being that he established a cooking school for the benefit of his wives. Anne Boleyn, whether or not she actually made syllabub, left her handwritten recipe for it for posterity. In later years, Queen Victoria had her own version of the drink-dessert, which was slightly richer and depended on beaten egg whites to produce a frothy topping, rather than the earlier version, which called for placing the syllabub bowl under the cow and milking directly into it.

Sponge cake, or Spanish cake, was made in England for the first time when Mary I married Philip II of Spain, and the cake became the inspiration for tipsy pudding, or trifle, when it was soaked with Spanish sherry and layered with custard.

The most historically famous English sweet tooth was owned by Queen Elizabeth I, and under her reign queen and populace must have nearly drowned in a sea of sugar. Sweetmeats of every kind were favored by the queen, with emphasis on meringue kisses, marzipan, which was then called marchpane, candied root of sea holly, called eringo, jams, jellies, marmalades, and preserves, pyramids of pastries, Naples biscuits, tarts, and custards in profusion. The first vanilla to be used in desserts flavored Elizabeth's marzipan, which was sometimes served with other sweets before a meal began, as well as at the end. The queen was known to have carried sweetmeats around in her pockets ready for consumption at any hour of the day, and it probably goes without saying she is reported to have had very bad teeth in her later years.

The English propensity for sweets endured in the person of Queen Victoria, who was often known to cook for Prince Albert in their private apartments at Windsor Castle. Three-quarters of Victoria's recipe collection was devoted to desserts and confections, among them gingerbread, a favorite of her German prince.

Chefs took the limelight and became the leaders of gastronomy after the French Revolution, foremost among them being Antonin Carême. A creator and designer of cuisine and a genuine genius of the kitchen, he was so inspired by pastry that he named confectionery as the main branch of the fine art of architecture. He cooked for Talleyrand, Baron de Rothschild, the Prince Regent of England, Russia's Czar Alexander, and France's King Louis XVIII, among others, and was the founder of classic French cookery. Carême devoted his life to perfecting the subtle preparation of food and writing detailed volumes on the subject complete with meticulously executed drawings of food arrangements, and he is probably best remembered for his dessert masterpieces called *pièces montées*, or "set pieces," some of which he made early in his career for Napoleon's table. Set pieces were formal, involved, intricately designed architectural arrangements of pastry and sugar made according to detailed plans, and were set on the table at the beginning of a dinner. When dessert time arrived, more sweets were arranged around the central structure—which might be in the shape of a classic vase or a windmill—in a well-ordered pattern to produce the most formal and at the same time most spectacular of meal endings.

Carême, like other great chefs of his era, at one time presided over the kitchen of a Parisian restaurant. Restaurants, practically unknown before the Revolution, blossomed in peacetime when an aristociacy no longer existed to hire great cooks. Former chefs to the rich found themselves in the position of going without employment or opening restaurants, and a new era in dining was born. The best and most varied cooking was suddenly available to the general public, and those who had a bit of money in their pockets could dine on the creations of France's most famous chefs.

In bygone days, the traveler or diner had been able to eat at inns, but the food was something less than perfect. No choice of menu was offered, and consuming the food could hardly be considered dining. Now restaurants presented a bill of fare with staggeringly long lists to select from. Beauvilliers, one of the most famous of these early French restaurants, offered no less than 115 sweets, desserts, and pastries.

While France was dining at elegant tables, America was being peopled by hearty settlers whose interest in food was often by necessity restricted to finding enough of it to keep alive. These people brought whatever culinary knowledge they had from Europe and, with little time to spare for fussing over the cooking hearth, and, as often as not, few ingredients to work with, depended on Providence and their wits to produce enough good food to keep up their strength and pioneer spirit. They soon learned from the Indians—and from trial and error—how to adapt the native foods of the New World to the cooking they were familiar with, and from this pioneer experimentation emerged a wealth of dessert and other recipes unique in Indian, English, Dutch, German, Spanish, French, Irish, Scotch, Welsh, Swiss, Swedish, Finnish, and African influence.

The Indians, without whose help the early settlers would have starved, taught the colonists how to grow corn and use it in their cooking. Indian pudding became such a mainstay that it was eaten not only as a dessert but sometimes at the beginning of a meal, with butter and molasses. Hasty pudding came into being and was nothing more than the well-known cornmeal mush served with maple syrup.

The settlers also learned from their native teachers how to sweeten a dish of berries with the dew of milkweed, how to collect the sap from maple trees and convert it into maple syrup or sugar, how to grow pumpkins and cook them or preserve them for making midwinter pies and puddings, how to use flowers, herbs, and roots for flavoring—including marigolds, nasturtiums, geraniums, and wild licorice (which is still used today in making commercial licorice)—how to use leaves and flowers for making teas (a specialty of Indians on the trail who knew better than to drink strange water without boiling it), how to collect rose hips for making jams and jellies, where to gather berries and how to keep them for winter use, how to plant millet to supplement the grain supply, as well as how to make rice, dried potatoes, roots, and nuts into flour for baking, and how to utilize sunflower seeds and oil in cooking and baking.

For their favorite dessert, the colonists made pies from wild berries, pies from cultivated apples, and pies from almost anything that was available. In the North, corn and pumpkin dishes were served with butter and sugared water or molasses, cornmeal mush was sometimes topped with a sweet pumpkin sauce, squashes were candied along with fruits, and sweet potatoes were mixed with molasses and nuts for puddings.

Fruit was particularly abundant in the South, where the growing season was long, and choices for picking ranged from mulberries, introduced by the Indians, to persimmons or melons or cultivated strawberries, raised from transplanted English varieties. Spanish settlers in Florida raised mangoes, figs, guavas, pomegranates, peaches, grapes, lemons, limes, mandarin oranges, and plaintains. Those intent on emulating local Indians could have a kicky dessert by filling hollowed-out oranges with honey and waiting for the mixture to ferment.

As colonial life became less harsh, food choices began to widen. Soon settlers fared well on desserts of cobblers, gingerbread, fruitcake, cheesecake, spicecake, and puddings of all kinds—bread, cranberry, carrot, or beggar's pudding, which was a sort of poor man's trifle made from leftover bread.

The Dutch, who gave the doughnut to the New World, sprinkled chopped nuts and fruit on their puddings and creams, made cookies, marzipan, peppermint drops, and horehound drops, and candied coriander, caraway, almonds, angelica, and lemon peel.

With the establishment of plantations, businesses, and trade in the colonies, dining took on a new sophistication, and there were more desserts and treats to be enjoyed. Rich creams, fools, gelatin-thickened flummery, ice creams, and syllabubs appeared among the dessert selections in manor houses. Some of these desserts might be topped with nuts, syrups, fruit preserves, or candied roses, violets, marigolds, clove pinks, or other flowers. Waffles and cookielike wafers that looked like thin waffles could be made with fine white flour, butter, cream, sugar, eggs, wines, spices, and nuts.

Imports brightened the tables of the affluent—refined sugar, oranges and lemons from Barbados, pineapples from the West Indies, delicacies, wines, and Champagnes from France, Sherry and Madeira from Spain, and confections, marmalades, and raisins from England. Other dessert choices were macaroons, glazed almonds, sugared raisins, prunes, and sweet relishes. Fortunately, these foods eventually found their way to the tables of nearly everyone.

The evolution of desserts in America can best be traced since colonial times through the introduction of refinements in certain ingredients such as vanilla, chocolate, flour, sugar, and baking powder, the invention of kitchen equipment such as the refrigerator, freezer, and electric beater and blender, and the development of food storage and packaging.

Vanilla, the bean of an orchid vine, was Mexico's gift to the world of sweets, and now flavors a vast number of desserts. Before its introduction, there was little in the way of subtle dessert flavoring, with almonds being the most commonly known.

Chocolate, another Mexican contribution, was introduced into Southwestern cooking from over the border, and was combined with milk and eggs for custards and puddings, added to batters to make baked goods, and boiled up to serve as hot chocolate. The first of North America's chocolate factories began operating before the American Revolution and ensured the housewife of a good supply of the necessary ingredient for making the roster of chocolate desserts that have become American favorites.

Highly refined flour, while lacking in the food benefits of whole-grain flours, nevertheless has made it possible for us to make fine-grained, beautiful cakes. Equally responsible for fine light baked goods is the American invention of baking powder. This product has been easily obtainable since 1891, when the leading manufacturer offered a thousand-dollar reward, apparently never claimed, to any competitor whose product could produce better baked goods.

Although sugarcane had been grown in the Caribbean for decades, it was available to the colonial housewife only in hard, compressed loaves that had to be hacked and pounded into powder before being used. It was a boon to dessert makers when Etienne de Bore, a Mississippi plantation owner, discovered how to granulate sugar, and the time-consuming and wearying task of sugar preparation in the home came to an end.

With the demise of the icebox and the invention of refrigeration came the safekeeping of butter, eggs, cheese, milk, cream, and other perishable products used for desserts. Reliable temperature maintenance now keeps charlottes and other molded desserts in shape, protects pastries and doughs during preparation, and prevents spoilage of cooked foods and overripening of fruits. Freezers make it possible for us not only to make ice cream and other frozen desserts with confidence but to store them, as well as pastries, crêpes, cookies, cakes, and other baked goods and desserts, for instant, on-hand use. Electric mixers, beaters, and blenders allow us to beat egg whites and batters with no effort, to turn out finished products as good or better than those made laboriously by hand.

The stove itself has brought one of the greatest advances in making desserts. Baking, which first became easier when ovens replaced primitive hearths, was further improved when wood- or coal-burning stoves took the cook away from the dangers of direct flames so she could concentrate more on what was being prepared than on fire prevention. With the coming of the gas range, top-of-the-stove heat as well as the oven could be reliably regulated for the first time, and custards, soufflés, baked goods, and just about anything else could be made with assurance.

Airtight preservation of food in corked bottles was the invention of a French chef during Napoleonic times, and his idea was perfected by an Englishman who in the early 1800s converted the process to use metal cans for packing and preserving foods. Since that time, canning and packaging processes have been perfected so that it's now possible to buy almost any special ingredient we need for making a dessert no matter where we happen to live.

Sweets have always been as popular eaten outside the home as in it, and have been sold on the streets for centuries. Middle Eastern street vendors in the early centuries A.D. sold sweet cakes and sugarcane for strollers to munch on. In the Middle Ages, those who could afford it carried spices such as cloves and coriander around in their pockets to pop into their mouths and eat like candy. Fifteenth-century London street criers offered the passerby a multitude of goodies that included everything from hot baked pears to Dutch biscuits, lemons, oranges, and the long-time English favorites, ripe cherries and strawberries. Some of these treats were, of course, destined for home consumption, as had been the cakes ancient Greeks once bought at their local bakeries and the candies Romans picked up from their neighborhood candy shops on their way home.

It was common for people to eat fruit in the streets and at all sorts of places of entertainment in the sixteenth and seventeenth centuries, and toward the latter part of that period Parisians frequented cafés at all hours to have ices and sherbets. The urge to stop for between-meal sweets or refreshment began in relatively modern times with the coffee-houses of Turkey. Here one could have as much conversation and thickly brewed, creamy-headed coffee as one wanted. Parisian coffee-houses opened some hundred years after the Turkish ones, and England and other countries followed suit. Vienna's coffeehouses and their fan-tastic pastries became the most famous of all. Chocolate shops sprang up in Spanish settlements in the New World to cater to the sweet tooth of the colonist and his newly found craving for chocolate drinking. Million-dollar ice-cream businesses are supported today by the many Americans unwilling to pass roadside ice-cream havens without stopping for a sample of the wares.

Sometimes desserts and sweets seem to mean different things to dif-ferent people. A sweet, according to American dictionaries, is a food high in sugar content, and to some it means a candy or bonbon. Yet to the British a sweet is not only that but a pudding, custard, or tart served after a dinner. Desserts to them are heavier concoctions, such as cakes, and are reserved for teatime.

A sweetmeat in olden times was a sweet delicacy prepared with sugar or honey, such as preserves, candied fruits, sugared nuts, sugarplums, bonbons, candy sticks, cakes, and pastries.

Dessert to the French is a course served with the cheese. In Italy, dessert at home consists of fruit or cheese, and pastries are bought from professional pastry chefs for special occasions or eaten when dining out. Restaurants in Italy often have a dessert specialty for this reason.

In Greece, a sweet may be served not only at mealtime but at any time throughout the day as mood dictates, and it is often served with brandy, ouzo, or strong Greek coffee. Desserts are so highly favored in India that they're sometimes served at the beginning of a meal. But no matter when dessert may appear at the table throughout the world, history has shown that no one wants to do without it.

CHAPTER 2

Desserts Now

*A man cannot have a pure mind
who refuses apple dumplings.*
—*Charles Lamb*

Probably no other part of a meal is so pleasing as dessert. A course that plays a supporting role on the menu, it delights nearly everyone with its gustatory uniqueness—traditionally the only sweet part of the meal. Since hardly anyone is truly hungry by the time the last course arrives, it must be the most inspired part of dinner, and for that reason can be the most fun to plan and prepare. Ideally, dessert should be able to pique waning appetites, excite the imagination, arouse curiosity, delight the eye, create a stir of surprise or gasp of admiration, and leave a feeling that something special has been shared. The finishing touch to dinner, and therefore the last impression that lingers, dessert should be a joy. To make it so is the goal of this book.

Within the wide range of dishes that make up the dessert family there are marvelous textures, incomparable temperature ranges, rainbows of color, and flavor combinations of endless shading and nuance to choose from. And there is a diversity of mood, feeling, and character among dessert dishes. The many and varied attributes of desserts are a boon in planning memorable meals, since you can use their properties as foils for the textures, flavors, and temperatures of other dishes on the menu, complementing or contrasting with them as you like.

For instance, if you plan to serve smooth-textured foods during the main course, emphasize those textures by serving a contrasting flaky, crumbly type of pastry for dessert. Or let dissimilarity of texture work within the dessert itself sometimes. You might, for example, serve a wedge of satiny-smooth Brie with slices of crisp, crunchy apple. Temperatures can bring interest through variation throughout the meal; it would be pleasing to have a hot chocolate soufflé served after a salad luncheon, or a frozen dessert after a hot soup and entrée. It's also fun to serve a dessert that has both hot and cold elements within itself, such as baked Alaska with its veiling of hot meringue over an ice-cream center.

Consider dessert colors and how they would best set off your dinner—and your dinnerware, for that matter. If a shade of red seems appropriate, you can choose anywhere between the palest pink of a strawberry ice cream dessert and the brightest red of a cherry tart. Or if yellow seems right, that color within dessert choices ranges from the faintest tint in lemon ice to the boldest yellow of a rich egg yolk custard.

In flavors, let tart ones follow the bland, exotic ones follow the easily identified, and so on. Vanilla desserts, for example, are custom-made to serve after spicy meals, while pungent gingerbread is good after, say, a mildly seasoned roasted chicken, and a pomegranate mousse would probably best end a dinner made up of otherwise familiar dishes.

Always try to serve light desserts after heavy meals, and vice versa. Crêpes for lunch followed by cake for dessert would put something of a strain on the stomach, but having a fruit for dessert instead would be very pleasant.

The mood a dessert can create is probably one of its most useful and captivating qualities. You can end a meal on a note of frivolity with a basket of meringues, folksiness with Indian pudding, exotica with Violet Cake, drama with flaming fruits, amusement with Funny Cake, purity with a perfectly ripe peach, and so on, as you see fit. There's a dessert to fit any feeling you want to evoke.

While they may often seem frivolous things, desserts do have a serious role to play in the diet. There are sound nutritional reasons for including them in your menu plans. The wholesome fruits, eggs, cheese, milk, cream, butter, honey, grains, nuts, and cereals which are the essential ingredients of dessert making are laden with the vitamins, minerals, and other food elements everyone needs to maintain a balanced diet. Nearly every dessert should serve a purpose in this direction, balancing the menu by filling in with any missing nutrients. A dessert omelet might be served after a meal scant on proteins, a fruit dessert chosen to supply vitamins that might otherwise be missed, or a rice dessert selected to top off a starchless dinner.

Along with adding to the enjoyment of the entire meal, a little sweetness rightfully belongs in every diet. Use raw sugar or turbinado sugar instead of white sugar for added food value in nearly any recipe. To benefit more from the flour you use, substitute unbleached white flour or whole wheat flour in whole or in part in any recipe where it seems appropriate. Whole-grain flour is particularly nice in recipes where a nutty taste is desirable.

A unique aspect of many desserts, in contrast with any other component of a meal, is its appropriateness and adaptability for serving at any occasion, day or night. For instance, if you baked a Poppy-Seed Horseshoe, you could serve it variously for breakfast, to morning-coffee visitors, for afternoon tea, as a dessert with any meal, or for an after-school or late-evening snack. Any fruit tart could as easily fill the same bill. Consider the versatility of things like strawberries, cheeses, or crêpes for round-the-clock serving.

Most desserts, like other good foods, should be simple, and the recipes in this book have been assembled with that thought in mind. But once in a while, for the sheer fun of it, do have one of the rich or elaborate desserts. They're true spirit lifters, and if you keep in mind that even rich desserts would become monotonous if eaten every day, you can feel free to enjoy them now and then.

With this attitude, once in a while let dessert be the main star of the meal, and perhaps let yourself show off in the bargain. There are several ways of doing this. If you feel like creating a dessert masterpiece that takes time and patience to prepare, build your meal around it, allow it to be a production, and underplay everything else on the menu leading up to the grand dessert. Buffets are a perfect place for making dessert the focal point. Select decorations, linens, china, and colors and flavors of other foods to point up your dessert, and let your guests see at a glance what a spectacular thing you've done for them.

If you want dessert to be impressive without spending the day in the kitchen, and at the same time put yourself onstage, you can choose a flaming dessert. Most can be quickly assembled in the kitchen, brought to the table flaming, and never fail to captivate onlookers.

Some people feel it's a good idea to serve a salad course separately just before dessert on the theory it clears the palate for sweet tastes. This is something you might want to consider when you plan to have a number of courses and your dessert is an extraspecial one.

If you build a small repertoire of desserts that you make well and easily, you can draw on these standbys when you have guests, whether by plan or unexpectedly. A fruit compote is always dependable, and you can use whatever fruits are in season to make shopping easy and economical. Learn to make one of the simple tart pastries so you have the basis for any number of filled tart desserts—another way to take advantage of fruits in season. Try your hand at soufflés, which aren't at all frightening after you get to know them, and can usually be made with ingredients on hand. Crêpes are simple to make, can be kept in your freezer to use on short notice, and can be filled with just about anything you can find in your pantry or refrigerator. Keep cheese-and-fruit combinations in mind for dessert—nearly everyone loves them and they're effortless. Knowing how to make a good custard or pastry cream and a simple but perfect basic cake would round out your repertoire and give you a very solid base to build dessert dreams on.

Please read through the following chapter, "Methods, Ingredients, and the Final Touch," before starting to cook.

And now, girl, bring me the dessert.
—Pierrette Brillat-Savarin

CHAPTER 3

Methods, Ingredients, and the Final Touch

Methods

Please read each recipe all the way through before starting to cook to prevent any surprises in procedure or time requirements that might not be obvious at a casual glance at the recipe. The following are some terms and procedures used in the book.

TO BEAT EGG WHITES. Have eggs at room temperature. Separate eggs, making certain no yolk at all is with the whites. Use a spotlessly clean and dry glass or ceramic bowl and equally clean beater or whisk. If you use a whisk, the best type is a long one with many thin wires. Start beating or whisking slowly until egg whites become foamy, and then beat faster—but steadily and without stopping—until the egg whites are as stiff as required in the recipe.

TO FOLD IN. Combine two or more mixtures or ingredients in a bowl by pushing a rubber spatula straight down through the center of the ingredients, bringing it across the bottom and toward the side of the bowl nearest you, up to the top, and back to the center. Give the bowl a quarter turn and repeat the down, across, up, and over movement. Continue this procedure, using thorough but gentle strokes, until the ingredients are blended.

TO COOK TO THE SOFT-BALL STAGE. The soft-ball stage, while referred to throughout the book as 238°, can be anywhere between 234°

and 240°F. If you do not have a candy thermometer, test for the soft-ball stage by dropping a small amount of the liquid into a cup of ice water. It should form a small ball that will flatten out but not disintegrate when pinched between the fingers.

TO PREPARE FRUITS FOR USE IN RECIPES. Remove any stems, hulls, or leaves from the fruit, wash it in cold water, and, where necessary, pat or wipe it dry with paper towels before using.

TO MAKE GRATED ZEST OF LEMON PEEL OR ORANGE PEEL. Wash the lemon or orange and dry it with paper towels. Using a sharp grater or a lemon zester, grate or scrape off only the colored part of the peel. Do not use any of the white part, which has a bitter taste.

TO SKIN A PEACH. Stab at the stem end with a sturdy fork and plunge the peach into boiling water. Let it remain in the water for a few seconds, then remove it. The skin should have loosened enough to be slit and pulled off easily with the aid of a knife. Repeat the process if necessary. Be certain to use ripe peaches, as no amount of coaxing will remove the skin from an unripe peach.

TO CUT UP A PINEAPPLE. Cut the pineapple into crosswise slices about ½ inch thick. Remove the core with a doughnut-hole cutter. Trim away the outside, including the eyes, using a small, sharp knife. Cut the slices into chunks if required.

TO GRIND NUTS. Use a nut grinder, electric blender, or food processor. Do not use a meat grinder, which tends to mash or crush the nuts instead of grinding them.

TO BLANCH ALMONDS. Place the shelled almonds in a bowl and pour boiling water over to cover. Let stand about 2 minutes, then drain. Cover with cold water. Squeeze each almond between the thumb and index finger to slip off the brown skin. Pat the almonds dry in paper towels.

TO MAKE DECORATIVE VENTS IN THE TOP OF PIECRUST OR TO CUT PRESERVED GINGER INTO FANCY SHAPES. Use a truffle cutter.

TO COOL CAKES, PASTRIES, AND SO ON. Unless otherwise directed, remove all baked goods from baking pans and cool them right-side up on wire racks immediately upon taking them from the oven.

TO UNMOLD DESSERTS WITHOUT STICKING. Before filling the mold, oil it very lightly with a fine, mild, high-quality oil. Do not use a strongly flavored oil for this purpose.

TO UNCURDLE CUSTARD. If a custard should curdle, beat it vigorously with a rotary eggbeater or a large wire whisk.

TO MAKE VANILLA SUGAR. Put 2 to 4 cups superfine sugar in a glass jar and push a 2-inch piece of vanilla bean down into the sugar. Seal the jar tightly with a screw-top lid. Allow it to remain for several days. Sugar may be replenished as it is used in recipes without changing the vanilla bean for some time. Vanilla sugar can be used in any recipe calling for sugar and vanilla extract. Simply omit the vanilla extract.

TO MELT CHOCOLATE. Cut, chop, or break chocolate up into small pieces. Put it into the top of a double boiler and set it over hot water. Stir with a wooden spoon until it has melted. Remove from the stove and leave it over hot water until ready to use it.

TO MAKE GRATED CHOCOLATE. Have the chocolate at room temperature, or a little warmer if possible during cool weather. Use a coarse grater, potato peeler, rotary grater, or the grating blade of a food processor. If using a hand grater, grate over waxed paper. Sprinkle the grated chocolate over the dessert with a small spoon.

TO MAKE CHOCOLATE TRIANGLES (The Alternative to Chocolate Curls). Like the weather, people talk a lot about making chocolate curls, but are seldom able to do anything about it. But don't blame the people; blame the chocolate. Most of the beautiful chocolate curls you see on professionally made cakes have been created with commercial chocolate that is easy to work with because of its high fat content. There is little sense in trying to achieve the same results with the chocolate available to consumers, since it tends to crack or break and be generally disagreeable and frustrating to work with.

An easy-to-make and very attractive substitute for chocolate curls is Chocolate Triangles. To make enough triangles to decorate one cake or a good number of individual desserts, place about 3 ounces of broken-up semisweet chocolate in the top of a double boiler and set over simmering water. Stir constantly until smooth and completely melted. Have ready a sheet of waxed paper placed on a board that will fit into the refrigerator. Pour the chocolate out onto the waxed paper, using a rubber spatula to scrape it out of the pan. With a metal spatula, spread out the chocolate thinly and as evenly as possible on the waxed paper.

Don't worry about how the edges look. Let it stand in the refrigerator for several minutes until the chocolate just sets. Remove from the refrigerator and with the point of a sharp knife mark the chocolate into diamonds, cutting through to the waxed paper and spacing the marks about 2 inches apart. Then cut into triangles by running the knife point through the widest part of the diamonds. Peel the triangles off the waxed paper and set on fresh waxed paper on a plate. Store in the refrigerator until ready to use, or wrap and freeze until needed. The chocolate is very easy to work with and can be cut into squares or any desired shapes with cookie cutters or other small cutters. Remelt any chocolate pieces that don't come out the way you want them, and use in the same manner as before. Stand the triangles up when you use them for trimming desserts.

Ingredients

The following are standards, suggestions for handling of, substitutions for, and sources for some of the ingredients called for in the recipes.

EGGS. Unless otherwise specified, all eggs used in these recipes are medium size. Eggs should be brought to room temperature before using.

BUTTER OR MARGARINE. Butter is called for in most recipes, but if you wish to substitute margarine you may do so, although at some sacrifice to flavor. Do not, however, substitute margarine when sweet butter is asked for, when making shortbread or any recipe where butter is a principal flavoring ingredient, when using melted butter to brush over phyllo pastry, when making puff pastry, or when the recipe is very specific about using butter. Butter or margarine should be taken from the refrigerator to soften slightly before creaming.

HEAVY CREAM. To whip properly, the cream, bowl, and beater should be well chilled.

LIGHT CREAM. If light cream is called for and is not available in your market, use ¾ cup heavy cream and ¼ cup milk as a substitute for 1 cup light cream.

HALF-AND-HALF. This refers to the so-called half-milk and half-cream dairy product. If it is not available in your market, substitute ⅓ cup heavy cream and ⅔ cup milk for 1 cup half-and-half.

SUGAR. Use plain white granulated sugar for all recipes unless otherwise directed. If you wish to substitute turbinado sugar (sometimes called raw sugar) for a little more food value, you may do so in recipes for desserts that will not be unattractive if they are darker in appearance.

BROWN SUGAR. Pack firmly when measuring unless otherwise instructed. Store unused brown sugar in a glass jar with a tight-fitting lid. Brown sugar that has hardened can usually be softened by spreading it on a baking sheet and placing it in a low oven for a short time.

FLOUR. Unless otherwise specified, ordinary white flour should be used in all recipes. Unbleached white flour is preferable since it contains fewer chemicals. In certain recipes where appropriate, you may substitute whole wheat flour for white flour by reducing the amount of flour used (use ¾ cup whole wheat in place of 1 cup white), adding a little more liquid, and using a little less butter or other fat called for. This will require individual experimentation and should not be tried with cakes that require a fine texture and white color.

CAKE FLOUR. Do not use any substitute if cake flour is called for.

SPICES. Unless otherwise specified, all spices in the recipes should be ground or powdered spices.

VANILLA BEAN. The fermented and cured whole bean from a certain orchid. It is imported in glass tubes, and its flavor is far superior to the extract made from the same bean.

HAZELNUTS AND FILBERTS. Filberts are a variety of hazelnut, but both the names and the nuts are interchangeable in the recipes.

NUT MEATS. Store raw nuts in tightly sealed glass jars in the refrigerator.

MARRONS (Chestnuts). Marrons are available in a number of forms.

> MARRONS GLACES (Glazed Chestnuts). Whole chestnuts which have been cooked in, and then glazed or iced with, sugar. They are imported from France and usually packed in round tin boxes wrapped in patterned paper. Use in recipes or serve with after-dinner coffee.
> MARRONS AU SIROP (Chestnuts in Syrup). Chestnuts packed in jars with vanilla-flavored syrup.
> CREME DE MARRONS (Chestnut Spread). Chestnut puree

---

sweetened with sugar and vanilla. Comes packed in cans of various sizes.

PUREE DE MARRONS AU NATUREL (Chestnut Puree). Unsweetened chestnut puree. Packed in cans.

MARRONS ENTIERS AU NATUREL (Whole Natural Chestnuts). Unsweetened whole chestnuts packed in water. Comes in cans.

SULTANAS. Sultanas are raisins made from white grapes. Do not confuse them with "golden" raisins, which are bleached raisins that will revert to their original dark color when cooked or used in baking.

EAGLE SWEET CHOCOLATE. This domestically processed chocolate is a little sweeter than semisweet. Probably the oldest and best-known brand is Maillard's, although other firms, such as Ghiradelli, also make it.

PRESERVED GINGER IN SYRUP. Fresh ginger cooked in heavy syrup, in which it is packed. Sliced and packed in jars. Both ginger and syrup are used in dessert cookery.

ROSEWATER *(Eau de Roses)*. This is a liquid made by distilling fragrant rose petals in water. Usually imported from France in 3-ounce bottles or from Greece in larger-size bottles.

ROSE ESSENCE *(Crème de Rose-Essence)*. Heavier, thicker, and more concentrated than rosewater, rose essence should be used by the drop rather than by the spoonful.

ORANGE FLOWER WATER *(Eau de Fleurs d'Orange)*. This is a fragrant liquid made by distilling orange blossoms in water. Usually imported from France in 3-ounce bottles or from Greece in larger bottles.

ORGEAT. Almond syrup from France. If not available, use other almond syrup.

BAR-LE-DUC RED CURRANT PRESERVES. Small jars of preserved currants from which the seeds have been removed by a painstaking process. Color and flavor are exceptional. Imported from France.

CANNED SWEETENED COCONUT CREAM. Often called cream of coconut on the can label, the best-known brands are Siboney and Coco Lopez. Most people know this product as an ingredient used in making the tropical drink piña colada.

CANDIED ORANGE SLICES OR CANDIED LEMON SLICES. Crosswise slices of oranges or lemons which have been cooked in and glazed with sugar to preserve them. Should be stored airtight.

CRYSTALLIZED VIOLETS, LILACS, ROSE PETALS, MINT LEAVES. Real flowers or leaves which have been treated with sugar and coloring and dried in repeated processes to preserve them for use as dessert decorations. Usually imported from France, they should be kept away from light and tightly sealed. Very long lasting.

CRYSTALLIZED OR CANDIED GINGER. Pieces of fresh ginger processed in heavy syrup and coated with sugar crystals. Comes in jars or boxes. Once opened, store tightly sealed in glass jar.

PHYLLO PASTRY. Sometimes called filo pastry or strudel leaves, phyllo is tissue-paper-thin raw pastry sheets which are stacked, rolled up, and packaged in long, thin boxes. Usually frozen except in ethnic markets in large cities where it can be bought fresh. Thaw frozen phyllo, unopened, before using.

CASSIS. Syrup made from the black currants of Burgundy in France. Other black currant syrup may be used if cassis is not available.

KIRSCH. A colorless brandy distilled from the fermented juices of cherries and their pits. Comes from France, Germany, or Switzerland and may also be labeled Kirschwasser or Schwarzwalder.

LIQUEURS. The following liqueurs are the most versatile and well-known in dessert cookery, but there are many others that can be used. The price and quality of a liqueur is largely determined by the method used in making it and the quality of its ingredients.

>STRAWBERRY LIQUEUR *(Crème de frais* or *crème de fraises des bois).*
>
>CASSIS LIQUEUR OR *CREME DE CASSIS.* French liqueur made from black currants.
>
>RASPBERRY LIQUEUR *(Crème de framboise).*
>
>ORANGE LIQUEUR (Curaçao, Grand Marnier, Cointreau, Triple Sec).
>
>COFFEE LIQUEUR (Kahlua, Tia Maria, Bahia).
>
>MARASCHINO LIQUEUR. Made in Italy from Marasca cherries. Brand generally seen is Stock.

CHOCOLATE OR COCOA LIQUEUR *(Crème de cacao).*
BANANA LIQUEUR *(Crème de banana).*

SOURCES. Ingredients and utensils which may be difficult to find outside of general food stores, supermarkets, department stores, and hardware stores can usually be located by visiting specialty food stores, ethnic markets, gourmet shops, candy and confectionery shops, cookware shops, and the like. Some firms fill mail orders for specialty foods and/or utensils and will send price lists on request. One such firm is Gourmets' Bazar, Inc., 3 Purdy Avenue, Rye, New York 10580. Some department stores with food and cookware departments also provide such services. Sources are sometimes given in food articles in magazines and newspapers, where specialty foods and cookware are sometimes also advertised.

The Final Touch
Nearly every recipe in this book includes a suggestion for appropriate decoration. You may, however, wish to omit decorations or alter them to suit your own taste. The following sauces may also be used as decorations to be spooned over ice cream, simple puddings, custards, cakes, and so on, or may be used as specified in dessert recipes.

APRICOT SAUCE. See page 239.

BLUEBERRY SAUCE. Combine 1 tablespoon cornstarch with ¼ cup water in a small saucepan. Add ¼ cup sugar, a pinch of salt, and 1 teaspoon lemon juice. Stir in 1 pint blueberries and cook over medium heat, stirring, until slightly thickened and clear. Serve warm or at room temperature.

BRANDY SAUCE. Whip 1 cup heavy cream until soft peaks form. Fold in 3 tablespoons apricot brandy or peach brandy a tablespoon at a time, and 2 tablespoons sifted confectioners' sugar. Serve immediately.

BRANDY HARD SAUCE. Cream ½ cup butter until very soft. Gradually add 1½ cups sifted confectioners' sugar and beat until fluffy. Beat in 2 or 3 tablespoons brandy. Refrigerate until serving time.

BUTTERSCOTCH SAUCE. Melt ⅓ cup butter in a heavy saucepan. Add ⅓ cup heavy cream and 1 cup brown sugar, firmly packed. Bring to boil and simmer 5 minutes, without stirring. Remove from heat and beat for a minute or two. Serve warm.

CASSIS SAUCE. Stir ½ cup black currant jam or preserves until smooth. Add enough cassis (black current syrup) or raspberry syrup, a tablespoon at a time, to make a sauce of a nice consistency to spoon over the dessert. If desired, add 1 tablespoon *crème de cassis* (cassis liqueur).

CHOCOLATE SAUCE. See page 202.

FLUFFY ORANGE SAUCE. Put 5 egg yolks and ½ cup sugar in the top of a double boiler. Set over simmering water and beat about 10 minutes with an eggbeater until very thick and pale. Remove from the heat and stir in ¼ cup orange liqueur. Cool, cover, and chill. Beat 1 cup heavy cream until stiff, and fold into sauce. Serve immediately.

MELBA SAUCE. Thaw a 10-ounce package frozen raspberries and combine the juice with 1 teaspoon cornstarch. Combine the raspberries with ½ cup red currant jelly in a heavy saucepan, cook over low heat, stirring constantly, until jelly is melted. Put the mixture through a fine sieve and return to the saucepan. Add the cornstarch mixture and ¼ cup sugar, and cook until slightly thickened and clear, stirring constantly. Cool and chill.

MOCHA SAUCE. Melt 6 ounces semisweet chocolate, broken up, and ¼ cup butter in the top of a double boiler over simmering water, stirring constantly. Add ½ cup sifted confectioners' sugar, ½ cup light corn syrup, ½ cup hot water, and 2 teaspoons instant espresso coffee powder, and cook until smooth and slightly thickened. Remove from the heat and add 1 teaspoon vanilla extract or 1 tablespoon rum. Serve at room temperature.

PASTRY CREAM. See page 293, English Trifle (custard).

PRALINE POWDER. Make as in PRALINE ICE CREAM recipe (page 169), omitting ice cream and garnish portion of recipe.

RUM SAUCE. Make the custard portion of recipe (page 293). Using ½ cup of the sauce, combine with ¼ cup rum. Whip ½ cup heavy cream until stiff, and fold into the sauce. Serve chilled.

STRAWBERRY SAUCE. Whirl together briefly in food processor or electric blender 1 pint strawberries, 2 or more tablespoons confectioners' sugar, and 1 or 2 tablespoons orange, strawberry, or raspberry liqueur or cassis liqueur if desired. Do not process this sauce long enough for it to become a puree.

VANILLA SAUCE. Whip ½ cup heavy cream until stiff. Soften 1 cup vanilla ice cream and fold the whipped cream into it. If desired, fold in 1 tablespoon kirsch, brandy, rum, or fruit liqueur. Serve immediately.

VANILLA CUSTARD SAUCE *(Crème anglaise)*. Make custard sauce portion of recipe (page 223) substituting 1 teaspoon vanilla extract for 2 tablespoons rum.

ZABAGLIONE SAUCE. See page 130.

NOTE

When the recipe for one dish included in this book is listed as an ingredient in another recipe here, the name of the former will be printed in small capital letters (for example, VANILLA BUTTER CREAM FROSTING). You can locate it quickly then, using the index at the back of the book.

CHAPTER 4

Cakes of All Kinds

*It is heavenly fare to lunch on grapes
and fresh baked hearth cakes.*
—*François Rabelais,* Gargantua

Since earliest times, cake has been regarded as a special, often festive, and sometimes symbolic food. Weddings seem incomplete without a towering, white, elaborately decorated cake, birthdays demand a gaily frosted and candle-festooned creation, and holidays of all kinds are accentuated the world over by the serving of traditional baked favorites.

At Christmastime, the French look forward to a rich butter-cream-filled cake log called *bûche de Noël,* the Germans to currant-studded stollen, the English to fruit-laden Christmas pudding (actually a steamed cake), and Americans to old-fashioned fruitcake heavy with nuts and fruits and perfumed with brandy or rum. To help celebrate the Easter holidays, Russians bake coffeecake-textured kulich, and in parts of Italy, *pizza pasqualina,* a cake of ricotta, eggs, and honey is made. Mexicans, in their never-ending round of fiestas, bake *pan de muertos,* a frosted and pink-sugar-dusted, anise-flavored cakebread, for All Saints' Day.

The baking of cakes with religious significance dates back to primitive times when cakes were used as offerings to the gods, and many nations today continue the age-old practice of commemorative baking to celebrate religious occasions.

It isn't surprising that many of the tradition-steeped cakes lean to the texture of sweet breads, since cakes and breads seem to have evolved from the same early baking experiments. The words *cake* and *bread* are even interchangeable at times, as when, for example, Scottish oatcakes turn out to be a kind of flatbread, and gingerbread a form of spicecake.

While the Egyptians were unique among ancient peoples in using leavening to make raised baked goods, and such a process was known in the Middle East long before the time of Christ, European cultures knew no such sophistication in baking.

Everyday cakes made at home during the Middle Ages were called hearth cakes or ash cakes, so-called because they were originally baked in the ashes of the hearth. These simple, unleavened wheat-flour cakes were shaped small and rather flat, turned once during baking to harden them on both sides, and by today's standards must have been quite crude. However, when baking was switched from the hearth to the oven, hearth cakes became commercial products and were sold for centuries at fairs and on market days throughout Europe. The town of Lerne in France enjoyed a reputation for making some of the best hearth cakes, and the ovens where they baked their hearth cakes, hewn out of solid rock, have endured until this day.

The first raised cakes were made with yeast and differed from bread mainly in that they were sweetened—usually with honey—and had eggs, fruits, nuts, or seeds such as caraway, and, of course, spices added. The major refinement in cake making came with the advent of the quick-raised cake. Until fairly recent times, this feat was accomplished by the use of myriads of eggs in the mixing of the cake. Beating egg whites high trapped millions of tiny air bubbles into the whites, and folding this mass into cake batter produced a cake that held its airiness during baking, resulting in a light texture without the necessity of leavening.

The dependency on eggs for making light-textured cakes accounts for some of the seemingly outrageous quantities of ingredients and exhaustion-inducing instructions in colonial cake recipes. A Mount Vernon recipe from 1781, for example, advised the cook to "take forty eggs and divide the whites from the yolks" as the first step in making a cake. Directions for a nun's cake of the 1700s, calling for thirty-five eggs and beating for two solid hours, were specified for the sole purpose of making the massive cake rise, though it might seem more a test of the physical endurance of the cook who had to do the work.

The practice of using egg whites to produce fine-textured cakes is still followed in many of France's most famous *gâteaux* today, such as *génoise*. Other cakes, traditionally unleavened, remain as popular and delicious today as they were several centuries ago. A case in point is the pound cake, which has been relatively unchanged for more than two hundred years in its proportion of one pound each of butter, sugar, eggs, and flour. Few fruitcakes require leavening, and are loved instead for their sheer weight and density of ingredients.

The majority of today's cakes are of a light and tender crumb, thanks to the discovery of adding one ingredient or another to cake batters to cause them to rise during baking. The first of these, potash, was used as early as the eighteenth century, and soon afterward a form of baking soda, known as saleratus, appeared. It was also found that egg whites would hold together and help the cake rise better if they were beaten with some cream of tartar.

The giant step in baking came with the invention of baking powder, and cream of tartar. Although no one really knows where the first baking powder was made, credit is given to America, where the first commercially produced product became available to housewives all over the nation a little more than a hundred years ago. Easy access to baking powder probably accounts for the tremendous popularity of the high layered cake in the United States.

Outstanding in the world of baking is the torte, which differs from the cake or the *gâteau* in that it usually is made either with very little flour or with no flour at all, crumbs or ground nuts making up the bulk of the dry ingredients. An abundance of eggs and a scarcity of butter results in a texture rich and different from other kinds of cake.

The torte, along with scores of other pastries of all sizes, shapes, and flavors, originated in Vienna during the height of popularity of that city's famous coffeehouses. It was at these opulent cafés that everyone—the rich and not-so-rich, the famous and infamous—met to gossip, flirt, exchange news, debate politics, and savor some of the world's most fantastic baking. There were tiny pastries shaped like violins, flowers, or even people. There was the ultimate in coffeecake, the *Kugelhopf*, and there were strudels bursting with nuts or fruit. There were tortes piled high with swirls, puffs, and rosettes of butter cream, layered with apricot preserves, or glazed with caramel. And there was coffee served in infinite variety from light to dark, thin to heavy, with pourings of milk or with mounds of whipped cream.

While the origins of many of the pastries served can be traced to Turkey, Hungary, and other places, it was the Viennese who adapted them, perfected them, raised their making and serving to a high art, and popularized them to the point where they are still made and enjoyed not only in Vienna but all over the world.

Some torte recipes are best left to the skills of the professional pastry chef, as are the most elegant cakes of France, Switzerland, and Austria, among other countries, but many tortes can be made to perfection at home, and recipes for them are included in this chapter. Here also is a

---

well-rounded representation of cake and *gâteau* recipes, and in addition you will find the following cake recipes in other chapters:

Austrian Linzer Torte
Blueberry Roll
Chestnut Meringue Cake
Cheesecake Epicurean
Chocolate Chiffon Cake
Devil's Food Cake
Gâteau Pithiviers
Gâteau Saint-Honoré
German Black Forest Cake
Gingerbread
Honey Plum Kuchen
Jelly Roll
Kugelhopf
Mango Shortcake
Meringue Butter Cream Cake
Meringue Nut Layer Cake
Strawberry Meringue Cake
Strawberry Shortcake
Thousand Leaves Cake

Since much has been written in standard cookbooks about the do's and don't's of cake baking, it doesn't seem necessary to detail them here. Nineteenth-century bakers were faced with vague instructions like the one that appeared in a cake recipe in *Godey's Lady's Book* telling one to "bake in a tolerably quick oven." But recipes now are explicit, equipment is time- and energy-saving, and quality ingredients are available everywhere. All one generally needs to do to turn out a good cake is to measure accurately and follow recipe instructions to the letter.

HAZELNUT CREAM CAKE

1 cup heavy cream
2 eggs
1 teaspoon vanilla extract
1½ cups flour
¾ cup sugar
2 teaspoons baking powder

Pinch of salt
3 tablespoons butter
¼ cup free-flowing brown sugar
½ cup chopped hazelnuts
1 tablespoon flour

Preheat the oven at 350°. Reserve 1 tablespoon of the heavy cream and whip the balance until stiff. Beat in the eggs, 1 at a time, mixing well each time. Add the vanilla extract. Sift the 1½ cups flour, the sugar, baking powder, and salt together twice, and stir into batter. Pour into a buttered, floured 9-inch spring-form pan and bake for 35 minutes, or until a cake tester inserted in the center comes out clean.

While the cake is baking, combine the butter, brown sugar, hazelnuts, 1 tablespoon flour, and the reserved 1 tablespoon heavy cream in a small saucepan. Heat until the butter has melted and all ingredients are blended.

When the cake has baked for 35 minutes, spread the topping over the cake and return to oven for 10 minutes. Cool on a cake rack, removing the side of the pan when cool.

Makes 8 servings.

GLAZED CHESTNUT CAKE WITH BLACK CURRANT SAUCE

Chestnuts, cassis, and currant jelly give this magnificent cake a flavor very French and quite extraordinary. If you can find a jar of Bar-le-Duc red currant preserves, by all means use it in place of ordinary currant jelly in this recipe. Each currant in the French preserves has had its seeds removed by hand by means of a goose feather, and the fruit has been cooked quickly in hot syrup, allowing it to retain its distinct flavor and bright color. The preserves have been made in the town of Bar-le-Duc in much the same way since the fourteenth century, when they were a delicacy reserved for the tables of lords and ladies.

2⅔ cups sifted cake flour
2¼ teaspoons baking powder
½ teaspoon salt
1 cup butter
2 cups sugar
4 egg yolks
1 teaspoon vanilla extract
1 tablespoon grated zest of
  orange peel
1 cup milk
1 cup slivered toasted almonds

1 ten-ounce can whole natural
  marrons (unsweetened
  chestnuts)
4 egg whites
1 three-ounce jar Bar-le-Duc red
  currant preserves or ¼ cup
  currant jam or currant jelly
Whole *marrons glacés* (glazed
  chestnuts) (optional)
1 cup heavy cream
¼ cup cassis (black currant
  syrup)

Preheat the oven at 350°. Butter and flour a 2-quart fancy tube pan such as a *Kugelhopf* mold or similar tube pan. Sift the cake flour, baking powder, and salt together twice. Cream the butter and add the sugar gradually. Beat in the egg yolks, 1 at a time. Add the vanilla extract and orange peel. Add the flour mixture alternately with the milk, beating well after each addition. Stir in the almonds and natural *marrons* (which have been thoroughly drained, dried with paper towels, and very finely crumbled). Beat the egg whites until stiff but not dry. Fold lightly into the batter and pour into the mold. Bake 1¼ to 1½ hours, or until a cake tester inserted in the center comes out clean. Cool on a wire rack.

In a small saucepan, melt the currant jelly and brush over the cake while it is still warm. When cool, garnish the cake with whole *marrons glacés* if desired. To serve, whip the heavy cream until stiff, and fold in the cassis. Slice the cake thinly and spoon the sauce over each serving.

ORANGE CREAM ROLL

For the cake:
5 egg yolks
¼ cup sugar
¼ cup sifted cake flour
5 egg whites
½ teaspoon vanilla extract
1 teaspoon frozen orange juice
  concentrate, thawed

For the filling:
4 tablespoons plain gelatin

3 tablespoons orange juice
1 tablespoon frozen orange juice
  concentrate, thawed
2 egg yolks
⅔ cup milk
3 tablespoons sugar
Grated rind of 1 orange
2 egg whites
3 tablespoons sugar
⅔ cup heavy cream
1 teaspoon vanilla extract

For the cake: Preheat the oven at 400°. Beat the egg yolks well. Add the sugar gradually and continue beating until the mixture is thick and pale. Fold in the cake flour with a rubber spatula. Beat the egg whites until stiff, then fold them into the egg yolk mixture. Fold in the vanilla extract and orange juice concentrate.

Pour the batter onto a buttered jelly roll pan, approximately 11x15 inches, which has been lined with buttered waxed paper. Spread the batter out evenly with a rubber spatula. Bake for about 12 minutes, or until lightly browned. Remove from the oven, loosen the waxed paper from the sides of the pan, and invert the cake onto a sheet of aluminum foil.

For the filling: Soften the gelatin in the orange juice (which has been combined with the orange juice concentrate). Beat the milk and egg yolks together and combine in a saucepan with the gelatin mixture. Add 3 tablespoons sugar. Cook over low heat, stirring, until the gelatin and sugar have completely dissolved. Remove from the heat, stir in the orange rind, and allow to cool. Chill until slightly thickened, checking the mixture every 10 minutes.

Beat the egg whites until stiff and gradually beat in 3 tablespoons sugar. Fold the egg white mixture into the gelatin mixture with a rubber spatula. Beat the heavy cream until stiff. Stir in the vanilla extract. Fold the whipped cream into the orange mixture with a rubber spatula.

Peel the waxed paper off the cake. Spread with the orange mixture and roll up lengthwise, using the aluminum foil to help lift and roll the cake, ending with the seam side down. Wrap the aluminum foil around the cake and refrigerate for several hours. Transfer to a board or long plate before serving.

MAPLE WALNUT ROLL

For the cake:
7 egg yolks
⅓ cup sugar
7 egg whites
Pinch of salt
¾ cup ground walnuts
1 teaspoon maple extract

For the filling:
2 teaspoons plain gelatin
3 tablespoons water
1½ cups heavy cream
½ cup maple syrup

For the cake: Preheat the oven at 350°. Beat the egg yolks until frothy. Add the sugar gradually and continue beating until a ribbon forms when the beater is lifted. Beat the egg whites until stiff, adding the salt. Fold one-fourth of the egg whites into the yolk mixture until no streaks appear. Fold the yolk mixture into the remaining egg whites along with the ground walnuts and maple extract, and fold until no streaks appear. Pour the batter onto a buttered jelly roll pan measuring approximately 11x15 inches, which has been lined with buttered waxed paper. Spread the batter out evenly with a rubber spatula. Bake for about 25 minutes until the cake is lightly browned. Loosen the waxed paper from the sides of the pan and invert the cake onto a sheet of aluminum foil. Allow to cool and remove the remaining waxed paper.

For the filling: Soften the gelatin in the water. Place the mixture in the top of a double boiler and set over hot water, stirring until the gelatin has dissolved completely. Remove from the heat. Beat the heavy cream until it begins to hold its shape. Add the gelatin and maple syrup and continue beating until stiff.

Spread the cooled cake with the filling and roll it up length wise, using the aluminum foil to help lift and roll the cake. Transfer to a board or long serving plate, seam side down.

CHOCOLATE CREAM ROLL

1 teaspoon instant espresso coffee
   powder
3 tablespoons cold water
6 ounces Eagle sweet chocolate
5 egg yolks
¾ cup sugar
1 teaspoon vanilla extract

5 egg whites
Pinch of salt
Cocoa (preferably Dutch)
1½ cups heavy cream
½ teaspoon vanilla extract
Sugar

Preheat the oven at 350°. Dissolve the espresso coffee powder in the cold water and place in the top of a double boiler with the chocolate. Set over hot (not boiling) water and stir until melted. Remove from the heat and allow to cool. Butter a jelly roll pan measuring approximately 11x15 inches and line it with buttered waxed paper.

Beat the egg yolks until they are thick and pale in color. Add ¾ cup sugar gradually and continue beating until the mixture is very thick and forms a slowly dissolving ribbon when the beater is lifted. Add 1 teaspoon vanilla extract. Add the cooled chocolate mixture. Beat the egg whites with salt until stiff. Fold into the chocolate batter. Pour into the prepared jelly roll pan and spread out evenly with a rubber spatula.

Bake for 10 minutes. Reduce the oven temperature to 300° and bake 5 minutes longer until a cake tester inserted in the center comes out clean. Remove from the oven. Place a damp dish towel over the cake and allow it to sit for 45 minutes. Remove the towel. Dust the surface with a little sifted cocoa. Lay a sheet of waxed paper over the surface. Invert. Peel off the waxed paper from the bottom of the cake. Trim the edges of the cake with a sharp knife.

Whip the heavy cream until stiff, adding ½ teaspoon vanilla extract and sugar to taste, and spread evenly over the cake. Roll the cake up lengthwise, using waxed paper to help lift and roll. Transfer to a board or long serving plate, seam side down. If desired, sprinkle with a little more sifted cocoa.

VIOLET CAKE WITH LEMON FROSTING

For the cake:
1 cup butter
2 cups sugar
4 eggs
2¾ cups sifted cake flour
3 teaspoons baking powder
½ teaspoon salt
1 cup less 2 tablespoons milk
2 tablespoons violet liqueur
(*crème de violette*) or 2
tablespoons violet syrup
¼ cup crystallized violets
Lemon curd or lemon marmalade

For the frosting and decorating:
¼ cup butter
2 cups sifted confectioners' sugar
¼ cup lemon juice
1 tablespoon heavy cream
1 to 1½ cups sifted confectioners'
sugar
Grated zest of 1 lemon
Crystallized violets
Crystallized mint leaves (optional)

For the cake: Preheat the oven at 350°. Cream the butter and add the sugar gradually, blending well. Add the eggs and mix well. Sift together the cake flour, baking powder, and salt, and add to the butter-egg mixture alternately with the milk. Stir in the violet liqueur or syrup. Pour into 2 buttered and floured round 9-inch cake pans. Chop the violets into small pieces and sprinkle them evenly over the top. Bake for 30 to 35 minutes, or until a cake tester inserted in the center comes out clean. Remove from the pans and cool on a wire rack.

When cool, spread one layer with lemon curd or lemon marmalade and place the second layer on top. Frost the top and sides with the following frosting.

For the frosting and decorating: Cream the butter until very fluffy and add 2 cups sifted confectioners' sugar alternately with the lemon juice and heavy cream. Add 1 to 1½ cups more sifted confectioners' sugar until the frosting is of the proper spreading consistency. Add the grated zest of lemon. Frost the top and sides of the cake and decorate it with crystallized violets and, if desired, crystallized mint leaves.

CHESTNUT ALMOND TORTE

A moist cake with a subtle chestnut and almond flavor, glazed first with raspberry jam, then chocolate, and served with a rum-chocolate whipped cream sauce.

For the torte:
4 egg yolks
¾ cup sugar
1 ten-ounce can whole natural
  marrons (unsweetened
  chestnuts)
2 tablespoons rum
1 cup finely ground blanched
  almonds
4 egg whites

¼ cup seedless raspberry jam or
  strained apricot jam
3 ounces sweet or semisweet
  chocolate
3 tablespoons butter, cut into
  small pieces

For the sauce:
3 ounces semisweet chocolate
3 tablespoons rum
1 cup heavy cream

For the torte: Preheat the oven at 350°. Beat the egg yolks with an electric mixer until very thick. Add the sugar gradually and continue beating until the mixture is very thick and pale and forms a slowly dissolving ribbon when the beater is lifted. Drain the chestnuts and put them through a ricer, the medium blade of a food mill, or the fine shredding blade of a food processor. Add them to the egg yolk mixture. Stir in the rum and ground almonds and mix well. Beat the egg whites until stiff and stir a small amount into the chestnut batter. Fold the remaining egg whites in and pour into a well-buttered and floured 10-inch spring-form pan. Bake for 10 minutes. Reduce the oven temperature to 325°and bake 45 minutes longer, or until a cake tester inserted in the center comes out clean. Remove from the oven, remove the sides from the pan, and cool the cake on a wire rack.

When the cake is cool, melt the raspberry or apricot jam in a small saucepan and brush over the cake. Melt the chocolate in the top of a double boiler set over hot water, stirring. Remove from the heat and add the butter, cut into small pieces. Stir until the butter has melted. Pour over the glazed cake, using a spatula to spread it evenly over the top and to coat the sides. Refrigerate while the chocolate sets.

For the sauce: Melt the chocolate with the rum in the top of a double boiler set over hot water, stirring until it has melted. Remove from the heat and allow to cool. When cool, whip the cream until stiff. Fold the chocolate mixture into the whipped cream. Refrigerate if not serving immediately. To serve, cut the cake into serving pieces and spoon the sauce over each piece.

Makes 12 servings.

PECAN COFFEE TORTE

For the torte:
8 egg yolks
1¼ cups sugar
1 teaspoon vanilla extract
8 egg whites
Pinch of salt
2 tablespoons sugar
1½ cups coarsely ground pecans

For the sauce:
2 eggs
2 teaspoons instant espresso
   coffee powder
½ cup hot water
¼ cup sugar
Pinch of salt
½ cup heavy cream

For the torte: Preheat the oven at 350°. Beat the egg yolks until very thick. Add 1¼ cups sugar gradually and continue beating until the mixture is very thick and pale and forms a slowly dissolving ribbon when the beater is lifted. Add the vanilla extract. Beat the egg whites until foamy, and add the salt. Continue beating until stiff. Add 2 tablespoons sugar, 1 tablespoon at a time, and continue beating until the mixture is thick and glossy. Stir a little of the egg white mixture into the egg yolk mixture. Then fold the balance of the egg white mixture into the egg yolk mixture. Fold in the pecans gently but thoroughly until no streaks of egg white or nuts show. Pour into a buttered and floured 10-inch spring-form pan, and bake for 45 to 50 minutes, or until a cake tester inserted in the center comes out clean. Remove the cake from the oven and set the pan on a wire rack. When cool, remove the sides of the pan.

For the sauce: Prepare while the cake is baking. Beat the eggs in the top of a double boiler. Dissolve the espresso powder in hot water. Add to the eggs slowly, stirring constantly. Add the sugar and salt. Place over hot water and heat until the sauce thickens and coats a metal spoon, stirring constantly. Remove from the heat, cool, and chill. Whip the cream until stiff, then fold into the coffee mixture. To serve, cut the cooled torte into wedges and spoon sauce over each serving.

Makes 8 servings.

KIRSCH TORTE IMPERIAL

2 nine-inch meringue layers
   (as for MERINGUE BUTTER
   CREAM CAKE)
1 nine-inch round GENOISE layer
1 recipe VANILLA BUTTER
   CREAM FROSTING

For the Currant Filling:
3 tablespoons cornstarch
⅓ cup sugar
¼ cup milk

¾ cup milk
⅓ cup currant jelly
¾ cup butter

For the Kirsch Solution:
3 tablespoons sugar
5 tablespoons water
5 tablespoons kirsch

For decoration:
Toasted, thinly sliced almonds
Currant jelly

For the Currant Filling: Combine the cornstarch, sugar, and ¼ cup milk. Heat ¾ cup milk in a saucepan to boiling. Remove from the heat and add the cornstarch mixture. Transfer to a saucepan and heat again just to boiling, stirring constantly. Remove from the heat and stir in the currant jelly. If the mixture does not become entirely smooth, put through a blender or food processor for a few seconds. Cream the butter until very soft and fluffy. Beat in the currant mixture gradually and blend well. Chill until of a spreading consistency.

For the Kirsch Solution: Combine the sugar and water in a saucepan and heat, stirring, until the mixture boils and the sugar dissolves. Remove from the heat and cool. Stir in the kirsch.

To assemble: Place 1 meringue layer on a serving plate. Cover with half the Currant Filling. Place the Génoise layer over the Currant Filling.

Pour the Kirsch Solution over the Génoise layer. Spread with the remaining Currant Filling. Place the remaining meringue layer on top. Frost the top and sides of the torte with Vanilla Butter Cream Frosting. Press toasted almonds onto the sides. Beat the currant jelly well to remove lumps, and make any desired design on the top of the cake or around the edges by forcing currant jelly through a pastry tube fitted with a small plain tip.

Makes 12 servings.

BRANDY TORTE

For the torte:
1 cup chopped dates
1 teaspoon baking soda
1 cup boiling water
2 tablespoons butter
1 cup sugar
1 egg
1¾ cups sifted flour
2 teaspoons baking powder
½ teaspoon salt
¼ cup chopped walnuts

For finishing:
1 cup sugar
¾ cup water
1 tablespoon butter
¾ cup brandy
1 teaspoon vanilla extract
Heavy cream (optional)

For the torte: Preheat the oven at 350°. Place the dates in a small bowl and sprinkle with the baking soda. Pour the boiling water over the dates and allow to stand. Cream the butter and add the sugar gradually. The mixture will be very crumbly. Beat in the egg. Sift the flour, baking powder, and salt together and add to the creamed mixture, mixing thoroughly. Add the date mixture, about one-third at a time. Stir in the walnuts. Pour into two round 9-inch cake pans which have been well buttered, floured, and the bottoms lined with buttered waxed paper. Bake for 20 minutes, or until a cake tester inserted in the center comes out clean, making sure not to run the tester through the dates, which will be sticky.

For finishing: While the cake is baking, combine the sugar, water, and butter in a saucepan and, stirring, bring to a boil. Reduce the heat and simmer for 4 minutes. Add the brandy and simmer for 1 minute. Remove from the heat. Add the vanilla extract.

Remove the baked cakes from the oven. Invert on wire racks, peel off waxed paper, and set the cakes right side up on the wire racks. Set the racks over large plates. Pour the hot syrup over the hot cakes and allow to cool. To serve, cut each cake into quarters and, if desired, pour heavy cream over each serving.

Makes 8 servings.

TREASURE CHEST TORTE

Besides being absolutely delicious, this is one of the most beautiful cakes imaginable.

For the torte:
6 egg yolks
1½ cups sugar
4 teaspoons hot water
2 teaspoons vanilla extract
2 cups sifted flour
3 teaspoons baking powder
¼ teaspoon salt
10 egg whites
½ cup strawberry jelly, raspberry jelly, or currant jelly

For the filling:
1 ten-ounce box frozen raspberries in syrup, thawed
1 cup fresh strawberries, hulled
1 envelope plain gelatin

2 tablespoons cold water
2 tablespoons superfine sugar
1 tablespoon strawberry liqueur, raspberry liqueur, or kirsch
1 cup heavy cream

For finishing:
¼ cup strawberry jelly, raspberry jelly, or currant jelly
2 teaspoons strawberry liqueur, raspberry liqueur, or kirsch
1 pint (or more) strawberries, hulled
¾ cup heavy cream
1 to 2 tablespoons sugar
1 teaspoon vanilla extract
Thinly sliced almonds or hazelnuts

For the torte: Preheat the oven at 375°. Beat the egg yolks until thick and pale in color. Add the sugar gradually and continue beating until the mixture is very fluffy and white in color. Beat in the hot water. Add the vanilla extract. Sift the flour, baking powder, and salt together and add to the batter gradually, mixing well. Beat the egg whites until stiff and stir half the egg whites into the batter. Fold the remaining egg whites into the batter. Pour into a well-buttered and floured 10-inch spring-form pan and bake 45 to 50 minutes, or until a cake tester inserted in the center comes out clean. Remove from the oven and remove the sides and bottom of the spring-form. Allow the cake to cool on a wire rack.

When cool, using a long, sharp knife, cut off a slice from the top of the cake about ½-inch thick to form a lid. With a small, sharp knife, cut around the sides of cake about 1 inch from the edge, making sure the knife does not pierce the bottom of the cake. Scoop out the center of the cake, leaving the 1-inch side and leaving about ½ to ¾ inch on the bottom. (The scooped-out cake can be used for another dessert such as toasted cake with ice cream, or a trifle, or it can be frozen.) Melt the jelly and brush over the exposed, cut parts of the lid and base of the cake.

For the filling: Puree the thawed raspberries in a blender or food processor. Put through a fine sieve to remove the seeds. Return to the blender or food processor and blend with the fresh strawberries. Soften the gelatin in the cold water. Place in the top of a double boiler and set over hot water, stirring until the gelatin has dissolved. Add to the berry mixture and blend again. Add the superfine sugar and liqueur or kirsch and blend again. Pour into a bowl. Whip the heavy cream until stiff and mix a little of the berry mixture into it. Fold the whipped cream into the berry mixture and pour into the hollowed-out cake, filling it just to the top. Place the cake lid over the top, glazed side down.

For finishing: Melt the jelly in a small saucepan, breaking up the lumps with a rubber spatula. Stir in the liqueur or kirsch, using whichever one was used in the filling. Brush the top of the cake to within 1 inch of the edge with melted jelly. Wash and thoroughly dry the strawberries and arrange them on top of the cake, pointed sides up, starting with the largest strawberries at the center and graduating to smaller ones at the outside, stopping 1 inch from the edge. Brush the strawberries with the remaining jelly glaze, reheating the glaze if necessary to spread easily.

Whip the heavy cream until stiff, adding sugar to taste and the vanilla extract. Spread it on the remaining exposed portions of the cake. Sprinkle and press the almonds or hazelnuts onto the whipped cream. Refrigerate until serving time, up to 24 hours.

BUTTER CREAM CROWN

½ cup butter
⅔ cup sugar
Grated zest of 1 lemon
4 eggs
¾ cup sifted flour
½ cup sifted cornstarch
2 teaspoons baking powder

Orange liqueur
Double recipe of VANILLA
  BUTTER CREAM FROSTING
PRALINE POWDER
Candied cherries or any glacéed
  fruits
Pistachio nuts

Preheat the oven at 350°. Cream the butter and add the sugar gradually, beating until fluffy. Add the lemon zest and eggs, 1 at a time, beating well after each addition. Sift the flour, cornstarch, and baking powder together and add gradually. Spoon into a well-buttered and floured 8- or 8½-inch tall ring mold or *Kugelhopf* mold. Bake for about 45 minutes, or until a cake tester inserted in the center comes out clean. Unmold and cool on a wire rack.

Cut the cake crosswise into 3 layers, using a long, very sharp knife. Sprinkle each layer lightly with the orange liqueur. Frost and stack the layers, and frost the outside of the cake with Vanilla Butter Cream Frosting. Sprinkle Praline Powder over all. Pipe butter cream rosettes around the top of the cake and decorate with candied cherries or any glacéed fruits and pistachio nuts to resemble jewels on a crown.

Makes 8 or more servings.

BABA AU RHUM

The Polish king Stanislas Leszczynski, who was known to putter about in the kitchen while in exile in France, one day baked some Kugelhopf, *a cake which had been made in his native land since the early 1600s, doused it with rum or some similar spirit, and set it aflame, thereby giving birth to the world's first baba. An inveterate reader of* The Thousand and One Nights, *he named his creation after one of his favorite characters, Ali Baba. When the cake later became popular in a Parisian bakery, its name was shortened to baba, and a further refinement was to immerse it in a rum-flavored syrup instead of sprinkling spirits over the top. Carême wrote, confoundingly, of the baba: "The true color of the baba should be reddish. It is a male pastry."* One can only suppose he meant that it was not a daintily adorned, fluffily frosted cake, but one can be certain that the baba is as attractive to the female appetite as it is to the male.

For the babas:
1 package active dry yeast
¼ cup lukewarm water (110°
    to 115°)
1 tablespoon sugar
¼ cup lukewarm milk (110°
    to 115°)
2 eggs
2 cups flour
¼ teaspoon salt
Grated zest of 1 lemon
½ cup melted butter, cooled

For finishing:
½ cup sugar
¾ cup water
1 teaspoon lemon juice
½ cup dark rum
¼ cup apricot jam
1½ teaspoons sugar
Red and/or green glazed cherries
    or other glazed fruits
Whole or slivered almonds

For the babas: Dissolve the yeast in the lukewarm water. Add the sugar and lukewarm milk and let stand in a warm place for about 5 minutes until the mixture starts to become bubbly. Add the eggs and beat in with a wire whisk. Stir in the flour. When combined, mix with the fingers for 2 minutes, raising the dough up with the fingers and allowing it to fall back into the bowl. Cover the dough with a dampened, wrung-out towel, and allow to rise in a warm spot for 1 hour, or until doubled in bulk.

Punch down the dough and stir in the salt, lemon zest, and melted butter, if possible blending in the butter with an electric mixer. Divide the dough into buttered baba molds, filling them one-half or less full. Cover and place in a warm spot again until the dough rises just to the tops of the molds. Meanwhile, preheat the oven at 350°. Bake for about 15 minutes, or until lightly browned and a cake tester inserted in the center comes out clean. Remove from the molds and allow to cool briefly on a wire rack.

For finishing: As soon as the babas come out of the oven, prepare the syrup. Combine ½ cup sugar, the water, and the lemon juice in a saucepan and, stirring, bring to a boil. Lower the heat and simmer for 5 minutes without stirring. Remove from the heat and add the rum.

Place the baked babas in a deep dish just large enough to hold them upright. Prick the tops with the tines of a fork. Pour the hot syrup over the babas, and with a bulb baster baste them with the excess syrup until it has all disappeared. Drain the babas on a wire rack.

Cakes of All Kinds

While the babas are draining, force the apricot jam through a strainer. Combine with 1½ teaspoons sugar and cook in a small saucepan, stirring, for about 5 minutes. Brush the apricot glaze over the tops of the babas. Decorate with glazed cherries or other glazed fruits, and almonds.

Makes about 12 babas, depending on the size of the molds used.

BLUEBERRY SAVARINS

First cousin to the baba is the savarin, which is made from the same dough. It was created in the mid-nineteenth century by a master pastry chef in Paris, who named it after the famous French gastronome Jean Anthelme Brillat-Savarin. Its original name of brillat-savarin was soon shortened to savarin.

1 recipe BABA AU RHUM dough
Double recipe of syrup for
   BABA AU RHUM
1 recipe of apricot glaze for
   BABA AU RHUM

1 pint blueberries
1 cup heavy cream (or more
   if desired)
Sugar
½ teaspoon vanilla extract

Prepare the dough as for the Baba au Rhum and, after the first rising, divide into 12 buttered individual savarin or ring molds. Follow the same procedure for baking, soaking with syrup (using half of the double recipe) and brushing with apricot glaze. Soak the blueberries in the balance of the syrup for 1 hour or longer. At serving time, arrange the blueberries around each savarin. Whip the cream until stiff, adding sugar to taste and the vanilla extract. Fill the centers with whipped cream. If desired, serve with additional whipped cream.

Makes 12 servings.

SAVARIN SUPREME

To fill the center:
¼ cup rum or brandy
Sugar
1 can mandarin orange
    segments, drained
1 cup seedless white grapes
1 cup fresh or canned bing
    cherries, pits removed
1 cup fresh strawberries, hulled
1 banana, sliced

1 recipe BABA AU RHUM dough
1 recipe of syrup for BABA AU
    RHUM

For finishing:
½ cup apricot jam
1 tablespoon sugar
Chopped pistachio nuts
Whole blanched almonds
Vanilla ice cream balls

To fill the center: Combine the rum or brandy with sugar to taste in a glass or ceramic bowl. Add the orange segments, grapes, cherries, and strawberries. Cover and allow to macerate in the refrigerator for several hours while preparing the savarin.

Prepare the dough as for Baba au Rhum. After the first rising, put the dough in a buttered savarin or ring mold. Cover and place in a warm spot until the dough rises just to the top of the mold. Meanwhile, preheat the oven to 350°. Bake 30 to 40 minutes, or until lightly browned and a cake tester inserted in the center comes out clean. Remove from the mold and allow to cool briefly on a wire rack while preparing the syrup. Follow the same procedure for making the syrup and soaking the savarin with it as in Baba au Rhum. While the savarin is draining, force the apricot jam through a strainer. Combine it with the sugar and cook in a small saucepan, stirring, for about 5 minutes. Brush the apricot glaze over the top of the savarin. Decorate with the pistachios and almonds.

To serve, combine the banana with the macerated fruits. With the savarin on a serving plate, fill the center with the fruits. Serve with a bowl of vanilla ice cream balls.

WALNUT ROUND

3 eggs
1 cup sugar
1 cup flour
1 teaspoon baking powder

Pinch of salt
1 cup chopped pitted dates
1 cup chopped walnuts
Confectioners' sugar (optional)

Preheat the oven at 350°. Beat the eggs until very thick, and add the sugar gradually, beating well. Sift the flour, baking powder, and salt together. Toss the dates and walnuts in the flour mixture and fold into the egg mixture until well blended. Turn into a buttered and floured 9½-inch spring-form pan and bake for 30 to 35 minutes, or until a cake tester inserted in the center comes out clean. Remove from the pan and cool on a wire rack. If desired, dust with sifted confectioners' sugar. Cut into wedges and serve.

Makes 6 to 8 servings.

POUND CAKE

1 cup butter (at room
   temperature)
1⅔ cups sugar
5 eggs
Grated zest of 1 lemon

2 cups flour
¼ teaspoon mace
⅛ teaspoon salt
Confectioners' sugar (optional)

Preheat the oven at 350°. Cream the butter until it has the consistency of mayonnaise. In another bowl, beat together the sugar and eggs with the lemon zest, using an electric mixer, until the mixture is doubled in volume and very fluffy. Sift the flour, mace, and salt together and add gradually, but do not overmix. Fold the well-creamed butter into the batter with a rubber spatula. Turn into a well-buttered and floured 9-inch tube pan and smooth out the top. Drop the pan once on a table sharply to remove any air holes. Bake for about 1 hour, or until a cake tester inserted in the center comes out clean. Cool on a wire rack. Dust the top with sifted confectioners' sugar if desired.

VARIATIONS

Walnut Pound Cake

Fold in 1 cup finely chopped walnuts after the butter is folded in.

Rose Marble Pound Cake

(Especially lovely in appearance and flavor). Omit the mace. Divide the finished batter into two bowls. To one, stir in 1 teaspoon almond extract and 2 tablespoons ground almonds. To the other, stir in 1 teaspoon rosewater or a few drops rose essence and 1 or 2 drops of red food coloring. Spoon the batters alternately into the pan to produce a marbled effect.

Ginger Pound Cake

When adding the mace, also add ½ teaspoon nutmeg and 2 teaspoons ground ginger. Stir in 2 tablespoons brandy after the butter is added.

RYE HONEY CAKE

1 cup rye flour	⅛ teaspoon cloves
1 cup white flour	½ teaspoon allspice
½ cup sugar	2 teaspoons cinnamon
2 teaspoons baking powder	½ cup honey
¼ teaspoon salt	½ cup milk
1 teaspoon ginger	1 teaspoon grated zest of lemon
1 teaspoon nutmeg	2 teaspoons grated zest of orange

Preheat the oven at 350°. Sift together the rye flour, white flour, sugar, baking powder, salt, ginger, nutmeg, cloves, allspice, and cinnamon. Add the honey, milk, lemon zest, and orange zest, and mix well. Pour into a buttered and floured 4½ x 8½-inch loaf pan and bake about 50 minutes, or until a cake tester inserted in the center comes out clean. Remove from the pan and cool on a wire rack.

Store, wrapped, for several days before eating to allow the cake to mellow. Slice thinly.

CRUSTY SAND CAKE

Not so heavy as pound cake, but of a similar texture, this sand cake has a delicate flavor and aroma and a thick, delicious crust sandy to the touch because of its bread-crumb-coated baking pan.

---

1 cup butter
1 cup sugar
4 eggs
1 tablespoon brandy
1 teaspoon vanilla extract
1 teaspoon grated zest of lemon

2 cups sifted flour
1 tablespoon cornstarch
¼ teaspoon salt
2¼ teaspoons baking powder
Fine dry bread crumbs

Preheat the oven at 350°. Cream the butter and add the sugar gradually. Beat in the eggs, 1 at a time. Beat in the brandy, vanilla extract, and lemon zest. Sift together the flour, cornstarch, salt, and baking powder, and add it all at once to the batter, beating until thoroughly blended. Spoon into an 8½-inch tube pan that has been well buttered and dusted with fine dry bread crumbs. Drop the pan once on a table sharply to remove any air holes. Bake for about 55 minutes, or until a cake tester inserted in the center comes out clean. Remove from the pan and cool on a wire rack.

VANILLA HAZELNUT CAKE

5 eggs
1 cup sugar
2 cups plus 2 tablespoons sifted
  cake flour
¼ teaspoon salt

½ cup ground hazelnuts or
  filberts
1 teaspoon vanilla extract
Confectioners' sugar
Coffee ice cream (optional)

Preheat the oven at 350°. Beat the eggs well and add the sugar gradually. Sift the cake flour with the salt and add, mixing well. Add the nuts and vanilla extract. Pour into a buttered and floured 10-inch tube pan or spring-form pan with a tube insert. Bake for 45 to 50 minutes or until a cake tester inserted in the center comes out clean. Turn out on a wire rack to cool.

To serve, dust with sifted confectioners' sugar. The subtle nut flavor of this even-grained and light-textured cake is particularly nice served with coffee ice cream.

OLD ENGLISH SEEDCAKE

1 cup butter
2 cups sifted flour
1 teaspoon baking powder
¼ teaspoon salt
4 large eggs

1 cup sugar
1 teaspoon vanilla extract
½ teaspoon grated zest of lemon
2 tablespoons caraway seeds

Preheat the oven at 350°. Cream the butter. Sift the flour, baking powder, and salt together, and add to the butter gradually. Add the eggs, 1 at a time, mixing well after each addition. Add the sugar and mix well. Add the vanilla extract, lemon zest, and caraway seeds and combine well. Spoon into a buttered and floured 9-inch tube pan and bake for 1 hour, or until a cake tester inserted in the center comes out clean. Cool on a wire rack.

To serve, slice thinly.

PUMPERNICKEL SPICECAKE

2 cups fine pumpernickel
  crumbs
¼ cup brandy
1½ squares grated baking
  chocolate (1½ ounces)
⅓ cup ground hazelnuts or
  filberts
5 large or 6 medium egg yolks
1 rounded tablespoon finely
  chopped candied lemon peel
1 rounded tablespoon finely
  chopped candied orange peel
1 tablespoon orange juice

1 tablespoon lemon juice
Pinch of cloves
¼ teaspoon nutmeg
½ teaspoon cinnamon
5 large or 6 medium egg whites
¼ teaspoon salt
1 cup sugar
Orange marmalade
1 cup heavy cream
1 tablespoon sugar
1 teaspoon orange flower water
  (optional)

Preheat the oven at 350°. Make the pumpernickel crumbs by grating them or putting them through a food processor or blender. Toss with the brandy. Add the grated chocolate and nuts and set aside. Beat the egg yolks slightly and stir in the candied peels, orange juice, lemon juice, cloves, nutmeg, and cinnamon. Beat the egg whites until foamy. Add the salt and continue beating until the egg whites hold their shape. Add 1 cup sugar gradually and beat until thick and glossy. Fold half the egg whites into the egg yolk mixture. Fold in the remaining egg whites. Fold in the pumpernickel crumb mixture. Pour into a well-greased 8½- or 9-inch tube pan. Bake for 50 to 60 minutes, or until the cake springs back when touched lightly. Cool the cake in the pan.

To serve, remove the cake from the pan. Spread a thin layer of orange marmalade over the top. Whip the cream and add the sugar and orange flower water if available. Slice the cake into serving pieces and serve with the whipped cream.

SESAME CRUNCH CAKE

½ cup butter
2 cups turbinado sugar
2 eggs
1 tablespoon instant espresso
  coffee powder

½ cup milk
2 cups flour
2 teaspoons baking powder
¼ teaspoon salt
¼ cup sesame seeds

Preheat the oven at 350°. Cream the butter and add the turbinado sugar gradually. Add the eggs, 1 at a time, beating well after each addition. Dissolve the espresso coffee powder in the milk. Sift the flour, baking powder, and salt together and add to the batter alternately with the coffee mixture, beating until the mixture is smooth.

Butter a 10-inch spring-form pan thoroughly. Sprinkle the sesame seeds evenly over the bottom. Spoon in the batter and smooth it out with a rubber spatula. Drop the pan once on a table sharply to remove any air bubbles. Bake about 1 hour, or until a cake tester inserted in the center comes out clean. Remove from the oven and remove the cake from the pan. Cool on a wire rack, sesame-seed side up.

Makes 8 to 10 servings.

GENOISE

¼ cup butter
6 large or 7 medium eggs
1 cup superfine sugar

1½ teaspoons vanilla extract
Pinch of salt
1 cup sifted cake flour

Select the cake pans to be used, choosing two or three 8-inch round or square cake pans, two 9-inch round or square cake pans, or one large pan with high sides. Grease the pans lightly, line the bottoms with waxed paper, and grease the waxed paper lightly. Melt the butter in a small saucepan and set it aside. Have all other ingredients at room temperature before starting to mix the batter.

Preheat the oven at 350°. Place the eggs in a warm electric mixer bowl and beat, first warming the beaters, until frothy. Add the superfine sugar gradually, beating at high speed, until the mixture has doubled in volume and forms a heavy, slowly dissolving ribbon when the beater is lifted. This takes about 10 minutes. Stop occasionally to scrape the sides and bottom of the bowl with a rubber spatula. Beat in the vanilla extract and salt. With the rubber spatula, fold the flour into the batter, a heaping tablespoonful at a time. Fold in the melted butter, which must be just lukewarm, a teaspoonful at a time, being careful not to include the residue at the bottom of the pan in which the butter was melted. When all the butter has been incorporated into the batter, pour it into the cake pans. Drop the pans gently on a table once. Bake 30 to 40 minutes, or until a cake tester inserted in the center comes out clean. Turn the cakes out of the pans and remove the waxed paper from the bottoms. Cool on wire racks.

CLASSIC SPONGE CAKE

6 egg yolks	1 tablespoon lemon juice
1 cup plus 2 tablespoons superfine sugar	1 teaspoon vanilla extract
	6 egg whites
1 teaspoon grated zest of lemon, firmly packed	¼ teaspoon salt
	1½ cups sifted cake flour

Have all the ingredients at room temperature. Preheat the oven at 325°. Put the egg yolks in a warm electric mixer bowl and beat with warmed beaters until they are thick and lemon-colored, about 5 minutes. Add the superfine sugar, a small spoonful at a time, beating well. This will take about 10 minutes. Beat in the lemon zest, lemon juice, and vanilla extract.

Beat the egg whites until they are foamy. Add the salt and continue beating until they are stiff but not dry. Pile the egg whites on top of the egg yolk mixture. Sift the cake flour over the egg whites. With a rubber spatula, fold the flour and egg whites into the egg yolk mixture gently but thoroughly. Turn the batter into an ungreased 9- or 10-inch tube pan, 3½ to 4 inches deep. Bake 50 to 60 minutes, or until a cake tester inserted in the center comes out clean. Invert on a wire rack and allow to cool. Remove the pan and set the cake top side up on the wire rack.

ORANGE GLAZED ANGEL CAKE

For the cake:
1 cup sifted cake flour
½ cup sugar
¼ teaspoon salt
1⅓ cups egg whites (about 12 egg whites)
1½ teaspoons cream of tartar
1 cup sugar, sifted

1 teaspoon vanilla extract
½ teaspoon almond extract

For the glaze:
1¼ cups sifted confectioners' sugar
Grated zest of 1 orange
2 tablespoons orange juice
1 teaspoon lemon juice

For the cake: Preheat the oven at 325°. Sift the cake flour, ½ cup sugar, and salt together several times. Beat the egg whites in a large bowl with a whisk, rotary beater, or electric beater until foamy and white. Add the cream of tartar and continue beating until soft peaks form. Sprinkle 1 cup sugar over the egg whites, 2 tablespoonsful at a time, beating in each time until just blended. When all the sugar has been beaten in, add the vanilla and almonds extracts and beat them in.

With a rubber spatula, fold in the flour mixture, ¼ cup at a time. Pour into a 9-inch ungreased tube pan and bake for about 45 minutes, or until the cake is lightly browned and springs back when touched lightly. Remove from the oven and invert on a wire rack. Allow it to stand for 1 hour before removing it from the pan, loosening the sides with a spatula if necessary. Frost with the following glaze, or serve the cake plain if desired.

For the glaze: Combine the confectioners' sugar, orange zest, orange juice, and lemon juice, and spoon over the top and outside of the cooled cake. Spread with a spatula or knife. Allow the cake to stand until it is set before cutting. To serve, cut with 2 forks or an angel food cake cutter, not with a knife. Leftover unfrosted angel cake is nice toasted.

RICH BUTTER CAKE

1 cup butter
2 cups sugar
4 eggs
2¾ cups sifted cake flour

3 teaspoons baking powder
½ teaspoon salt
1 cup milk
2 teaspoons vanilla extract

Preheat the oven at 350°. Cream the butter and add the sugar gradually. Add the eggs and mix well. Sift the cake flour, baking powder, and salt together and add alternately with the milk and vanilla extract. Pour into 2 buttered and floured round 9-inch cake pans and bake 30 to 35 minutes, or until a cake tester inserted in the center comes out clean. Remove from the pans and cool on a wire rack.

This cake may also be baked in an 8x12-inch pan for about 45 to 50 minutes.

ROYAL WHITE FRUITCAKE

The Romans baked a fruitcake called satura, *which is the root of our word* saturate. *The traditional fruitcake they made, like the ones we bake today, was saturated with good things—raisins, nuts, pomegranate seeds, spices, and honeyed wine. Their fruitcake-making approach was faultless, for a really good fruitcake should be so laden with fruit that there's just enough batter to hold it all together. While there's much to be said in defense of each kind of present-day fruitcake, be it black, dark, light, or white, the latter seems to best point up the beauty of the fruits themselves, as in this recipe.*

1 cup butter
2 cups sugar
4 egg yolks, lightly beaten
1 teaspoon almond extract
2½ cups sifted flour
1 cup sifted cake flour
½ cup dry sherry
2 cups slivered blanched almonds
1½ cups cut-up candied red or
 green cherries

1½ cups cut-up candied
 pineapple
1½ cups chopped candied lemon
 and/or orange peel
1 cup cut-up candied or dried
 apricots
1 pound sultanas (about 3 cups)
½ cup cake flour
6 egg whites, stiffly beaten

Preheat the oven at 300°. Cream the butter and add the sugar gradually. Beat in the egg yolks and almond extract. Sift 2½ cups of flour and the cake flour together, and add it alternately with the sherry. Dredge the nuts and fruits in ½ cup flour, tossing well. Stir into the batter. Fold in the egg whites.

Line 2 greased 4x8½-inch loaf pans with aluminum foil. Butter well, flour, and shake out any excess flour. Divide the batter between the 2 pans. Bake about 2½ hours, or until a cake tester inserted in the center comes out clean. Remove the foil and cool the cakes on a wire rack.

If desired, the cakes can be decorated when completely cooled by putting dots of thick jam, such as apricot, on them to use as anchors for holding nut meats or candied fruits in place. If you wish to frost the cakes, use ROYAL ICING.

VANILLA BUTTER CREAM FROSTING

½ cup sugar
Generous pinch of cream of tartar
2 tablespoons water

2 egg yolks
½ cup butter (at room temperature)
1½ teaspoons vanilla extract

Combine the sugar, cream of tartar, and water in a small saucepan and bring to a boil over medium heat, stirring constantly until the sugar is dissolved. Raise the heat and cook to 240°, or until the mixture spins a long thread without stirring. Remove the saucepan from the heat and set it aside.

Beat the egg yolks, preferably with an electric beater, until they are thick and pale in color. Beat in the syrup gradually. Beat in the butter, 1 tablespoon at a time, until well blended. Beat in the vanilla extract. Chill the mixture until it stiffens a little, and beat it with a wooden spoon. Chill again until it is of spreading consistency.

Makes about 1½ cups.

VARIATIONS:

Chocolate Butter Cream

Melt 2 squares (2 ounces) unsweetened chocolate in the top of a double boiler over hot water, stirring. Set the chocolate aside to cool while making the above frosting, and mix it in when adding the vanilla extract.

Coffee Butter Cream

Dissolve 2 teaspoons instant coffee powder in the vanilla extract.

Rum Butter Cream

Stir 2 tablespoons dark rum into the frosting when adding the vanilla extract.

Other Flavors

Add any flavor you like in extracts, liqueurs, and so on, to the basic recipe, with or without vanilla extract. A drop or two of food coloring may also be added if desired.

ROYAL ICING

2 egg whites
1 tablespoon lemon juice

1⅔ cups sifted confectioners'
sugar

Beat the egg whites just enough to break them up. With a wooden spoon, stir in the lemon juice and about 1 cup of the confectioners' sugar, and beat until smooth. Add the balance of the confectioners' sugar gradually until the icing has a smooth, thick consistency.

With a spatula or knife, ice the cake with a thin coating of icing. Allow it to dry completely. Keep the icing bowl covered with a damp towel when not working with it. Apply a second, thicker coat of icing to the cake and allow it to dry.

CHAPTER 5

Fruit Desserts

And feed upon strawberries,
Sugar and cream.
—nursery rhyme

Fruit, the oldest of all desserts, still walks away with top honors because of its utter simplicity, eye appeal, and health-giving properties. Arranged in a lovely bowl or handsome basket, fruit can provide the most beautiful of all centerpieces for a table and the easiest-of-all-to-serve desserts. The French, Italians, and other Europeans known for making some of the world's most delightful desserts instinctively include fruit, and often cheese, on their everyday menus, reserving pastries and other sweets for special dinners and holiday fare.

Ancient peoples valued fruit highly, and whether or not they called their fruit course dessert, they consumed many varieties. A poem written in India in the second century tells of peddlers in the streets selling mangoes. Melons were favorites of the Persians, who also had an abundance of other fruits, such as limes, rhubarb, cherries, and peaches, the latter probably originating in that land. The Sumerians grew dates, figs, and grapes on the site of the present-day Libyan desert. The clay tablets they left behind attest to the variety of their fruits, listing apricots, prunes, and raisins as proper foods for the gods—and no doubt for Sumerians, too.

The Romans enjoyed a profusion of fruits that included peaches, apricots, cherries, quinces, plums, pomegranates, blackberries, citron, carob, elderberries, melons, mulberries, strawberries, blueberries, sloes, and the staples of that time, figs and dates. Many of these fruits, or the plants from which they grew, were brought home from conquered lands by the Romans. These people often made a meal of fruit alone, and they dried plums, apples, and other fruits to eat when fresh fruit wasn't available, pears being considered the ultimate in dried fruit. Fruits were also preserved in wine concentrate, much as we make rumtoff or brandied fruits today. So fond of fruit and horticulture were the Romans that they developed forty-one varieties of pears and twenty-nine varieties of figs alone.

In medieval times, a popular and healthful dessert was honeyed fruit. Even the most lowly of serfs is said to have had his own beehive to ensure his being able to make a continual supply of the concoction.

Some exotic fruits found their way to Europe when Spanish conquerors returned from Mexico and Central and South America with samples of guavas, avocados, and pineapples. Another New World treat they discovered was the papaya, a favorite meal ending of the Aztecs, who wisely treated it as an aid to digestion as well as a tenderizer of meat.

Desserts in England around the time of Henry VIII consisted of things like perfumed fruits and various kinds of candied flowers. The English seem always to have had a fondness for fruit, and early cookbooks advised the housewife to dry apricots, plums, and pears, to preserve olives and all kinds of fruits, to brandy fruits, and to serve them all in an elaborate manner when special guests were entertained during the winter. Cherry trees were first planted in quantity in England during the reign of Queen Elizabeth I. That lady, to satisfy her notorious sweet tooth, established orchards to ensure a supply of cherries to be made into pies, one of her favorite desserts. These cherry pies are said to be the forerunners of fruit pies as we know them today.

The cultivation of fruit began early in America with Ponce de León's planting of orange and lime seedlings in Florida. These he brought from the island of Hispaniola, where the fruits had been planted previously by Columbus.

Colonists in Virginia found native fruits growing plentifully, and they also had seeds and plants of English favorites sent over for their gardens. Cherries, strawberries, persimmons, mulberries, and melons were common, and lemons, oranges, prunes, and raisins could be bought for a price. The fruits were eaten raw or made into preserves, pickled fruits, brandied fruits, or fruit cordials with fine French brandy as a base, or they were dried or made into wine.

Housewives in the New England colonies depended on native plants and trees to provide them with fruit. Pumpkins were popular and were often prepared by cutting off the top, scooping out the seeds, and baking the shell. Milk was poured into the cooked pumpkin, which was eaten straight out of the shell. Apples and berries as well as pumpkins were dried for winter use. Cranberries grew in great quantity in parts of Massachusetts, where the eating of the fruit warded off scurvy in the early days of the settlers.

Pioneers who settled the West were guided by the Indians, who in turn were often guided by the bears, in their quest for the many fruits growing wild over the land. Bears, Indians, and pioneers all feasted throughout the summer on blueberries in the vast Rocky Mountain area. The Indians gathered their berries in fern-lined baskets to preserve the freshness of the fruit, and they taught the pioneers how to dry blueberries as well as currants and other berries for cold-weather eating. Red raspberries were gathered in the foothills of the Rockies to be eaten, dried, or used in making hot or cold drinks. Strawberries grew in abundance, and when they were in season, the Indians satiated themselves by having strawberries served for breakfast, strawberries made into soup, strawberries sprinkled with milkweed dew, and strawberries as seasoning for meat dishes. More strawberries were used to make medicines for a variety of ills, and more still to make strawberry bitters. The Indians ate all kinds of fruits and berries, such as gooseberries (which they ate raw or sometimes cooked with young corn), grapes, and elderberries. The settlers learned to make a drink from the elderberries, as well as jelly, chutney, and fried elderberry flower heads.

Necessity no longer requires us to dry or preserve fruits to ensure a steady supply through the winter. Nevertheless, we like to buy dried fruits the year round because of their unique flavor and texture, the convenience of having them on hand, and for the storehouses of nutrition that they are. Many people still preserve their own fruits in preference to buying commercially prepared ones if they happen to have an abundance of fruit, special preserving recipes, or a love for the old-fashioned goodness of simple foods.

The best and most popular fruit is, of course, fresh fruit, and generally the best of the fresh fruits are those grown and sold locally. These in-season fruits have had the advantage of ripening partially or completely on the tree, bush, or vine to ensure the best flavor and texture. Hothouse fruits, while beautiful, seldom match local produce in taste. Quality, not appearance, is what to look for when buying fruits. Next to locally grown fruit, the best buy is fruit shipped in from other regions or nations. If it were not for modern packaging and transportation methods, we would never be able to have melons in New York, apples in Florida, or grapefruit in Alaska. We'd never know the joy of eating tropical treats like papayas or mangos, or even the now-commonplace banana.

Fruits that are exceptionally perishable, extraordinarily exotic, or not in great demand everywhere at all times, can be bought in jars or cans in specialty food shops or supermarkets to be used whenever needed. Mandarin orange segments, Chinese gooseberries, guava shells, and mango slices, for example, can all be waiting on your pantry shelf ready to become out-of-the-ordinary desserts.

Since fruit is so essential a part of the diet that it should be eaten every day, and because it lends itself so well to being prepared in so many ways, nearly a quarter of this book is devoted to fruit recipes. Serving fresh fruit by itself of course requires no recipe, but it's good to keep in mind that you can make fresh fruit interesting by serving it in an unusual basket or bowl and by serving several color-complementing kinds and a variety of sizes of fruit together—red apples, yellow bananas, and purple grapes, for instance, or golden apricots, dark-red cherries, and green plums. If they're available, tuck a few leaves in among the fruit—grape, boxwood, or small rhododendron leaves. Nuts, in the shell or out, are natural companions for fresh fruit. Supply each person with a small plate and a knife for cutting or peeling the fruit, and if you do serve nuts, put out nutcrackers and picks.

Another easy yet ideal way of serving fruit is with cheese, and suggestions for doing this are thoroughly covered in "Cheese and Fruit for Dessert" in Chapter 11.

A step beyond the simplicity of serving fresh fruit to be eaten whole is to cut up two or more kinds of fruits, add sugar or honey and a bit of liqueur or wine, and allow the mixture to macerate for an hour or so in a glass or china bowl in the refrigerator before serving. Fruit prepared in this manner is called a macédoine. Recipes will be found in this chapter, or you can make your own combinations of berries and cut-up fruits with a liqueur such as Grand Marnier or any orange liqueur, a fruit liqueur such as apricot, strawberry, currant (cassis), raspberry, or cherry (kirsch), or with a wine such as champagne, ginger wine, light white wine, or rosé, or a heavier wine such as Port, Sherry, Marsala, or Madeira, or with brandy, rum, or a liqueur like Benedictine, chartreuse, or anisette.

When you prepare a syrup and poach fruit in it, it becomes a compote. Recipes for compotes are in this chapter, as are those for baked fruit, fruit fritters, puddings, molds, fruit soups, cakes, fruit sauces, and so on. Some recipes for hard-to-find fruits such as quinces and mulberries are included for anyone lucky enough to come across the fruits but lacking ways in which to use them. Most of the recipes here are for easy-to-find fruits running the gamut from apples to strawberries, and can be made use of every day. In addition to these recipes, you will find the following fruit recipes in other chapters:

Normandy Apple Tart
Easy Apple Strudel
Apple Charlotte
Apple Pandowdy
Apple Duff
Cherry Apple Bake with Cherry Heering Sauce
Minted Apricots
Apricot Soufflé
Frozen Apricot Mousse
Apricot Honey Ice Cream
Vanilla Converts to Apricot Ice Cream
Frozen Banana Cream
Banana Soufflé
Blackberry Bavarian Cream
Blackberries in Port Cream
Blueberry Soufflé
Blueberry Streusel
Deep-Dish Blueberry Pie
Blueberry Babas
Blueberries in Kahlua Cream
Cherries Jubilee
Cherry Pudding
Cranberry Pudding with Honey Eggnog Sauce
Vanilla Converts to Cranberry Ice Cream
Fig Pudding
Fig Ice Cream
Gooseberry Pie
Grapefruit Sherbet
Deep-Dish Mango Pie
Mango Ice Cream
Melon Sherbet
Melon Cream
Gingered Honeydew
Cantalope Ice Cream
Mulberry Rhubarb Pie
Deep-Dish Nectarine Pie
Double Orange Meringue
Mandarin Oranges in Lime Juice
Peach Cobbler
Peach Mousse
Peach Tart
Pears Hélène
Pear Tarts Bourdaloue

Pears Schouvaloff
Persimmon Ice Cream
Pineapple Mousse
Green Plum Pie
Plum Pudding
Prunes in Port with Gervais
Raspberry Sherbet
Raspberry Bavarian Cream
Rhubarb Crisp
Frozen Strawberry Mousse
Strawberry Shortcake
Quick-as-a-Wink Strawberry Soufflé
Strawberry Tarts
Fresh Strawberry Omelet
Strawberry Soufflé
Treasure Chest Torte
Brandied Fruits in Champagne and Orange Jelly
Iced Fruit in Ginger Wine

MAPLE MINCEMEAT BAKED APPLES

Firm apples   **Mincemeat**
Butter   **Maple Syrup**
Rum

Preheat the oven at 350°. Allowing 1 apple per serving, core the apples, making sure not to cut through the blossom end. Pare off the skin on the upper third of the apples. Place them in a baking dish just large enough to hold them. Put a small piece of butter and 1 teaspoon rum in the cavity of each apple. Fill to the top with mincemeat. Pour maple syrup over the apples and to a depth of ¼ inch in the bottom of the baking dish. Bake for 30 to 40 minutes, or until the apples are tender but not mushy when pierced with a fork, basting every 10 minutes during the baking time. Serve warm.

NUT BAKED APPLES WITH SOUR CREAM-BRANDY SAUCE

6 firm apples
2 tablespoons soft butter
6 tablespoons chopped almonds
  or other chopped nuts
6 tablespoons sugar
½ teaspoon cinnamon
¼ teaspoon nutmeg

1 cup sugar
1 cup water
1 cup sour cream
2 tablespoons confectioners'
  sugar
2 tablespoons brandy

Preheat the oven at 350°. Core the apples, making sure not to cut through the blossom end. Pare off the skin on the upper third of the apples. Place them in a baking dish just large enough to hold them. Combine the butter, chopped nuts, 6 tablespoons sugar, cinnamon, and nutmeg, and fill the apple cavities with the mixture.

Combine 1 cup sugar and the water in a saucepan and bring to a boil, stirring to dissolve the sugar. Cook several minutes longer until the mixture becomes a light syrup. Pour over the apples and to a depth of ¼ inch in the bottom of the baking dish. Bake for 30 to 40 minutes, or until the apples are tender but not mushy when pierced with a fork, basting every 10 minutes during the baking time. Remove from the oven. Cool and refrigerate.

At serving time, combine the sour cream, confectioners' sugar, and brandy, and spoon some of the mixture on each apple.

Makes 6 servings.

APPLE BEIGNETS

1 egg yolk
3 tablespoons oil
Scant ¾ cup stale beer
2 teaspoons brandy
Pinch of salt
Pinch of sugar

1 cup sifted flour
3 or 4 large tart apples
1 tablespoon kirsch, rum, or
  lemon juice
1 egg white
Fat or oil for frying

Place the egg yolk, oil, beer, brandy, salt, sugar, and flour in the container of an electric blender or food processor and whir until blended, if necessary stopping to scrape down the sides of the container. Pour into a mixing bowl, cover, and set in a warm place for several hours.

Core and peel the apples and cut them into ¼- to ½-inch-thick crosswise slices. Place them in a glass or ceramic bowl and sprinkle with the kirsch, rum, or lemon juice. Cover the bowl and allow it to stand at room temperature for 30 to 60 minutes, turning the apples occasionally. Drain the apple slices and pat them dry with paper towels.

Beat the egg whites until stiff and fold it into the batter. Place 3 or 4 apple slices at a time in the batter, turning each piece over to coat it well. Plunge the coated apples into deep fat heated to 375° and fry until puffed and brown on both sides, turning once. Drain on paper towels. Continue until all slices have been fried. Serve immediately.

Makes 4 servings.

CHILLED PINK APPLE SOUP

2 or 3 large tart red apples	2 tablespoons water
4 cups water	¼ cup dry white wine
3 strips lemon peel	Sweetened whipped cream
1 stick cinnamon	Toasted slivered almonds
2 whole cloves	ALMOND MACAROONS
½ cup sugar	(homemade or bought)
2 tablespoons cornstarch	(optional)

Core and slice the apples but do not peel them. Place them in a saucepan with 4 cups water, the lemon peel, cinnamon, and cloves, and bring to a boil. Lower the heat, cover, and simmer 5 minutes or so until the apples are tender. Rub them through a sieve and return them to the saucepan. Add the sugar and cornstarch (which has been combined with 2 tablespoons water), and cook, stirring, until the mixture thickens. Remove from the heat and stir in the wine. Cool and refrigerate.

Serve very cold in chilled bowls. Garnish each bowl with a dollop of sweetened whipped cream sprinkled with toasted slivered almonds. If desired, serve with almond macaroons.

Makes 4 to 6 servings.

APRICOT POACHED APPLES
WITH ORANGE CREAM

For the apples:
½ cup water
½ cup apricot preserves
2 tablespoons sugar
1 teaspoon grated zest of orange
    peel
3 large apples
Lemon juice

For the orange cream:
1¾ cups milk
½ cup sugar
¼ cup cornstarch
Pinch of salt
4 large or 5 medium egg yolks
¼ cup cold milk
1 teaspoon vanilla extract
1 tablespoon orange liqueur

For the apples: Combine the water, apricot preserves, sugar, and orange zest in a small saucepan. Bring to a boil, stirring, and simmer over low heat for a few minutes. Peel and core the apples and cut them in half. Rub them all over with the lemon juice. Place them in a skillet or saucepan wide enough to hold them, and pour the apricot mixture around them. Cover and simmer over low heat until the apples are tender but still firm, basting a few times during cooking. This will take about 15 minutes. Remove the apple halves to a serving dish, core side up, and cool. Cover and refrigerate until serving time.

For the Orange Cream: Heat 1¾ cups milk until hot but not boiling. Combine the sugar, cornstarch, and salt in the top of a double boiler and add the heated milk gradually, using a wire whisk if necessary to blend. When the mixture is smooth, place it over direct heat and cook, stirring, until it becomes very thick. Remove the mixture from the heat. Beat the egg yolks, combine them with ¼ cup cold milk, and add to the first mixture. Place it over hot water and cook, stirring, until the mixture thickens again. Remove it from the heat and stir in the vanilla extract and orange liqueur. Allow the mixture to cool, stirring it often to prevent a skin from forming on top of the cream. Cover and refrigerate until serving time.

To serve, spoon the Orange Cream over the apples, allowing it to run around them. Spoon the apricot sauce over the apples.

Makes 6 servings.

APRICOTINA

A tangy summer dessert.

**8 ripe apricots, thoroughly
    chilled
1 cup sour cream**

**Seville orange marmalade
    (vintage Seville orange
    marmalade if available)**

Remove the pits from the apricots and slice them. Arrange the apricot slices in 4 dessert glasses alternately with spoonsful of sour cream and dabs of orange marmalade, ending with sour cream topped by a bit of marmalade.

Makes 4 servings.

APRICOTS A LA CREME

**2 cups dried apricots
4 cups water
½ cup sugar
2 teaspoons lemon juice
½ teaspoon almond extract**

**1 cup heavy cream
¼ cup blanched slivered almonds
Whipped cream
Thinly sliced unblanched almonds**

Bring the apricots and water to a boil in a saucepan. Add the sugar and stir until it is dissolved. Lower the heat and simmer, uncovered, for about 30 minutes, or until the apricots are tender. Drain. Put the apricots in the container of an electric blender or food processor and blend them until smooth, or put them through a food mill. Transfer the mixture to a bowl. Add the lemon juice and almond extract. Whip the heavy cream until stiff. Stir about one-third of the whipped cream into the apricot mixture and combine them well. Fold in the remaining whipped cream. Fold in the blanched slivered almonds. Spoon into 6 to 8 ramekins or *pots au crème* cups. Chill well.

To serve, decorate with whipped cream and sprinkle with thinly sliced unblanched almonds.

Makes 6 to 8 servings.

APRICOTS CONDE

A molded apricot-rice dessert.

½ cup sugar
1 cup water
8 fresh apricots
1 teaspoon vanilla extract
¾ cup rice
2 cups scalded milk
¼ teaspoon salt
⅓ cup sugar
1 two-inch piece vanilla bean
1½ tablespoons plain gelatin

¼ cup cold water
2 tablespoons butter
3 egg yolks
1 teaspoon rosewater
½ cup heavy cream
Green cherries, citron, angelica,
    or candied mint leaves
    (optional)
1 recipe APRICOT SAUCE

Combine ½ cup sugar with the water in a saucepan and bring to a boil, stirring, until the sugar dissolves. Simmer for 5 minutes. Add the apricots, which have been halved and pitted. Simmer for several minutes until the apricot halves are just tender. Remove from the heat and stir in the vanilla extract. Turn the mixture into a bowl, cool, cover, and refrigerate.

Meanwhile, put the rice in the top of a double boiler and cover with some boiling water. Cover and allow to stand for 30 minutes. Drain. Add the scalded milk, salt, ⅓ cup sugar, and vanilla bean. Place over simmering water, cover, and cook about 45 minutes, or until the rice is tender and has absorbed all the liquid.

Shortly before the rice has finished cooking, soften the gelatin in the cold water. When the rice has finished cooking, remove the vanilla bean and stir in the softened gelatin until it has dissolved. Add the butter and stir until it has melted. Remove from the heat. Beat the egg yolks lightly and stir a spoonful of the rice mixture into them. Then stir the egg yolk mixture into the rice mixture and combine gently but well. Add the rosewater. Turn the mixture into a bowl, cool slightly, and refrigerate it until slightly chilled.

Whip the heavy cream until it is stiff. Stir about one-third of the whipped cream into the rice mixture. Then fold in the balance of the whipped cream. Turn into a lightly oiled plain shallow mold. Cover and refrigerate until the mixture is well chilled and firm.

To serve, unmold on a serving plate and arrange the apricot halves over the top and sides. If desired, decorate with bits of green cherries, citron, or angelica, or candied mint leaves. Serve with Apricot Sauce.

Makes 8 servings.

BANANAS PAOLINA

¾ cup heavy cream
¾ cup canned sweetened
  coconut cream
Pinch of salt
1 teaspoon rosewater*
1 drop red food coloring*
1 tablespoon sugar

1 can mango slices, chilled and
  drained, or 1 fresh mango,
  chilled and sliced
1 can Chinese gooseberries,
  chilled and drained, or ¾ cup
  chilled fresh pineapple chunks
  or canned pineapple chunks,
  drained
2 bananas

Combine the heavy cream, coconut cream, salt, rosewater, and food coloring. Cover and chill until serving time.

To serve, toss together the mangos, Chinese gooseberries or pineapple chunks, and bananas (which have been cut into ½-inch diagonal slices). Arrange in dessert glasses. Spoon a generous amount of the chilled coconut cream sauce over each serving.

Makes 6 servings.

* If rose essence is available, use a drop or two in place of the rosewater and omit the red food coloring. Also add more sugar to taste if necessary.

BANANAS A LA CREME

4 well-ripened bananas
6 tablespoons lemon juice
½ cup heavy cream
2 tablespoons sugar

1 or 2 tablespoons orange liqueur
  (optional)
6 candied violets or lilacs
  (optional)
1 recipe CAT TONGUES (optional)

Mash the bananas and add the lemon juice, heavy cream, and sugar, and mix well. If desired, put the mixture in an electric blender at medium speed for 5 seconds or in a food processor for 1 second for a smoother texture. Cover and refrigerate until chilled.

To serve, stir in the orange liqueur if desired, and spoon the mixture into stemmed sherbet glasses. Top with a candied violet or lilac if desired. Serve with Cat Tongues if desired.

Makes 6 servings.

BAKED GUAVA ALMOND BANANAS

½ cup guava jelly
2 tablespoons water
2 tablespoons butter

½ cup canned sweetened
  coconut cream
¼ cup toasted slivered almonds
6 bananas

Preheat the oven at 375°. Melt the guava jelly in a saucepan with the water and butter. Stir in the coconut cream and almonds and heat slightly. Peel the bananas and arrange them in a shallow buttered baking dish. Pour the guava mixture over the bananas and bake about 15 minutes, basting once or twice, until the bananas are just tender but not mushy. Serve them immediately, spooning the sauce over each serving.

Makes 6 servings.

RUM BANANAS WITH KUMQUATS

3 tablespoons butter
4 bananas
8 kumquats
1 tablespoon lemon juice
4 tablespoons brown sugar

½ teaspoon cinnamon
4 tablespoons rum
Vanilla or orange ice cream
  (optional)

Melt the butter in a skillet or the blazer pan of a chafing dish. Peel and slice the bananas in half lengthwise, and cut the kumquats in half. Sauté the fruit briefly in the butter until the bananas are lightly browned on both sides. Sprinkle with the lemon juice, brown sugar, and cinnamon. Warm the rum and pour it over the fruit. Ignite the mixture and serve immediately. If desired, serve with vanilla or orange ice cream.

Makes 4 servings.

Fruit Desserts

BANANA FRITTERS WITH BLACK CHERRY SAUCE

For the fritters:
1 egg yolk
3 tablespoons oil
Scant ¾ cup stale beer
2 teaspoons kirsch
Pinch of salt
Pinch of sugar
1 cup sifted flour
6 bananas
1 tablespoon confectioners' sugar

2 tablespoons rum
1 egg white
Cooking oil
For the sauce:
1 14–16 ounce can pitted bing
  (or other dark) cherries
2 teaspoons cornstarch
2 tablespoons lemon juice
⅓ cup sugar
1 tablespoon kirsch

For the fritters: Combine the egg yolk, oil, beer, kirsch, salt, sugar, and flour in an eletcric blender at high speed for 1 or 2 minutes, stopping to scrape down the sides if necessary, or in a food processor for several seconds. Transfer the mixture to a bowl, cover, and allow to stand in a warm place for 2 hours.

Cut the bananas in half lengthwise, and in thirds crosswise. Place them in a shallow glass or ceramic dish and sprinkle the confectioners' sugar and rum over them. Cover the mixture and allow it to stand at room temperature for 30 to 60 minutes, turning the bananas occasionally.

For the sauce: Drain the cherries and combine ¼ cup of the drained syrup with the cornstarch. Place the balance of the syrup (about ¾ cup) in a saucepan with the lemon juice and sugar. Bring to a boil, stirring, and simmer for 2 minutes. Stir in the cornstarch mixture and continue stirring until the mixture is thickened and smooth. Remove from the heat. Stir in the cherries and kirsch. Set aside.

To finish fritters: Drain the banana pieces and pat them dry with paper towels. Beat the egg white until stiff and fold it into the batter. Heat the cooking oil in a deep-fat fryer or wok to 375°. Place a few pieces of banana in the batter and coat them well. Plunge them, a few at a time, into the hot fat and fry, turning once, until puffed and brown on both sides. Drain on paper towels. Continue frying the remaining pieces.

Serve immediately, allowing 6 pieces per serving and spooning the cherry sauce over each serving.

Makes 6 servings.

BLACKBERRY FLUMMERY

2 cups blackberries
1 cup water
¼ cup cornstarch
¾ cup sugar

Pinch of salt
1 tablespoon lemon juice
1 cup heavy cream
1 or 2 tablespoons sugar

Put the blackberries and water in a saucepan, bring to a boil, and simmer about 5 minutes. Remove the mixture from the heat and pass it through a sieve or food mill. Add enough cold water to measure 2½ cups, and return it to the saucepan. Combine a small amount of the blackberry mixture with the cornstarch, stirring until it is smooth. Pour into a saucepan. Add ¾ cup sugar, a pinch of salt, and the lemon juice. Cook, stirring, until the mixture thickens. Cool and refrigerate.

To serve, whip the heavy cream until it is stiff, and add 1 or 2 tablespoons of sugar to taste. Spoon the blackberry mixture into serving glasses and top with the whipped cream.

Makes 4 servings.

POACHED SPICED BLUEBERRIES

¼ cup water
¼ cup sugar
Juice of ½ lemon
Strip of lemon peel

1 cinnamon stick
1 whole clove
Pinch of salt
1 pint fresh blueberries

Combine the water and sugar in a saucepan and bring to a boil. Add the lemon juice and peel, cinnamon stick, clove, and salt, and simmer a few minutes. Add the blueberries and simmer several minutes until the blueberries are cooked but still retain their shape. Cool the mixture and allow to macerate in the refrigerator for 24 hours. To serve, spoon into dessert glasses.

Makes 4 servings.

BLUEBERRIES LIMOUSIN

This dish, known in the Limousin area of France as clafouti, *may also be made with cherries, which can be macerated in kirsch before baking.*

2 cups fresh blueberries	**2 teaspoons vanilla extract**
1 cup milk	**Pinch of salt**
⅓ cup sugar	**1 cup flour**
2 eggs	**Confectioners' sugar**

Preheat the oven at 350°. Wash the blueberries and dry them well. Turn them into a buttered shallow baking dish 1½ inches deep. (A round 9-inch cake pan will do nicely.)

In the container of an electric blender or food processor, blend the milk, sugar, eggs, vanilla extract, and salt for a few seconds. Add the flour and blend the mixture until smooth. Pour over the blueberries. Bake for about 1 hour or until it is puffy and a cake tester inserted in the center comes out clean.

Serve warm, if possible, as it will deflate as it cools. Sprinkle heavily with sifted confectioners' sugar.

BLUEBERRY ROLL

2 cups flour	**1 teaspoon crystallized ginger,**
½ teaspoon salt	**finely chopped**
1 tablespoon baking powder	**1 cup heavy cream**
3 tablespoons butter	**2 tablespoons sugar or**
¾ cup milk	**(preferably) 1 tablespoon**
1 tablespoon melted butter	**syrup from a jar of preserved**
2 cups fresh blueberries	**ginger in syrup**
2 tablespoons corn syrup	

Preheat the oven at 400°. Sift the flour, salt, and baking powder into a bowl and cut in the butter with a pastry blender or two knives. Quickly stir in the milk, knead gently for a moment, and turn the dough out onto floured board. Roll out into a rectangle ⅛-inch thick. Brush with the melted butter.

Wash and dry the blueberries thoroughly and combine them with the corn syrup and crystallized ginger. Spoon the blueberry mixture over the dough. Roll it up in jellyroll fashion. Brush the edges with water and seal well. Brush the top of the pastry with milk. Place on a greased baking sheet and make 4 gashes on the top to allow for escaping steam. Bake 25 minutes. Transfer to an oval serving plate or long board.

Whip the heavy cream just enough for it to begin to hold its shape. Add the sugar or ginger syrup. Transfer the cream to a serving bowl and serve with the Blueberry Roll.

BURGUNDY CHERRY SOUP

1 sixteen-ounce can dark pitted cherries in syrup	Pinch of salt
	1 one-inch piece cinnamon stick
1 strip orange peel	1½ cups red Burgundy wine
1 strip lemon peel	Slightly sweetened whipped
1 tablespoon cornstarch	cream
2 tablespoons water	

Put the cherries with their liquid through a food processor or electric blender until they are pureed. Empty them into a saucepan and add the orange peel, lemon peel, cornstarch mixed with water, salt, and the cinnamon stick. Place the mixture over heat and stirring, bring to a boil. Remove from the heat and stir in the wine. Cool and chill.

To serve, remove the cinnamon stick and citrus peels and pour into small, fancy bowls or cups. Put a dollop of sweetened whipped cream on top of each serving.

Makes 4 or 5 servings.

CHERRY MOUSSE

1 envelope plain gelatin
¼ cup sherry
1¼ cups canned drained bing
   cherries, cut into quarters
1 tablespoon lemon juice

Grated zest of 1 lemon
1 tablespoon kirsch
2 egg whites
⅓ cup sugar
1 cup heavy cream

Soften the gelatin in the sherry. Place in the top of a double boiler, set over hot water, and stir until the gelatin has dissolved. Remove from the heat. Stir in the cherries, lemon juice, lemon zest, and kirsch. Beat the egg whites until soft peaks form, and beat in the sugar, a little at a time, until the mixture is stiff and shiny. Stir a little of the cherry mixture into the egg whites. Then fold the egg whites into the cherry mixture.

Beat the cream until stiff. Stir a little of the cherry mixture into the whipped cream. Then fold the whipped cream into the cherry mixture. Turn into a 1½-quart container, cover, and freeze until firm. To serve, spoon into dessert glasses.

Makes 6 servings.

CHERRIES IN CLARET

1 pound fresh ripe cherries
1 cup Bordeaux (claret) wine
½ cup sugar
1 stick cinnamon
2 whole cloves

2 tablespoons currant jelly
Whipped cream (optional)
LADYFINGERS (homemade or
   bought from bakery) (optional)

Remove the stems and pits from the cherries and place them in a saucepan with the wine, sugar, cinnamon stick, and cloves. Bring to a boil, reduce the heat, cover, and simmer for 10 minutes. Remove the cherries and reduce the syrup to ½ cup. Stir in the currant jelly. Place the cherries back in the syrup. Cool and chill.

To serve, spoon the cherries into dessert glasses and, if desired, top with whipped cream. LADYFINGERS are a nice accompaniment if desired.

Makes 4 servings.

STUFFED CHERRIES

1 pound fresh ripe cherries
Shelled whole hazelnuts
Sugar

2 tablespoons kirsch or
   Maraschino or Cherry Heering
Heavy cream, slightly whipped

Remove the stems and pits from the cherries and press 1 hazelnut into the cavity left by each pit. Place in a bowl and sprinkle lightly with the sugar and kirsch or Maraschino or Cherry Heering. Cover and refrigerate 1 hour or longer.

To serve, spoon the cherries into dessert glasses and top with slightly whipped cream.

Makes 4 servings.

CRANBERRY KISSEL

4 cups cranberries
2 cups water
1 cup sugar

1½ tablespoons cornstarch
1½ tablespoons water
1 cup heavy cream

Bring the cranberries and 2 cups water to a boil in a saucepan. Reduce the heat and simmer until the cranberries are tender. Rub them through a fine sieve or put them through a food mill fitted with a fine disk. Add the sugar, taste, and, if necessary, add a little more sugar. Return the mixture to the saucepan, bring to a boil, and stir in the cornstarch (which has been combined with 1½ tablespoons water). Cook for several minutes, stirring, until the mixture has thickened. Cool it to lukewarm and pour it into serving dishes. Refrigerate. Serve with heavy cream, plain or whipped.

Makes 6 servings.

STUFFED BAKED FIGS

8 to 12 fresh figs (2 or 3 per
   person, depending on size of
   figs)
½ cup chopped unsalted
   cashew nuts

3 tablespoons honey
¼ cup Port wine
¼ cup honey
6 tablespoons heavy cream

Wash the figs and place them in a saucepan with cold water to just cover. Bring to a boil, cover, lower heat, and simmer for 15 minutes. Drain and cool.

Preheat the oven at 350°. Combine the cashew nuts and 3 tablespoons honey. Make a small slit in the side of each fig and spoon in some of the cashew mixture. Arrange the figs in a buttered shallow baking dish and pour the Port over them. Bake for 15 minutes.

Combine ¼ cup honey and the heavy cream. Serve the figs while they are still warm, spooning some of the honey-cream mixture over each serving.

Makes 4 servings.

FIGS WITH RASPBERRY CREAM

12 fresh figs
1 ten-ounce package frozen
  raspberries, thawed

2 tablespoons superfine sugar
½ teaspoon lemon juice
½ cup heavy cream

Peel the figs, place them in a bowl, cover, and refrigerate. Put the raspberries through an electric blender or food processor until pureed. Put them through a fine strainer to remove the seeds. Combine them with the superfine sugar and lemon juice. Whip the cream until stiff and fold it into the raspberry mixture. To serve, place 2 or 3 figs in each serving dish and spoon the Raspberry Cream generously over each.

Makes 4 to 6 servings.

FIGS FLAMBE

12 ripe figs
3 tablespoons orange liqueur

3 tablespoons brandy
Heavy cream

Peel the figs, prick them with a fork, and arrange them in a chafing dish. Pour the orange liqueur and brandy over the figs and put the chafing dish over direct heat for a few seconds until the liqueur is just warm. Ignite immediately and shake the pan until the flames die. Serve immediately with any liqueur that may remain, and pour a little heavy cream over each serving.

Makes 4 to 6 servings.

Fruit Desserts

FIGS IN LIQUEUR

12 ripe figs
1 cup sour cream

2 tablespoons coffee liqueur or
    chocolate liqueur
Cocoa or grated chocolate

Peel the figs. Combine the sour cream and liqueur. Place 2 or 3 figs on each serving dish and spoon the sour cream mixture over each. Dust with a little sifted cocoa, or sprinkle with a little grated chocolate.

Makes 4 to 6 servings.

FIGS AND STRAWBERRIES

1 pint strawberries
1 sixteen-ounce jar figs
2 tablespoons kirsch
½ cup heavy cream
1 teaspoon sugar

2 teaspoons strawberry liqueur or
    raspberry liqueur
1 pint FIG ICE CREAM or 1 pint
    VANILLA ICE CREAM
    (homemade or bought)

Wash and hull the strawberries, and cut any large ones in half lengthwise. Drain the figs and combine them with the strawberries and kirsch, tossing lightly. Cover the mixture and refrigerate 1 hour. Whip the cream until it is stiff, and add the sugar and liqueur. Fold the whipped cream mixture into the chilled strawberry-fig mixture. Soften the ice cream and quickly fold it into the fruit mixture. Spoon into chilled dessert glasses and serve immediately.

Makes 6 servings.

GOOSEBERRY FOOL

2 cups fresh gooseberries
½ cup water
¼ cup sugar

½ cup heavy cream
1 recipe LACE COOKIES or
    PETITS CORNETS (optional)

Remove the blossom and stem ends of the gooseberries and wash them in cold water. Combine the water and sugar in a saucepan and bring to a boil, stirring. Simmer for 2 minutes. Add the gooseberries and cook for 10 minutes, or until they are tender. Puree the gooseberry mixture in an electric blender or food processor, or put it through a food mill. Refrigerate for 1 hour. Whip the cream until it is stiff, and fold it into the gooseberry mixture. Serve with cookies if desired.

Makes 6 servings.

BRANDIED GRAPEFRUIT

2 grapefruit	**¼ cup brandy**
¼ cup brown sugar	**Butter**

Cut the grapefruit in half crosswise. Remove the seeds, leaving a small cavity in the center of each half. Run a curved knife around the sides to loosen the fruit, and run a straight knife on the sides of each section to separate the sections from the membrane.

Preheat the broiler. Place the grapefruit halves in a shallow ovenproof dish just large enough to hold them. Sprinkle the top of each grapefruit half with 1 tablespoon brown sugar. Pour 1 tablespoon brandy in the center of each one. Place a pat of butter on each one. Broil for about 5 minutes until the butter and sugar are nicely blended into the grapefruit halves and the tops are slightly browned.

Makes 4 servings.

HONEY GRAPEFRUIT

2 grapefruit	**½ cup exotic or strongly flavored honey such as Attiki, heather, or buckwheat**

Cut the grapefruit in half crosswise. Remove the seeds, leaving a small cavity in the center of each half. Run a curved knife around the sides to loosen the fruit, and run a straight knife on the sides of each section to separate it from the membrane. Spoon 2 tablespoons honey in the center of each half and refrigerate, covered, for 1 or 2 hours until serving time.

Makes 4 servings.

GRAPE MELON MOUSSE

2 envelopes plain gelatin
½ cup cold apple juice
1 cup boiling apple juice
2 tablespoons lemon juice

½ cup heavy cream
½ cup sour cream
2 cups seedless white grapes
1 cup cantaloupe balls

Soften the gelatin in the cold apple juice. Add the boiling apple juice and the lemon juice, and stir until the gelatin has dissolved. Cool and chill until the mixture begins to set and is about the consistency of egg whites.

Whip the cream until stiff. Fold in the sour cream. Fold into the gelatin mixture. Fold in the grapes and melon balls. Pour the mixture into a lightly oiled 4-cup mold. Cover and chill until firm.

Makes 6 servings.

COUPE CAROLINE

2 tablespoons honey
1 teaspoon lemon juice
1 tablespoon brandy

½ pound seedless white grapes
4 scoops VANILLA ICE CREAM
   (homemade or bought)

Combine the honey, lemon juice, and brandy in a small bowl. Add the grapes and toss together. Cover and refrigerate for several hours or overnight.

To serve, place a scoop of ice cream in each dessert glass. Spoon the grape mixture over the ice cream.

Makes 4 servings.

MANGO SHORTCAKE

2 cups flour
1 tablespoon sugar
3 teaspoons baking powder
½ teaspoon salt
Generous pinch nutmeg
½ cup butter
1 egg
⅔ cup milk or cream
2 tablespoons rum

1 or 2 peeled ripe mangos, cut
into slices, or 1 can mango
slices, drained
1 cup heavy cream
1 tablespoon sugar
1 tablespoon rum
Finely sliced unblanched
almonds (optional)

Preheat the oven at 450°. Sift the flour, 1 tablespoon sugar, baking powder, salt, and nutmeg together in a bowl. Cut in the butter with a pastry blender until the mixture resembles coarse meal. Beat the egg with the milk or cream and stir into the flour mixture. Make sure the ingredients are well combined but avoid overmixing. Turn into a buttered, floured, round 9-inch cake pan. With floured fingers pat the dough out smoothly so that it reaches all sides of the pan, and pat the top so that it is even. Bake about 15 minutes. Cool on a wire rack.

Split the cake horizontally into 2 layers. Sprinkle the bottom layer with 2 tablespoons rum. Arrange half the mango slices on the bottom layer and set the other layer of the cake on top. Whip the cream until it is stiff, and add 1 tablespoon sugar and 1 tablespoon rum. Spoon the mixture over the cake and arrange the remaining mango slices in the whipped cream. If desired, strew finely sliced unblanched almonds over the top.

Makes 6 servings.

MANGO CREAM

2 ripe mangos
⅓ cup orange juice
2 teaspoons lemon juice

2 tablespoons confectioners'
sugar
1 cup heavy cream, whipped
Chopped pistachios or pecans

Peel and cut the mangoes into pieces. Puree in an electric blender or food processor with the orange juice, lemon juice, and confectioners'

sugar. Transfer the mixture to a bowl, and fold in the whipped cream. Chill. Spoon into serving dishes and sprinkle with the chopped nuts.
Makes 6 servings.

MANGOS WITH COINTREAU

2 ripe mangos
¾ cup free-flowing brown or
   turbinado sugar
¾ cup water

1 teaspoon lime juice
3 tablespoons Cointreau or other
   orange liqueur

Peel and slice the mangos. Combine the sugar and water in a sauce-pan and heat to boiling. Boil 2 minutes, add the mango slices, stir gently, and bring to a boil again. Turn off the heat immediately. Cool. Add the lime juice and Cointreau. Cover and chill. Spoon into serving dishes.
Makes 4 servings.

FILLED CANTALOUPE
A LA CREME

3 small cantaloupes
1 recipe VANILLA CONVERTS TO
   CANTALOUPE ICE CREAM,
   using meat from above
   cantaloupes

Whipped cream and melon balls,
   or whole strawberries, or fresh
   mint sprigs or crystallized
   mint leaves (optional)

Cut the cantaloupes in half, discard the seeds, and carefully scoop out the flesh, leaving the shells intact. Rinse with cold water. Freeze the shells for 1 hour or longer until they are solidly frozen.
Meanwhile, use the scooped-out flesh of the cantaloupes to prepare the ice cream. Spoon the ice cream into the frozen shells. Freeze the filled shells, covered with plastic wrap until they are firm. If desired, garnish with whipped cream and melon balls, or with whole straw-berries, or with fresh mint sprigs or crystallized mint leaves.
Makes 6 servings.

MELON BALL MIX

1 cantaloupe
1 honeydew melon
2 tablespoons white crème de
  menthe*

3 tablespoons white corn syrup
Sour cream (optional)
Fresh mint sprigs (optional)

Make melon balls from the cantaloupe and honeydew and combine them with the crème de menthe and corn syrup (which have been mixed together). Cover and refrigerate for 1 hour or longer, turning the balls occasionally. Spoon the mixture into serving glasses. If desired, garnish each glass with a dollop of sour cream and a mint sprig.

Makes 6 to 8 servings.

* Green crème de menthe can be used, but it will stain the fruit green.

MELON WITH PEACHES

1 cantaloupe
3 medium-sized ripe peaches
3 tablespoons honey

Pinch of salt
2 tablespoons lemon juice
1 tablespoon rosewater

Make melon balls from the cantaloupe and put them in a bowl with any juice from the melon. Peel the peaches and slice them very thin. Add them to the melon balls along with the honey, salt, lemon juice, and rosewater, and toss lightly. Cover the bowl and refrigerate for several hours or overnight. Spoon into serving dishes.

Makes 6 servings.

MOLDED CANTALOUPE

1 very ripe cantaloupe
1 envelope plain gelatin
2 tablespoons cold water
¼ cup boiling water
1¼ cups canned unsweetened
  pineapple juice

3 tablespoons rum
¼ cup maple syrup
Whipped cream flavored with a
  little rum and maple syrup
  (optional)

Peel the cantaloupe and cut enough long, curved strips to fit the lengthwise design in a 4-cup melon mold. Oil the mold lightly, and lay the melon strips in it. Chop the remaining cantaloupe meat.

Soften the gelatin in the cold water. Add the boiling water and stir until the gelatin has dissolved. Combine it with the pineapple juice, rum, and maple syrup. Pour a small amount of the liquid into the melon mold to come halfway up the melon strips. Refrigerate the mold until it is firm enough for the melon strips to hold in place. Refrigerate the balance of the liquid until it is mushy. Fold in the chopped cantaloupe and fill the mold with the mixture. Cover and refrigerate until it is firm. Unmold on an oval serving dish. If desired, decorate with flavored whipped cream.

Makes 6 servings.

SHERRIED WATERMELON

5 cups bite-sized watermelon cubes, seeds removed

½ cup Sherry
Scant ½ teaspoon nutmeg

Toss the watermelon cubes, Sherry, and nutmeg together in a bowl. Cover and refrigerate at least 2 hours, stirring occasionally. Spoon the mixture into dessert glasses.

Makes 6 servings.

NECTARINES WITH SOUR CREAM

6 to 8 large, ripe nectarines
1 cup sour cream

¼ cup maple syrup
Maple sugar (optional)

Chill the nectarines. Peel, slice, and divide them into serving dishes. Combine the sour cream and maple syrup, and spoon over the nectarines. If desired, sprinkle maple sugar over the top. Serve immediately.

Makes 6 servings.

NECTARINES WITH GINGER WAFFLES

6 medium-sized ripe nectarines
⅓ cup green ginger wine (such as Stones)
1½ cups crushed gingersnaps (about 6 ounces)
2 teaspoons baking powder

Pinch of salt
2 egg yolks
½ cup milk
2 tablespoons melted butter
2 egg whites
1 cup heavy cream

Peel and slice the nectarines and combine them with the ginger wine in a bowl. Cover and refrigerate for 1 hour, turning the fruit a few times.

Combine the gingersnaps, baking powder, and salt. Beat the egg yolks lightly and add the milk and melted butter. Add to the gingersnap mixture. Beat the egg whites until they are stiff, and fold them into the batter. Bake the batter in a waffle iron on low heat, making 6 waffles.

Arrange the waffles on serving dishes. Drain the nectarines and spoon the ginger wine over the waffles. Whip the cream until it is stiff, and divide it evenly over the waffles. Spoon the nectarines over the whipped cream and serve immediately.

Makes 6 servings.

NECTARINES GRANDMERE

1 cup water
1 cup brown sugar
6 to 8 large nectarines
1 tablespoon brown sugar
¼ teaspoon ground cardamon

¼ cup sour cream
½ pint VANILLA ICE CREAM (homemade or bought)
Unblanched thinly sliced almonds (optional)

Combine the water and 1 cup brown sugar in a saucepan and, stirring, bring to a boil. Simmer for 5 minutes. Meanwhile, peel and slice the nectarines and add them to the syrup at the end of 5 minutes. Simmer for several minutes until the nectarine slices are just tender. Remove from the heat, transfer to a bowl, cool, and refrigerate, covered.

Combine 1 tablespoon brown sugar, the cardamom, and the sour cream. Soften the ice cream and quickly combine it with the sour cream mixture. Fold in the drained nectarines. Spoon into serving glasses. If desired, strew almonds over the top.

Makes 6 servings.

NECTARINES FLAMBE

1 cup water
½ cup sugar
1 two-inch piece vanilla bean
6 to 8 large nectarines

⅓ cup warmed rum
6 scoops maple walnut or
    pistachio ice cream

Combine the water, sugar, and vanilla bean in a saucepan and bring to a boil, stirring until the sugar has dissolved. Simmer for 5 minutes. Meanwhile, peel and slice the nectarines. Add the fruit to the syrup and simmer for several minutes until just tender. Remove the vanilla bean. Transfer the mixture to the blazer pan of a chafing dish and place it over direct heat. Pour the warmed rum over the top and ignite. When the flames die, spoon the mixture into serving glasses. Top each serving with a scoop of ice cream.

Makes 6 servings.

ORANGES WITH ROSEMARY

4 large oranges
¼ cup sugar
½ cup water

1 teaspoon rosemary
    (preferably fresh)
½ teaspoon vanilla extract

Peel the oranges with a sharp knife, removing all membranes. Cut out segments, discarding the membrane, pith, and any pits. Combine the sugar, water, and rosemary in a saucepan and, stirring, bring to a boil. Simmer for 5 minutes until the mixture is slightly thickened. Add the orange segments and simmer for 1 minute or less. Remove from the heat. Transfer the mixture to a bowl and stir in the vanilla extract. Cool, cover, and refrigerate until it is well chilled. Spoon into serving glasses.

Makes 4 servings. (To make 6 servings, use 6 oranges and proceed as above.)

CANDIED ORANGES IN WHITE WINE JELLY

6 candied orange slices*
1½ envelopes plain gelatin
¼ cup cold water
½ cup boiling water
2 tablespoons strained lemon juice

½ cup sugar
2½ cups Riesling wine
Whipped cream
Sugar
½ teaspoon orange flower water (optional)

Cut the orange slices into quarters and place 1 piece in each of 6 tall, narrow, clear dessert glasses or wineglasses. Soften the gelatin in the cold water. Add the boiling water and stir until the gelatin has dissolved. Add the strained lemon juice, ½ cup sugar, and wine. Pour the liquid into each dessert glass to a level of ½ inch above the orange piece. Refrigerate until firm, about 1 hour. Place another orange piece in each glass, and another ½ inch of liquid. Refrigerate again until firm, and continue until all orange pieces have been used, ending with a covering of liquid. Set the orange pieces at different angles as you jell them so that they will appear to be suspended in the wine jelly. Refrigerate until set. To serve, decorate the tops with whipped cream to which has been added a little sugar to taste and orange flower water if desired.

Makes 6 servings.

* Available in specialty food shops and candy shops. *Note:* These are actual orange slices which have been candied, not candy gums in the shape of orange slices.

ORANGE SLICES IN RED WINE

4 large oranges
¼ cup sugar
½ cup water
¾ cup red wine

1 one-inch piece cinnamon stick
⅛ teaspoon nutmeg (preferably freshly ground)
2 whole cloves

Peel the oranges with a sharp knife, removing all membranes. Slice them crosswise into ⅓-inch slices, removing any seeds. Combine the sugar, water, red wine, cinnamon stick, nutmeg, and whole cloves in a glass or ceramic bowl. Add the orange slices and stir the mixture gently.

Fruit Desserts

Cover and allow it to macerate at room temperature for about 8 hours, stirring several times. Refrigerate the mixture until serving time. Serve it well chilled. Spoon it into dessert glasses.

Makes 4 servings. (To make 6 servings, use 6 oranges and proceed as above.)

BAKED ORANGES MADEIRA

4 large seedless oranges
6 tablespoons Madeira wine
3 tablespoons melted butter
3 tablespoon brown sugar

½ cup orange juice
¼ cup brown sugar
1 tablespoon lemon juice

With a small, sharp knife, peel the zest from 1 orange, making certain not to include any of the white part of the rind. Cut the orange zest into narrow strips like matchsticks. Place them in a small bowl and cover with the Madeira. Allow the mixture to steep for 30 minutes.

Preheat the oven at 350°. Peel all 4 oranges with a sharp knife, making sure to remove all outside membranes. Place the oranges in a buttered shallow baking dish just large enough to hold them. Combine the melted butter with 3 tablespoons brown sugar and spoon over the oranges. Bake for 12 minutes in the upper third of the oven.

While the oranges are baking, place the steeped orange peel and Madeira in a small saucepan with the orange juice, ¼ cup brown sugar, and lemon juice. Bring to a boil, stirring, and boil down until the quantity is reduced by half. When the oranges have baked 12 minutes, run them under the broiler for 1 or 2 minutes to brown the tops. Spoon the syrup over the oranges and serve immediately.

Makes 4 servings.

ROSY PEACH COMPOTE

6 large, ripe freestone peaches
⅔ cup water
½ cup sugar
2 teaspoons rosewater

1 teaspoon vanilla extract
1 tablespoon crystallized rose
    petals

Peel the peaches and cut them in half, removing the pits. Combine the water and sugar in a saucepan and bring to a boil, stirring until the sugar has dissolved. Simmer for 5 minutes. Add the peach halves, a few at a time, and poach for about 2 minutes, turning and basting them. Remove the peach halves to a shallow bowl or large soup plate and remove the syrup from the heat. Stir the rosewater, vanilla extract, and crystallized rose petals into the syrup and pour over the peaches. Cool them, turning them occasionally. Cover the mixture and chill it well. Serve in dessert glasses.

Makes 6 servings.

HONEY PEACHES

¼ cup orange juice
2 tablespoons orange liqueur
3 tablespoons honey

4 large, ripe peaches
Fresh mint sprigs (optional)

Combine the orange juice, orange liqueur, and honey in a bowl. Peel and slice the peaches and add them to the orange mixture, stirring gently to make sure all the peach pieces have been coated. Cover and refrigerate for 1 hour. To serve, spoon the peaches into dessert glasses and decorate them with fresh mint sprigs if desired.

Makes 4 servings.

PEACHES IN RED WINE

4 large, ripe freestone peaches
2 tablespoons sugar
1½ cups red wine
   (perferably Bordeaux)

2 tablespoons sugar
1 one-inch piece cinnamon stick

Peel the peaches and cut them in half, removing the pits. Place them in a shallow dish with any juice that exudes, sprinkle them with 2 tablespoons sugar, and allow the mixture to stand at room temperature for 30 minutes.

Combine the red wine, 2 tablespoons sugar, and cinnamon stick in a saucepan and, stirring, bring to a boil. Lower the heat and place the peach halves in the wine, allowing them to poach gently until they are

---

tender. Remove the peach halves to a bowl. Boil the wine down to one-third of its original volume. Remove the cinnamon stick. Pour the wine over the peaches. Cool, cover, and chill the mixture. Serve in dessert glasses.

Makes 4 servings.

PEACHES WITH MINTED CREAM

2 cups water
1 cup sugar
1 one-inch piece vanilla bean*
6 ripe freestone peaches

¼ cup mint jelly
⅔ cup heavy cream
Crystallized mint leaves or fresh
    mint sprigs (optional)

Combine the water and sugar in a saucepan and bring to a boil, stirring until the sugar has dissolved. Add the vanilla bean, lower the heat, and simmer for 5 minutes. Meanwhile, peel the peaches and cut them in half, removing the pits. Add the peach halves to the syrup (half of them at a time if necessary) and simmer gently until they are just tender. Remove them from the heat, cool, and cover. Refrigerate until they are chilled.

In a small bowl, work the mint jelly with a rubber spatula until it is very smooth. Beat with a fork or whisk to aerate it. Beat the cream until it is stiff. Fold the mint jelly into the whipped cream with a rubber spatula. To serve, place 2 peach halves and a small amount of syrup in each serving glass. Top generously with minted cream and, if desired, decorate with a crystallized mint leaf or fresh mint sprig.

Makes 6 servings.

* If vanilla bean is not available, add 1 teaspoon vanilla extract after removing the syrup from the heat.

Fruit Desserts

PEACHES CARDINAL

2 cups water
1 cup sugar
1 one-inch piece vanilla bean*
3 large, ripe freestone peaches
1 ten-ounce box frozen
   raspberries, thawed

1 or 2 tablespoons sugar
1 tablespoon kirsch
1 cup heavy cream
1 tablespoon sugar
½ teaspoon vanilla extract
Thinly slivered blanched almonds

Combine the water and sugar in a saucepan and bring to a boil, stirring until the sugar has dissolved. Add the vanilla bean, lower the heat, and simmer for 5 minutes. Meanwhile, peel the peaches and cut them in half, removing the pits. Add the peach halves to the syrup (half of them at a time if necessary) and simmer them gently until just tender. Remove the peaches from the heat and cool. Cover and chill.

Puree the raspberries in an electric blender or food processor. Put the puree through a fine sieve to remove the seeds. Stir in 1 or 2 tablespoons sugar to taste and the kirsch. Cover and chill.

To serve, place a peach half, round side up, in each dessert glass. Spoon the raspberry puree over the peaches. Whip the cream until stiff and add 1 tablespoon sugar and the vanilla extract. Pipe the cream around the sides of the peaches through a pastry bag fitted with a fluted tip. Sprinkle with almonds.

Makes 6 servings.

* If vanilla bean is not available, add 1 teaspoon vanilla extract after removing the syrup from the heat.

BOURBON PEACHES

8 canned Elberta freestone peach
   halves
½ cup brown sugar

8 teaspoons butter
⅓ cup bourbon, warmed

Preheat the broiler. Drain the peach halves and arrange them, cut side up, in a buttered shallow ovenproof serving dish. Put 1 tablespoon brown sugar and 1 teaspoon butter in the hollow of each peach half. Broil until the sugar melts and the peaches are heated, making sure the sugar does not scorch or burn. Remove the peaches to the serving table.

Pour the warmed bourbon over the peaches and ignite. Spoon the liquid over the peaches until the flames die.

Makes 4 servings.

PEACHES PIEMONTE

4 ripe freestone peaches
¼ cup sugar
1 egg yolk
1 tablespoon lemon juice

¼ cup crushed almond
   macaroons
2 tablespoons apricot jam
Butter
Apricot nectar

Preheat the oven at 350°. Peel the peaches and cut them in half. Remove the pits and scoop out a little pulp from each half. Arrange the peach halves, cut side up, in a buttered shallow baking dish just large enough to hold them. Chop the peach pulp and combine it with the sugar, egg yolk, lemon juice, macaroons, and apricot jam. Spoon the mixture into the peach halves and dot them with butter. Pour enough apricot nectar into the baking dish to just cover the bottom. Bake for about 30 minutes, or until the peaches are just tender, checking during the baking time to make sure the peaches do not scorch or become too dry and adding more apricot nectar as necessary.

Serve hot or cold.

Makes 4 servings.

PEARS WITH BLACKBERRY SAUCE

For the pears:
2 cups water
1¼ cups sugar
1 one-inch piece vanilla bean*
6 to 8 fresh pears

For the sauce:
6 tablespoons sugar
¼ cup water
1 pint blackberries
½ teaspoon lemon juice
Superfine sugar
1 cup heavy cream

For the pears: Combine the water and sugar in a saucepan and bring to a boil, stirring until the sugar has dissolved. Add the vanilla bean, lower the heat, and simmer for 5 minutes. Meanwhile, peel, halve, and core the pears. Place them in a saucepan with the syrup and simmer gently until just tender, poaching half the pears at a time if necessary, and turning them so that they poach on both sides. Transfer the pears to a bowl. Cool, cover, and chill them.

For the sauce: Combine the sugar and water in a saucepan and heat, stirring, until the sugar has dissolved. Add the blackberries and simmer for 3 minutes. Puree the mixture in an electric blender or food processor. Strain it through a fine sieve into a bowl. Add the lemon juice and a little superfine sugar to taste. Cover and chill. Whip the heavy cream and fold it into the blackberry puree.

To serve, place 2 pear halves on each dessert plate. Spoon the blackberry sauce over the pears to cover completely.

Makes 6 to 8 servings.

Note: This dish may also be made with canned pear halves if fresh pears are not available.

* If vanilla bean is not available, stir in 1 teaspoon vanilla extract after removing the syrup from the stove.

ORANGE GINGER PEARS

⅓ cup Seville orange marmalade (preferably vintage Seville orange marmalade)
¾ cup orange juice
2 tablespoons preserved ginger in syrup, chopped

1 teaspoon lemon juice
Pinch of salt
4 fresh pears, peeled, cored, and halved
½ teaspoon vanilla extract

Combine the marmalade, orange juice, preserved ginger, lemon juice, and salt in a saucepan and cook, stirring, until the marmalade has melted. Add the pear halves, bring to a boil, lower the heat, cover, and simmer for about 8 minutes, or until the pears are just tender. Remove the pear halves to a serving dish and boil the liquid down to about ½ cup. Remove the liquid from the heat, stir in the vanilla extract, and pour it over the pears. Cool, cover, and chill.

Makes 4 servings.

PEARS IN PORT

6 medium-sized, firm pears
1½ cups red wine
½ cup Port
½ cup water
1 cup sugar

1 two-inch piece cinnamon stick
1 whole clove
Brie or Camembert with
   crackers (optional)

Peel the pears but do not remove the stems. Combine the red wine, Port, water, sugar, cinnamon stick, and whole clove in a saucepan and stirring, bring to a boil. Lower the heat and simmer for 5 minutes. Add the pears, cover, and simmer until the pears are tender but not soft, occasionally turning them gently so that they cook and color evenly. If necessary, cook half the pears at a time. Remove the pears and put them in a bowl. Boil down the syrup until it is slightly thickened. Remove the cinnamon stick and clove and pour the syrup over the pears. Cool, turning the pears occasionally. Cover them and chill well. Serve in dessert glasses, spooning the syrup over each pear. If desired, serve with soft, ripened cheese such as Brie or Camembert with crackers.

Makes 6 servings.

BLUSHING CRANBERRY PEARS

6 fresh pears
1 can whole berry cranberry
   sauce
½ cup water
1 tablespoon lemon juice

⅛ teaspoon allspice
⅛ teaspoon cinnamon
¼ cup green ginger wine (such
   as Stones)

Peel, halve, and core the pears. Melt the cranberry sauce in a saucepan with the water, lemon juice, allspice, and cinnamon, stirring continuously. Add the pear halves, cover, and simmer until the pears are just tender. Remove them to a serving dish. Boil the cranberry mixture down until it is reduced to about 1 cup. Remove it from the heat and stir in the ginger wine. Pour the mixture over the pears. Cool, cover, and chill.

Makes 6 servings.

MOLDED CARAMEL PEARS

2 cups milk
5 egg yolks
3 tablespoons sugar
Pinch of salt
1 envelope plain gelatin
2 tablespoons cold water
1 teaspoon vanilla extract

¼ teaspoon nutmeg, preferably
   freshly grated
6 canned pear halves
½ cup sugar
¼ cup hot water
½ teaspoon vanilla extract

Scald the milk in the top of a double boiler over direct heat. Beat the egg yolks lightly and add 3 tablespoons sugar and a pinch of salt. Stir a little of the hot milk into the egg yolks. Then stir the egg yolks into the milk and place over simmering water, making sure the water does not touch the bottom of the pan. Cook slowly, stirring constantly, until the custard thickens. Meanwhile, soften the gelatin in the cold water. When the custard has thickened enough to coat a spoon, remove it from the heat immediately and set the pan in a bowl of cold water and ice to stop the cooking and prevent curdling. Add the softened gelatin, 1 teaspoon vanilla extract and the nutmeg, and stir until gelatin has dissolved. Allow to cool.

Drain the pear halves and arrange in a simple 4- or 5-cup mold or bowl. Pour the cooled custard over and around the pears. Cover and chill until firmly set.

Melt ½ cup sugar in a heavy saucepan over moderate heat, stirring with a wooden spoon. Remove from the heat and add the hot water. This will cause lumps to form. Return to the heat and cook until the lumps have dissolved. Remove from the heat and stir in ½ teaspoon vanilla extract. To serve, unmold the pears and custard on a serving dish and pour the caramel sauce over the top. Serve immediately.

Makes 6 servings.

SPICED PEARS FLAMBE

6 hard-ripe pears
¾ cup orange juice
1 tablespoon lemon juice
1 tablespoon brandy
¼ cup sugar

1 two-inch piece cinnamon stick
2 whole cloves
3 tablespoons brandy
2 small lumps sugar

Preheat the oven at 350°. Peel, halve, and core the pears. Place them, cut side down, in a baking dish just large enough to hold them. Combine the orange juice, lemon juice, 1 tablespoon brandy, ¼ cup sugar, cinnamon stick, and whole cloves in a saucepan and, stirring, bring to a boil. Pour over the pears. Cover and bake for 30 to 40 minutes, or until the pears are just tender, removing the cover after 20 minutes.

Warm the 3 tablespoons brandy and pour into a soup ladle. Add the sugar lumps. Ignite and pour the flaming brandy over the pears. Serve at once.

Makes 6 servings.

PERSIMMONS IN CREAM

4 ripe persimmons
2 tablespoons rum
1 tablespoon sugar
1 cup heavy cream

6 slices toasted pound cake,
angel cake, sponge cake, or
GENOISE

Peel the persimmons and slice them crosswise. Place in a bowl with the rum and sugar, and chill, covered, for 30 minutes. Stir them gently once while they macerate. Whip the cream until it is stiff, and fold in the persimmon slices. Arrange the toasted cake on serving dishes and spoon the persimmon cream over it.

Makes 6 servings.

PERSIMMONS A L'ORANGE

4 ripe persimmons
4 tablespoons orange juice

4 teaspoons lemon juice
4 teaspoons orange liqueur

Peel the persimmons and remove their stems. Cut them in quarters from the pointed end down, without cutting all the way through to the bottom. Arrange them tulip-fashion in dessert glasses. Pour 1 tablespoon orange juice, 1 teaspoon lemon juice, and 1 teaspoon orange liqueur over each persimmon. Chill for 30 minutes before serving.

Makes 4 servings.

HONEY PERSIMMON PUDDING

1 egg
2 or 3 very ripe persimmons
1 cup sifted whole wheat flour
2 teaspoons baking powder
1 teaspoon salt
¼ teaspoon nutmeg

½ cup honey
1 tablespoon melted butter
1 teaspoon vanilla extract
½ cup finely chopped walnuts
Whipped cream (optional)

Preheat the oven at 350°. Beat the egg lightly. Remove the stems from the persimmons, chop them coarsely, and puree in an electric blender or food processor to make 1 cup of persimmon puree. Add to the beaten egg. Sift the whole wheat flour, baking powder, salt, and nutmeg together and add it to the persimmon mixture. Stir in the honey, melted butter, and vanilla extract. Add the walnuts and mix well. Pour the mixture into a 1-quart buttered baking dish. Cover and bake for 50 to 60 minutes. Spoon it into dessert cups while it is still warm, or cool and chill it before serving. If desired, garnish with whipped cream.

Makes 4 to 6 servings.

SAUTEED PINEAPPLE IN CREAM

Once you've cut up the pineapple, it's easy to assemble this dessert, and you can do it at the table in front of your guests if you like. The flavor combination is really distinctive. If you can't get a fresh pineapple, substitute canned unsweetened pineapple.

1 ripe pineapple
2 tablespoons butter
1 tablespoon sugar

3 tablespoons kirsch
⅔ cup heavy cream

Peel, core, and cut the pineapple into bite-sized pieces. Melt the butter in the blazer pan of a chafing dish on the stove. Sauté the pineapple wedges, half of them at a time, until they are lightly browned, adding more butter if necessary. Place all the browned wedges in the blazer pan and sprinkle with the sugar. Toss well. Add the kirsch, 1 tablespoonful at a time, stirring, and allowing the kirsch to evaporate each time before adding the next spoonful.

Remove the blazer pan from the stove and place it on the chafing-dish stand over the lit burner. Heat for 1 or 2 minutes, stirring. Pour the heavy cream over the pineapple without stirring at all. When the cream is heated through, serve.

Makes 4 to 6 servings, depending on the size of the pineapple.

APRICOT BAKED
STUFFED PINEAPPLE

1 large pineapple	½ cup apricot preserves
½ cup crumbled almond	1 tablespoon sugar
macaroons	1 tablespoon Falernum*
¼ cup dried apricots, chopped	(optional)

Preheat the oven at 400°. Cut the top off the pineapple about 1 inch below the crown, and discard. Cut and scoop out the pulp, leaving a ½-inch shell all around. Discard the core and chop the pulp coarsely. Combine with the crumbled macaroons, chopped apricots, apricot preserves, sugar, and Falernum (if available). Spoon into the shell and set it in a small baking pan. Cover the top of the pineapple with aluminum foil. Bake for 1 hour, removing the foil halfway through the baking time.

Makes 4 to 6 servings.

---

*Falernum is a syrup with an unusual almondlike flavor. Include it in the ingredients if you can.

ICY FILLED PINEAPPLE

Fresh pineapple, as in this recipe, is considered a good choice for dessert after a heavy meat meal, as it acts somewhat as a digestive aid. The reason is that uncooked pineapple contains an enzyme that breaks down protein—the same reason that uncooked pineapple will not allow a gelatin dessert to set, since it keeps breaking down the protein in the gelatin.

Water
1 large pineapple
1 teaspoon sugar
1 teaspoon kirsch
½ cup canned or fresh black
cherries, pitted

1 tablespoon sugar
2 tablespoons strawberry jelly
(not jam)
2 tablespoons kirsch
Strawberry ice cream

Fill a small ring mold, about 6½ inches in diameter, with water, and freeze. When it is frozen, unmold the ring and store it in plastic wrap in the freezer until serving time.

Cut the top off the pineapple about 1 inch below the crown, and reserve it for a lid. Cut and scoop out the pulp, leaving a ½-inch shell all around. Sprinkle the inside of the shell with 1 teaspoon sugar and 1 teaspoon kirsch. Replace the pineapple lid and refrigerate until serving time.

Discard the pineapple core and chop the pulp into dice-size pieces. Combine them in a bowl with the black cherries, 1 tablespoon sugar, strawberry jelly (which has been mashed with a rubber spatula), and 2 tablespoons kirsch. Cover and chill for 2 hours or more, stirring occasionally.

To serve, place the ice ring on a serving plate. Set the pineapple shell in the ice ring. Fill it with alternate layers of the macerated fruit and strawberry ice cream. Replace the lid or serve with the fruit mounded up over the top of the shell.

Makes 4 to 6 servings.

PINEAPPLE ORANGE COMPOTE

1 pineapple
¾ cup sugar
1½ cups water
1 three-inch piece vanilla bean
1 tablespoon lemon juice

Pinch of salt
1 can mandarin orange segments,
drained
2 tablespoon kirsch

Peel, core, and slice the pineapple, and cut it into bite-sized wedges. Combine the sugar, water, vanilla bean, lemon juice, and salt in a saucepan, and bring to a boil, stirring. Lower the heat and simmer for 5 minutes. Add the pineapple wedges and simmer a few minutes longer. Remove the pineapple wedges and place them in a bowl with the mandarin orange segments. Boil the syrup down until it measures ¾ cup. Remove it from the heat. Remove the vanilla bean and stir in the kirsch.

Pour the liquid over the fruit. Cool. Cover and chill, stirring once or twice. Spoon into serving glasses.

Makes 4 to 6 servings.

PLUM YUM

¼ cup water
¼ cup sugar
3 cups sliced fresh purple or
 red plums
2 tablespoons lemon juice
1 tablespoon cornstarch

2 tablespoons water
1 tablespoon butter
2 tablespoons dry white wine
Generous pinch of nutmeg
8 scoops VANILLA ICE CREAM
 (homemade or bought)

Combine the ¼ cup water and the sugar in a saucepan. Bring to a boil slowly, stirring until the sugar has dissolved. Add the plum slices and lemon juice, and bring to a boil again. Add the cornstarch (which has been mixed with 2 tablespoons water) and simmer, stirring constantly, until the mixture thickens. Remove from the heat and stir in the butter, white wine, and nutmeg.

Put scoops of vanilla ice cream in serving glasses and spoon the hot plum sauce over the top. Serve immediately.

Makes 8 servings.

HONEY PLUM KUCHEN

1 cup unbleached white flour
¼ cup whole wheat flour
¼ cup sugar (preferably
 turbinado sugar)
1½ teaspoons baking powder
¼ teaspoon salt
¼ cup butter
1 egg

¼ cup milk
1 teaspoon vanilla extract
4 cups sliced fresh, firm purple
 or red plums
2 tablespoons butter
½ teaspoon cinnamon
½ cup honey

Preheat the oven at 400°. Sift the white flour, whole wheat flour, sugar, baking powder, and salt into a bowl and cut in the ¼ cup butter with a pastry blender until the mixture resembles coarse crumbs. Beat the egg lightly, add the milk and vanilla extract, and add to the flour mixture, stirring with a fork just enough to combine the ingredients. Spread the batter on the bottom of a greased 9-inch-square baking pan. Arrange the plum slices in 4 parallel rows over the batter, letting the slices overlap one another a little.

Melt 2 tablespoons butter in a small saucepan. Remove from the heat and stir in the cinnamon and honey. Pour the mixture over the plum slices. Bake for about 30 minutes. Serve warm or cold.

Makes about 9 servings.

MOLDED PURPLE PLUMS IN CLARET

2 envelopes plain gelatin
¼ cup cold water
1½ cups boiling syrup from canned plums (with water added if necessary)
6 tablespoons sugar

1 cup Bordeaux (Claret) wine
6 tablespoons orange juice
2 tablespoons lemon juice
20 to 24 canned purple plums, pits removed
Heavy cream (optional)

Soften the gelatin in the cold water. Add the boiling syrup and stir until the gelatin has dissolved. Add the sugar, wine, orange juice, and lemon juice, and stir until the sugar has dissolved. Drain the plums very well and arrange them in a well-oiled simple 6-cup mold, leaving some plums whole, halving some, and cutting others to make an attractive decoration within the mold. Pour in the gelatin mixture and refrigerate until firm. Unmold on a serving plate. If desired, serve with heavy cream.

Makes 8 to 10 servings.

MOLDED GREENGAGE PLUMS IN SAUTERNES

2 envelopes plain gelatin
¼ cup cold water
1½ cups boiling syrup from canned greengage plums (with water added if necessary)
¼ cup sugar
1½ cups Sauternes

2 tablespoons lemon juice
1 large can (about 1 pound 14 ounces) greengage plums (no substitutes will do)
Whipped cream
Nutmeg

Soften the gelatin in the cold water. Add the boiling syrup and stir until the gelatin has dissolved. Add the sugar and stir until it has dissolved. Add the Sauternes and lemon juice. Drain the plums very well and arrange them in a lightly oiled 6-cup decorative mold, leaving some plums whole, slicing others in half, and cutting others in smaller pieces to make an attractive decoration within the mold. Pour in the gelatin mixture and refrigerate until firm. Unmold on a serving plate and decorate with whipped cream. Dust lightly with nutmeg.

Makes about 8 servings.

POMEGRANATES BAVARIAN

The pomegranate, an old Semitic symbol of life, fertility, and abundance, and a fruit that was eaten in Mesopotamia over four thousand years ago, is, strangely, unfamiliar to many of us today. Most pomegranates, it would seem, are grown for the manufacturers of grenadine syrup, who discard the thick skins and inside pulp and make their product from the juicy red part interspersed throughout the fruit. It is this same juicy red part that we use for making pomegranate desserts such as the one below. Although the color is akin to that of cranberries, the flavor is delicate and has none of the tartness of cranberries. To extract the juice from pomegranates, roll them on a wooden board to soften their interiors, cut off the tufted ends, and squeeze the juice out by hand. Another method, perhaps less messy, is to cut the fruits in half, making sure to save any juice that escapes, and to ream out the juice gently on an orange squeezer.

6 pomegranates (more or less)	2 tablespoons cold water
¼ cup sugar	1 egg white
1 envelope plus 1 teaspoon plain gelatin	½ cup heavy cream

Squeeze enough pomegranates to make 2 cups of strained pomegranate juice. Place the juice in a saucepan with the sugar, and slowly bring the mixture just to the boiling point, stirring continuously to dissolve the sugar. Meanwhile, soften the gelatin in the cold water. Remove the pomegranate juice from the heat, and add the softened gelatin, stirring until it has dissolved. Transfer the mixture to a bowl and refrigerate until it thickens to the consistency of egg whites.

Beat the egg white until it is stiff. Fold it into the pomegranate mixture. Beat the cream until it is stiff. Fold the pomegranate mixture into the whipped cream. Pour into a lightly oiled 3½- or 4-cup mold. Cover and refrigerate until the mixture is firm. Unmold onto a serving plate. Makes 4 to 6 servings.

ORANGE CREAM WITH PRUNE SAUCE

½ pound pitted prunes
Cold water
½ cup orange juice
3 tablespoons sugar
½ teaspoon vanilla extract
3½ cups milk
⅓ cup honey

Grated zest of 1 orange
4 egg yolks
1 envelope plus 1 teaspoon plain gelatin
1 tablespoon plus 1 teaspoon cold water

Place the prunes in a saucepan and add cold water to cover. Bring to a boil and simmer until the prunes are tender. Drain. Transfer the prunes to an electric blender or food processor and blend with ¼ cup of the orange juice until smooth. Transfer the mixture to a saucepan and stir in the remaining ¼ cup orange juice and the sugar. Cook the mixture over medium heat, stirring, until it bubbles and the sugar has dissolved. Remove from the heat and stir in the vanilla extract. Cool the mixture to room temperature and transfer it to a small bowl or sauce serving dish. Cover and set it aside.

Scald the milk in a nonaluminum pan. Remove from the heat and stir in the honey and orange zest. Cool slightly. Beat the egg yolks lightly and stir a little of the milk mixture into them. Then combine the yolk mixture and the milk mixture. Soften the gelatin in 1 tablespoon plus 1 teaspoon water. Add it to the milk-egg yolk mixture, and return it to the stove. Cook the mixture over medium heat, stirring constantly, until the gelatin has completely dissolved and the mixture has thickened slightly and will coat a metal spoon. Remove it from the heat and pour it into a 4-cup nonaluminum mold. Cool, cover, and chill it until firm. Unmold and serve with the prune sauce.

Makes 6 servings.

RASPBERRY FOOL

1 cup fresh raspberries
  (reserve 3 or 4 whole berries)
3 tablespoons superfine sugar

2 teaspoons strawberry liqueur,
  kirsch, or orange liqueur
½ cup heavy cream

Wash and puree the raspberries in an electric blender or food processor. Put the puree through a fine sieve to remove the seeds. Combine it with the sugar and liqueur. Whip the cream until it is stiff, and fold it into the puree. Chill well. Spoon into serving dishes. Top with 1 whole raspberry on each dish.

Makes 3 or 4 servings. The recipe may be doubled.

RASPBERRIES WITH LIQUEUR

1 tablespoon sugar
2 tablespoons strawberry liqueur
  or raspberry liqueur

½ pint fresh raspberries, rinsed
  and patted dry

Combine the sugar and liqueur. Add the raspberries and toss gently. Refrigerate for 1 hour. Spoon into dessert glasses.

Makes 2 servings. The recipe may be doubled.

HONEY RHUBARB WITH RASPBERRY ICE

1 bunch rhubarb
½ cup honey

6 scoops raspberry water ice or
  raspberry sherbet

Preheat the oven at 350°. Wash and cut the rhubarb into ¾-inch pieces. Place the pieces in a baking dish, cover, and bake for 20 to 25 minutes until the rhubarb is tender but still retains its shape. Stir in the honey and set the mixture aside to cool. Taste and add more honey if desired. Cover and chill. Divide the mixture among 6 sherbet glasses and put a scoop of raspberry water ice or raspberry sherbet in each glass.

Makes 6 servings.

RHUBARB MOUSSE

2½ cups 1-inch pieces of rhubarb
1 tablespoon lemon juice
¼ cup sugar
5 eggs
4 egg yolks

¼ cup sugar
Grated zest of 1 lemon
2 envelopes plain gelatin
¼ cup cold water

Preheat the oven at 350°. Put the rhubarb pieces in a baking dish and sprinkle them with the lemon juice and ¼ cup sugar. Bake for 20 minutes, remove from the oven, and cool.

Put the eggs, egg yolks, ¼ cup sugar, and lemon zest in a bowl and beat with an electric mixer for about 15 minutes until the mixture is very thick and stiff. Meanwhile, soften the gelatin in the cold water. Place it in the top of a double boiler and set it over hot water, stirring until the gelatin has dissolved. With the beater running, add the dissolved gelatin to the thickened egg mixture. Fold in the baked, cooled rhubarb. Pour the mixture into a serving bowl. Cover and refrigerate until it has set.

Makes 4 to 6 servings.

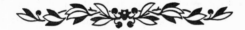

RHUBARB CREAM

4 or 5 cups rhubarb cut into
   1-inch lengths
½ cup orange juice
½ cup strawberry preserves

2 egg yolks
2 egg whites
½ cup heavy cream*

Put the rhubarb and orange juice into a saucepan and bring to a boil. Lower the heat, cover, and simmer until the rhubarb is tender, about 8 to 10 minutes. Transfer to an electric blender or food processor and add the strawberry preserves. Blend. Beat the egg yolks and add the rhubarb mixture gradually, stirring constantly to make sure the eggs are not scrambled by the hot rhubarb mixture. Cool, cover, and chill the mixture

* If you wish a less rich dessert, you may omit the heavy cream. The dessert will still have an excellent texture and flavor.

for about 1 hour. Beat the egg whites until stiff and glossy, and fold them into the rhubarb mixture with a rubber spatula. Beat the cream until stiff, and fold it into the rhubarb mixture. Spoon into dessert glasses.

Makes 8 servings.

RHUBARB PUFF-OVER

The batter shell puffs up around the sides and partway over the top to partially hide the rhubarb filling.

2 eggs	1½ cups rhubarb cut in 1-inch
¾ cup milk	pieces
¾ cup flour	½ cup grape jelly
½ teaspoon salt	¼ cup water
¼ cup butter	

Preheat the oven at 425°. Beat the eggs with the milk. Stir in the flour and salt, and beat until the mixture is smooth. Put the butter in a 9-inch pie tin and warm it in the oven until it is bubbly. Pour the batter into the buttered pan immediately, and pour the rhubarb into the center. Bake for 25 minutes.

While the puff-over is baking, make the sauce by melting the grape jelly with the water in a saucepan. Remove the puff-over from the oven and serve it immediately, spooning the sauce over each portion.

Makes 6 servings.

STRAWBERRIES CASSIS

1 pint strawberries	¼ cup black currant syrup
1 ten-ounce package frozen	(cassis)
raspberries, thawed	Sugar

Wash and hull the strawberries and cut them in half lengthwise. Puree the raspberries in an electric blender or food processor. Put them through a fine sieve to remove the seeds. Combine them with the cassis. Taste, and, if necessary, add a little sugar. Pour over the strawberries in a bowl. Cover and chill the mixture. Spoon it into dessert glasses.

Makes 4 servings.

STRAWBERRIES ROMANOFF

1 quart strawberries	½ cup heavy cream
¼ cup orange juice	Sugar
2 tablespoons orange liqueur	1 teaspoon vanilla extract
1 pint VANILLA ICE CREAM (homemade or bought)	

Wash and hull the strawberries and combine them with the orange juice and orange liqueur in a bowl. Cover and refrigerate for 1 hour or so. Spoon the fruit into serving dishes.

Soften the ice cream. Whip the cream until it is stiff, adding sugar to taste and the vanilla extract. Fold the whipped cream into the ice cream. Spoon over the berries and serve immediately.

Makes 8 servings.

STRAWBERRY ORANGE FLAMBE

1 orange	2 tablespoons sugar
1 cup boiling water	3 tablespoons orange juice
1 pint strawberries	2 tablespoons orange liqueur
1 tablespoon butter	

With a vegetable peeler or a small, sharp knife, remove the zest from the orange and cut it into julienne strips. Simmer the strips in the boiling water for 5 minutes. Drain and set them aside. Wash and hull the strawberries and set them aside.

Melt the butter in the blazer pan of a chafing dish over direct heat. Add the sugar and cook until the mixture begins to brown slightly. Add the julienne strips and cook, stirring, for a minute. Add the orange juice and heat it to boiling. Add the strawberries and stir them gently. Warm the orange liqueur, pour it over the strawberries, and ignite. When the flames die out, spoon the fruit into serving glasses.

Makes 3 to 4 servings.

STRAWBERRIES BEAUJOLAIS

1 quart strawberries   **Beaujolais wine**
Sugar

Wash and hull the strawberries. Place them in a bowl and sprinkle them with sugar to taste. Cover and allow the fruit to macerate in the refrigerator for 1 hour. Divide it among dessert glasses or wineglasses. Pour the Beaujolais into each glass, leaving the top berries almost completely exposed.

Makes 6 to 8 servings.

SUMMER FRUIT COMPOTE

1 cup sugar   **4 ripe apricots**
1 cup water   **4 purple or red plums**
1 tablespoon lemon juice **¾ cup blueberries**
2 firm, ripe pears   **1 tablespoon kirsch**
2 ripe peaches

Combine the sugar, water, and lemon juice in a saucepan and bring to a boil, stirring until the sugar has dissolved. Lower the heat and simmer for 5 minutes. Meanwhile, peel, halve, and core the pears, peel, halve, and remove the pits from the peaches, cut the apricots in half and remove the stones, and score the plums into quarters all around, but leave them intact. Add the fruits to the syrup and simmer until they are tender. Test gently and remove the fruit as it becomes ready, placing it in a serving bowl. Do not allow the plums to overcook or their skins to peel off. When all the fruit has been removed, add the blueberries and cook them for 30 seconds. Remove the blueberries to the serving bowl. Boil the syrup down to measure ¾ cup. Remove it from the heat. Stir in the kirsch. Pour the liquid over the fruit. Cool, cover, and chill the mixture for 1 to 2 hours before serving.

Makes 4 servings.

MACEDOINE OF FRESH FRUITS

3 cups honeydew melon balls
2 cups strawberries cut in half
  lengthwise
6 preserved kumquats

2 tablespoons gin
2 tablespoons syrup from
  preserved kumquats
3 juniper berries, bruised

Combine the melon balls, strawberries, and kumquats in a bowl.
Combine the gin, kumquat syrup, and juniper berries and pour over the
fruits. Toss lightly. Cover and refrigerate the mixture for several hours
before serving.
Makes 6 to 8 servings.

FRUIT MELANGE WITH YOGURT

*While nearly any combination of fruits would be good served this
way, this is a particularly pleasing one.*

3 peaches, peeled and sliced
1 red- or green-skinned apple,
  cut into small chunks
1 large banana, cut into
  diagonal, ¼-inch slices

1 cup vanilla yogurt
Turbinado or brown sugar

Combine the peaches, apples, and bananas, and divide the fruit
among 4 serving glasses. Stir the yogurt until it is smooth, and spoon
it on top of the fruit. Sprinkle with sugar and serve immediately.
Makes 4 servings.

WINTER FRUIT COMPOTE

2 cups water
1¼ cups sugar
1 two-inch piece vanilla bean
3 firm, ripe pears
1 cup pitted prunes
¾ cup dried apricots
1 lemon slice

1 pint VANILLA ICE CREAM,
  or APRICOT HONEY ICE
  CREAM, or VANILLA
  CONVERTS TO APRICOT ICE
  CREAM, or bought vanilla ice
  cream

Combine the water, sugar, and vanilla bean in a saucepan and bring to a boil, stirring until the sugar has dissolved. Simmer for 5 minutes. Meanwhile, peel, halve, and core the pears. Add them to the syrup and simmer gently until they are just tender, turning them occasionally. Remove the pears from the syrup and set them aside to cool. Cut each pear half in thin slices, lengthwise.

Add the prunes, apricots, and lemon slice to the syrup. Bring to a boil, lower the heat, and simmer the fruit until it is tender. Remove the fruit and let it cool. Cut the prunes in half lengthwise, removing the pits. Boil the syrup down to measure ¾ cup. Return all the fruit to the syrup to heat. Spoon the ice cream into dessert glasses. Spoon the hot syrup and fruit over the ice cream and serve immediately.

Makes 4 servings.

BAKED TUTTI-FRUTTI

You will need enough of each canned fruit to arrange a single layer in your casserole.

¾ cup chopped walnuts or
  pecans
¾ cup sultanas
3 tablespoons brown sugar
Canned dark sweet cherries,
  drained
Canned pineapple chunks,
  drained
Canned purple plum halves,
  drained

3 tablespoons melted butter
Canned peach or apricot halves,
  drained
⅓ cup brandy
2 tablespoons butter
1 tablespoon brown sugar
½ cup crushed almond macaroon
  crumbs
Heavy cream (optional)

Preheat the oven at 350°. Butter a 1½-quart casserole, soufflé dish, or deep baking dish. Combine the walnuts or pecans, sultanas, and brown sugar. Arrange a single layer of dark sweet cherries in the bottom of the casserole, and sprinkle one-third of the nut mixture over them. Cover with a layer of pineapple chunks and sprinkle another third of the nut mixture over them. Cover with a layer of purple plum halves and sprinkle the remaining third of the nut mixture over them. Pour the melted butter over all. Cover with a layer of peach or apricot halves, round side up. Pour the brandy over all.

Cream the butter with the brown sugar. Add the macaroon crumbs and mix well. Sprinkle the mixture evenly over the peach or apricot halves. Bake for 30 minutes. Serve warm, or, if desired, serve cold with heavy cream.

Makes 6 servings.

CHAPTER 6

Cobblers and Puddings

Who wants some pudding nice and hot!
  'Tis now the time to try it;
Just taken from the smoking pot,
  And taste before you buy it.
—old London street cry

Fortunately, puddings have come a long way since the ancient Greek versions made from appalling ingredients that included gruel, blood, and animal intestines. Far from the dessert world, these formidable concoctions were eaten as the mainstays of the day, just as they were in England many centuries later, when, mercifully, more palatable puddings were devised. "Pudding and beef make Britons fight," went a verse of the early 1700s, and puddings certainly became one of that country's most popular stick-to-the-ribs foods. Plum pudding, probably the first of all fruit puddings, was originally eaten as a nondessert food during the twelve days of Christmas feasting instituted during the reign of Henry VIII. From this pudding have evolved any number of dessert puddings, both with and without fruit.

In steaming a pudding, the procedure is to fill a mold about two-thirds full, and seal the top well. Use either a pudding mold that has its own top that clamps on, or use an open-top mold and tie aluminum foil firmly over the top. Set the pudding on a metal rack or steamer inside a large pot. Unless the recipe specifies otherwise, pour in boiling water to a depth of one inch, cover the pot, and simmer slowly. Check the water level regularly throughout the steaming to see that the level is maintained.

Other hearty hot desserts which are baked rather than steamed are cobblers, crisps, streusels, and duffs. Distinct from crisps or streusels, which have crumbly tops, cobblers are baked with biscuit dough or batter topping arranged over hot fruit fillings. Deep-dish pies, or duffs, have pastry tops, the latter name being simply a variation of the word *dough*.

Other pudding recipes in this book include:

Bread and Butter Pudding
Chocolate Sponge Pudding
Indian Pudding
Honey Persimmon Pudding

SPOTTED DOG

My grandmother made this pudding for her family when my mother was a little girl. Apparently, the entire family rejected the common, unappealing names for the dessert, "suet pudding" or "bag pudding," and my mother called it, instead, "Spotted Dog" because of the vast numbers of currant and raisin "spots" in the pudding, which varied in number from one making to the next in accordance with the state of family finances. My uncle remembers the desserts as "Roly-Poly" and used to eat his portion with honey or molasses, while my mother had hers with butter. When trimmed with a holly sprig and set aflame with brandy, this fruit-laden pudding makes a gorgeous holiday dessert.

8 eggs	1 tablespoon salt
1 pound beef kidney suet	1 pound raisins
(no substitutes)	1 pound currants
1 cup sugar	1 cup flour
3½ cups flour	Holly sprig, ½ cup warmed
1 tablespoon nutmeg	brandy, and BRANDY HARD
1 teaspoon ginger	SAUCE (optional)

Beat the eggs lightly in a large bowl. Grind enough suet to end up with 1 pound, and combine with the eggs. Add the sugar and mix well. Sift the 3½ cups flour, nutmeg, ginger, and salt together, and add gradually. Toss the raisins and currants with 1 cup flour. Add the raisins and currants to the dough, but do not include any flour which does not adhere to the fruit. Mix into the dough, using your hands if necessary to combine well.

In warm water, wet thoroughly a 1-yard-square piece of clean, unbleached muslin. Wring it out well and place it on the work table. Sprinkle all over with flour, shaking off the excess. Turn the pudding mixture into the center of the cloth. Bring up all sides of the cloth and, allowing for a small amount of expansion during cooking, tie the top of the bag securely with very strong twine, making a loop in the twine for the removal of the hot pudding after cooking.

Plunge the pudding bag into a large kettle of boiling water—it should be covered by the water. Cover the kettle, lower the heat, and simmer (undisturbed except for checking the water level) for 4 hours. Remove the pudding from the kettle by looping the string over a large fork or spoon and lifting it onto a platter. Cut the string and roll the pudding out of the bag onto the platter. If desired, decorate with a holly sprig stuck into the pudding's top, pour warmed brandy over the pudding, and ignite it. When the flames die, slice the pudding and serve with Brandy Hard Sauce.

Makes 20 or more servings. The pudding may be reheated by steaming.

CABINET PUDDING

¼ cup raisins
Boiling water
¼ cup assorted candied fruit peel
1 tablespoon kirsch
3 eggs
2 egg yolks
½ cup sugar

2 cups scalded milk
1 teaspoon vanilla extract
1 recipe LADYFINGERS
Kirsch
Apricot jam
ZABAGLIONE SAUCE (optional)

Cover the raisins with the boiling water and set them aside for 10 minutes. Drain the raisins and pat them dry. Combine with the assorted candied fruit peel and 1 tablespoon kirsch, and set aside.

Preheat the oven at 350°. Beat the eggs and egg yolks with the sugar. Add the scalded milk gradually, beating constantly. Stir in the vanilla extract. Butter and sugar a 6-cup charlotte mold. Sprinkle half the fruit mixture over the bottom of the mold. Brush the ladyfingers with the kirsch and arrange a single layer over the fruit. Dot with the apricot jam. Pour half the custard over the top. Add another layer of kirsch-brushed ladyfingers, then the balance of the fruit. Pour the remaining custard over the top.

Set the charlotte mold in a pan and pour hot water around it up to a level of one-half the height of the mold. Bake for about 45 minutes, or until a knife inserted in the center comes out clean. Remove the mold from the oven and allow it to stand for about 10 minutes. Unmold on a serving plate. If desired, serve with Zabaglione Sauce.

Makes 6 servings.

MARMALADE PUDDING

¼ cup butter
½ cup turbinado or free-flowing brown sugar
2 eggs
1 cup sifted cake flour
1½ teaspoons baking powder
¼ teaspoon ground cardamom
¼ teaspoon salt

½ cup skimmed milk
1 teaspoon grated zest of lemon peel
½ cup Seville orange marmalade
½ cup apricot jam
Whipped cream (optional)
Candied orange slices (optional)

Preheat the oven at 400°. Cream the butter until fluffy, and add the sugar, creaming well. Add the eggs, 1 at a time, beating well after each addition. Sift the cake flour, baking powder, ground cardamom, and salt together, and add to the butter-egg mixture alternately with the skimmed milk. Stir in the lemon zest.

In a small saucepan, heat the marmalade and apricot jam, and pour the mixture into the bottom of a 4½x8½-inch loaf pan. Pour the batter over the jam. Bake for about 30 minutes, or until a cake tester inserted in the center comes out clean. Remove from the oven and unmold on a serving dish. If desired, serve with whipped cream or decorate with a whipped cream border and candied orange slices.

Makes 6 servings.

CRANBERRY PUDDING WITH HONEY EGGNOG SAUCE

2 cups fresh cranberries
½ cup molasses
1 egg
2 teaspoons baking soda
½ cup boiling water
1½ cups flour
¼ teaspoon cinnamon
¼ teaspoon ground ginger

Pinch of cloves
½ cup chopped blanched almonds
1 cup light cream
¼ cup honey
4 egg yolks, beaten
Pinch of salt

Chop cranberries coarsely and combine cranberries with the molasses and egg. Add the baking soda (which has been dissolved in the boiling water). Sift the flour, cinnamon, ginger, and cloves together, and add to the cranberry mixture along with the chopped blanched almonds, mixing well. Pour the batter into a well-greased 6-cup mold or clean coffee can, filling it about two-thirds full. Place aluminum foil over the top, tying it on tightly with string.

Place the mold on a rack in a large pot and pour in boiling water to a level of 1 inch. Cover the pot and simmer gently for 1½ hours, checking occasionally to see that the water level is maintained, and pouring in additional boiling water if needed. When the pudding has finished steaming, remove it from the pot. Remove the aluminum foil, and allow the pudding to set and for steam to escape before unmolding.

Meanwhile, scald the cream in the top of a double boiler over direct heat. Place over hot water and stir in the honey, egg yolks, and salt. Cook the mixture until it is slightly thickened. Serve hot over the unmolded hot pudding.

Makes 6 servings.

POUND CAKE PUDDING

½ cup milk	1 tablespoon lemon juice
2 cups crumbled pound cake or similar cake, with or without fruits or nuts	½ teaspoon vanilla extract
	4 tablespoons melted butter
	Whipped cream (optional) or
2 eggs	APRICOT SAUCE (optional)
1 cup pineapple preserves	

Preheat the oven at 350°. Pour the milk over the crumbled pound cake and set aside. Beat the eggs lightly and beat in the pineapple preserves, lemon juice, and vanilla extract. After the crumbled cake has soaked for at least 5 minutes, add it to the batter. Beat in the melted butter. Pour the mixture into a buttered 1-quart baking dish and bake for 50 to 60 minutes until it is well browned. Remove from the oven, cool, and refrigerate, covered. To serve, cut the pudding into wedges or slices and, if desired, serve with whipped cream or Apricot Sauce.

Makes 6 servings.

RHUBARB CRISP

4 to 5 cups 1-inch pieces
  rhubarb*
1½ cups free-flowing brown
  sugar

1 cup oatmeal
½ cup flour
½ teaspoon cinnamon
½ cup butter

Preheat the oven at 350°. Place the rhubarb in a buttered shallow 1½-quart baking dish. Sprinkle with ½ cup free-flowing brown sugar. Combine the oatmeal, 1 cup free-flowing brown sugar, flour, and cinnamon. Cut in the butter with a pastry blender until the mixture is crumbly. Sprinkle over the rhubarb and bake for 30 minutes.

Makes 4 servings.

  * The exact quantity of rhubarb isn't too important. You can use more if you would like to make another serving or two.

BLUEBERRY STREUSEL

½ cup butter
½ cup sugar
1 egg, beaten
Grated zest of 1 lemon
2 cups flour
2½ teaspoons baking powder
¼ teaspoon salt

½ cup milk
2 cups blueberries
½ cup sugar
½ cup flour
½ teaspoon ground ginger
⅛ teaspoon ground cardamom
¼ cup butter

Preheat the oven at 350°. Cream ½ cup butter and gradually add ½ cup sugar. Add the beaten egg and lemon zest. Sift the 2 cups flour, baking powder, and salt together and add to the butter-egg mixture alternately with the milk. Pour into a buttered 9-inch-square baking pan. Sprinkle with the blueberries.

Mix together the ½ cup sugar, ½ cup flour, ground ginger and ground cardamom, and work the mixture with the ¼ cup butter until it is crumbly. Sprinkle over the blueberries. Bake for 40 to 50 minutes until the top is nicely browned and a cake tester inserted in the center comes out clean. Serve warm.

Makes 8 servings.

PEACH COBBLER

1½ tablespoons cornstarch
¼ cup brown sugar, firmly
  packed
½ cup water
4 cups peeled, sliced fresh
  peaches
1 tablespoon butter
1 tablespoon lemon juice

1 tablespoon sugar
⅓ cup sour cream
1 tablespoon milk
1 cup buttermilk biscuit mix
1 tablespoon sugar
⅛ teaspoon nutmeg
Cream, whipped cream, or sour
  cream (optional)

Preheat the oven at 400°. Mix the cornstarch, brown sugar, and water together in a saucepan. Cook, stirring, until the mixture is thickened. Add the peach slices and heat a few minutes longer. Remove the saucepan from the heat, and stir in the butter and lemon juice. Pour the mixture into a buttered 1-quart baking dish.

Combine the 1 tablespoon sugar, sour cream, milk, and buttermilk biscuit mix, and spoon over the hot peaches. Combine 1 tablespoon sugar with the nutmeg and sprinkle over the top. Bake for 20 to 25 minutes, or until nicely browned. Serve warm or cold with cream, whipped cream, or sour cream if desired.

Makes 6 servings.

CHERRY APPLE BAKE WITH
CHERRY HEERING SAUCE

1⅓ cups flour
1½ teaspoons baking powder
¼ teaspoon salt
⅓ cup sugar
⅛ teaspoon mace
¼ cup butter
1 egg, lightly beaten
¼ cup milk
1 teaspoon vanilla extract
1 teaspoon grated zest of lemon

4 cups peeled, cored, and thinly
  sliced apples
1 or 2 1-pound cans pitted dark
  cherries, well drained
¼ cup sugar
½ teaspoon cinnamon
¼ cup melted butter
¼ cup currant jelly
1 cup heavy cream
2 tablespoons Cherry Heering

Preheat the oven at 400°. Sift the flour, baking powder, salt, ⅓ cup sugar, and mace together into a bowl. Cut in the butter with a pastry blender or work it in with the fingers. Add the egg, milk, vanilla extract, and lemon zest, and mix well. Spread the mixture in a buttered shallow rectangular or oval baking dish measuring about 9x13 inches. Arrange the apple slices in rows over the dough, with the apple slices closely overlapping each other, and leaving about ½ inch between the rows. Place rows of dark cherries in the spaces between the apple slices. Combine ¼ cup sugar with the cinnamon and sprinkle over the fruit. Drizzle melted butter over the top. Bake for 35 minutes.

Shortly before removing the baking dish from the oven, melt the currant jelly in a saucepan over low heat. Brush the jelly over the top of the Cherry Apple Bake after removing it from the oven. Allow it to cool. To serve, whip the heavy cream until it is stiff, and stir in the Cherry Heering. Spoon the sauce over individual portions.

Makes 10 to 12 servings.

LEMON SHERRY PUDDING

½ cup butter
¾ cup sugar
4 eggs
2 cups sifted flour
2 teaspoons baking powder
Pinch of salt

¼ cup lemon juice
¼ cup Sherry
1 tablespoon grated zest of lemon
    peel
Candied lemon slices (optional)

Cream the butter, and gradually add the sugar. Beat in the eggs, 1 at a time, mixing well after each addition. Sift the flour, baking powder, and salt together and add about one-third of it to the batter. Add the lemon juice and mix well. Add another third of the flour mixture. Add the Sherry and mix well, then the balance of the flour mixture. Stir in the lemon zest. Pour the mixture into a buttered 1½-quart pudding mold and cover with a lid or with heavy-duty aluminum foil tied securely with string.

Place the mold on a rack in a large kettle and pour in boiling water to a level halfway up the mold. Cover the kettle and allow the pudding to steam for 2½ to 3 hours, checking the water level occasionally and adding more boiling water if necessary to maintain the level. Test the pudding by opening the mold and inserting a cake tester in the center. Serve the pudding hot, decorated, if desired, with candied lemon slices.

Makes 6 servings.

CHERRY PUDDING

¾ cup sugar
⅔ cup red wine (such as
　Bordeaux)
2 cups fresh black cherries, pitted
½ cup butter
1 cup fine dry bread crumbs

½ cup sugar
3 egg yolks
1 teaspoon vanilla extract
5 egg whites
3 tablespoons kirsch
2 tablespoons currant jelly

Preheat the oven at 375°. Combine ¾ cup sugar and the wine in a saucepan and, stirring, bring to a boil. Add the cherries and simmer for 5 minutes. Remove the cherries and set them aside, allowing the syrup to remain in the saucepan off the heat.

Cream the butter and add the bread crumbs. Add ½ cup sugar and blend well. Add the egg yolks, 1 at a time, mixing well after each addition. Add the vanilla extract and the cherries, mixing gently but thoroughly until well combined. Beat the egg whites until they are stiff. Mix one-fourth of the egg whites into the cherry batter. Then fold in the balance of the egg whites and turn the mixture into a 1½-quart pudding mold which has been heavily buttered and coated with fine dry bread crumbs.

Place the mold, uncovered, in a pan of boiling water and set it in the oven. The water should come halfway up the mold. Bake for 35 to 40 minutes, or until a cake tester inserted in the center comes out clean. Remove from the oven and loosen the sides. Unmold the pudding onto a serving plate. Heat the saucepan of syrup, adding the kirsch and currant jelly. Pour over the pudding and serve immediately.

Makes 6 servings.

PECAN DATE PUDDING

2 eggs
½ cup honey
¼ cup heavy cream
5 tablespoons instant free-
　flowing flour

1½ teaspoons baking powder
1 cup coarsely broken pecans
1 cup cut-up, pitted dates
Whipped cream flavored with
　brandy or rum (optional)

Beat the eggs until they are very frothy. Gradually add the honey and continue beating. Add the cream, instant flour, and baking powder, and mix well. Stir in the pecans and dates. Turn the mixture into a well buttered 1-quart mold. Seal the top with a lid or securely tie on heavy-duty aluminum foil. Place the mold on a rack in a large kettle containing 1½ inches of boiling water. Place a lid on the kettle and, keeping the water at a simmer, steam the pudding for 2 hours, occasionally checking the water level. Test the pudding by inserting a cake tester in the center, which should come out clean. Remove the pudding and unmold it on a serving dish. If desired, serve with whipped cream flavored with brandy or rum.

Makes 6 servings.

CHESTNUT PUDDING WITH BRANDY SAUCE

6 tablespoons butter	¼ cup sugar
2 egg yolks	1 teaspoon cornstarch
1 seventeen-ounce can chestnut spread (*crème de marrons*)	¾ cup milk
	1 cup heavy cream
2 egg whites	1 tablespoon lemon juice
⅓ cup very finely chopped pecans	½ teaspoon grated zest of lemon
	2 tablespoons Armagnac or other
4 egg yolks	brandy

Preheat the oven at 350°. Cream the butter and beat in the 2 egg yolks, 1 at a time, beating well after each addition. Add the chestnut spread and mix well. Beat the egg whites until they are stiff and gently but thoroughly fold them into the chestnut mixture. Fold in the pecans. Turn the mixture into a buttered and sugared 1-quart baking dish, such as a soufflé dish. Bake for about 40 minutes until the pudding is puffy.

While the pudding is baking, beat the 4 egg yolks until thick. Add the sugar gradually and continue beating until the mixture is thick and light in color and forms a slowly dissolving ribbon when the beater is lifted. Add the cornstarch and beat again. Very gradually add the milk and cream (which have been scalded together in the top of a double boiler), beating constantly. Turn the mixture into the top of a double boiler and cook over simmering water, stirring constantly, until the mixture coats a metal spoon. Remove it from the heat and stir in the lemon juice, lemon zest, and Armagnac or other brandy. Set the double-boiler top in a bowl of water and ice cubes to cool quickly. Refrigerate the sauce until the pudding is done. Serve the pudding warm, with the sauce chilled.

Makes 6 servings.

PUMPKIN PUDDING WITH CORIANDER SAUCE

For the pudding:
½ cup butter
1 cup turbinado or free-flowing
  brown sugar
2 eggs
1¾ cups buttermilk biscuit mix
½ teaspoon salt
1 teaspoon ground coriander
½ teaspoon cinnamon
⅛ teaspoon cloves
1 cup pumpkin

For the sauce:
1 egg
3 tablespoons melted butter
¾ cup sifted confectioners' sugar
½ teaspoon ground coriander
½ teaspoon vanilla extract
½ cup heavy cream

For the pudding: Cream the butter and gradually add the sugar. Add the eggs, 1 at a time, beating well after each addition. Sift together the biscuit mix, salt, coriander, cinnamon, and cloves, and add it to the butter-egg mixture alternately with the pumpkin. Spoon the mixture into a buttered 1½-quart mold and cover it with a buttered lid or tie buttered aluminum foil securely over the top. Set the mold on a rack in a large kettle and pour in boiling water to a depth of about 1½ inches. Cover the kettle and simmer for 3 hours, or until a cake tester inserted in the center of the pudding comes out clean. Check the water level occasionally, adding more boiling water if necessary. Remove the pudding and unmold it on a serving plate.

For the sauce: Beat the egg until thick. Add the melted butter, confectioners' sugar, coriander, and vanilla extract, and blend well. Whip the heavy cream and fold it into the sauce. Serve on warm or cool pudding.

Makes 8 servings.

FIG PUDDING

½ pound dried figs
Cold water
¼ cup molasses
½ cup brown sugar, firmly
  packed
½ cup finely chopped suet
  (preferably beef kidney suet)
4 eggs
1 cup peeled, cored, chopped
  apples

¼ teaspoon salt
1 teaspoon cinnamon
½ teaspoon nutmeg
3 cups slightly dry, crumbled
  bread crumbs
½ cup flour
1 cup milk
½ cup chopped pecans

Cover the figs with cold water, bring to a boil, and simmer for about 30 minutes, or until tender. Drain and chop the figs and combine them with the molasses, brown sugar, and suet. Add the eggs, 1 at a time, combining well after each addition. Add the apples, salt, cinnamon, and nutmeg. Add the bread crumbs and flour alternately with the milk. Add the pecans and mix well.

Spoon the mixture into a buttered and sugared 1½-quart mold. Cover with a lid or aluminum foil tied on securely. Set the mold on a rack in a kettle and pour in boiling water to a level halfway up the side of the mold. Cover the kettle and steam the pudding for 5 hours, checking the water level occasionally and adding more boiling water if necessary. Remove the pudding and unmold it onto a serving plate.

Makes 8 servings.

PLUM PUDDING

This recipe for genuine English Plum Pudding has been in our family for at least five generations.

1 pound fine dry bread crumbs
(about 4⅔ cups)
½ pound flour (about 2 cups)
⅔ cup brown sugar, firmly
packed
1 tablespoon nutmeg
5 tablespoons cinnamon
3 tablespoons ground ginger
6 eggs
1½ cups milk

1 pound beef kidney suet, ground
(no substitutes)
1 pound raisins
1 pound currants
½ pound sultanas
8 ounces mixed preserved citrus
peel
¾ cup flour
½ cup brandy (more or less)
BRANDY HARD SAUCE

Combine the bread crumbs, ½ pound flour, brown sugar, nutmeg, cinnamon, and ginger. Beat the eggs in a large bowl. Add the milk. Stir in the ground suet. Add the bread-crumb mixture and mix well. Combine the raisins, currants, sultanas, and preserved citrus peel. Sprinkle with ¾ cup flour and toss well so that each piece of fruit is well coated. Add the fruit to the bread-crumb mixture and combine well. (This is best done with the hands.)

Pack the mixture into greased molds. Pudding molds, crocks, or clean, empty cans, such as coffee cans, may be used. Fill the molds about two-thirds full. Cover the tops with greased waxed paper. Tie cheesecloth over the tops. Wrap each mold in aluminum foil, laying the foil on the top and folding it down over the sides. Wrap each mold in another piece of aluminum foil, from the bottom up over the top. Set the molds on wire racks in large kettles, and fill the kettles halfway up the molds with boiling water. Place lids on the kettles and simmer the puddings for 6 hours, checking the water level occasionally and adding more boiling water if necessary.

Remove the puddings from the kettles carefully, and allow them to cool until they are comfortable to the touch. Remove all wrappings. Pour 2 or more tablespoons of brandy over each pudding. Place fresh waxed paper over each, and replace the cheesecloth. Wrap each pudding in aluminum foil and keep them in a cool place for at least 3 weeks before eating. If they are made long before the holidays, check the puddings each month and, if desired, add a little brandy now and then.

To serve, steam the puddings again for 3 hours. Serve with Brandy Hard Sauce.

Makes about 4 puddings, depending on the sizes of the molds.

CHAPTER 7

Charlottes, Creams, and Custards

From many a berry,
*   and from sweet kernels press'd,*
She tempers dulcet creams.

—*John Milton,* Paradise Lost

When *Godey's Lady's Book* began to include recipes and menus among its fashion plates in 1860, some of the first recipes published were for custards. Sweetened milk curds, a forerunner of custards, had been served at least as far back as the 1500s, and the Italians during the Renaissance enjoyed custard cakes and almond pastry creams very much like our own today.

The simple perfection of these desserts seems to have appealed to nearly everyone since they were first made. A baked custard or flan is grand in its plainness and can also form the base for a more elegant creation. An unsophisticated soft custard turns, Cinderella-like, into a dazzling dessert when it appears as *oeufs à la neige* ("snow eggs"). A Bavarian cream, rich and delicious in its own right, becomes the ultimate in impressiveness when made into a diplomate pudding.

All these desserts have two things in common—their basic ingredients are eggs and milk or cream, and their names are tantalizing. James Beard has said that if anyone says "cup custard" to him in a resturant, he finds himself ordering it because he can't resist the sound of its name. Mousse, zabaglione, *crème brûlée,* and *pots de crème* are all names that roll appealingly off the tongue, and are just as appealing to eat.

Custards and creams are an excellent way to get milk and eggs into the diet. Serve them as the recipes here suggest, and also use the thinner custards as sauces on poached fruit, use the thicker ones for filling tart or cake shells topped off with fruit, or serve any custard-style dessert with a fruit sauce, nuts, or honey.

Although custards need to be made with care, they're relatively easy if you give them your complete attention. To assure a nice texture, keep the temperature low when cooking custard—that is, keep the flame low when cooking top-of-the-stove custards, and keep the oven temperature no higher than 325° or 350° when baking them. No custard should ever be boiled, even though some recipes have the misnomer of "boiled custard" and must be stirred constantly during cooking. If a custard seems about to curdle, plunge the pan into ice water or ice cubes so it will stop cooking immediately. Stirring vigorously with a wire whisk can repair a custard that begins to lump slightly.

If you want baked creams and custards to have smooth, uncolored tops, be sure to scoop the foam off the top with a spoon before they go into the oven. On the other hand, if you want a rich brown top, beat the eggs very well and leave all the bubbles on. A custard that is being made to unmold will turn out better if the eggs are not beaten too much.

Some cream desserts are thickened by egg yolks—the more egg yolks, the thicker and richer they become—and others by cornstarch, flour, or gelatin, depending on the nature of the recipe. Evidently it has not always been an easy matter to thicken creams and custards. An old English recipe for steeple cream, for example, sounds more masonrylike than culinary when it tells the cook to put some hartshorn and ivory together in a stone bottle as the first step in preparing the dish. A colonial recipe for blancmange thickens the dessert with isinglass soaked and boiled in water, and one feels grateful these methods have passed out of use.

A word of caution regarding kitchen utensils will be useful in preventing your ending up with a custard or cream of a greenish or grayish cast: Never use aluminum pots or pans with these mixtures; use only stainless-steel or heavy enameled or porcelainized pans. Avoid stirring with a spoon that is not made of stainless steel or wood, and use only a stainless-steel whisk. Porcelain, pottery, or ovenproof glass can be used for baked custards.

In addition to the recipes in this chapter, other custard and cream recipes in this book are:

Chocolate Mousse
Chocolate Pots de Crème
Crème Brûlée
English Trifle
Frozen Apricot Mousse
Pomegranates Bavarian
Snow Eggs

COCONUT CALENDULA CUSTARD

2 cups milk
1 tablespoon dried calendula
  or marigold petals
2 tablespoons unsweetened
  flaked coconut
3 egg yolks, slightly beaten
¼ cup sugar

Pinch of salt
Pinch of nutmeg
Pinch of allspice
1 teaspoon vanilla extract
Whipped cream (optional)
4 marigold buds (optional)

Combine the milk, dried flower petals, and coconut in a saucepan and heat over a low flame until the milk is scalded. Stir in the egg yolks, sugar, salt, nutmeg, and allspice, and cook, stirring, until the mixture coats a metal spoon. Remove from the heat and stir in the vanilla extract. Pour the custard into dessert glasses or cups. Cool, cover, and chill.

To serve, garnish with whipped cream if desired, with a marigold bud atop the whipped cream.

Makes 4 servings.

RICH RUM CUSTARD

7 egg yolks
2 tablespoons half-and-half
1 cup half-and-half
2 tablespoons sugar
Pinch of salt
1 teaspoon vanilla extract

2 tablespoons rum
¼ cup finely chopped candied
  fruits or bottled nesselrode,
  drained (optional)
12 CAT TONGUES (homemade
  or bought)

Beat the egg yolks with 2 tablespoons half-and-half until the mixture is light and creamy. Combine 1 cup half-and-half, the sugar, and the salt in the top of a double boiler. Set it over hot water and cook, stirring, until the mixture is quite hot. Stir in the egg yolks and, stirring constantly, cook until the mixture coats a metal spoon. Remove from the heat and stir in the vanilla extract and rum. If desired, stir in the candied fruits or nesselrode. Pour the custard into sherbet glasses and allow it to cool slightly. Stick 3 Cat Tongues in each custard so that they stand upright but flare slightly outward. Refrigerate until well chilled.

Makes 4 servings.

PUMPKIN FLAN

An ethereal dessert that may make you forever forget its humble cousin, the pumpkin pie.

½ cup sugar
5 eggs
1 cup pumpkin (canned or freshly made thick puree)
½ cup sugar
¼ teaspoon salt
1 teaspoon cinnamon

1½ cups evaporated milk
⅓ cup milk
1½ teaspoons vanilla extract
1 cup heavy cream
2 tablespoons syrup from preserved ginger in syrup

Melt the ½ cup sugar in an 8-inch-square baking pan or flameproof dish over medium heat, stirring constantly. When it has melted, tilt the pan to distribute the caramel evenly over the bottom and sides of the pan. Set aside.

Preheat the oven at 350°. Beat the eggs lightly and combine them with the pumpkin. Add ½ cup sugar, the salt, and the cinnamon, and mix well. Stir in the evaporated milk, milk, and vanilla extract. Pour into the prepared pan and set in a pan of hot water. Bake for 1 hour, or until a knife blade inserted in the center comes out clean. Remove from the pan of water. Cool and refrigerate until it is well chilled. Unmold on a serving plate. Whip the cream until it is stiff, and fold in the ginger syrup. Spoon onto individual portions when serving the flan.

Makes 8 servings.

VANILLA POTS DE CREME

1 cup cream
1 one-inch piece vanilla bean*
¼ cup sugar

3 egg yolks
6 crystallized flowers (optional)

Preheat the oven at 350°. Scald the cream in a saucepan with the vanilla bean and sugar, stirring. Set aside.

Beat the egg yolks until they are very thick and pale in color. Stir the cream mixture into the egg yolks gradually, stirring constantly. Remove

* If vanilla bean isn't available, stir in 1 teaspoon vanilla extract after the cream and egg yolks have been combined.

Charlottes, Creams, and Custards

the vanilla bean. Pour into 6 *pots au crème* cups or custard cups and spoon off any foam from the tops. Set the cups in a baking pan. Pour boiling water around the cups to a level two-thirds of the way up the sides of the cups. Place covers on the *pots au crème* cups, or cover the custard cups with aluminum foil. Bake for 15 to 20 minutes, or until a knife blade inserted in the center comes out clean.

The pan should be set in the lower third of the oven, and the water should not be allowed to boil. Adjust the oven temperature if necessary, and take care not to overcook the crèmes. Remove them from the pan of water, cool, and refrigerate until they are chilled. If desired, decorate each cup with a crystallized flower.

Makes 6 servings.

VARIATION:

Coffee Pots de Crème

Add 1 tablespoon instant coffee powder when scalding the cream.

ALMOND CHARLOTTE

Charlottes are charming desserts first made some 150 years ago by Carême, one of France's most famous chefs. The original dessert was an apple charlotte he created while chef to the prince regent of England (later to become King George IV) and named for George's daughter, Charlotte. It was made in a charlotte mold lined with buttered bread, filled with an apple mixture, and served hot. Later, when Carême went to Russia to become chef for Czar Alexander, he created the cold charlotte (charlotte russe) which we know so well today. It consisted of a cream mixture in a casing of ladyfingers.

A charlotte is made in a plain, round tin-washed metal mold with high, slightly sloping sides. While a charlotte mold can be used for many other dishes, including meat and vegetables, only the special desserts made in it are called charlottes. Look for a charlotte mold with little side handles, or "ears," set about half an inch down from the top, which will give you useful finger room when you unmold the dessert. If you don't have a genuine charlotte mold (avoid those made of aluminum, which don't stand up well and can't be used over direct heat), use a glass oven-ware dish of a size similar to that of a charlotte mold.

The Almond Charlotte which follows, sometimes known as Charlotte Malakoff, is one of the classic charlottes, and is delicious served as is, or with a strawberry or raspberry sauce.

2 tablespoons kirsch or orange
   liqueur
4 tablespoons water
10 to 14 LADYFINGERS
   (homemade or bakery
   ladyfingers)
⅔ cup blanched slivered almonds
2 tablespoons superfine sugar

½ cup sweet butter
½ cup superfine sugar
2 tablespoons kirsch or orange
   liqueur
1 teaspoon vanilla extract
2 cups heavy cream
Whipped cream (optional)

Cut a circle of waxed paper to fit the bottom of a 6-cup charlotte mold. With a fine light oil, oil the mold lightly and place the circle in the bottom. Combine the 2 tablespoons kirsch or orange liqueur with the water in a shallow bowl. Dip the Ladyfingers into the solution and drain on a wire rack, making more solution if necessary. Arranging the Lady-fingers upright, line the inside wall of the mold, placing them closer together.

Blend the almonds and 2 tablespoons superfine sugar in an electric blender or food processor until the mixture is completely pulverized and without lumps. Cream the butter and add the ½ cup superfine sugar gradually, beating well after each addition. Continue beating until the mixture is very fluffy and pale in color. Add the almond mixture and beat until it is well blended. Add the 2 tablespoons kirsch or orange liqueur and the vanilla extract. Whip the cream until stiff, and fold a little into the mixture. Then fold in the balance. Turn into a lined charlotte mold and cover with a lid or aluminum foil. Chill for 6 hours or over-night.

To serve, unmold on a serving plate and peel off the waxed-paper circle. If desired, decorate the top with whipped cream forced through a pastry bag fitted with a fluted tip.

Makes 6 to 8 servings.

APPLE CHARLOTTE

About ½ loaf firm-textured,
   thinly sliced white bread
1 generous cup butter
6 cups peeled, sliced firm apples
3 tablespoons sugar

1 tablespoon lemon juice
Generous pinch of salt
¼ teaspoon vanilla extract
1 recipe APRICOT SAUCE

Cut 2 semicircles of bread to fit into the bottom of a 6¼-inch charlotte or similar mold. Sauté the bread in a tablespoon or so of butter in a skillet until it is lightly browned, and place it in the bottom of the mold. Melt ½ cup butter and pour it into a flat soup plate. Cut strips of bread, removing the crusts, about 1½ inches wide, tapering a bit toward the ends. Dip the bread strips into the melted butter, coating both sides, and, fitting them close together, line the sides of the mold.

Preheat the oven at 375°. Melt ½ cup butter in a skillet and add the apple slices. Cover and cook, shaking the pan occasionally, until the apples are just tender. Add the sugar, lemon juice, salt, and vanilla extract, and spoon into the lined mold. Cut additional bread strips to cover the top of the mold, dipping them in melted butter before laying them over the apples. Set the mold on a baking sheet and bake for about 35 minutes. Remove from the oven and allow to stand for 15 to 25 minutes. Unmold on a serving plate. Serve with Apricot Sauce.

Makes 6 servings.

CHARLOTTE RUSSE

½ cup chopped candied or
   preserved fruits
2 tablespoons kirsch
1 recipe LADYFINGERS, or
   bakery ladyfingers, or bought
   champagne biscuits
4 egg yolks
1 cup milk

1 envelope plain gelatin
⅓ cup sugar
1 teaspoon vanilla extract
1 cup heavy cream
Whipped cream
Candied violets, currant jelly,
   candied cherries, or stemmed
   maraschino cherries

Combine the candied or preserved fruits with the kirsch and allow the mixture to macerate at room temperature for 30 minutes. Meanwhile, line the bottom and sides of an 8-inch spring-form pan or 8 to 10 indi-

---

Charlottes, Creams, and Custards

vidual molds with Ladyfingers or champagne biscuits. Beat the egg yolks in the top of a double boiler. Add the milk and mix. Sprinkle the gelatin over the top and allow it to soften. Add the sugar. Set over hot water and cook, stirring, until the gelatin and sugar have dissolved. Remove from the heat. Add the vanilla extract and the macerated fruits with the kirsch. Set the double boiler top into a bowl of ice, and stir until the mixture becomes thick enough to mound slightly when lifted and dropped back onto the surface. Whip the cream until stiff, and fold it into the custard mixture. Chill until firm.

Pour the chilled custard into the lined spring-form pan or molds. Remove the sides from the spring-form pan, and set the dessert on a serving plate. Decorate the tops of large or individual desserts with whipped cream piped through a pastry bag fitted with a large star tip. Set candied violets, dabs of currant jelly, candied cherries, or stemmed maraschino cherries on top of the whipped cream as desired.

Makes 8 to 10 servings.

MOCHA PISTACHIO CREAM

Legend has it that the Queen of Sheba ordered the nuts of the very best pistachio trees to be harvested yearly for her exclusive use. She was a wise if somewhat greedy lady, for the pistaschio is one of the most beautifully colored nuts in the world—a lovely green that can enhance scores of desserts, as it does this one—and is one of the most distinguished in flavor. When selecting pistachios, look for those with the darkest green color (you can tell this only by opening one). The very darkest come from Italy. While some pistachios are grown in California, the bulk of the crop comes from the Middle East, where pistachios have been used in making such treats as baklava and Turkish delight for centuries. The largest nuts come from Iran, and the smallest from Afghanistan. To save time and work, you can buy pistachios already shelled. Store them in the refrigerator in a glass jar with a tightly fitting lid.

1 envelope plain gelatin	½ cup heavy cream
⅓ cup cold strong coffee	4 tablespoons crème de cacao
1½ cups hot strong coffee	⅓ cup chopped pistachios
6 tablespoons sugar	Chopped pistachios (optional)
Pinch of salt	Grated chocolate (optional)

In a bowl, soften the gelatin in the cold coffee. Add the hot coffee and stir until the gelatin has dissolved. Add the sugar and salt, and stir until it has dissolved. Chill the mixture until it is slightly thickened then beat with a rotary or electric beater until it has about doubled in volume. Whip the cream until it is stiff, and stir in the crème de cacao. Fold the whipped-cream mixture into the coffee mixture. Fold in the chopped pistachios. Turn into a 4-cup mold which has been lightly rubbed with fine, light oil. Cover and chill until it is firm.

To serve, unmold on a serving plate and, if desired, garnish with chopped pistachios and grated chocolate.

Makes 6 servings.

CHESTNUT CREAM

1 envelope plain gelatin
½ cup cold milk
½ cup scalded milk
½ cup sugar
4 egg yolks
2 cups chestnut puree (*purée de marrons au naturel*)

¼ cup Italian maraschino liqueur
½ cup sugar
1 teaspoon vanilla extract
1 cup heavy cream
Whipped cream (optional)
Candied red and green cherries (optional)

Soften the gelatin in the cold milk. Add the scalded milk and stir until the gelatin has dissolved. Place in a saucepan with ½ cup sugar. Add the egg yolks, one at a time, beating well after each addition. Place over low to medium heat and cook, stirring, until the mixture thickens. Remove from the heat immediately, and set the saucepan in a bowl of ice cubes for a few minutes until cooled. Turn the mixture into a bowl.

Combine the chestnut puree, maraschino liqueur, ½ cup sugar, and vanilla extract. Add to the egg yolk mixture, and combine well. Whip the cream until stiff, and fold it into the chestnut mixture. Turn into a simple 6-cup mold. Cover and chill until firm, preferably overnight.

To serve, unmold on a serving plate and, if desired, decorate with whipped cream and candied red and green cherries.

Makes 8 servings.

ZABAGLIONE
OR
ZABAGLIONE SAUCE

1 egg yolk
¼ cup Marsala wine
2 teaspoons sugar

Shaved chocolate or crystallized
flowers (optional)

Beat the egg yolk, Marsala, and sugar together in the top of a double boiler. Place over hot water and cook, beating constantly with a rotary beater, until the mixture is thick, foamy, and creamy. Use as a dessert sauce or spoon into dessert glasses and serve immediately as a dessert. If desired, decorate each glass with shaved chocolate or a candied flower.
Makes 3 or 4 dessert servings or a sauce for 6 or more servings.

CREME BEAU RIVAGE

¼ cup sugar
6 eggs
2 egg yolks
½ cup sugar
1 cup cream
1½ cups milk

1½ teaspoons vanilla extract
1½ cups heavy cream
1 ten-ounce package frozen
    strawberries, thawed
1 recipe PETITS CORNETS

Preheat the oven at 350°. Heat ¼ cup sugar in a saucepan over medium heat, stirring until melted. Pour into a ring mold and tilt the mold to coat the bottom and partway up the sides. Set aside.

Beat the eggs and egg yolks well, and add ½ cup sugar gradually, beating until the mixture is very thick and pale in color. Scald the cream and milk together, and add to the egg-sugar mixture gradually, stirring constantly. Add the vanilla extract and pour the mixture into the prepared mold. Set the mold in a pan of hot water and bake for about 45 minutes, or until a knife blade inserted in the center comes out clean. Remove from the pan of water and cool. Refrigerate until chilled, and unmold on a serving plate.

Whip the heavy cream until stiff, and fill the Petits Cornets with the whipped cream. Fold the thawed strawberries into the balance of the whipped cream and spoon into the center of the ring. Arrange the Petits Cornets around the edge of the plate.

Makes 8 servings.

EMPRESS RICE

⅔ cup assorted preserved or
   candied fruits, finely diced
3 tablespoons kirsch
¾ cup long-grain rice
2 cups milk, scalded
¼ teaspoon salt
⅓ cup sugar
1 two-inch piece vanilla bean

1½ tablespoons plain gelatin
¼ cup cold water
2 tablespoons butter
3 egg yolks
½ cup heavy cream
Candied cherries, angelica, or
   other candied fruits
¾ cup currant jelly

Combine the assorted fruits and kirsch, and set the mixture aside to macerate. Put the rice in the top of a double boiler and pour boiling water over it to cover. Cover and set aside for 30 minutes. Drain well. Add the scalded milk, salt, sugar, and vanilla bean. Place over simmering water, cover, and cook for 45 minutes, or until the rice is tender and has absorbed all the liquid.

Shortly before the rice has finished cooking, soften the gelatin in the cold water. When the rice has cooked, remove the vanilla bean and add the softened gelatin, stirring until it has dissolved. Add the butter and stir until it has melted. Remove from the heat. Beat the egg yolks lightly and stir a spoonful of the rice mixture into them. Then stir the egg yolk mixture into the rice and mix well but gently. Turn the mixture into a bowl, cool it slightly, and refrigerate until it is slightly chilled.

Drain the macerated fruits, reserving the liquid, and add the fruits to the rice mixture. Whip the heavy cream until it is stiff. Stir about one-third of the whipped cream into the rice mixture. Then fold in the balance of the whipped cream. Turn the mixture into a lightly oiled mold. Cover and chill until it is firm. Unmold on a serving plate and decorate with cherries, angelica, or other candied fruits. Whip the currant jelly with a fork, and beat in the reserved kirsch from the macerated fruits. Pour around the mold, and serve.

Makes 8 servings.

Charlottes, Creams, and Custards

ORANGE RICE

1 cup long-grain rice
2⅓ cups milk, scalded
¼ teaspoon salt
1 two-inch piece vanilla bean
2 oranges
⅓ cup sugar
½ teaspoon grated zest of lemon
  peel

¼ cup (or less) orange juice
3 or 4 tablespoons orange liqueur
¾ cup heavy cream
2 cans mandarin orange segments
2 tablespoons apricot jam

Put the rice in the top of a double boiler and pour boiling water over it to cover. Cover and set aside for 30 minutes. Drain the rice well, and add the scalded milk, salt, and vanilla bean. Place over hot water, cover, and cook for 45 minutes or until the liquid is absorbed and the rice is tender. Remove the vanilla bean.

Meanwhile, with a vegetable peeler or a small, sharp knife, peel the zest from the oranges. Place the zest in a small saucepan, cover with boiling water, and blanch for 2 minutes. Drain it and pat dry. Slice it into very thin julienne strips.

Turn the cooked rice into a bowl and add the julienne strips of orange zest, the sugar, lemon zest, orange juice (the amount depending on the firmness of the rice mixture), and 1 tablespoon of the orange liqueur. Allow the mixture to cool. Beat the heavy cream until it is stiff, and fold it, one-half at a time, into the rice mixture. Pack into a lightly oiled 4-cup ring mold, cover, and refrigerate until it is firm.

Meanwhile, drain the mandarin orange segments and place them in a bowl with the apricot jam and 2 or 3 tablespoons of the orange liqueur.

To serve, unmold the rice mixture onto a serving plate and fill the center with the mandarin-orange-segment mixture.

Makes 6 servings.

ORANGE FLAN

1 cup brown sugar
2 tablespoons water
3 tablespoons orange marmalade
3 egg whites

¾ cup sugar
2 cups evaporated milk
8 egg yolks
2 teaspoons vanilla extract

Preheat the oven at 350°. In a saucepan over moderate heat, melt the brown sugar with the water, stirring constantly. Heat until it is syrupy. Pour into a large ring mold and tilt the mold to coat the bottom and partway up the sides. Cut the marmalade finely, and distribute it evenly over the bottom of the mold.

Beat the egg whites until they form soft peaks. Add the sugar gradually, continuing to beat until stiff peaks form. Stir in the evaporated milk. Beat the egg yolks lightly, and stir them in. Add the vanilla extract. Pour the mixture into the prepared mold.

Set the mold in a pan of hot water, and bake for 1 hour, or until a knife blade inserted in the center comes out clean. Cool and chill. Unmold onto a serving plate.

Makes 8 servings.

MAPLE SYRUP CUSTARD

4 eggs, beaten	½ teaspoon vanilla extract
3 cups milk	Pinch of salt
¾ cup maple syrup	Finely chopped walnuts

Preheat the oven at 350°. Combine the eggs with the milk, maple syrup, vanilla extract, and salt. Pour the mixture into custard cups or *pots au crème* cups, and set in a pan of hot water so that the water level is the same as the level of the custard. Bake for 35 to 45 minutes, or until a knife blade inserted in the center of the custard comes out clean. Remove the cups from the hot water, cool, and refrigerate until the custard is chilled. To serve, sprinkle with a small amount of finely chopped walnuts.

Makes 8 servings.

ORANGE COFFEE CREAM

1 envelope plain gelatin	2 tablespoons orange liqueur
¼ cup heavy cream	1¼ cups crushed ice
¼ cup scalded heavy cream	Liquid-center candy coffee beans
2 tablespoons coffee liqueur	(optional)

Soften the gelatin in ¼ cup heavy cream and place in the container of an electric blender. Add the scalded heavy cream, and blend at high speed for 30 seconds. Add the coffee liqueur and orange liqueur along with the crushed ice, and blend at high speed for 30 seconds. Pour the mixture into small sherbet glasses and chill until set. To serve, decorate each dessert with 2 or 3 liquid-center candy coffee beans.

Makes 4 servings.

HONEY PARFAIT

6 tablespoons honey   1 cup heavy cream, whipped
2 eggs

Heat the honey in a small saucepan, but do not allow it to boil. Transfer the honey to a bowl, and with an electric beater add the eggs, 1 at a time, and continue beating for 5 to 10 minutes until the mixture is pale and very thick and forms a slowly dissolving ribbon when the beater is lifted. Fold in the whipped cream. Pour the mixture into a 6-cup plastic container. Cover and freeze until it is firm.

Makes 6 servings.

RASPBERRY BAVARIAN CREAM

1 ten-ounce package frozen   2 eggs
  raspberries, thawed   1 heaping cup shaved or finely
¼ cup milk   crushed ice
2 envelopes plain gelatin   1 cup heavy cream
¼ cup sugar   Whipped cream (optional)

Drain the juice from the thawed raspberries into a small saucepan. Puree the raspberries in an electric blender. Put the puree through a fine sieve to remove the seeds. Lightly oil a 4-cup mold. Pour the milk into the container of an electric blender. Sprinkle the gelatin over the milk. Heat the raspberry juice to boiling, and pour it into the blender. Blend for 40 seconds.

Add the sugar and eggs, and blend for 5 seconds. Add the pureed raspberries and blend for 5 seconds. Add the ice and heavy cream, and blend for 20 seconds. Immediately turn the mixture into a mold. Cover and refrigerate until it is firm. To serve, unmold on a serving plate. If desired, decorate the dessert with whipped cream piped through a pastry bag fitted with a star tip.

Makes 6 servings.

VARIATION:

Strawberry Bavarian Cream

Substitute 1 ten-ounce package frozen strawberries for the raspberries, but do not puree and strain them.

GINGER BAVARIAN CREME

2 egg yolks
¼ cup sugar
Pinch of salt
1 cup milk, scalded
1 envelope plain gelatin
¼ cup cold water
1 teaspoon vanilla extract
2 tablespoons syrup from
preserved ginger in syrup

1 cup heavy cream
¼ cup very finely shredded
preserved ginger in syrup,
drained
Whipped cream (optional)
Preserved ginger, sliced
(optional)
Glazed green cherries or
angelica (optional)

In the top of a double boiler, combine the egg yolks, sugar, and salt. Add the scalded milk gradually, stirring constantly. Set over hot water and cook until the mixture coats a metal spoon. Meanwhile, soften the gelatin in the cold water. Remove the milk mixture from the heat and stir in the vanilla extract and the syrup from the preserved ginger. Add the softened gelatin, and stir until it has dissolved. Chill the mixture until it begins to thicken slightly.

Whip the heavy cream until it is stiff, and fold it into the gelatin mixture. Fold in the shredded ginger. Turn the mixture into a lightly oiled 4-cup mold, cover, and refrigerate until it is firm.

To serve, unmold on a serving plate and, if desired, decorate with whipped cream, sliced preserved ginger, and glazed green cherries or angelica cut into fancy shapes.

Makes 8 servings.

Charlottes, Creams, and Custards

PEACH MOUSSE

2 tablespoons plain gelatin
¼ cup cold water
¼ cup boiling orange juice
2 large plums
3 medium-sized peaches
1 tablespoon lemon juice
¼ cup orange juice
½ cup sugar

2 tablespoons Cognac
¼ teaspoon almond extract
2 egg whites
1 cup heavy cream
Sweetened whipped cream
 (optional)
Crystallized rose petals
 (optional)

Soften the gelatin in the cold water. Add the boiling orange juice and stir until the gelatin has dissolved. Peel the skin from the plums and peaches and cut up the fruit coarsely. Place it in the container of an electric blender or food processor with the lemon juice and ¼ cup orange juice, and blend just until the fruit has broken up. Do not allow it to become pureed. In a bowl, combine the gelatin mixture and the fruit mixture. Add the sugar, Cognac, and almond extract.

Beat the egg whites until they are stiff but not dry. Fold them into the fruit mixture. Whip the heavy cream until it is stiff, and fold it into the fruit mixture. Pour into a lightly oiled 6-cup mold. Cover and refrigerate for several hours until set.

To serve, unmold on a serving plate. This may be done an hour or two before serving time. If desired, decorate the dessert with sweetened whipped cream forced through a pastry bag fitted with a star tip, and with crystallized rose petals.

Makes 8 servings.

CHESTNUT MOUSSE

1 eight-ounce package cream
 cheese
¾ cup chestnut puree (*purée
 de marrons au naturel*)
½ cup sugar
1 ounce semisweet chocolate

½ cup mixed preserved or
 candied fruit, finely cut
1 cup heavy cream
Pieces of preserved chestnuts
 (optional)

Cream the cream cheese until soft. Add the chestnut puree and mix well. Add the sugar, semisweet chocolate (which has been melted and slightly cooled), and finely cut fruits. Whip the heavy cream until stiff, and fold it into the chestnut mixture. Spoon the mixture into ramekins or *pots au crème* cups and chill well. To serve, decorate the dessert with pieces of preserved chestnuts if desired.

Makes 8 servings.

RASPBERRY MACAROON MOUSSE

1 ten-ounce package frozen
  raspberries, thawed
1 cup heavy cream
2 egg whites
¼ cup sugar

⅓ cup almond macaroon crumbs
Whole raspberries (optional)
Crystallized mint leaves
  (optional)

Puree the raspberries in an electric blender. Put the puree through a fine sieve to remove the seeds. Whip the heavy cream until stiff, and fold in the raspberries. Beat the egg whites until soft peaks form. Add the sugar gradually, and continue beating until the mixture is thick and glossy. Fold the egg whites into the raspberry mixture. Freeze for 30 to 45 minutes, or until the mixture firms slightly.

Remove from the freezer and, without blending them well, fold in the almond macaroon crumbs. (The crumbs should be left in streaks throughout the raspberry mixture.) Turn the mixture into a plastic container, cover, and freeze until firm. To serve, spoon into dessert glasses and, if desired, garnish with whole raspberries and crystallized mint leaves.

Makes 6 servings.

PINEAPPLE MOUSSE

3 egg yolks
¼ cup sugar
1½ envelopes plain gelatin
½ cup canned pineapple juice
1 small can crushed pineapple,
  drained (juice reserved)

1 cup heavy cream
1 tablespoon rum
Candied pineapple and citron or
  angelica (optional)

Beat the egg yolks until thick. Add the sugar gradually, and beat until the mixture is thick and pale and forms a slowly dissolving ribbon when the beater is lifted. Soften the gelatin in the pineapple juice. Pour the juice from the can of crushed pineapple into a small saucepan and heat to boiling. Pour the boiling juice over the softened gelatin and stir until the gelatin has dissolved. Add the crushed pineapple.

Combine the pineapple mixture with the egg yolk mixture and refrigerate for 10 minutes. Stir up the mixture from the bottom to distribute the pineapple throughout. Refrigerate for 10 minutes more, or until the mixture begins to thicken slightly. Stir again. Whip the heavy cream until stiff and fold it into the pineapple mixture. Fold in the rum. Cover and chill.

To serve, spoon the mousse into dessert glasses. If desired, decorate with candied pineapple and citron or angelica cut into attractive shapes.

Makes 6 servings.

COGNAC CREAM

5 egg yolks	**½ cup Cognac**
¾ cup sugar	**1 cup heavy cream**
1 envelope plain gelatin	**Whipped cream (optional)**
¼ cup cold water	**Crystallized lilacs (optional)**

Beat the egg yolks until thick and pale in color. Add the sugar gradually, and beat until the mixture is very thick. In the top of a double boiler, soften the gelatin in the cold water and ¼ cup of the Cognac. Place over hot water and heat, stirring, until the gelatin has dissolved. Pour into the egg yolk mixture, stirring briskly. Add the remaining ¼ cup Cognac. Whip the heavy cream until stiff, and fold into the Cognac mixture. Spoon the mixture into dessert glasses, cover, and chill until set.

To serve, decorate with dollops of whipped cream topped with candied lilacs if desired.

Makes 8 servings.

FRIED CREAMS

1 cup heavy cream
2 egg yolks
2 tablespoons sugar
1 teaspoon rum
Pinch of cinnamon
2 tablespoons cornstarch

1 tablespoon milk
2 eggs
1 cup rusk crumbs
1 cup blanched almonds, finely
   ground
Fat or oil for frying

Scald the heavy cream and set it aside. Beat together the egg yolks, sugar, rum, and cinnamon. Combine the cornstarch and milk, and stir into the egg yolk mixture. Add the slightly cooled heavy cream gradually, and transfer the mixture to the top of a double boiler. Cook over hot water, stirring, until the mixture thickens. If the mixture lumps, stir briskly with a wire whisk to remove the lumps. Turn the mixture into a shallow buttered pan to a depth of about ¾ inch. Cool, cover, and chill until very firm.

Beat 2 eggs in a shallow soup plate. Combine the rusk crumbs and finely ground blanched almonds in another shallow soup plate. Remove the cream from the refrigerator and cut it into small squares. Dip the squares in the rusk mixture, then in the beaten egg, and then again in the rusk mixture. Arrange the squares on a flat plate and chill again.

At serving time, heat the fat in a deep fryer to 375° to 390°. Fry the squares, turning once, until they are lightly browned. Drain on paper towels and serve immediately.

Makes 4 servings.

COFFEE CIRCLE

1 envelope plain gelatin
¾ cup cold coffee
1 cup hot coffee
⅓ cup sugar
2 tablespoons coffee liqueur
2 tablespoons rum

Whipped cream
Candy coffee beans with liquid
   centers (optional)
Crystallized mint leaves
   (optional)

Soften the gelatin in the cold coffee. Add the hot coffee and stir until the gelatin has dissolved. Add the sugar and stir until it has dissolved. Stir in the coffee liqueur and rum. Pour the mixture into a lightly oiled

---

2-cup ring mold (sometimes called a rice ring), or into 4 dessert glasses if preferred. Cover and chill until firm.

To serve, unmold the ring on a serving plate. Fill the center with whipped cream. If desired, decorate with candy coffee beans and crystallized mint leaves.

Makes 4 servings.

PRUNE WHIP WITH PORT

½ pound pitted prunes
Cold water
2 tablespoons sugar
Piece of zest of lemon peel

½ cup Port wine
½ cup heavy cream
Whipped cream (optional)

Place the prunes in a saucepan and cover with cold water. Add the sugar and lemon zest and bring to a boil. Reduce the heat and simmer for 3 minutes. Drain and add the Port. Cover and simmer for 3 minutes longer. Remove the lemon zest. Turn the mixture into the container of an electric blender or food processor and blend until pureed, if necessary stopping to scrape down the sides of the container. Turn the mixture into a bowl.

Whip the heavy cream until stiff, and fold it into the prune mixture. Spoon into dessert glasses. Cover and chill thoroughly. To serve, top with whipped cream if desired.

Makes 4 servings.

CHAPTER 8

Crêpes

*Very merry, and the best pancakes
that ever I ate in my life.*
—*Samuel Pepys,* Diary,
February 26, 1661, Shrove Tuesday

Though crêpes have only recently become popular in the United States—
with the notable exception of long-famed Crêpes Suzette—thin pancakes
called by one name or another have been eaten in different parts of the
world for hundreds of years.

The first "crêpes" may well have been tortillas that the ancient Mexicans made from cornmeal and filled with strawberries. The crêpe itself,
made of buckwheat flour, was born in France just about the time
Columbus was off discovering new lands to the west, and tissue-thin
pancakes were even made in Colonial America. These were called appropriately, paper pancakes, and the batter used to make them was
called "a quire of paper." It became a tradition to serve them on Saint
Valentine's day in old Virginia.

Today, whether they're dished up with lingonberries in Sweden and
called Swedish pancakes, rolled up in China and called Mandarin pancakes, or stacked up in Hungary and called *palacsinta*, it seems everyone
everywhere loves crêpes. One reason is they adapt themselves to being
filled with just about anything. While they're temptingly fragile and
delicate in appearance, they're really sturdy and can hold practically
any ingredient you decide to put in them. After you've made some of
the recipes in this chapter, you'll probably come up with some original
ideas for your own dessert crêpe fillings. You'll find the possibilities
endless.

Crêpes can be made in almost any skillet, but for ease in turning them
and for even browning, the French iron crêpe pan is ideal. A 6½- or

---

7½-inch-diameter pan (measured across the top) is a good size to use. Before using a new iron crêpe pan, cure it by washing it once with soap and water. Fill it with milk, then heat, but don't boil the milk. Turn off the heat and allow to stand for eight hours or overnight. Rinse the pan with water, dry it with paper towels, and rub it all over with oil. Thereafter, never wash it, and rub it with oil after using to prevent rusting between crêpe-making sessions. Remove any stubborn spots by rubbing them with salt.

For the sake of convenience, you can make crêpes one or two days ahead, wrap them in plastic wrap or aluminum foil, and store them in the refrigerator until ready to use. Or, since they freeze beautifully, they can be wrapped in plastic wrap or foil with a piece of waxed paper between each crêpe, and frozen in lots of a dozen for easy thawing and counting.

To defrost frozen crêpes, leave them at room temperature until the crêpes easily peel off the waxed paper. Don't try to force them, or they'll break. If your recipe doesn't call for heating the filled crêpes in the oven, warm the thawed crêpes in a 300° oven for several minutes before filling and serving.

Always serve crêpes on warmed plates, even though the filling may be cold or even frozen, because crêpes should always convey the feeling they're "fresh off the griddle."

BASIC CREPES

This crêpe batter ensures a tender crêpe and, as opposed to most other recipes, uses instant or quick-mixing flour in place of ordinary flour. This method eliminates the usual waiting period of several hours for the flour to expand and absorb the other ingredients. Look for quick-mixing flour under various trade names such as Gold Medal Wondra or Pillsbury's Sauce 'n Gravy Flour. Please read the chapter introduction before making crêpes for the first time.

1 cup instant or quick-mixing flour	**Pinch of sugar**
⅔ cup cold milk	**Pinch of salt**
⅔ cup cold water	**2 tablespoons melted butter**
3 eggs	**Melted butter or oil for greasing crêpes pan**

Blend flour, milk, water, and eggs in bowl with wire whisk. Add sugar, salt, and 2 tablespoons melted butter.

Heat the crêpes pan over a medium flame and brush with melted butter or oil. Pour in a ladleful of batter, using a small ladle that holds between 2 and 3 tablespoonsful. The size of the ladle you use depends on the size of your crêpes pan, and after the first crêpe you will be able to judge how much batter to pour for each one. Tilt the pan immediately to make the batter thinly cover the entire bottom of the pan. Pour any excess back into the bowl of batter immediately, before it has time to set.

As soon as the crêpe has browned on one side, turn it over with a spatula and briefly brown the other side. The first side that you browned is the "outside." The other side does not brown as prettily and should be the side you place the filling on and fold in.

Continue making crêpes, brushing the pan with melted butter or oil as necessary, until all the batter has been used. As you make the crêpes, place them on a large plate. You can put them on top of one another without fear of sticking.

Makes about 2 dozen.

CREME DE MARRONS CREPES

12 BASIC CREPES
4 egg yolks, beaten
3 tablespoons sugar
½ cup hot water
1 tablespoon instant espresso
    coffee powder

½ cup heavy cream
Canned chestnut spread (crème
    de marrons)
12 spoonsful vanilla ice cream,
    softened
Grated chocolate

Combine the egg yolks and sugar in the top of a double boiler. Dissolve the instant espresso coffee powder in the hot water and add to the egg yolk mixture along with the heavy cream. Place over hot water and cook, stirring, until the mixture coats a metal spoon, making sure it does not boil. Remove from the heat.

Spread the crêpes with the canned chestnut spread. Place a spoonful of softened vanilla ice cream on each crêpe. Sprinkle with grated chocolate and roll up. Put 2 crêpes on each serving dish and spoon the warm coffee sauce over each one. Serve immediately.

Makes 6 servings.

CREPES MELBA

12 BASIC CREPES
1 large can freestone sliced
   Elberta peaches, drained
   (reserving syrup)
½ cup sugar
1 teaspoon vanilla extract
12 spoonsful vanilla ice cream,
   softened

3 tablespoons butter
½ cup MELBA SAUCE or 1
   ten-ounce package frozen
   raspberries, thawed
¼ cup kirsch or peach brandy,
   warmed

Drain 1 cup of syrup from the peaches, adding water if necessary to make 1 cup, and combine with the sugar in a saucepan. Heat, stirring, until the sugar dissolves and the mixture comes to a boil. Boil down until ½ cup of the liquid remains. Remove from the heat and add the vanilla extract.

Arrange the drained peach slices over the crêpes, dividing them evenly. Place a spoonful of softened vanilla ice cream on each crêpe. Roll them up. Place the butter and the boiled-down peach syrup in a chafing dish at the table or in a shallow baking dish on the stove, and allow the mixture to heat well. Arrange the rolled crêpes in the syrup and pour the Melba Sauce or raspberries (which have been pureed and put through a fine sieve to remove the seeds) over the top. Pour the warmed brandy over all, ignite, and spoon the sauce over the crêpes until the flames die. Serve 2 crêpes on each serving dish.

Makes 6 servings.

STRAWBERRY MINCEMEAT CREPES

12 BASIC CREPES
1 package frozen sliced
   strawberries, thawed

1 fourteen-ounce jar brandied
   mincemeat
Confectioners' sugar, sifted

Preheat the oven at 375°. Combine the strawberries and mincemeat and place a generous spoonful of the mixture on each crêpe. Roll up and arrange the crêpes side by side in a shallow buttered baking dish. Bake for 10 minutes.

Remove the baking dish from the oven, and spoon over the crêpes any juices that may have exuded. Sprinkle the confectioners' sugar over the crêpes and serve them while warm.

Makes 6 servings.

CHOCOLATE CREPES CHANTILLY

For the chocolate crêpes:
2 eggs
½ cup instant or quick-mixing flour
2 tablespoons cocoa
¼ cup sugar
1 cup half-and-half
1 teaspoon vanilla extract
1 tablespoon melted butter

For finishing:
1 cup heavy cream
1 or 2 tablespoons sugar
¼ teaspoon almond extract or 2 teaspoons chocolate liqueur or coffee liqueur
Chopped toasted almonds
CHOCOLATE SAUCE (homemade or bought)

For the chocolate crêpes: Beat the eggs lightly and add the flour. Sift together the cocoa and sugar, and add gradually to the egg-flour mixture. Add the half-and-half gradually, along with the vanilla extract and melted butter, beating well after each addition.

Prepare the crêpes as in the recipe for Basic Crêpes, using a lower heat and making sure the crêpes do not scorch or burn. Turn them with a wide spatula. If made ahead, stack the crêpes on a plate with waxed paper between each one, and enclose the plate in a plastic bag to keep the crêpes from becoming dry. These crêpes can be frozen, and any unused batter can be stored in a covered glass jar in the refrigerator for a day or two.

For finishing: Whip the heavy cream until stiff, and add sugar to taste. Stir in the almond extract or liqueur. Spoon over 8 crêpes, sprinkle them with chopped toasted almonds, and roll them up. Arrange 2 crêpes on each serving dish and pour Chocolate Sauce sparingly over the top.

Makes 4 servings, plus additional crêpe batter.

CREPES SUZETTE

18 BASIC CREPES, made by
   increasing sugar to 1
   tablespoon and adding 2
   tablespoons orange liqueur
   to batter
½ cup butter

⅓ cup sugar
Grated zest of 1 orange
⅓ cup orange juice
1 teaspoon lemon juice
½ cup orange liqueur
¼ cup brandy or Cognac

Cream the butter until it is very fluffy. Add the sugar gradually, beating well after each addition. Add the grated orange zest. Gradually add the orange juice and lemon juice. Add the orange liqueur and set the sauce aside until serving time.

To serve, heat the above mixture in a chafing dish until bubbly. Add the crêpes, one at a time, turning each to coat with the sauce. After coating with the sauce, fold each crêpe in half, then in half again, so that they are folded into quarters. Put them to the side of the chafing dish and continue coating and folding until all the crêpes have been folded.

Heat the brandy and pour it over the crêpes. Ignite the brandy and spoon it over the crêpes until the flames die. Serve 3 crêpes on each warmed serving dish, unfolding them so they will be in halves. Spoon some of the sauce over each serving.

Makes 6 servings.

CREPES A LA CREME

12 BASIC CREPES
1¾ cups milk
½ cup sugar
¼ cup cornstarch
Pinch of salt
4 egg yolks

¼ cup cold milk
1 teaspoon vanilla extract
1 tablespoon orange liqueur
½ cup apricot jam
¼ cup butter
1 tablespoon kirsch

Scald 1¾ cups milk in a saucepan. Combine the sugar, cornstarch, and salt in the top of a double boiler. Add the scalded milk gradually, using a wire whisk to combine. Place over direct heat and cook, stirring constantly, until the mixture becomes very thick. Remove from the heat and add the egg yolks (which have been beaten with ¼ cup cold milk). Place over hot water and cook, stirring, until the mixture thickens. Remove from the heat and stir in the vanilla extract and orange liqueur. Cool slightly. Spoon onto the crêpes, roll them up, and arrange them on a serving dish.

In a saucepan, melt the apricot jam, stirring. Add the butter and heat until it has melted. Remove from the heat and stir in the kirsch. Pour over the crêpes and serve.

Makes 6 servings.

ALMOND CREPES

12 BASIC CREPES	Apricot jam
4 ounces almond paste	Sour cream
¼ cup sour cream	Chopped toasted almonds

Soften the almond paste in a bowl, and add ¼ cup sour cream gradually until the mixture is well blended. Spread on the crêpes. Spoon some apricot jam on each crêpe. Roll up the crêpes and arrange them on a serving plate. Top with sour cream and chopped toasted almonds.

Makes 6 servings.

BANANA CREAM CREPES

8 BASIC CREPES	1½ medium-sized bananas, very
1 cup heavy cream	thinly sliced
2 tablespoons sugar	Confectioners' sugar, sifted
2 tablespoons banana liqueur	
(*crème de banane*) or 1	
teaspoon vanilla extract	

Whip the heavy cream until stiff. Stir in the sugar and banana liqueur or vanilla extract. Fold in the bananas. Spoon the mixture on the crêpes, roll them up, and arrange 2 crêpes on each serving dish. Sprinkle sifted confectioners' sugar over each serving.

Makes 4 servings.

DATE NUT CREPES

16 BASIC CREPES **or chocolate
crêpes as in** CHOCOLATE
CREPES CHANTILLY
**1 cup chopped walnuts
1 cup chopped dates**

**1 cup sour cream
¼ cup brown sugar
1 tablespoon finely chopped
crystallized ginger
Confectioners' sugar, sifted**

Preheat the oven at 300°. Combine the walnuts, dates, sour cream, brown sugar, and ginger, and spoon onto the crêpes. Roll them up and arrange them in a buttered shallow baking dish. Heat them in the oven for about 10 minutes. Sprinkle with sifted confectioners' sugar and serve.
Makes 8 servings.

CHAPTER 9

Frozen Desserts

I love snow, and all the forms
Of the radiant frost.
—*Percy Bysshe Shelley, "Rarely, Rarely,*
   Comest Thou"

Ice cream lovers everywhere owe a debt of gratitude to the two Italians who first shared the wonders of frozen desserts as we know them with the rest of the world—Catherine de Medici, the Renaissance tastemaker, and Francisco Procopio, a Sicilian born about a hundred years later. When Catherine journeyed to France to marry the future King Henry II, she took along a cortege of cooks with a collection of recipes for ice cream and other sophisticated Florentine foods until then unknown in France. The dessert was, of course, an instant success among those lucky enough to eat in the royal dining rooms, but the directions for making it were well guarded for the enjoyment of that select few. It was Procopio who brought ice cream to the people when he opened a café in Paris, forerunner of our own ice cream parlors, specializing in countless flavors of frosty delights. His café was so popular that before long more than two hundred similar ice cream havens had popped up throughout the city.

In America, cookbooks of the early 1800s included good recipes for ice cream and ices, and these products were first sold commercially, if on a small scale, around that time. Thomas Jefferson introduced ice cream to the nation's capital, having learned to make it while in France. With the freezer he brought back, he produced the first ice cream dessert served at a state dinner, and went on to invent at least one dessert of his own, a hot flaky pastry filled with ice cream.

Edible ice cream cones appeared at the St. Louis International Exposition in 1904, and for the first time ice cream could be sold in the streets. Nowadays, millions of gallons are made and sold yearly all over the country. Some of these store-bought varieties are so good that by stirring a few ingredients of your own into them, plain flavors can be converted into exotic treats. There's also a tremendous thrill in making your own frozen treats from scratch.

The ice cream family is made up of water ice, sherbet, ice cream, frozen mousse, and various combinations of these products, all of which you'll find in this chapter. Water ices are simple frozen desserts made of sugar syrup combined with fruit or other flavoring. Sherbets, or sorbets, are elaborations of water ices that owe their lighter texture to the addition of egg whites or whipped cream. Sometimes flavored with liqueurs or wines instead of fruit, sherbets can be served either between courses as palate refreshers or at the end of meals as desserts.

Mousses are unlike other frozen desserts in that they're never stirred during the freezing process. Not only do they require less attention than other frozen desserts, but they seem to resist ice crystals quite success-fully. Well named for their inviting texture, mousses, meaning "foam" or "froth," lend themselves to any number of styles of serving. Freeze them in any ordinary container and spoon them out onto dessert plates, mold them in individual or full-sized molds, pour them into little paper cups or individual soufflé dishes or ramekins, or use them as fillings for bombes or any layered dessert.

One of the most festive desserts, and one that never fails to produce oohs and ahs when unmolded and sliced, is the bombe. This is made by lining a mold with one kind of ice cream or ice and filling it with another kind or with a mousse (or with as many of these as time and fancy allow). Bombes, as the name would imply, were first made in cannon-ball shapes, but times have changed and almost any container that's freezable makes for an interestingly shaped dessert. A stainless-steel mixing bowl, for example, would be perfect.

Coupes (*coupe* means "cup," and simply refers to the container in which the dessert is served) are lovely combinations of ice cream and/or ices with generous sprinklings of nuts, fruits, liqueurs, and so on. They're marvelous time-saving desserts, and many of them appear in Chapter 21, "Superfast Desserts." But any frozen desserts in this chapter may be used to make coupe combinations of your own. Other frozen dessert recipes in this book are:

Baked Alaska
Midnight Sun Baked Alaska
Bombe Rothschild
Cherry Mousse
Frozen Port Meringue with Apricot Sauce

FROZEN LIME CREAM

5 egg yolks
⅓ cup sugar
⅔ cup fresh lime juice
Grated zest of 1 lime

5 egg whites
Pinch of salt
⅓ cup sugar
1 cup heavy cream

Beat the egg yolks in the top of a double boiler until very thick. Add ⅓ cup sugar gradually, and continue beating until the mixture forms a slowly dissolving ribbon when the beater is lifted. Stir in the lime juice and lime zest. Set over hot water and cook, stirring, until the mixture thickens slightly, taking care it does not boil. Remove from the heat and cool to room temperature.

Preheat the oven at 350°. Beat the egg whites with the salt until they form soft peaks. Add ⅓ cup sugar gradually, and continue beating until stiff peaks form. Stir a little of the egg white mixture into the egg yolk mixture. Then fold in the balance of the egg white mixture. Turn into a buttered 1-quart soufflé dish and bake for 15 minutes. Cool. Cover tightly with plastic wrap. Chill, and then freeze. To serve, whip the heavy cream and swirl it over the entire surface of the lime cream.

Makes 8 servings.

WALNUT BISQUE

3 egg yolks
⅓ cup sugar
2 cups milk, scalded
⅔ cup sugar

⅔ cup finely chopped walnuts
1 cup heavy cream
1 teaspoon vanilla extract

Beat the egg yolks until they are thick and pale in color. Gradually beat in ⅓ cup sugar. Beat in the scalded milk. Turn the mixture into the top of a double boiler and set it over simmering water. Cook, stirring, until the mixture coats a metal spoon. Remove from the heat. Cool, cover, and chill.

Heat ⅔ cup sugar in a skillet over low heat, stirring, until it has completely melted and is a light reddish-brown in color. Stir in the walnuts and pour the mixture immediately onto a sheet of buttered aluminum foil. When the mixture is cool and hard, break it into pieces and pulverize them in an electric blender, food processor, or with a mortar and pestle. Stir into the chilled custard. Beat the heavy cream until stiff, and add the vanilla extract. Fold into the custard with a rubber spatula. Turn the custard into a mold, cover with aluminum foil, and freeze for 6 hours or overnight. To serve, unmold on a serving plate.

Makes 6 servings.

APRICOT HONEY ICE CREAM

1 cup dried apricots
2 cups water
3 tablespoons lemon juice

3 egg yolks
¾ cup honey
1 cup heavy cream

Place the apricots and water in a saucepan and bring to a boil. Cover and simmer for 10 minutes. Remove the apricots from the liquid and place them in an electric blender or food processor. Boil the liquid down to measure ¼ cup. Add it to the apricots along with the lemon juice, and blend.

Beat the egg yolks until they are thick and pale in color. Add the honey gradually, beating until the mixture becomes very thick. Fold the pureed apricots into the honey mixture. Whip the heavy cream until stiff and fold it into the apricot mixture. Pour into a plastic container, cover and freeze until firm.

Makes 6 servings.

VANILLA ICE CREAM

4 egg yolks
Pinch of salt
½ cup sugar
1 one-inch piece vanilla bean*

2 cups plus 2 tablespoons milk
1 tablespoon sweet butter
1 cup heavy cream

Beat the egg yolks until they are very thick, adding a pinch of salt. Add the sugar gradually, and continue beating until the mixture forms a slowly dissolving ribbon when the beater is lifted.

Slit open the piece of vanilla bean and place it in a nonaluminum

* Vanilla bean gives a rich, distinctive vanilla flavor and should be used if at all possible. If you can't get a vanilla bean, substitute 1½ teaspoons vanilla extract, which should be stirred in with the butter after cooking.

saucepan with the milk. Place over moderate heat and bring to a boil. Remove the saucepan from the heat and take out the vanilla bean. Pour the milk over the egg yolk mixture gradually, beating constantly with a wire whisk. Transfer the mixture to a saucepan and place it over moderate heat, or place it in the top of a double boiler over hot water, and cook, beating constantly, until the mixture thickens slightly. Do not allow it to boil.

Remove from the heat and stir in the butter. Allow the mixture to cool, and stir in the heavy cream. Freeze in a manual or electric ice cream freezer according to the manufacturer's instructions, or place the mixture in a freezing tray or plastic container and freeze until it becomes mushy. Beat with an electric beater until smooth. Replace in the container and freeze until nearly firm. Beat again with the electric beater until smooth. Place the ice cream in 1 or 2 plastic containers, cover tightly, and freeze until firm.

Makes about 1 quart.

PUMPKIN PARFAIT

2 cups cooked mashed pumpkin (either fresh or canned)
½ cup brown sugar, firmly packed
1 teaspoon cinnamon
½ teaspoon ground ginger
¼ teaspoon ground nutmeg
⅛ teaspoon ground allspice
Pinch of salt
1 quart eggnog ice cream or vanilla ice cream
Sweetened whipped cream
Crystallized ginger cut into small pieces

Combine the pumpkin, brown sugar, cinnamon, ginger, nutmeg, allspice, and salt. Soften the ice cream and stir the pumpkin mixture into it. Turn the mixture into a mold or plastic container. Cover and freeze until firm. To serve, unmold on a serving plate or spoon into parfait glasses. Decorate the dessert with sweetened whipped cream and pieces of crystallized ginger.

Makes 8 servings.

FROZEN BANANA CREAM

2 medium-sized bananas
2 tablespoons lemon juice
⅓ cup superfine sugar
1 cup heavy cream
Toasted sweetened coconut (optional)

Cut the bananas into chunks and place in the container of an electric blender or food processor. Add the lemon juice. Blend. Add the sugar and blend again, stopping if necessary to scrape down the sides of the container. Whip the heavy cream until stiff, and fold it into the banana mixture. Pour into a 1-quart plastic container. Cover and freeze until the ice cream is firm but not hard. To serve, spoon the dessert into serving glasses and garnish with toasted sweetened coconut if desired.

Makes 4 servings.

PISTACHIO CREAM GLACE

8 ounces cream cheese
1 teaspoon vanilla extract
½ cup sifted confectioners'
   sugar
1 tablespoon orange liqueur
1 eight-ounce container sour
   cream

½ cup pistachio nuts (unsalted)
Whipped cream
Finely chopped pistachios
Orange liqueur (optional)

Soften the cream cheese by hand in the bowl of an electric mixer. Add the vanilla extract and beat with the electric mixer. Add the confectioners' sugar and 1 tablespoon orange liqueur, and beat well. Whip the sour cream until stiff. (This will take considerably longer than beating heavy cream.) Fold the whipped cream into the cream cheese mixture. Chop ½ cup pistachio nuts coarsely and fold them into the mixture.

Line a small loaf pan or round, 1-quart casserole with plastic wrap. Pour the mixture in and cover it with another piece of plastic wrap. Freeze until firm. Remove the top sheet of plastic wrap, unmold onto a serving plate, and remove the remaining plastic wrap. Decorate with whipped cream forced through a pastry bag fitted with a star tip. Sprinkle with finely chopped pistachios. Replace in the freezer. Thirty minutes before serving, transfer to the refrigerator. To serve, spoon out small portions. Pour a little orange liqueur over each serving if desired.

Makes 8 servings.

FROZEN VIOLET MOUSSE

1 teaspoon plain gelatin
1 tablespoon cold water
2 tablespoons boiling water
2 cups milk
2 tablespoons sugar
3 egg whites

1 cup heavy cream
1 tablespoon lemon juice
2 tablespoons violet liqueur
   (*crème de violette*)
Crystallized violets or fresh
   violet blossoms and leaves

Soften the gelatin in the cold water. Add the boiling water and stir until the gelatin has dissolved. Place it in a saucepan with the milk and sugar, and heat over a moderate flame. Beat the egg whites until stiff and fold in some of the milk mixture, a tablespoonful at a time, until the egg whites are light in consistency. Then fold the egg whites into the remaining milk. Cook over moderate heat, beating constantly with an eggbeater, until the mixture comes to a boil and increases in bulk. Remove from the flame and cool.

Whip the heavy cream until stiff, and fold in the lemon juice and violet liqueur. Add some of the egg white mixture, and fold it in. Add the whipped cream to the remaining egg white mixture, and thoroughly fold it in. Pour the mixture into a rectangular pan and freeze until it becomes mushy. Beat it until smooth with an electric beater. Pour it into a 6-cup mold (which has been rinsed in cold water). Cover the top tightly with plastic wrap and secure with a rubber band. Place a lid on the mold if available. Freeze until firm. Unmold on a serving plate and garnish with crystallized violets or fresh violet blossoms and leaves.

Makes 8 to 10 servings.

FROZEN STRAWBERRY MOUSSE

4 cups fresh strawberries
⅔ cup sugar
⅓ cup water
2 egg whites
¼ teaspoon cream of tartar

2 cups heavy cream
1 teaspoon vanilla extract
Macaroon crumbs (optional)
Whole fresh strawberries
   (optional)

Puree the strawberries in an electric blender or food processor. Set them aside. In a saucepan, combine the sugar and water and bring to a boil, stirring constantly. Cover, and boil over high heat until the mixture reaches the soft-ball stage, about 238°. Remove from the heat.

Beat the egg whites until they are foamy. Add the cream of tartar and continue beating until stiff peaks form. Continue beating while pouring the syrup over the egg whites in a steady stream. Beat until the mixture is thick and glossy. Fold the strawberry puree into the egg white mixture. Whip the heavy cream until stiff. Add the vanilla extract. Fold the whipped cream into the strawberry mixture, combining them well. Pour the mixture into plastic containers, a freezable decorative deep serving dish or bowl, or a collared 1½-quart soufflé dish. Cover the container tightly with plastic wrap, and seal with lid if available. Freeze for several hours.

To serve, spoon the mousse into serving dishes, unmold it onto a serving plate, or remove the collar from the soufflé dish. If desired, garnish with macaroon crumbs and whole fresh strawberries.

Makes 8 or more servings.

FROZEN ORANGE LIQUEUR MOUSSE

6 egg yolks	**3 tablespoons orange liqueur**
½ cup sugar	**Candied orange peel (optional)**
1 cup heavy cream	**Whipped cream (optional)**

In a mixing bowl, beat the egg yolks until thick. Add the sugar and continue beating until the mixture is very thick and pale in color. Whip the heavy cream until stiff, and stir it into the egg yolk mixture. Add the orange liqueur. Set the bowl in a container of cracked ice, and beat the mixture until frothy. Pour it into a 3-cup mold. Seal the top with plastic wrap and cover tightly with aluminum foil. Freeze for 8 hours or overnight. Unmold the mousse onto a serving plate and return it to the freezer until serving time. If desired, decorate the dessert with candied orange peel and/or whipped cream piped through a pastry bag fitted with a star tip.

Makes 6 servings.

FROZEN APRICOT MOUSSE

¾ cup dried apricots, firmly
    packed
1 cup water
½ cup sugar
1 teaspoon vanilla extract
1 teaspoon lemon juice
Canned apricot nectar (about
    1 cup)

8 egg yolks
3 egg whites
⅓ cup sugar
1 cup heavy cream
Dried on glacéed apricots
    (optional)
Whipped cream (optional)

In a saucepan, bring the apricots and water to a boil. Lower the heat, cover, and simmer for 10 mintues. Add ½ cup sugar and stir until it has dissolved. Remove the saucepan from the heat and add the vanilla extract. Transfer the mixture to an electric blender or food processor, and blend until pureed. Add the lemon juice and enough canned apricot nectar for the mixture to measure 2 cups in all. Blend until smooth.

Beat the egg yolks until they are thick and pale in color. Gradually beat in the apricot mixture. Transfer the mixture to the top of a double boiler and place over hot water. Cook over low heat, stirring, until it is very thick, about 15 minutes, making sure the spoon keeps cleaning the entire bottom and sides of the pan as you stir. Remove the top of the double boiler from the heat and set it in a bowl of ice. Stir until the mixture cools.

Beat the egg whites until soft peaks form, and continue beating, while gradually adding ⅓ cup sugar, until stiff peaks form. Fold the apricot mixture into the beaten egg whites with a rubber spatula. Beat the heavy cream in a chilled bowl until stiff. Fold the whipped cream into the apricot mixture with a rubber spatula. Pour the mixture into a plain, 8-cup mold, or, if you wish to serve the mousse on more than one occasion, pour into 2 or 3 smaller molds equaling 8 cups, or, if you plan to spoon it into dessert glasses, freeze it in a plastic container. Cover the mold or other container tightly with plastic wrap, aluminum foil, or a lid. Freeze overnight.

To serve, spoon the mousse into dessert glasses, or unmold it on a serving plate and return it to the freezer until serving time. If desired, decorate the dessert with dried or glacéed apricots cut into designs, and/or with whipped cream piped through a pastry bag fitted with a star tip.

Makes 12 to 16 servings.

CHOCOLATE ICE CREAM

⅓ cup water
1 cup sugar
3 egg whites
¼ teaspoon cream of tartar
Pinch of salt
2 tablespoons instant espresso
  coffee powder

¼ cup water
1 cup milk
5 ounces Eagle sweet chocolate
2 ounces baking chocolate
2 teaspoons vanilla extract
1 cup heavy cream

In a saucepan, combine ⅓ cup water and the sugar, and bring to a boil over medium heat, stirring constantly. Cover and boil the syrup over high heat until it reaches the soft-ball stage, about 238°. Remove from the heat. Beat the egg whites until they are foamy. Add the cream of tartar and a pinch of salt, and beat until stiff peaks form. Continue to beat while pouring in the syrup in a steady stream until the mixture is thick and shiny. Set aside.

Dissolve the espresso powder in ¼ cup water and place the mixture in a saucepan with the milk. Chop the sweet and baking chocolate finely and add it to the milk. Place the saucepan over low to medium heat, and cook, stirring, until the chocolate has completely melted. Simmer a few minutes longer, stirring, making sure the mixture does not stick to the bottom of the pan. Remove the pan from the heat and set it in a bowl of ice. Stir until steam no longer rises from the chocolate mixture. Stir in the vanilla extract. Fold the chocolate mixture into the meringue mixture. Whip the heavy cream until it just holds its shape. Fold the whipped cream into the chocolate mixture. Pour into plastic containers. Cover with plastic wrap and put lids on the containers. Freeze the ice cream until firm.

Makes about 2 quarts.

THE VERSATILE BOMBE

The possibilities for combining flavors of ice creams, sherbets, mousses, and other frozen desserts to make bombes are infinite, but the procedure for putting together a bombe is a simple matter. First, make sure your freezer is set below 0°F. Then, choose a mold such as a bombe mold, charlotte mold (both of which are nice because they usually have fitted covers), melon mold, mixing bowl, loaf pan, or any tin, copper, stainless-steel, aluminum, or other metal container of a suitable size and character for filling and freezing. The simpler the mold, the easier the unmolding will be. Rub the mold very lightly with a fine, light oil and chill. Decide on the ice cream flavor to be used to line the mold (don't use sherbet or mousse for the lining because they aren't heavy enough), and one or two flavors of mousse, sherbet, or other ice cream flavors to fill the center. (Suggestions follow.) There's no reason why good commercially made ice creams can't be used for all or part of the bombe construction.

Working as quickly as possible, use a wooden spoon to soften the ice cream to be used for the lining, and spread an even layer 1 to 2 inches thick on the bottom of the mold. Work up the sides, filling in any pattern on the mold and making the sides the same thickness as the bottom, leaving a hollow center. A rubber spatula will be helpful in shaping the ice cream. Keep the mold in the freezer for 1½ to 2 hours, until the ice cream is solidly frozen. Fill the center with mousse or sherbet, or spread a second flavor of ice cream over the first, and freeze again. Continue this procedure until the mold is filled. You can sprinkle toasted almonds, macaroon crumbs, grated chocolate, or similar ingredients between layers if you wish. It's best to top the mold off with an inch of the ice cream that lines the mold. Smooth the top evenly. Cover with plastic wrap or waxed paper, then aluminum foil or a lid. Set the mold in the freezer on top of something else, such as a box of frozen vegetables, instead of placing it directly on the freezer shelf. Freeze for 8 hours or overnight. Bombes can be made as much as a week ahead of time if they are well sealed.

Before unmolding, chill the serving plate. Dip the mold quickly in and out of hot water, or press a towel wrung out in hot water around it, with particular emphasis on the bottom of the mold. Dry quickly. Invert on a chilled plate. Repeat the procedure if necessary. Place the bombe on a serving plate in the freezer to firm up again before serving.

Decorate the bombe with any ingredient that enhances its particular flavors or the occasion on which it is being served. Some possibilities are: preserved or crystallized ginger, sliced, chopped, or cut into shapes; glacéed cherries; pineapple; angelica or other candied fruits or candied chestnuts; fresh whole strawberries or raspberries; marzipan colored and shaped into various forms; real flowers for a birthday; holly for Christmas; chopped pistachios, pecans, almonds, or other nuts, either toasted or plain; shaved chocolate; crystallized flowers; fresh mint sprigs; fresh orange-peel curls; whipped cream; dustings of cocoa or praline powder and so on. To serve a bombe, cut up into wedges or slices, depending on the shape of the mold you use, so that the layerings will be shown to their best advantage on the individual serving plates.

Some suggestions for flavor combinations follow, but to produce your own unique bombe, simply keep colors and flavors in mind with an eye to how they will complement and contrast with one another to achieve the most pleasing appearance and taste.

Lining	Filling(s)	Decoration(s)
pineapple ice cream	RASPBERRY CREAM SHERBET; a layer of sponge cake at the top of the mold; with final coating of pineapple ice cream	candied or canned pineapple pieces and chopped pistachios
cherry ice cream sprinkled with macaroon crumbs	GINGER ICE CREAM and MACAROON ICE CREAM mixed together or used in separate layers	whipped cream, chopped candied ginger, toasted almonds, or whole fresh cherries with stems
VANILLA ICE CREAM sprinkled with chopped pistachios	FROZEN ORANGE LIQUEUR MOUSSE	whipped cream and candied orange slices, chopped pistachios, or crystallized violets
PRALINE ICE CREAM sprinkled with toasted chopped coconut	lining of CHOCOLATE ICE CREAM sprinkled with macaroon crumbs; filled with APRICOT HONEY ICE CREAM	candied apricots and/or toasted almonds
coffee ice cream sprinkled with chopped toasted filberts	lining of CHOCOLATE ICE CREAM; filled with PRALINE ICE CREAM	shaved chocolate, candy coffee beans, or whipped cream dusted with praline powder
pistachio ice cream sprinkled with chopped pistachios	FROZEN BANANA CREAM	whipped cream and chopped pistachios, or angelica and candied cherries for Christmas, or tiny marzipan fruits, including bananas
VANILLA ICE CREAM	FROZEN APRICOT MOUSSE or PUMPKIN PARFAIT	glacéed apricot pieces or tiny marzipan pumpkins

TORTONI

1½ cups heavy cream
½ cup sifted confectioners' sugar
3 tablespoons brandy or rum
1 egg white

½ cup finely crumbled ALMOND MACAROON crumbs (homemade or bought)
Finely chopped toasted almonds

Whip the heavy cream until slightly thickened. Add the confectioners' sugar gradually, and continue to beat until stiff. Stir in the brandy or rum. Beat the egg white until stiff, and fold it into the whipped cream. Puree the Macaroon Crumbs in an electric blender or food processor, or reduce them to fine crumbs with a rolling pin. Fold them into the whipped cream mixture. Spoon the mixture into fluted cupcake-sized paper cups which have been set into muffin tins. Sprinkle the tops with finely chopped toasted almonds. Freeze until firm. Cover the tortoni with plastic wrap if they will not be served the same day.

Makes 12 servings.

ALMOND ICE MILK

1 envelope plain gelatin
¼ cup cold water
2 cups milk
1 cup (2.3 ounce envelope) dry milk powder

½ cup sugar
1 teaspoon almond extract
Whole blanched almonds (optional)

Soften the gelatin in the cold water. Combine the milk and milk powder in a saucepan, and stir in the sugar and the softened gelatin. Cook over low heat, stirring constantly, until the gelatin has completely dissolved. Remove the saucepan from the heat and add the almond extract. Pour the mixture into a rectangular metal pan and freeze it until set. Scrape the mixture into a bowl and beat with an electric beater until smooth. Freeze it again until firm, then beat it again until smooth. Pour into a 1-quart plastic container, cover, and freeze until firm.

To serve, spoon the dessert into serving glasses. If desired, decorate the top of each serving with a whole blanched almond.

Makes 1 quart.

Substitute any desired flavor of extract, such as vanilla or maple, for the almond extract.

GRAPEFRUIT SHERBET

Peeled zest of 2 grapefruit
Boiling water
3 cups grapefruit segments, all
   membranes removed
⅓ cup cold water

1¼ cups sugar
3 egg whites
¼ teaspoon cream of tartar
Pinch of salt

Put the peeled grapefruit zest in a saucepan and cover with boiling water. Bring to a boil again, and boil for 15 minutes. Drain. Place the grapefruit zest in an electric blender or food processor with 1½ cups of the grapefruit segments, and blend for a few seconds. Transfer the mixture to a bowl. Chop the remaining grapefruit segments finely and combine with the first grapefruit mixture. Set aside.

Combine the cold water and sugar in a small saucepan. Cook, stirring constantly, over low heat until sugar has dissolved and the mixture begins to boil. Cover and boil over high heat, testing every minute or so with a candy thermometer, until the mixture reaches the soft-ball stage, about 238°. Remove from the heat.

Beat the egg whites with an electric beater until they are foamy. Add the cream of tartar and salt, and continue beating at high speed until the mixture forms stiff peaks. Pour the syrup over the beaten egg whites in a stream, beating at high speed all the while, and continue beating until the mixture is very stiff. Allow it to cool for 5 minutes or more. Add the grapefruit mixture and combine well. Pour the mixture into a rectangular pan or freezer tray and freeze until it becomes mushy, about 1 hour. Transfer to a bowl and beat with an electric beater until smooth. Spoon the dessert into chilled sherbet glasses. Freeze until it becomes firm.

Makes about 8 servings.

RASPBERRY CREAM SHERBET

2 ten-ounce packages frozen
  raspberries, thawed
1 tablespoon lemon juice
¾ cup sugar
⅓ cup water

1 tablespoon corn syrup
3 egg whites
Pinch of salt
¼ teaspoon cream of tartar
½ cup heavy cream

Puree the raspberries in an electric blender or food processor. Put the puree through a fine sieve to remove the seeds. Add the lemon juice. Combine the sugar, water, and corn syrup in a saucepan, and bring to a boil, stirring until the sugar has dissolved. Cook to the soft-ball stage, about 238°.

Meanwhile, beat the egg whites until they are foamy. Add the salt and cream of tartar, and continue beating until stiff peaks form. Pour the sugar syrup in a fine stream over the beaten egg whites, beating continually, until well combined. Fold in about one-third of the raspberry puree. Whip the heavy cream until it holds its shape but is not too stiff. Fold it into the egg white mixture. Fold in the remaining raspberry puree, one-half at a time, until the mixture is well combined. Pour it into a rectangular pan or freezer tray, and freeze until it becomes mushy, about 1 hour. Stir the mixture well, scraping down the sides and all over the bottom of the pan, until the mixture is completely smooth. Pour the sherbet into plastic container(s) and cover tightly with plastic wrap and container lid(s). Freeze until firm.

Makes 1 generous quart.

MELON SHERBET

2 medium cantaloupes
½ cup sugar
¼ cup heavy cream

2 tablespoons kirsch
Chopped pistachios (optional)

Peel, seed, and cut up the cantaloupes, and puree enough in an electric blender or food processor to measure 6 cups. Transfer to a bowl, add the sugar, and stir until it has dissolved. Add the heavy cream and kirsch and combine well. Pour the mixture into a rectangular pan or freezer tray and freeze until it becomes mushy, about 1 hour. Transfer the mixture to a chilled bowl and beat with an electric beater until smooth. Return the mixture to the pan and place it in the freezer again. When the mixture is almost firm, beat it again. Spoon it into plastic containers, cover them closely with plastic wrap, and seal them with lids. Freeze the sherbet until it is almost firm, and serve it fairly soft, spooning it into dessert glasses. If desired, sprinkle each serving with chopped pistachios. If the mixture becomes too firm, place it in the refrigerator and allow it to stand for 1 or 2 hours until serving time.

Makes about 1½ quarts.

ORANGE POMEGRANATE SHERBET

6 to 8 seedless oranges
⅓ cup grenadine syrup
⅓ cup superfine sugar
1 egg white, slightly beaten

3 cups carbonated mineral water
(preferably Perrier water)
Mint leaves (optional)

With a sharp knife, cut the skins and outside membrane from the oranges. Cutting between the membranes, remove the orange segments. Place the segments in a bowl with any juice that exudes during cutting. Cut them up fine, making enough to measure 2½ cups of pulp and juice combined. Add the grenadine syrup, superfine sugar, egg white, and carbonated mineral water. Place the mixture in a rectangular pan or freezer tray and freeze until it becomes mushy, about 1 hour. Turn it into a chilled bowl and beat with an electric beater until it becomes smooth. Turn the mixture into plastic containers, cover them closely with plastic wrap, and seal them with lids. Freeze the dessert until it is almost firm. Spoon it into sherbet glasses. If desired, garnish with mint leaves.

Makes about 1½ quarts.

ROSE PETAL WATER ICE

2 cups sugar
4 cups water
¼ cup lemon juice

2 teaspoons grated zest of lemon
peel
3 tablespoons rose petal jam
(jam of roses, not rose hip jam)

In a saucepan, combine the sugar and water. Place over medium heat and bring to a boil, stirring until sugar has dissolved. Simmer for 5 minutes. Remove the saucepan from the heat and add the lemon juice, lemon zest, and rose petal jam. Stir well until the jam has melted and is evenly distributed throughout the mixture. Cool.

Pour the mixture into a rectangular pan or freezer tray and freeze until it becomes mushy, about 1 hour. Transfer the mixture to a chilled bowl and beat with an electric beater until it becomes smooth. Return the mixture to the freezer. When it is almost firm, beat it again. Spoon the mixture into plastic containers, cover them closely with plastic wrap, and seal them with lids. Freeze the dessert until serving time. If the mixture becomes too hard, place it in the refrigerator and allow it to stand for 1 or 2 hours before serving.

Makes about 1 quart.

LEMON HONEY WATER ICE

½ cup sugar
1½ cups water
½ cup honey

½ cup lemon juice
1½ teaspoons grated zest of
    lemon peel

In a saucepan, combine the sugar, water, and honey, and bring to a boil, stirring constantly. Cover and boil for 5 minutes without stirring. Remove the saucepan from the heat and add the lemon juice and lemon zest. Pour the mixture into a rectangular pan or freezer tray and freeze until firm, about 45 minutes. Scrape the mixture into a chilled bowl, and beat with an electric beater until it becomes fluffy. Refreeze and beat again. Place the mixture in a plastic container, cover it closely with plastic wrap, and seal it with a lid. Freeze until it is firm but not hard.

Makes 1 generous pint.

VANILLA ICE CREAM
CONVERTS TO . . .

There are so many good commercially prepared ice creams in the United States that it makes sense to utilize them in preparing frozen desserts with plain vanilla as their base, making exotic ice cream flavors that cannot be bought. Vanilla ice cream converts beautifully to a vast number of interesting flavors, as follows.

Ginger Ice Cream

½ cup drained preserved ginger in syrup, very finely chopped

2 tablespoons syrup from ginger jar
1 quart vanilla ice cream

Combine the chopped ginger with the ginger syrup. Soften the ice cream, and quickly stir the ginger mixture into it. Pack the mixture in plastic containers, cover, and freeze until firm.
Makes about 1 quart.

Macaroon Ice Cream

1 cup almond macaroon crumbs
2 tablespoons orgeat or Falernum syrup, or ½ teaspoon almond extract

1 quart vanilla ice cream

Crush the macaroon crumbs finely, and toss with the orgeat or Falernum syrup or almond extract. Soften the ice cream and quickly stir the macaroon mixture into it. Pack the ice cream in plastic containers, cover, and freeze until it is firm.
Makes about 1 quart.

Mango Ice Cream

1 mango, peeled and cut into pieces
1 tablespoon plus 1 teaspoon lime juice

2 tablespoons honey
1 pint vanilla ice cream

Blend the mango pieces, lime juice, and honey briefly in an electric blender or food processor. Soften the ice cream and quickly stir the mango mixture into it. Pour the ice cream into a plastic container, cover, and freeze it until firm.

Makes 1 scant quart.

Cantaloupe Ice Cream

1 or 2 cantaloupes
1 tablespoon honey
1 tablespoon orange liqueur
1 quart vanilla ice cream

Melon balls (optional)
Mint sprigs or crystallized mint
leaves (optional)

Pare, seed, and cut up the cantaloupe. Put it through an electric blender or food processor, pureeing enough to measure 2 cups. Combine with the honey and orange liqueur. Soften the ice cream, and quickly stir the melon mixture into it. Pack the ice cream in plastic containers, cover, and freeze it until firm. At serving time, spoon the ice cream into dessert glasses and, if desired, decorate the portions with melon balls and mint sprigs or crystallized mint leaves.

Makes about 1½ quarts.

English Toffee Ice Cream with Praline Sauce

3 one-and-one-eighth-ounce
chocolate-coated English toffee
bars (such as Heath's)
1 quart vanilla ice cream

1 ounce sweet chocolate (such as
Eagle sweet chocolate)
½ cup heavy cream

Crush 2 of the candy bars with a rolling pin, or break them up and put them through a food processor. Soften the ice cream and quickly stir the crushed toffee into it. Pack the ice cream in plastic containers, cover, and freeze until firm.

Break up the remaining candy bar and place it in a small saucepan with the sweet chocolate and heavy cream. Heat the mixture over a low flame, stirring constantly, until the chocolate has completely melted. Serve it hot or at room temperature, spooned over servings of the ice cream.

Makes about 1 quart ice cream and enough sauce for 6 servings.

Apricot Ice Cream

12 or more canned, peeled, pitted
 apricots
2 teaspoons lemon juice or
 apricot brandy

1 quart vanilla ice cream
Chopped pistachios or whipped
 cream and glazed apricot
 pieces (optional)

Puree enough apricots in an electric blender or food processor to measure 1 cup. Add the lemon juice or apricot brandy. Soften the ice cream and quickly stir the apricot mixture into it. Pack the ice cream in plastic containers, cover, and freeze until firm. To serve, spoon the ice cream into dessert glasses and, if desired, decorate with chopped pistachios or whipped cream and glazed apricot pieces.

Makes 1 generous quart.

Cranberry Ice Cream

2 cups cranberries
1¼ cups sugar

1 pint vanilla ice cream
Whipped cream (optional)

Preheat the oven at 350°. Spread the cranberries in a buttered shallow baking dish and sprinkle them with the sugar. Cover with aluminum foil and bake for 1 hour. Cool. Soften the ice cream and quickly mix in the cooled cranberries, reserving 4 for garnishing if desired. Spoon the ice cream into a plastic container or individual serving glasses. Cover, and freeze until firm. If desired, decorate with dollops of whipped cream and a reserved cranberry atop each serving.

Makes 4 servings.

Bali Parfait

1 banana
¾ cup drained unsweetened
 crushed pineapple
3 tablespoon unsweetened flaked
 coconut

2 tablespoons brown sugar
¼ teaspoon cinnamon
Pinch of mace
1 quart vanilla ice cream

Mash the banana and combine it with the crushed pineapple, coconut, brown sugar, cinnamon, and mace. Soften the ice cream and quickly stir the banana mixture into it. Pack the ice cream in plastic containers, cover, and freeze until firm.

Makes 1 generous quart.

Fig Ice Cream

10 canned green figs, drained   **1 quart vanilla ice cream**
2 teaspoons lemon juice   **Candied figs (optional)**

Puree the figs in an electric blender or food processor. Add the lemon juice. Soften the ice cream and quickly stir the fig mixture into it. Turn the mixture into a rectangular pan or freezer tray and freeze until slightly firmed. Stir it up from the bottom. Turn the ice cream into plastic containers, cover, and freeze until firm. To serve, decorate with candied figs if desired.

Makes about 1 quart.

Persimmon Ice Cream

6 very ripe persimmons   **1 quart vanilla ice cream**
1 teaspoon lemon juice

Peel the persimmons and chop them coarsely, removing any surrounding hard substance and seeds. Combine with the lemon juice. Soften the ice cream and quickly stir the persimmon mixture into it. Pack the ice cream in plastic containers, cover, and freeze until firm.

Makes 1 generous quart.

Praline Ice Cream

½ cup slivered blanched almonds   **1 quart vanilla ice cream**
½ cup sugar   **Toasted slivered blanched**
3 tablespoons water   **almonds (optional)**
⅛ teaspoon cream of tartar

Spread out ½ cup slivered blanched almonds on a baking sheet and toast them in a moderate oven for 5 to 7 minutes until they are lightly browned. Watch carefully to see that the nuts do not scorch, and turn them once during toasting.

Combine the sugar, water, and cream of tartar in a small saucepan, and heat, stirring constantly, until the mixture comes to a boil and the sugar has completely dissolved. Stir in the toasted nuts, and cook over medium heat without stirring until the mixture is golden-brown in color. Pour the mixture out onto a piece of buttered aluminum foil and allow it to cool. When it has cooled, break up the praline and crush with a rolling pin or with a mortar and pestle, or put it through an electric blender or food processor until the mixture has been reduced to a powder.

Soften the ice cream and quickly stir the praline mixture into it. Pack the ice cream in plastic containers, cover, and freeze until firm. To serve, spoon into serving glasses and, if desired, decorate the portions with toasted slivered blanched almonds.

Makes about 1 quart.

SHELLS TO FILL WITH FROZEN DESSERTS

An attractive way to serve ice cream, sherbet, water ice, mousse, or any other frozen dessert is to scoop it into balls and set them into some sort of edible dessert shell. This turns them into a more festive and special dessert. Some ideas for types of shells and suggestions for filling follow, but feel free to fill shells, whether homemade or bought, with whatever filling appeals to you. For flavorings of fillings and for decorating ideas, follow the suggestions outlined in THE VERSATILE BOMBE.

Cookie Cups

½ **cup flour**	**Pinch of salt**
½ **cup sugar**	**1 egg plus 1 egg white**

Preheat the oven at 350°. Sift together the flour, sugar, and salt. Add the egg and egg white and mix until thoroughly combined. With a toothpick, mark 6 circles on buttered baking sheets by tracing around a small plate or saucer about 5 inches in diameter. Do not place more than 3 circles on each sheet. Place one-sixth of the batter in the center of each circle, and spread out the batter with a rubber spatula to fill in the circles. Bake, 1 sheet at a time, until the circles begin to brown lightly around the edges, about 6 or 7 minutes. Remove the circles from the baking sheets with a spatula and invert each one over the back of a buttered custard cup. Working quickly but gently, form them into fluted shells with your hands by molding them down the sides of the custard cups. Don't try to bake more than 3 at a time or the circles will harden before you have time to mold them. Continue baking the remainder of the shells, and when all have cooled, set them open side up on individual serving plates or group them on one large serving plate.

Pineapple Cookie Cups

Combine 1½ cups well-drained crushed pineapple with 2 tablespoons sweetened canned coconut cream and ½ teaspoon almond extract or 2 teaspoons Falernum syrup. Place a scoop of vanilla ice cream in each Cookie Cup and spoon the pineapple mixture over the top. Decorate with whipped cream and a sprinkling of finely shredded toasted almonds.

Giant Cookie Cup

Prepare the batter as above, and bake one very large circle. Invert it over a large buttered casserole or mixing bowl. Set it on a serving dish and fill with ice cream scoops. Top with a fruit sauce, chocolate sauce, or other sauce, and decorate as desired.

Chocolate Cups

Make CHOCOLATE CUPS or use bought chocolate cups. Fill them with balls of ENGLISH TOFFEE ICE CREAM WITH PRALINE SAUCE, RASPBERRY CREAM SHERBET, or any frozen dessert.

Meringue Shells

Make MERINGUE SHELLS or use bought meringue shells. Set a ball of ice cream in each. APRICOT ICE CREAM or ROSE PETAL WATER ICE would be nice flavors to use.

Nutted Meringue Shells

Make NUTTED MERINGUE SHELLS. Set a ball of chocolate ice cream, FROZEN ORANGE LIQUEUR MOUSSE, or other flavor frozen dessert in each shell.

Orange Shells

Cut a thick slice from the stem end of each orange. If necessary, trim a small amount from the bottom of any orange that tends to tip, so that all sit squarely on a serving plate. Carefully cut out the orange segments and remove the membrane, keeping the rind intact. Scrape out the orange cases to remove all the membrane. Notch the edges with scissors. Fill the cases with ORANGE POMEGRANATE SHERBET, LEMON HONEY WATER ICE, or bought orange, lemon, or lime sherbet or water

---

ice. Trim with a twist of orange peel, or with some of the segments taken from the oranges.

VARIATION:

Tangerines may be similarly used to make tangerine shells.

Sweet Pastry Tart Shells

Make individual shells of SWEET TART PASTRY. Fill with any desired flavor of frozen dessert.

CHAPTER 10

Drink-Desserts

Eat a bit before you drink.
—old English proverb

Whether you call them liquid desserts or thick drinks, these desserts are festive to look at and relaxing to eat or sip. Since they have few, if any, solid ingredients, they're good to serve after hearty dinners.

Drink-desserts simplify the serving of dessert and after-dinner liqueurs by combining the two in a single glass. In two of the recipes in this chapter, hot coffee is included with the other ingredients, eliminating the separate serving of coffee to ease entertaining even more.

LA SAULAIE BRAZILIAN COFFEE

Learning to make La Saulaie Brazilian Coffee is an absolute guarantee of dazzling dinner guests with an end-of-dinner coffee, fantastic dessert, and after-dinner liqueur all combined with flair and artistry in one luxurious glassful. This is a specialty that delights diners at La Saulaie Restaurant in Boucherville, just outside of Montreal in Quebec, Canada.

Lemon wedge	Hot coffee
Sugar	Whipped cream
1 ounce Grand Marnier	1 ounce Cognac
½ ounce Tia Maria	

Wet the rim of a 10-ounce stemmed goblet with the lemon wedge. Dip the rim into the sugar to frost it. Heat the glass over alcohol heat and pour in the Grand Marnier. Flame the Tia Maria and add it to the Grand Marnier. Fill the glass with hot coffee and place a dollop of whipped cream on top. Flame the Cognac in a ladle and pour it over the whipped cream. Serve immediately.

Makes 1 serving.

IRISH COFFEE

¾ cup hot coffee
2 teaspoons brown sugar

1½ ounces Irish whiskey
Whipped cream

Pour the hot coffee into a tall, stemmed glass. Add the brown sugar and Irish whiskey, and stir until sugar has dissolved. Top with a spoonful of whipped cream.

Makes 1 serving.

MINTED ORANGE SNOW

1 small can frozen concentrated
  orange juice, slightly thawed
¼ cup confectioners' sugar

2 strips zest of lemon peel
3 cups crushed ice
¼ cup green crème de menthe

Blend the orange juice, confectioners' sugar, and zest of lemon peel in an electric blender or food processor for a few seconds (10 seconds in the blender, less in the food processor). Add the crushed ice and blend until it is smooth and has the texture of snow, stopping if necessary to push the ice down from the sides of the container. Spoon into sherbet glasses and pour a tablespoonful of crème de menthe over each serving. Arrange a tiny straw in each glass and supply a spoon to each diner.

Makes 4 servings.

MELON CREAM

1 cantaloupe
½ cup heavy cream
2 tablespoons orange liqueur

1 teaspoon lemon or lime juice
1 tablespoon sugar
1 pint vanilla ice cream

Peel the cantaloupe, remove the seeds, and cut it up coarsely. Blend the cantaloupe pieces in an electric blender or food processor with the heavy cream, orange liqueur, lemon or lime juice, and sugar until the mixture is smooth. Spoon in the ice cream and blend for 1 or 2 seconds or longer. Pour into tall, stemmed glasses and serve immediately.

Makes 4 to 6 servings.

SYLLABUB

Syllabub has resisted being categorized since it was first created in England during Elizabethan times. Its name literally means "bubbling wine drink," coming from the words Sillery, *the area where the wine for it was originally produced, and* bub, *slang in those days for a bubbling drink. Since then, it has alternately been called a "rich dessert" and a "frothy punch" by those willing to define it, and "an English country concoction" or simply a "famous English recipe" by those preferring to skirt the issue. Hannah Glasse, who wrote* The Art of Cookery, *something of a bible to eighteenth-century English cooks, seems to have come closest to defining syllabub by calling it a "whipt" drink. Light and fluffy, it differs from other milk- or cream-based drinks in that it is always made with wine rather than liquor, such as one finds, for example, in a Tom and Jerry or an eggnog. Syllabub, being rather too thick to drink, is best served in a chilled glass and eaten with a spoon.*

2 cups heavy cream
¾ cup medium-dry-to-sweet
　Sherry, Port, or Madeira
¼ cup sugar

1 teaspoon orange flower water
　or ¼ teaspoon orange extract
8 strips zest of lemon peel

Beat the heavy cream until very stiff. Combine the Sherry, Port, or Madeira with the sugar and orange flower water or orange extract, and stir to dissolve the sugar as much as possible. Fold the mixture into the whipped cream with a rubber spatula, a spoonful at a time, turning the bowl with one hand as you fold with the other hand. Cover and chill thoroughly. At serving time, fold the mixture one more time, and spoon it into dessert glasses. Twist a strip of zest of lemon peel over each glass and decorate the top of the dessert with it.

Makes 8 servings.

DOUBLE MOCHA

1 tablespoon chocolate syrup
Double-strength hot coffee
1 scoop coffee ice cream

1 tablespoon coffee liqueur
1 tablespoon crème de cacao

Pour the chocolate syrup into a mug or a tall, footed cup, and fill the container three-quarters full with hot coffee. Top with a scoop of coffee ice cream, and stir lightly. Pour the liqueurs over the top and serve immediately.

Makes 1 serving.

CHAPTER 11

Cheese Desserts

I will make an end of my dinner;
There's pippins and cheese to come.

—*William Shakespeare,* The Merry
Wives of Windsor

PART I: CHEESES FOR DESSERT

Choose Brie, the queen of cheeses, Roquefort or Stilton, which vie
for the title of king, or any one of a vast array of delectable dessert
cheeses you can buy today, but do choose cheese for the most regal
yet easiest-of-all-to-serve desserts. Everyday serving of cheese as the
last course is a time-honored tradition in Europe, particularly in France,
where some of the best dessert cheeses are made, and it seems a habit
worth copying.

Though often eaten with fruit and sometimes followed by a sweet
dessert course, cheese is probably most delectable and voluptuous when
served alone and followed by no other food. An old English saying,
"After cheese comes nothing," sums it up neatly.

There are, of course, times when cheese isn't at all appropriate for
dessert, but these exceptions are few. It would not be good, for example,
to serve it after a meal in which it has already played a principal role,
such as a cheese fondue, quiche Lorraine, or dish containing a cheese
sauce or rich cream sauce. It would seem odd, too, to serve it following
a dinner where cheese is alien to the nature of the national cuisine served,
such as Indian, Indonesian, or Chinese food. Because cheese is a genu-
inely solid food, it's best served as a dessert after a reasonably light lunch
or dinner, and the best choices generally are the soft-textured, gentle
cheeses.

The texture of cheese is one of the best guides in choosing the right dessert cheese. Hard cheeses should be avoided almost without exception, because their nature is more suited to satisfying hunger than to ending a meal. All excellent in their place, but not as the last course, are the Swiss cheeses Emmenthal (Swiss cheese), Gruyère, and Appenzell, and their American counterparts, hard Italian cheeses such as provolone, Cheddars of all kinds, or any of the grating-type cheeses. Bypass also the Dutch table cheeses: Edam, Gouda (whether young or aged), and seeded Leyden. Some of these bland cheeses can very well be served with fruit, as discussed further on in this chapter, but are not interesting in themselves at the meal's end. Other cheeses that are unsuitable as dessert cheeses are those containing herbs, seeds, pepper, garlic, or spices, those that are smoked or those preserved in brine, such as feta, those that are manufactured as process cheeses and are for the most part lacking in any real flavor or distinction, and strong cheeses such as Limburger, Liederkranz, French Muenster, Danish Tilsit, or Swiss Raclette, which are best served with drinks or as snacks.

A list of so many "no's" for dessert cheeses automatically turns almost every other cheese into a "yes." The remaining cheeses, for easy discussion and remembering, are divided into four categories: the soft-ripening cheeses, including the double crèmes and triple crèmes; the semisoft cheeses; the goat cheeses; and the blue cheeses.

The soft-ripening cheeses are without a doubt the most luxurious, luscious cheeses ever made. Heading off the list is Brie (pronounced *bree*), satiny in texture, pale in color, and unequaled in smooth, rich, gentle, yet earthy flavor. It is the most difficult cheese to buy, but one of the most rewarding to eat. The first thing to remember when you buy Brie is to buy only French Brie, for the imitations made in other countries are usually disastrous, as are the Bries that are packed in tin cans.

Brie is a large, disk-shaped cheese and one of the few soft-ripened cheeses sold in bulk. The best way to buy it is from a wheel which has been ripened, then cut and wrapped in clear plastic wrap so you can see its exact state of being. It should bulge a little, showing that it's ripe and ready to run, and it should have a velvety texture from top to bottom with no chalky center which would indicate that it had been cut before being properly ripened. It should have a pale-brown or white-streaked crust, and no hard-ridged or cracked edges, which would mean that it is overripe and drying out. If in doubt, ask your cheese dealer if he can open the wrapping enough for you to smell the cheese, and if he is reputable, he will have no reason to refuse.

Expect a smell like cheese, possibly even faintly ammoniated, but not overpoweringly so, for it will then be a strong and unpleasant cheese. Look for a crust that is thin, as the entire cheese should be eaten, crust and all. And look for texture that is even and runny or near-runny, so that when left at room temperature the cheese will be beautifully soft and spreading. For the best of all Bries, buy Brie de Meaux if your dealer carries it. Its flavor and texture are unequalled by any other Brie.

If you can't locate good Brie sold in bulk, your next best bet is to buy a Baby Brie or Petit Brie, which comes in a pancake-shaped chipboard box about five inches in diameter. This cheese will not have quite the character of its larger sister, but it can still be very nice. Open the box before you buy, select one that gives slightly in the center to your touch, and leave it at room temperature the maximum time, as discussed at the end of this section. Whenever you buy cheese, ask your cheese dealer for his advice on the length of time to leave it out. He knows the age and state of each cheese and can be your best guide. Further on in this section is a detailed discussion on how to store, handle, and serve all the dessert cheeses. In general, avoid buying cheese that has shrunken away from the sides of the box or where the wrapping is stuck to the cheese in dark spots or gummy collections.

Also in the Brie family is Coulommiers (*koo-loh-m'YAY*), which comes in a round box a little larger than a Baby Brie's, has a slightly thicker crust than Brie, and a flavor leaning toward that of Camembert. Buy and serve it with the same care you would give to Brie.

Even richer than Brie, though slightly milder in flavor, is Brie Nouveau, which is sold in bulk. One of its attractive qualities is that it is not subject to as many ripening problems as Brie, and it remains at a just-ripe point much longer.

If you're planning to serve a large group of people and want to buy a whole Brie, the wheel will weigh two pounds or more and will serve a dozen or more people for dessert. Here you will not have the benefit of buying a Brie whose interior you can see, and you will have to depend on your dealer to select a cheese that will be ripe when you want to use it. Order it ahead of time so it can be ripened for you. While a popular belief is that one good Brie in ten is a fair average, the reverse is actually true of a cheese dealer who gives his attention to his stock. He can ripen an excellent Brie nine times out of ten, making some allowance for the capriciousness of the cheese. Learn to buy and serve Brie, providing, of course, it appeals to you, and all the other cheeses will be easy to understand and handle.

Another undisputed leader among soft-ripened cheeses is Camembert (*KAH-mehm-bair*), and again it should be French if you are to avoid disappointment. It comes in the same kind of chipboard box as Brie, but its size is never over eight ounces. Anything larger isn't Camembert. Buy the whole round Camembert in preference to the half-moon-shape Camembert or the Camembert packaged in wedges, because these cheeses, having been cut before packaging, will probably never ripen properly. Camembert should have a texture similar to Brie—that is, suave and nearly runny. It should be a creamy yellow color, its edible crust white to golden and turning slightly red all over when ripe, and no strong odor should come from the box when you open it. Its flavor is smooth, sweeter and subtler than Brie's, and pleasingly different.

Cheeses that resemble the classic Camembert in flavor and that should be bought and cared for similarly are the square-shaped Four Seasons and Carré de l'Est (*kah-REH deh-LEST*), the latter having a faintly sharp aftertaste.

One of the few relatively recent cheeses that belong to the soft-ripening family is not French but Danish. Called Crema Danica (*KREH-mah DAH-nee-kah*), or Crema Dania, and available in a surprising number of stores, this cheese is more reliable than Brie because it almost always ripens with no chalky center after being left at room temperature for several hours. It has a texture similar to Brie's and a delicate flavor. Look for it in a square box with two loaf-shaped pieces inside. Some stores will sell you half a box. Make sure that you open the cheese before buying, especially in supermarkets, where the stock may not be carefully watched. If there is an offensive odor, if the rind is not all white, or if the cheese you can see is not a pale-yellow color, choose another cheese.

There are several other excellent soft-ripening cheeses to keep your eye open for, all creamy and white-crusted. (Incidentally, the cheeses discussed up to this point have crusts which should be eaten right along with the rest of the cheese.) One of the nicest of these cheeses is Fol Amour (*fohl-ah-MOOR*), an oval-shaped cheese that comes in a chipboard box. Bûche Lorraine (*boosh loh-REHN*) is, as its name implies, shaped like a log, and comes wrapped in white, red, or blue foil, the cheese in each package being identical regardless of wrapping color. Port Fleuri (*pohr floh-REE*), which comes in a small round box, is an extremely mild soft-ripening cheese. These cheeses, which are all French, are good choices for dessert and well worth trying. Don't hesitate to try any other soft-ripening cheese you come upon in your cheese hunting. It's the only way you'll find out if it's a cheese you want to include on your list of favorites in the future.

The ultimate in richness and sheer indulgence is the family of double crème and triple crème cheeses. Certainly not to be eaten every day but a treat of the highest order when you do have them, these cheeses are milder yet shamelessly richer than the Brie-type cheeses, and it's easy to become addicted to them. The category "double" means that the cheese has at least 60 percent butterfat, and "triple" means that it has at least 75 percent, accounting for the extreme richness and creaminess of the cheeses.

The double crèmes to look for are Caprice de Dieux (*kah-PREES deh d'YEW*), an edible-crusted, oval-shaped cheese that comes in a box; Monsieur Fromage (*mah-SYEW fram-MAHZH*), a small, round boxed cheese with an edible crust; Excelsior, also with an edible crust, a cheese nearly rich enough to be classified as a triple crème, packed in a small round box; and Crème Chantilly (*krehm shahn-tee-YEE*), a Swedish cheese—as opposed to the others in this category, which are all French—with a very delicate flavor and edible crust. It is packaged in a triangular-shaped box. Inclined to be perishable, this cheese should be bought with care.

Included among the double crèmes are some of the fresh cheeses that are flown to the United States from France. These are lovely, mild, delicate cheeses with a faintly sour taste compared with their nearest American counterpart, cream cheese. Petit Suisse (*peh-TEE swees*) comes in little cup-shaped plastic cylinders, each one holding an individual serving. When you remove the cheese from the cup, you find it wrapped in a little white paper jacket which needs to be taken off before serving. (See the end of this chapter for more about caring for this cheese.) Gervais (*zhehr-VAY*) is square and comes wrapped in foil similar to American cream cheese. Cream cheese lovers will like its gentle tang.

The triple crèmes are richer and even more enticing than the double crèmes, with Explorateur and Triple Crème Parfait probably two of the richest of all available cheeses. Explorateur, round and wrapped without a box is as creamy, smooth, and buttery as a cheese can be without actually being butter. Triple Crème Parfait has an orange-white edible crust and is packed in a round box. Other triple crèmes are: Brillat-Savarin (*bree-YAH sah-vah-RAN*), similar in character to Triple Crème Parfait; Boursault (*boor-SOH*), which comes wrapped in white paper and is exceedingly smooth and crustless; and Boursin Natural (*boor-SAN*), meltingly delicious, crustless, wrapped in foil in its round five-and-a-quarter-ounce shape and then packaged in a square cardboard box. (Avoid this cheese in its various smaller packagings unless you enjoy fusing with the unwrapping of a number of small-size cheeses.) All these cheeses should retain their shapes, smell cheesy yet clean, and have no discoloration.

The semisoft cheeses are easy to buy and tend as there is no ripening procedure to worry about or "running" to wait for. You need only bring them to room temperature to be pleased with them nearly every time. Any of the cheeses in this group, though fairly soft, are firm enough to be sliced, and are therefore neater to serve than soft cheeses. There's a large selection of this type of cheese well suited for dessert. Not all of them are French, and some of the most delightful are, in fact, Italian.

If you think of Italian cheeses as things to grate up and sprinkle over pasta, then be happily surprised to take your first taste of Taleggio (*tah-LEH-joe*). It's a square-shaped cheese sold in bulk, which means you can buy any amount you like, and taste, too, if you like. Off-white in color and bearing a wax rind, Taleggio has a pleasingly mellow flavor with an enticingly smooth texture and a glowing aftertaste.

Another lovely Italian cheese is Fontina (*fahn-TEE-nah*), not to be confused with any name of a similar spelling or with Swedish fontina, an altogether different and undistinguished cheese. Italian fontina, like all semisoft cheeses, has a rind that must be removed before eating. Inside this grayish-red-brown rind is a cheese with a texture nearly glossy and a flavor subtly nutlike and rich. Its ivory color is sprinkled with tiny eyes or holes. This cheese, cut from a thick, good-sized wheel, is also sold in bulk.

Cream-colored Bel Paese (*bell pah-AZE*) is a mild but distinctive cheese available almost everywhere. It can be bought in bulk or in small rounds that come with a map of Italy on the wrapper. The American version, which comes with a map of North and South America on the top, is good, but it lacks the full flowering of the original version. These cheeses both have inedible yellow-wax coatings.

A good Canadian semisoft dessert cheese is Oka. Pale yellow, smooth, and similar in flavor to Port Salut, which we discuss next, it has a thin golden rind. Buy it in a sixteen-ounce package or cut from a large wheel.

The classic of semisoft cheeses is France's Port Salut (*pohr sah-LOO*). You may find it under varying spellings and with or without hyphens, as Port Salut, Port du Salut, Port-Salut, or Port-du-Salut. Spell it as you will, Port Salut is a yellow, smooth, soft-textured cheese with an altogether pleasing flavor, mild yet with a distinctive, somewhat earthy edge. It can be had in bulk or in small plastic-wrapped rounds which are easily distinguishable by their dark-orange rinds showing through. A small cheese very much like Port Salut is French Gold, and quite an agreeable cheese it is. Saint Paulin (*sehn poh-LEHN*), another Port Salut although it cannot use that name, is equally good. Any of these are good standbys and probably the best semisoft cheeses to serve if you aren't sure of everyone's taste.

For a distinctive cheese quite different from other semisofts, choose Pont l'Évêque (*pohn leh-VECK*), another classic French cheese. Square-shaped, it is a pale yellow in color, with tiny eyes and a brownish-white crust. Its flavor is edged by an inviting pungency. It is plump, and while it does not actually run, it has a texture not unlike that of a soft-ripened cheese. Buy one that has not shrunken away from the sides of its chipboard box.

Other good small cheeses in the semisoft category are Mon Bouquet, a mild, round, creamy cheese with a red-wax coating that comes in a brightly decorated gold wrapping, and Reblochon (*reh-bloh-SHOHN*), one of France's best mountain cheeses. The latter is a round, paper-wrapped, ivory-colored cheese with a light-brown crust. Its flavor is nutlike and rich, its name having derived from the provincial dialect word *reblocher*, meaning "milking for a second time," when the milk is extremely rich.

Two bulk cheeses in this category are Beaumont (*bow-MOHN*) and Tomme de Savoie (*tohm deh sah-VWAH*), both French mountain cheeses. They are both pale, creamy yellow, have small eyes or holes, light-reddish-brown rinds, mellow flavors, and are cut in wedges from round wheels an inch or two thick.

If you can find a heart-shaped Coeur Rollot (*coor roh-LOH*), it's a great idea for a Valentine dessert or to end any romantic dinner. It is stronger in flavor than most other semisoft cheeses, its color is deep yellow, and the entire cheese is edible.

There are several "flavored" cheeses that are nice to include among the semisoft dessert cheeses. First is Gourmandise (*goor-mahn-DEEZ*), a smooth white cheese flavored with cherry or kirsch, almond or orange, and perfect for dessert. Nec Plus Ultra, which you can buy with walnut flavoring and which is exactly like Gourmandise in texture, is one of the nut-flavored or nut-studded cheeses available. Others are Rambol, which has a processed Emmenthal base and is covered with walnut halves, and Ground Reybino encased in whole almonds, pistachios, or hazelnuts, which also run through its center. La Grappe (*lah GRAHP*), also called Fondue du Risin, or simply grape cheese is similar in texture to Gourmandise, is made with Emmenthal or Gruyère cheese as a base, and is covered all around with grape seeds and pulp that remain after the grapes are pressed for wine. The crust can be eaten or not as you like, and the cheese can be bought in small rounds or cut in bulk from large rounds. A tiny bit of mold that may appear among the seeds is considered normal.

Goat cheese, or chèvre (*SHEV-reh*), is, regrettably, ignored or by-passed too often simply because it is not well understood in the United States. Try some of the goat cheeses suggested here for a lovely surprise in flavor, for they have a special tang unlike that found in any cow's-milk cheese. Many goat cheeses are deliciously mild, and once you have tried them it's easy to develop a yearning for them. If you've never had goat cheese, start off with an extremely mild one such as Chèvre Saint Mauré (*SHEV-reh sahn-maw-RAY*), entirely edible, which comes in a little loaf-shaped package for nice slicing. Saint Marcellin (*sahn mahr-seh-LEHN*), a small, round, creamy cheese with a soft consistency, is a good choice, as is Ile de France Chèvre, which comes packed in a miniature cardboard suitcase and is white throughout with an edible crust. The interior becomes beautifully creamy when left at room temperature for about eight hours.

Another goat cheese to try is Valencay (*vah-lehn-SAY*), which is shaped like a miniature pyramid and also becomes creamy inside when left out. Its crust is grayish-green and forbidding, but when you cut it open, you'll be pleasantly surprised. Don't try eating the crust, however, unless this sort of thing really appeals to you. For a variation on plain goat cheese, a good idea is log-shaped, cellophane-wrapped Montrachet (*mohn-trah-SHAY*), mild, very moist, and covered with an interesting charcoal blanket that you can eat or not as you see fit. Strands of straw run through its center, so don't be surprised when you cut into them. Banon (*bah-NOHN*) makes an attractive dessert, since it comes in a little patty shape and has been cured in brandy and wrapped in grape leaves—it's edible except for the leaves.

Blue cheeses have a piquancy found in no other cheeses, and deserve a top place among the best dessert cheeses. Roquefort (*ROHK-fohr*) is unique among cheeses in general, and blue cheeses in particular, for several reasons. It is one of the few sheep's-milk cheeses sold outside its native land, and it is cured in the famous limestone caves around the town of Roquefort in France, which give it a flavor impossible to duplicate anywhere else in the world. It has beautifully marked blue-green veining in its white body, a smooth texture, and a pleasant, tingly taste. Taste before you buy to avoid a Roquefort that may be too salty for you.

Stilton, which is made in England, is another hard-to-match blue cheese. It is made with richer milk than Roquefort, and its consistency is therefore creamier. Its flavor is mellow and faintly suggestive of good aged Cheddar. The rind is, properly, thick and ominously wrinkled, and is not edible. The cheese itself, a pale ivory with blue-green veining, becomes darker close to the rind and is quite crumbly when cut. Like Roquefort, Stilton is sold only in bulk, and it's best to buy at least half a pound or you may arrive home with a package of crumbs—delicious but hard to serve. If you plan on serving Port wine with Stilton, please read Chapter 25, on "Dessert Wines," first.

Gorgonzola is a superb Italian cheese with green veining, a soft, sometimes slightly grainy texture, and an agreeably pungent flavor. Like the blues mentioned above, Gorgonzola is cut in wedges from a large, round form of cheese. Less expensive than all these blues is Norwegian Blue, which has a not-so-creamy texture similar to that of Roquefort, and the distinctly veined Danish Blue, which is creamier but not so interesting in flavor as the Norwegian.

A differently shaped blue cheese is Pipo Crèm' from France. It comes in a large cylinder shape and is cut off and sold in slices of whatever width you want. This cheese is moist and among the more delicate of the blue cheeses. Bleu de Bresse is one of the few blue cheeses available in both individual packages and in bulk. Either way you buy it, it should be soft and creamy and have pronounced blue marbling and a rich flavor.

If you plan on serving more than one cheese for dessert, choose them from different categories—a soft-ripening cheese with a goat cheese, for instance, or a double crème with a semisoft and a blue. The following are a few suggested combinations:

Camembert	Coulommiers
Banon	Reblochon
	Gourmandise
Boursin (plain) or Boursault	
Roquefort	Excelsior
	Gorgonzola
Crema Danica	Fontina
Bel Paese	
	La Grappe
Brie	Ile de France Chèvre
Port Salut	Pont l'Évêque
Bleu de Bresse	Norwegian blue
Explorateur	
Taleggio	Brie Nouveau
Stilton	Gervais
	Saint Paulin
Monsieur Fromage	Chèvre Saint Mauré
Montrachet	Pipo Crèm'
Oka	

Accompany dessert cheeses with plain crackers, either unsalted or with just the tiniest suggestion of salt in their makeup. To complement the cheeses as much as possible, toast the crackers or heat them a little in the oven. This will do for your cheese course what heated plates have done for the main course of your dinner.

Serve the cheese itself on the most natural serving plate you can find, having allowed it to come to room temperature on that piece. A wooden board is perfect—or a marble slab—and serve the crackers in an attractive basket to carry out the natural feeling of the coarse. Provide each person with a small plate and spreader, and remember to put a cheese knife on the serving board for each kind of cheese served so the

---

flavors remain separate. Wine might be the only other thing you'll need on the table, as discussed in Chapter 25.

When you shop for cheese, try to estimate how much you will need to serve, particularly with the soft-ripening cheeses so you won't have much in the way of leftover cheese. While it will still be good and edible the following day, no cheese benefits greatly from being taken in and out of the refrigerator and repeatedly being brought to room temperature. If you're serving only one kind of cheese, a safe estimate for each serving would be about three ounces or about three-quarters of a pound for four people. If you're serving two or three kinds of cheese, then about half a pound of each kind would be about right for four or even six people.

Leftover cheese, whether soft or semisoft, can be used in making sauces, hot hors d'oeuvres, or open-face broiled sandwiches if you don't want to serve it as a cheese course again. Don't be disturbed by a little mold that may develop on cheeses you store, particularly semisoft or hard cheeses. It can easily be scraped off and is pretty much of a harmless thing. Mold is, after all the friend of cheese.

To select the best cheese store in your area, buy from as many as you can until you determine which one carries the superior cheeses and cares for them best. If possible buy from a place where enough cheese is sold to ensure a fresh supply at all times. The size of the store is not necessarily an indication of the quantity or quality of the cheeses sold. Some supermarkets, for example, stock and sell a number of good soft-ripened cheeses, while others allow them to become overhandled, over-ripe, and discouraging to buy. Good cheese sellers examine and care for their stock daily and remove any from sale that are questionable.

The first way to judge cheeses is by their appearance. Cheeses sold in bulk are cut from large loaves or wheels, leaving one or more exposed sides for you to look at. The conscientious cheese seller covers the exposed part of every cut cheese with heavy plastic wrap in order to keep the air from reaching it and drying it out, and to keep other flavors from penetrating it. If you buy at a delicatessen, make certain no salami, pickles, or other strong-flavored foods are kept exposed nearby to transfer their tastes to the cheese. Cheeses in small boxes should be stacked neatly, no boxes should be lying open, and no overripe or shrunken cheeses should be offered for sale. Small cheeses sold without boxes should be well sealed and in good shape, not mashed or crushed in any way.

Although you will probably not be able to ask for samples if you buy from a supermarket or from certain cheese stores that sell all their bulk cheeses in precut wedges, other cheese sellers will be more than happy to let you taste any semisoft or hard bulk cheese, and will willingly answer questions and help you in your selection and understanding of

Cheese Desserts

cheese. Soft-ripening cheeses cannot be cut for sampling, and so should be bought with the greatest care. When sampling cheese in a store, remember that the cheese has in most cases just been taken from the refrigerator and is being eaten cold. Any cheese eaten cold will not have its full flavor, aroma, or proper texture, and you must make allowance for that. Taste for the general idea of the cheese.

Don't ever feel embarrassed to ask about a cheese you aren't familiar with, can't pronounce properly, or are just curious about. Cheese sellers interested in their products are delighted to share their knowledge with you when you show a genuine interest in the subject. Get to know your cheese man or woman.

When you've made your selections and arrived home with them, wrap each one closely and separately in clear plastic wrap (not in foil or sandwich bags), forcing out all air. Refrigerate them immediately unless you intend to serve them in a few hours, since there are few, if any, places cool enough for storing cheese anywhere else in the home. This may not be true in European homes without central heating, but it is true in most homes and apartments in the United States. While cheese likes to stay cool and is happy in the refrigerator, never under any circumstances freeze it. Freezing may or may not destroy the flavor, but it will undoubtedly change the texture and is a risky business at best. The sole exception to this rule is Petit Suisse, a fresh cheese which has to be frozen before being shipped by air from France. It should be kept frozen in cheese stores, so look for it in the freezer rather than the refrigerator, or it will probably not be good. Having been frozen, Petit Suisse will not be perfect, as it would be if bought in France, but it is still worth the sacrifice in texture, for the flavor is one of the most delicate and delicious among dessert cheeses. Remove it from the freezer to thaw in the refrigerator eight hours or overnight, and leave it at room temperature not more than half an hour before serving.

All cheeses need to be taken from the refrigerator and allowed to stand at room temperature before serving. The length of time will vary with the type of cheese and the weather. Petit Suisse, Gervais, or any fresh cheese need be removed only half an hour before serving. Very soft, cheeses such as Boursin and Boursault need only one hour. Brie, Camembert, other soft-ripening cheeses, and all semisoft cheeses, goat cheeses, and blue cheeses need from two to three and occasionally four hours at room temperature to develop their flavors and textures properly. Judge the weather and room temperature and shorten the time in the summer or in a very warm room, and lengthen it in cold rooms or during the winter months. In the case of all soft-ripened cheeses, ask your dealer how long they should be left out, since each cheese has its moment of perfection in ripening and can probably be judged best by the person who sells it.

It's important to remove the paper or any other wrappings from a cheese before bringing it to room temperature in order to release any odors that may have built up under tight wrappings during storage in the refrigerator. Cheeses need to breathe to be at their best and do not want to be enclosed in any way when getting ready to be served. If you're serving two or more kinds of cheeses at the same time, arrange them on the serving board so that each one has enough space around it to prevent a mingling of flavors when they are cut. These few precautions will ensure your cheeses being faultless at dessert time.

PART II: CHEESES AND FRUIT FOR DESSERT

Simple, yet sophisticated as a dessert can be, fruit and cheese have long been a favorite meal ending, and the idea gains in popularity as more and more interesting cheeses, both domestic and imported, become readily available. Even more appealing than serving the classic fresh fruit bowl and tray of assorted cheeses is selecting just one fruit and serving it with the cheese that seems made for it alone, or, in reverse, choosing one cheese and finding the fruit that complements it best.

Experimenting with possible fruit-and-cheese combinations is as exciting and rewarding as the sampling you'd do at a wine-and-cheese tasting. However, it's also time-consuming. For this reason the following are suggestions for several dozen excellent fruit-and-cheese combinations you can serve at any time with certainty. If you like, you can make further discoveries by experimenting with your own choices when time and mood allow.

Before buying any cheese, please read the first section of this chapter, which tells how to buy, store, and handle cheeses.

With all cheese-and-fruit desserts, the keynote should be informality. Furnish everyone with a butter spreader or cheese knife along with a little dessert plate, and serve the cheese on its own wooden or marble board with a cheese knife. The fruit can be in a bowl or on a serving plate, depending on its nature. Everyone should feel free to eat both cheese and fruit with the fingers. Serve some simple unsalted crackers for anyone who may want them.

Good apples, which can be bought through most of the year, go well with cheese, and are probably the most familiar fruit in the cheese-fruit duos. A not-so-familiar but superb combination is sliced, crunchy red apples, such as Delicious, accompanied by wedges of satiny French Brie. The smoothness of the Brie is delightful with the crispness of the apple. Let everybody spread the cheese on the apple slices as they would on crackers.

For heartier tastes, serve whole, shiny apples and some good aged Gouda. Aged Gouda is altogether different from the buttery young Gouda that most of us know. It's full of character and a perfect mate to apples.

Apple pies, apple tarts, and similar apple desserts are good with slabs of Vermont, New York State, or Canadian Cheddar. These Cheddars range from mild to sharp in the order listed. In the same family, and equally good with this type of dessert, are domestic Colby, Brick, and Coon, and English Cheshire, Wensleydale, and Double Gloucester, all of which appeal very much to lovers of Cheddar. Another apple-pie idea is to mix generous gratings of Sapsago, a clover-flavored grating cheese from Switzerland, with a little butter, sprinkle it over the pie, and run it under the broiler a few minutes before serving. If you have a very tart apple pie, blue-veined Stilton would be a good choice.

Consider serving a bit of Calvados or applejack with any of the apple-cheese desserts.

Oranges and tangerines go well with Roquefort and make a tingling flavor combination. Another approach to citrus fruits would be to contrast their acidity with the creamy mildness of Monterey Jack. This California cheese, which has been made for some seventy-five years, is generally moist and much softer than the Cheddar-type cheeses. Wisconsin Muenster would also go well with fruits of the orange family.

Bananas are a natural with Gorgonzola. If you close your eyes and sniff this delicate green-veined cheese, you realize how similar the aroma is to that of ripe bananas. When you serve this combination, cut the bananas into wedges just before they're brought to the table to keep them from darkening.

Figs, either fresh or canned, blend beautifully in flavor with cream cheeses. Buy either American cream cheese or one of the fresh French cream cheeses, which are not so sweet as the American and have a faintly sour taste that's pleasant with fruits. Two kinds of French cream cheese are Gervais and the softer, fluffier Petit Suisse. Either stuff the figs with one of these cheeses or just serve them together on the same plate and eat them with a spoon

If you come upon a good, ripe pineapple, slice it into bite-sized pieces (see p. 16 "TO CUT UP A PINEAPPLE,") and serve it with a delicate Camembert. Fol Amour, a cheese similar to Camembert, would also be nice, as would be any of the cream cheeses mentioned in the paragraph above. Supply cocktail picks or forks for the pineapple along with the spreaders for the cheese.

Honeydew melon is good with Italian fontina, and cantaloupe's pronounced flavor is best offset by one of the cream cheeses. Red grapes team up pleasingly with Italian provolone, and the assertive taste of a Pont l'Évêque seems best with white grapes, especially the tart varieties.

When persimmons are in season, have some good ripe ones to eat "as is" with either Swiss Emmenthal, generally just called Switzerland Swiss, or its headier relative, Swiss Gruyère. (Incidentally, don't confuse the latter with process Gruyère, which is not at all distinctive and not the same cheese.)

Strawberries are perfect with one of the fresh French double or triple crème cheeses. The "double" and "triple" designations refer to the amount of butterfat in the cheese, and consequently their richness. These are Petit Suisse, which we've already discussed, Boursin (natural), Boursault, Belletoile, and Explorateur. Petit Suisse comes in small, cylindrical individual portions just the right size for putting on each dessert plate and surrounding with strawberries. The remaining cheeses are served whole for each person to help himself.

If you become addicted to this incredibly luscious group of cheeses, which is quite easy to do, and find that strawberries to serve with them are out of season, it's almost as nice to substitute good strawberry preserves for the fresh fruit. Just spoon some over each portion. If you can locate a jar of Bar-le-Duc wild strawberries or the same kind of currants, you'll have found the makings for a gourmet's dessert dream. The preserves, which the French have been making for some five hundred years, taste as fantastically good as they look in their whole-berry state. Frozen strawberries can be served with the cheeses, too—as can frozen raspberries—after being thawed.

Another way to serve Boursin (natural) or Boursault with fruit is to allow the cheese to come to room temperature in a bowl, soften it with a spoon, blend in a little Cognac and confectioners' sugar, and put a dollop of the luxurious blend on some fresh black cherries that have been pitted and steeped for half an hour in a little kirsch. This works equally well with canned bing cherries.

There are those who unswervingly swear by pears with Gorgonzola, and it is a lovely combination. But for a change of pace try juicy Bartlett pears with creamy slices of Bel Paese, either domestic or imported from Italy. Good choices to accompany firmer-type pears are Bleu de Bresse or creamier, milder, Wedgwood-blue-veined Pipo Crèm'. Both of the latter are French cheeses.

Some summer fruit-and-cheese ideas are blueberries with Port Salut, nectarines with Brie, fresh peaches with Gorgonzola, fresh cherries with Crema Danica (Danish) or Crème Chantilly (Swedish), purple plums with Stilton, and red plums with Appenzell (Swiss). There's a tantalizing interplay of flavors when you serve fresh apricots with one of the mild, creamy French goat cheeses, either the Ile de France Chèvre, which comes in a little cardboard container that looks like a suitcase or Chèvre Saint Mauré. Unless you know goat cheeses well, you'll need reliable help from your cheese dealer in choosing a mild goat cheese if you stray from these two varieties or the ones discussed in Part I of this chapter.

Think of having cheese with almost any fruit or berry pie. Have mince pie (and if you like it, why wait until November?) with a fine Norwegian or Danish blue cheese, or, similarly, have pumpkin pie with Gervais or Petit Suisse. Peach pie is good with Crème Chantilly, and banana pie with Gorgonzola. Whatever cheese goes well with a fruit will generally go just as well when you convert that fruit into a pie.

If you want one good all-around dependable cheese to serve with just about any fruit the choice would probably best be a French Port Salut. Its texture is semisoft, its flavor just tangy enough to be interesting, and there's hardly a cheese eater who wouldn't love it.

While there are really no hard-and-fast rules to follow for enjoying cheeses and fruit together, the key to success is often proper timing. Although mentioned in the first part of this chapter it's worth repeating that you should remove cheeses from the refrigerator and leave them at room temperature with their wrappers removed for two to three hours before serving in order to bring out their true flavors and textures. Two hours will generally be long enough in the summer, and three in winter. Boursin, Boursault, Petit Suisse, and other cheeses of this type need only about an hour at room temperature for their flavors and textures to be at their best. In the case of Brie, Camembert, and other soft-ripening cheeses, until you feel you can judge accurately for yourself, ask your cheese dealer to tell you how long to leave the cheese at room temperature. This will depend on how ripe the cheese is when you buy it. Sometimes you won't even need to refrigerate the cheese at all after you bring it home; other times you may need to refrigerate it only briefly.

Whatever fruit you're serving should be refrigerated up to serving time unless you have a definite prejudice against cold fruit. Most people prefer it pleasantly cool.

Allow, if you can, half an hour between the main part of dinner and the fruit-and-cheese course to let taste buds and appetites sharpen. Have a change of scenery, too, if you like, by serving this course in the living room or even out-of-doors in summer weather. In cool weather it's nice to pass around a bowl of nuts and a nutcracker—or nut meats, either salted or unsalted.

PART III: OTHER CHEESE DESSERTS

BRIE EN CROUTE

½ recipe PUFF PASTRY
1 Petit Brie, whole Camembert,
   or Coulommiers, just ripe

1 egg
1 teaspoon water

Roll out the chilled puff pastry ⅛-inch thick on a lightly floured board. Cut a circle of puff pastry 1 inch larger in diameter than the cheese. Cut another circle of puff pastry 3 inches larger in diameter than the cheese, or large enough to allow the pastry to cover the cheese, extend down the sides, plus ½ inch all around.

Place the smaller circle of pastry on a baking sheet. Set the unwrapped cheese on it, properly centered. Moisten the edges of the pastry with water. Place the larger circle of pastry over the cheese, allowing it to cover the sides, and press the edges of the circles well together all around against the baking sheet. With the tines of a fork, press a decorative border all around the bottom of the pastry. Refrigerate for 30 minutes on the baking sheet.

Meanwhile, preheat the oven at 450°. Beat the egg and water together lightly. After 30 minutes, remove the baking sheet from the refrigerator and brush the pastry with the egg mixture. Place it in the oven. After 5 minutes reduce the heat to 350°. Continue baking about 15 minutes longer, or until the pastry is puffed and nicely glazed. Remove from the oven and place on a serving dish. Allow to cool for 15 minutes at room temperature before cutting. Cut into 6 wedges and serve on small plates with forks. Serve with fruit if desired.

Makes 6 servings.

PRUNES IN PORT WITH GERVAIS

12 ounces ready-to-eat, pitted
   prunes
1 cup port
¼ cup water

1 tablespoon lemon juice
¼ cup sugar
2 small packages Gervais
1 or 2 tablespoons cream

Soak the prunes overnight in the port. Transfer the prunes to a saucepan and add the water, lemon juice, and sugar. Bring to a boil, lower the heat, cover, and simmer for 10 to 15 minutes until the prunes are tender but not mushy. Cool and chill. Divide the fruit among 5 dessert glasses.

Cream the Gervais until it is soft and fluffy. Beat in the cream to lighten the consistency. Spoon over the prunes.

Makes 5 servings.

CHEESECAKE EPICUREAN

2½ cups fine rusk crumbs
   (preferably made from
   imported rusk)
5 tablespoons melted butter
1 rounded tablespoon sugar
Generous pinch of cinnamon
1 pound cream cheese
2 cups ricotta cheese
1 cup sour cream

¼ cup sifted cake flour
5 egg yolks
⅓ cup sugar
1 tablespoon lemon juice
1 teaspoon vanilla extract
Grated zest of 1 lemon
5 egg whites
Pinch of salt
⅓ cup of sugar

Make the rusk crumbs by crushing the rusks with a rolling pin. Combine them with the melted butter, sugar, and cinnamon. Pat the mixture firmly onto the bottom and sides of a well-buttered 10-inch spring-form pan. Cream the cream cheese until it is soft and fluffy. Put the ricotta through a fine sieve and add it to the cream cheese. Beat until the cheeses are well blended and fluffy. Add the sour cream and mix well. Fold in the sifted cake flour.

Beat the egg yolks well, and add ⅓ cup sugar gradually. Continue beating until the mixture is very pale and thick and forms a slowly dissolving ribbon when the beater is lifted. Add the lemon juice, vanilla extract, and grated zest of lemon. Add a little of the cream cheese mixture and combine well. Then fold the egg yolk mixture into the cream cheese mixture.

Preheat the oven at 325°. Beat the egg whites with pinch of salt until soft peaks form. Add ⅓ cup sugar gradually and continue beating until stiff. Mix in a little of the cream cheese mixture. Then fold the egg white mixture into the cream cheese mixture. Pour into the prepared spring-form pan and smooth the top with a rubber spatula. Bake about 1¼ hours, or until the center of the cake does not jiggle when the pan is gently prodded. Turn off the oven, open the door, and allow the cake to cool in the oven. When it is cold, remove the sides of spring-form pan. Serve, or refrigerate, covered, until serving time.

Makes 12 or more servings.

COEUR A LA CREME
WITH STRAWBERRIES

This is probably the world's most romantic dessert. A mixture of cheeses molded in a heart-shaped basket or white porcelain mold with holes in the bottom for drainage, Coeur à la Crème unmolds as a beautiful snow-white heart. Serve it surrounded by bright-red strawberries or with strawberry sauce spooned on top for a classic cheese-and-fruit dessert.

8 ounces cream cheese or Gervais
1 cup ricotta cheese or cottage cheese which has been forced through a fine sieve
¾ cup heavy cream

1 pint strawberries
Confectioners' sugar to taste
2 tablespoons orange liqueur, strawberry liqueur, or raspberry liqueur (optional)

Put the cream cheese and ricotta in a bowl and allow to stand at room temperature until the cream cheese is slightly softened. Blend until smooth. Stir in the heavy cream and blend well. Cut a clean piece of cheesecloth to line 6 individual or 1 large *coeur à la crème* mold.* Dampen the cheesecloth with water, wring it out, and line the mold(s). Pack the cheese mixture into the mold(s) and set on a plate. Cover the top loosely with plastic wrap or waxed paper. Refrigerate for several hours or overnight.

To serve, unmold on individual plates or on 1 large serving plate. Surround the dessert with whole strawberries, or slice the strawberries, sweeten them to taste with confectioners' sugar, and spoon them around the heart(s), or make a sauce by whirling the strawberries, confectioners'

---

* *Coeur à la crème* molds can be purchased in specialty cookware shops and department stores. Heart-shaped baskets can also be purchased at basket shops and hardware stores.

sugar, and liqueur together in an electric blender or food processor and spoon over the heart(s).

Raspberries can be used instead of strawberries, or you can break with tradition and use any kind of sweetened fruit you like.

Makes 6 servings.

CREAM CHEESE TARTS

1 three-ounce package cream
   cheese
¼ cup heavy cream
1 teaspoon plain gelatin
1 tablespoon cold water
2 eggs
⅓ cup sugar

½ cup milk, heated
½ teaspoon vanilla extract
½ cup heavy cream, whipped
8 four-inch baked tart shells
   (TART PASTRY or bought)
Slivered toasted almonds

Cream the cream cheese until soft. Blend in ¼ cup heavy cream and beat until fluffy. Set aside. Dissolve the gelatin in the cold water.

In the top of a double boiler set over simmering water, beat the eggs and sugar together until creamy. Add the hot milk quickly and stir until the mixture begins to thicken. Remove from the fire. Add the gelatin and stir until it has dissolved. Add the vanilla extract, mix well, and cool. Add to the cream cheese mixture. Fold in the whipped heavy cream. Pour the mixture into the baked tart shells and sprinkle with the slivered toasted almonds. Chill for 1 or 2 hours before serving.

Makes 8 servings.

HONEY CHEESE PIE

1 cup flour
1 tablespoon sugar
5 tablespoons cold butter
2 tablespoons ice water
1 pound ricotta cheese

¼ cup sugar
½ cup honey
3 eggs
2 teaspoons grated zest of lemon

In a bowl, combine the flour and 1 tablespoon sugar. Cut the butter into small pieces and add to the flour mixture, working it with the fingers until the mixture resembles peas. Add the ice water and mix with the hands until the mixture can be formed into a ball. Cover with plastic wrap and chill for 1 hour.

Preheat the oven at 350°. Roll the pastry out on a floured board and line a 9-inch pie pan with it. Flute the edges. Place a sheet of waxed paper in the pie plate, fill it with some dry beans or rice, and bake for 10 minutes. Remove from the oven, turn out the beans or rice, and allow the pie shell to cool.

Meanwhile, combine the ricotta cheese with ¼ cup sugar. Add the honey and mix well. Beat the eggs lightly and add them to the cheese mixture. Stir in the lemon zest. Pour into the pie shell. Return the pie to the oven and bake for 45 minutes, or until lightly browned. Serve it warm or chilled. Grapes are a nice accompaniment.

Makes 6 to 8 servings.

In addition to the recipes in this chapter, other cheese recipes in this book are:

Italian Cannoli
Petit Suisse with Guava Shells
Pistachio Cream Glacé
Russian Paska

CHAPTER 12

Chocolate Favorites

*... he would hold his nose high in the
air and take long deep sniffs of the
gorgeous chocolatey smell all around him.*
—*Roald Dahl,* Willy Wonka and
    the Chocolate Factory

The Spanish conquistadores in ancient Mexico found Aztec emperors drinking frothy chocolate sweetened with honey, flavored with vanilla, chilled with snow carried down from the mountains, and served in golden goblets. Intrigued with this luxurious drink—not to mention the goblets—they carried not only the cocoa and vanilla beans back to Spain, but the recipe for making the exotic brew. The Spanish took chocolate to their hearts, and chocolate drinking became commonplace in that country long before the rest of Europe was aware of the practice.

When chocolate was introduced into France and the rumor began circulating that it had aphrodisiac qualities, its fame spread rapidly. Except for the fact that chocolate is quick-energy food, no one makes claims of therapeutic or other values of the cocoa bean nowadays. But as a favorite flavor it knows no equal. Before the Declaration of Independence was signed, the first chocolate factory was built in Massachusetts, and since then we've been importing and processing cocoa beans in ever-increasing tonnages yearly.

While it's impossible in this book to include everyone's favorite chocolate recipe—of which there must be thousands—the most luscious of the time-tested favorites are included. In buying chocolate for cooking or just plain eating, you'll find there are several kinds: bitter chocolate, or baking chocolate, which is without sweetening; bittersweet chocolate, which is slightly sweetened; semisweet chocolate, which has a little more sugar added; sweet chocolate, which has still more sugar added;

and milk chocolate, which has powdered or condensed milk as well as sugar added.

If you have chocolate that assumes a grayish cast, don't be alarmed. It's simply the butterfat rising to the surface, as it's inclined to do in hot weather, and affects the chocolate in no way other than appearance.

To melt chocolate, place chocolate which has been cut up into fairly small pieces in the top of a double boiler or a small saucepan, and set over hot (not boiling) water. Stir with a wooden spoon until it has completely melted. Allow the chocolate to remain over warm water until you're ready to add it to your recipe.

In addition to the recipes in this chapter, other chocolate recipes in this book are:

Chocolate Cream Roll
Chocolate Crêpes Chantilly
Chocolate Ice Cream
Chocolate Omelet
German Black Forest Cake
Profiteroles with Chocolate Sauce

CHOCOLATE MOUSSE

½ cup water
½ cup sugar
3 ounces baking chocolate, finely chopped
3 ounces semisweet chocolate, finely chopped
3 egg yolks
1 teaspoon vanilla extract
1⅓ cups heavy cream

Combine the water and sugar in a saucepan and heat, stirring constantly, to dissolve the sugar. Bring to a boil and simmer for 5 minutes. Pour into the container of an electric blender or food processor, and add the baking chocolate and semisweet chocolate. Process until the chocolate has completely melted and the mixture is blended. Add the egg yolks, one at a time, and blend for 1 or 2 seconds after each addition. Add the vanilla extract and blend again. Whip the heavy cream until stiff. Fold in the chocolate mixture, about one-third at a time, until the mixture is completely blended. Pour into a plastic 1-quart container, cover with a lid, and freeze for 2 hours or longer. Remove the container from the freezer and refrigerate it for 1 hour before serving time. To serve, spoon the mousse into dessert cups or glasses.

Makes 6 to 8 servings.

POTS DE CREME AU CHOCOLAT

Serve these lovely custards in little handled pots called pots au crème *cups, or make them in ramekins or custard cups. Top with a crystallized flower for the most elegant of desserts.*

1 cup heavy cream
4 ounces semisweet chocolate,
   broken up
3 tablespoons sugar
1 egg plus 2 egg yolks

1 tablespoon vanilla extract, or
   rum, or brandy
Crystallized flowers (preferably
   violets) (optional)

Place the heavy cream and chocolate (which has been broken up) in a saucepan over low heat, and stir until the chocolate has melted. Add the sugar. Beat the egg and egg yolks together lightly. Add the chocolate mixture to the eggs gradually, stirring constantly. Add the vanilla extract, rum, or brandy.

Preheat the oven at 350°. Pour the chocolate mixture into *pots au crème* cups or other baking cups. With a spoon, remove any bubbles or foam that floats to the top. Place covers on the pots or cover the cups with aluminum foil. Set the pots in a baking pan and pour boiling water into the pan to a level two-thirds of the way up the sides of the pots. Bake for about 15 to 20 minutes in the lower third of the oven, checking the water to see that it does not boil, and lowering the oven temperature if necessary. When a knife blade or needle inserted in the center of the custard comes out clean, remove from the oven and cool. Take care not to overcook. When cool, chill and serve with a crystallized flower atop each dessert if desired.

Makes 4 to 6 servings, depending on the size of the cups used.

CHOCOLATE SPONGE PUDDING

3 egg yolks
2 tablespoons butter, melted
   and cooled
½ cup sugar
¼ cup instant or quick-mixing
   flour
¼ teaspoon salt

2 cups milk
2 ounces baking chocolate,
   chopped
1½ teaspoons vanilla extract
3 egg whites
Heavy cream

Preheat the oven at 350°. Beat the egg yolks lightly. Add the butter. Add the sugar, instant flour, and salt, and combine well. Combine the milk and baking chocolate in the top of a double boiler. Heat over hot water, stirring, until the chocolate has completely dissolved. Remove from the heat and stir in the vanilla extract. Add to the egg yolk mixture gradually, stirring well.

Beat the egg whites until soft peaks form. Fold a few tablespoons of the chocolate mixture into the egg whites. Fold the egg whites into the chocolate mixture. Turn into a buttered round 1½-quart baking dish. Set in a shallow pan in the oven, and fill the pan with hot water to a level of 1 inch. Bake for about 45 minutes. Serve the pudding warm with heavy cream, or, if desired, chill and serve it with whipped heavy cream.

Makes 6 servings.

CHOCOLATE CUPS

**2 four-ounce bars Eagle sweet
chocolate or 8 ounces
semisweet chocolate**

Place the chocolate in the top of a double boiler, breaking up chocolate bars if they are used. Set over hot, not boiling, water and heat until the chocolate has melted. Remove from the heat. Spoon the chocolate into 8 cupcake-sized fluted foil or paper cups (if you are using foil cups, which are easier to peel off, set the foil cups into paper cups while working with the melted chocolate to protect your hands from the heat). With the back of a teaspoon spread the chocolate around to coat the entire inside of the cups evenly. Set the cups in muffin tins and chill for 30 minutes.

Peel the cups off the chocolate and store the Chocolate Cups in the refrigerator or other cool place until serving time. To serve, place a ball of ice cream sherbet, mousse, or water ice in each cup and decorate as desired. A dollop of whipped cream and a sprinkling of chocolate hail or shaved chocolate are nice.

Makes 8 Chocolate Cups.

Triple Chocolate Treat

Fill the Chocolate Cups with balls of CHOCOLATE ICE CREAM (home-made or bought) and spoon CHOCOLATE SAUCE over the ice cream. Sprinkle chocolate hail or shaved chocolate over all.

CHOCOLATE CHESTNUT LOAF

6 or 7 ounces semisweet
  chocolate
2 tablespoons milk
2 tablespoons rum
6 tablespoons butter

1 seventeen-ounce can chestnut
  spread (*crème de marrons*)
Whipped cream
Candied chestnuts (optional)

Grease a small loaf pan and line it with waxed paper. Butter the waxed paper and sprinkle with 3 or 4 ounces of the semisweet chocolate (which has been grated).

Combine the milk and 3 ounces semisweet chocolate (which has been broken up) in the top of a double boiler. Set over hot water and heat, stirring, until the chocolate has melted. Remove from the heat and stir in the rum, 1 tablespoon at a time, until thoroughly blended. Beat the butter with an electric beater until very creamy. Add the chestnut spread gradually, beating well. Add the chocolate mixture and blend until smooth and even in color. Turn into a lined loaf pan and smooth the top with a rubber spatula. Cover with waxed paper and refrigerate for 12 hours or longer, until the mixture is very hard. Unmold, removing the waxed paper. Decorate with whipped cream and, if desired, candied chestnuts. To serve, slice thin.

Makes 8 to 10 servings.

CHOCOLATE CREAM PIE

1 nine-inch baked pie shell
(OLD FASHIONED PASTRY or
any preferred pie shell)
2 ounces semisweet chocolate,
broken up
2 cups milk
2 tablespoons cornstarch
2 tablespoons instant or
quick-mixing flour

¼ teaspoon salt
⅔ cup sugar
3 egg yolks
1 tablespoon butter
1 teaspoon vanilla extract
Whipped Cream
Shaved Chocolate (optional)

Combine the semisweet chocolate (which has been broken up) and the milk in the top of a double boiler. Set over hot water and heat, stirring, until the chocolate has completely melted. Sift together the cornstarch, instant flour, salt, and sugar, and stir into the chocolate mixture. Blend well, making sure there are no lumps. Beat the egg yolks lightly and add them to the chocolate mixture. Cook stirring constantly, until the mixture thickens. (This will take about 7 minutes.) Remove from the heat and place the pan in a bowl of ice cubes or crushed ice. (Make sure not to overcook. However, if you do and the mixture lumps, beat briefly with a large wire whisk until the mixture becomes smooth.) Add the butter and vanilla extract and stir until butter has melted. Cool the mixture slightly. Stir again and pour into the baked pie shell. Chill well. Garnish with whipped cream and, if desired, shaved chocolate.

Makes 8 servings.

CHOCOLATE SAUCE

1¼ cups sugar
Pinch of salt
1 cup heavy cream

3 ounces baking chocolate,
chopped
1 teaspoon vanilla extract
1 tablespoon brandy

Combine the sugar, salt, heavy cream, and chocolate in a small saucepan and cook over medium heat, stirring constantly, until the chocolate has melted. Raise the temperature and bring to a boil. Cook, stirring, until the mixture reaches the soft-ball stage, about 238°. Remove from the heat and stir in the vanilla extract and brandy. Serve hot or at room temperature.

Chocolate sauce may be used as a cake frosting, in which case it should be spooned over the cake while warm; or it may be used as a sauce on frozen desserts, custards, or any dessert where a chocolate sauce is in order.

VARIATION:

Melt a few chocolate mint patties or chocolate bonbons with any desired flavor of cream filling in the top of a double boiler over hot water, and stir into the finished sauce.

CHOCOLATE SOUFFLE

1 cup milk
4 ounces sweet chocolate (such as Eagle sweet chocolate)
4 egg yolks
¼ cup sugar

3 tablespoons instant or quick-mixing flour
2 teaspoons butter
1 teaspoon vanilla extract
5 egg whites

Combine the milk and sweet chocolate (which has been broken up) in a heavy saucepan, and cook over low heat, stirring, until the chocolate has melted. Remove from the heat. Beat the egg yolks until thick. Combine the sugar with the instant flour and add to the egg yolks gradually, beating constantly, until the mixture is very thick and pale in color. Add to the chocolate mixture and combine well. Return to the stove and cook over low heat, stirring, until the mixture thickens. Remove from the heat and stir in the butter and vanilla extract. Cool for 15 minutes.

Meanwhile, preheat the oven at 350°. Butter and sugar a 1½-quart soufflé dish. Beat the egg whites until stiff peaks form, and fold the beaten egg whites into the chocolate mixture. Pour into the soufflé dish and bake about 35 minutes.

Makes 6 servings.

CHOCOLATE GRAND MARNIER SOUFFLE

3 tablespoons butter
3 tablespoons instant or
    quick-mixing flour
1 cup milk
1 ounce semisweet chocolate
½ cup sugar

¼ cup Grand Marnier
5 egg yolks
7 egg whites
½ teaspoon cream of tartar
Candied orange peel, finely
    chopped (optional)

Place the butter in the top of a double boiler and set over hot water. Stir until the butter has melted. Mix in the instant flour. Add the milk and blend until smooth. Add the chocolate and cook, stirring, until the chocolate has melted and the mixture is smooth and thick. Remove from the heat. Stir in the sugar and mix well. Add the Grand Marnier and set aside to cool for 15 minutes.

Meanwhile, preheat the oven at 350°. Beat the egg yolks and add to the chocolate mixture, blending well. Beat the egg whites until foamy. Add the cream of tartar and continue beating until stiff peaks form. Fold a little of the chocolate mixture into the egg whites. Then fold the egg whites into the chocolate mixture. Butter and sugar a 2-quart soufflé dish. Turn the mixture into the soufflé dish and bake for 25 to 30 minutes.

If desired, strew the soufflé with finely chopped candied orange peel before serving.

Makes 8 servings.

CHOCOLATE FONDUE

8 ounces semisweet chocolate,
    broken up
3 tablespoons heavy cream
1 or 2 tablespoons brandy

Toasted cake fingers, macaroons,
    banana wedges, strawberries,
    and pineapple chunks

Melt the chocolate with the heavy cream in a saucepan over a very low flame stirring constantly. Remove from the heat and stir in the brandy. Pour the mixture into a fondue and set over a lighted candle or other low flame.

Serve with a tray of toasted cake fingers, macaroons, banana wedges, strawberries, and pineapple chunks, which can be speared with fondue forks and dipped into the chocolate mixture by each person.

This recipe can be varied by substituting orange liqueur or other fruit liqueur for the brandy, or by adding some cream-filled mint patties or other flavors of cream-centered chocolate bonbons when melting the chocolate.

Makes 4 servings. The recipe can be doubled.

CHOCOLATE PECAN TORTE

For the cake:
1½ cups pecan halves, firmly
    packed
⅔ cup superfine vanilla sugar*
2 tablespoons instant or
    quick-mixing flour
5½ ounces semisweet chocolate,
    broken up
¾ cup butter
5 egg yolks
5 egg whites

For the frosting and finishing:
8 ounces sweet chocolate (such
    as Eagle sweet chocolate)
1 cup heavy cream
CHOCOLATE TRIANGLES or
    grated chocolate (optional)

For the cake: Place the pecan halves and 1 tablespoon of the superfine vanilla sugar in an electric blender or food processor, and blend until the nuts are completely pulverized. Transfer to a bowl and toss with the instant flour. Break up and melt the semisweet chocolate in the top of a double boiler over hot water, stirring constantly. Remove from the heat and set aside.

Preheat the oven at 350°. Cream the butter in the bowl of an electric mixer until very creamy. Add the remaining superfine vanilla sugar and continue creaming until the mixture is very light. Add the egg yolks, 1 at a time, beating for 2 minutes after each addition. Add the chocolate and combine well. Stir in the pecan mixture with a spoon and combine well.

* Superfine vanilla sugar is made by placing a piece of vanilla bean in a jar of superfine sugar for a day or two. After using the sugar, the jar may be refilled with sugar and stored for future use.

Beat the egg whites until stiff, and fold them into the batter with a rubber spatula. Turn the mixture into a buttered and floured 9-inch spring-form pan. Bake for about 40 minutes, or until a cake tester inserted in the center comes out clean. Cool the cake slightly on a wire rack and remove the spring-form rim. Continue to cool.

For the frosting and finishing: When the cake is cold, place the sweet chocolate in the top of a double boiler and set over hot water. Heat, stirring constantly, until the chocolate has melted. Remove from the heat and cool to lukewarm. Beat the heavy cream until stiff, and fold the chocolate into the whipped cream. Spread over the top of the cake. If desired, decorate with Chocolate Triangles or grated chocolate.

Makes 8 servings.

DEVIL'S FOOD CAKE
WITH FUDGE FROSTING

For the cake:
4 ounces baking chocolate, chopped
½ cup milk
¾ cup turbinado sugar
1 egg yolk, slightly beaten
2 cups sifted cake flour
1 teaspoon baking powder
1 teaspoon baking soda
½ teaspoon salt
½ cup butter
¾ cup turbinado sugar
2 egg yolks
¾ cup milk
2 teaspoons vanilla extract
2 egg whites

For the frosting:
1 cup milk
2 cups sugar
2 ounces baking chocolate, chopped
Pinch of salt
3 tablespoons butter
1 teaspoon vanilla extract

For the cake: Combine the baking chocolate, ½ cup milk, and ¾ cup turbinado sugar in the top of a double boiler. Add the egg yolk. Place over hot water and cook, stirring, until the chocolate melts and the mixture thickens. Remove from the heat and set aside.

Preheat the oven at 350°. Sift together the cake flour, baking powder, baking soda, and salt. Cream the butter and gradually add ¾ cup turbinado sugar. Add 2 egg yolks, 1 at a time, beating well after each addition. Add the flour mixture alternately with ¾ cup milk combined with the vanilla extract. Add the chocolate mixture and blend well. Beat the egg whites until stiff and fold them into the batter. Turn the mixture ino a buttered and floured 9x12-inch cake pan and bake for about 30 minutes, or until a cake tester inserted in the center comes out clean. Cool on a wire rack.

For the frosting: While the cake is cooling, combine the milk, sugar, chopped baking chocolate, and salt in a heavy saucepan. Cook over medium heat, stirring, until the chocolate has melted. Bring the mixture to a boil, lower the heat, and cook without stirring, partially covered, to the soft-ball stage, about 238°. Remove the pan from the heat and place it in a bowl of ice cubes or shaved ice. Stir the frosting until the temperature drops to about 130°. Add the butter and stir until it has melted. Add the vanilla extract. Beat until the frosting begins to stiffen and is of the proper spreading consistency. Spread on the cake immediately.

Makes about 15 servings.

BOURBON BROWNIES

3 ounces semisweet chocolate
5 tablespoons butter
2 eggs
¾ cup sugar
1 teaspoon vanilla extract
1 tablespoon bourbon*

½ cup flour
½ teaspoon baking powder
¼ teaspoon salt
1 cup coarsely chopped walnuts
   or pecans

Preheat the oven at 350°. Break up the chocolate and place it with the butter in the top of a double boiler. Set over hot water and heat, stirring, until the chocolate has melted. Remove from the heat and set aside. Beat the eggs well, add the sugar gradually, and beat until the mixture is light and fluffy. Add the vanilla extract and bourbon. Add the chocolate mixture and mix well.

Sift the flour, baking powder, and salt over the chocolate mixture. Mix well. Stir in the nuts and combine well. Turn into a buttered and floured 8-inch-square baking pan. Bake for 25 to 30 minutes, or until a cake tester inserted in the center comes out clean.

Makes 12 brownies.

* For rum brownies, substitute 1 tablespoon rum.

CHAPTER 13

Hot and Cold Together

Grateful coolness in the heat.
—*Caswell,* Hymns and Poems

A dessert guaranteed to intrigue is one that offers the drama of temperature difference within itself. People are fascinated by the phenomenon of a frozen and a hot food served on the same plate. The hot fudge sundae in its simplicity certainly has as many devotees as the king of all hot-and-cold desserts, Baked Alaska. This latter creation, consisting of a solidly frozen ice cream interior overcoated with swirls of meringue browned in the oven, was the invention of a New York chef in the 1800s who was inspired by the snowy lands of the newly purchased Alaskan territory and produced a dessert in its honor.

Lily gilders have gone on to serve Baked Alaska flaming—and there's something to be said for the idea. A few tablespoons of rum, brandy, or kirsch flamed over a dessert, be it ice cream and meringue, or fruit, or any other combination of fixings, produces an instant atmosphere of festivity. Flambéed desserts are hard to forget, as witness Cherries Jubilee, which owes more of its fame to the spell of flame than to its delicious blending of flavors.

There isn't any secret to making desserts flame properly, but there are two ways to handle the flaming. One is to pour flaming liquor over the dessert, and the other is to pour the liquor over the dessert and then flame it. In either case, the only rule for success is first to heat the liquor in a small, flat-bottomed pan or a ladle over a medium flame. A pan is usually more convenient since you can set it down while you light a match. Swirl the liquor around while it's heating, and let it just get warm, not hot. If you heat it too much, it won't light. Either flame it directly by holding a lighted match over it for a second while standing back and reaching your arm toward the liquor or pour the warmed liquor over the dessert and light it without delay. A little practice will give you assurance to flame away in front of an audience.

In addition to the recipes in this chapter, other hot-and-cold-together recipes in this book are:

Irish coffee
Plum Yum

ORANGE FLAPJACKS WITH VANILLA ICE CREAM

For the flapjacks:
¼ cup flour
3 tablespoons water
1 egg
1 teaspoon sugar
Pinch of salt
2 tablespoons butter

For the sauce and finishing:
1 tablespoon butter
1 tablespoon sugar
½ cup orange juice
Grated zest of 1 orange
3 tablespoons brandy
Vanilla ice cream

For the flapjacks: Combine the flour and water. Add the egg, sugar, and salt, and beat until smooth. Melt the butter in a skillet and pour in all the batter. Cook over a low flame for about 5 minutes. Turn and brown the other side for 1 or 2 minutes. Turn out onto a plate and cut into 1-inch squares.

For the sauce and finishing: Melt the butter in a skillet. Add the sugar, orange juice, and orange zest, and stir until the sugar has dissolved. Place the flapjack squares in the orange mixture and heat gently. Warm the brandy, pour it over the flapjacks, and ignite immediately. When the flames die out, divide the flapjacks and sauce among 4 warmed plates and top each with vanilla ice cream. Spoon some of the sauce over the ice cream.

Makes 4 servings.

CREME BRULEE

2 cups heavy cream
1 one-inch piece vanilla bean
4 egg yolks

¼ cup sugar
Additional sugar

Heat the heavy cream and vanilla bean in the top of a double boiler over low direct heat, but do not allow to boil. Remove from the heat. Beat the egg yolks until thick. Add ¼ cup sugar gradually and continue beating until the mixture is thick and pale and forms a slowly dissolving ribbon when the beater is lifted. Remove the vanilla bean from the cream and add the cream to the egg yolk mixture gradually, stirring constantly. Place the mixture in the top of a double boiler and cook, stirring, until the mixture coats a metal spoon. Pour into a very shallow ovenproof dish. Cool, cover, and chill, preferably overnight.

To serve, preheat the broiler. Cover the top of the custard evenly with a ¼-inch-thick layer of sugar. Embed the dish in a bowl or pan of chopped ice and set it under the broiler, about 5 inches from the flame. Watch carefully, and as soon as the sugar caramelizes, remove the dish from the broiler. Refrigerate 3 minutes and serve immediately. Crack the top with the back of a spoon before serving out portions.

Makes 6 servings.

GOLD BRICK SUNDAE

1 container Elmer's Gold Brick
   Chocolate Nut Topping*

1 quart VANILLA ICE CREAM
   (homemade or bought)

Place the container of Gold Brick in a saucepan of hot water for 5 minutes, or follow the package directions. Remove from the water and open. Stir well. Spoon the ice cream into serving glasses. Spoon the topping over each serving. The topping will form a nutted crust over the ice cream.

Makes 6 servings.

* Available at gourmet, specialty food, and fancy grocery shops.

BAKED ALASKA

1 recipe GENOISE
1 tablespoon kirsch
1 quart brick or round-shaped
   ice cream or ice (any flavor)

6 egg whites
¼ teaspoon salt
¼ teaspoon cream of tartar
¾ cup sugar
1 teaspoon vanilla extract

Prepare the Génoise, filling an 8 inch-square baking pan with a layer of batter ⅝-inch deep. Bake as directed, using the remaining batter for another recipe. Place the cooled baked cake on a wooden board or oven-proof serving platter. Sprinkle with kirsch. Place the ice cream on the cake, and trim the cake so that it extends 1 inch beyond the ice cream on all sides. Freeze until serving time.

To serve, preheat the oven at 475°. Beat the egg whites until foamy. Add the salt and cream of tartar, and continue beating until soft peaks form. Add the sugar gradually, and continue heating until the mixture is thick and glossy and stiff peaks form. Add the vanilla extract. Spread the mixture thickly over the ice cream and cake, using a rubber spatula. If desired, use some of the meringue to pipe designs over the surface with a pastry bag fitted with a star tip. Place in the oven and bake for 3 or 4 minutes until lightly browned. Serve immediately.

Makes 8 to 10 servings.

MIDNIGHT SUN BAKED ALASKA

1 recipe BOURBON BROWNIES
1½ quarts coffee ice cream
3 egg yolks
12 tablespoons sugar

½ teaspoon almond extract
8 egg whites
½ cup brandy

Bake the Bourbon Brownies substituting 1 tablespoon brandy for the bourbon and 1 cup slivered blanched almonds for the walnuts. Bake in a round 10-inch cake pan. Cool on a wire rack. Set on a wooden board, preferably round in shape.

Soften the ice cream sufficiently to shape into a round mound on the brownie base, leaving a 1-inch border of cake all around the ice cream. Freeze until serving time.

To serve, preheat the oven at 475°. Beat the egg yolks until thick,

---

and add 6 tablespoons sugar gradually, continuing to beat until the mixture is thick and pale and forms a slowly dissolving ribbon when the beater is lifted. Add the almond extract. Beat the egg whites until soft peaks form. Gradually add the remaining 6 tablespoons sugar, and continue beating until stiff peaks form. Fold very carefully and gently into the egg yolk mixture. Remove the cake from the freezer and, using a spatula, spread the meringue thickly all over the cake, piping some meringue through a pastry tube fitted with a star tip if you care to decorate it further. Place in the oven and bake for 3 to 4 minutes. Heat the brandy slightly. Remove the cake from the oven, ignite the brandy, and pour it over the cake. Bring the cake to the table flaming.

Makes 12 servings.

DOUBLE ORANGE MERINGUE

6 oranges (preferably navel)
Orange sherbet or orange
   water ice
3 egg whites

⅓ cup sugar
3 egg yolks
1 teaspoon orange flower water

Cut off the tops of the oranges about one-quarter of the way down. Remove the orange sections with the aid of a spoon and/or grapefruit knife, and reserve them for another use. With scissors, cut a zigzag pattern around the edge of each orange shell. Fill the shells full, but not mounded, with orange sherbet or water ice. Set them close together in an ovenproof baking dish. Freeze until serving time.

To serve, preheat the oven at 450°. Beat the egg whites until soft peaks form. Gradually add the sugar, and continue beating until the mixture is thick and glossy. Beat the egg yolks until thick, and fold them into the egg white mixture. Fold in the orange flower water. Place the mixture in a pastry bag fitted with a large star tip, and pipe the meringue onto the orange shells to cover the sherbet completely and to just meet the shells at their edges so that no air spaces remain. Place in the oven and bake for 3 to 4 minutes until the meringue browns lightly, watching carefully to be sure it does not burn.

Makes 6 servings.

CHERRIES JUBILEE

1 fourteen- or sixteen-ounce can
  or jar pitted bing cherries
1 tablespoon cornstarch
1 tablespoon lemon juice

¼ cup sugar
1 quart VANILLA ICE CREAM
  (homemade or bought)
¼ cup kirsch

Combine ¼ cup of the syrup from the cherries with the cornstarch. Drain the balance of the syrup into a saucepan. Add the lemon juice and sugar. Bring to a boil, stirring, and simmer for 1 or 2 minutes. Stir in the cornstarch mixture, and continue stirring until the mixture is thickened and smooth. Add the cherries and heat through.

Spoon the ice cream into a serving bowl. Top with the cherry mixture. Heat the kirsch slightly and pour over the ice cream and cherries. Ingite the kirsch immediately and bring the dish to the table flaming. When the flames die, spoon the dessert into serving glasses.

Makes 6 servings.

PEARS HELENE

2 cups water
1¼ cups sugar
1 one-inch piece vanilla bean
3 large pears

CHOCOLATE SAUCE
1 quart VANILLA ICE CREAM
  (homemade or bought)
6 crystallized violets

In a saucepan, combine the water, sugar, and vanilla bean, and bring to a boil, stirring. Simmer for 5 minutes. Meanwhile, peel, halve, and core the pears. Place them in saucepan with the syrup and simmer gently until the pears are just tender. Remove from the heat and allow the pears to cool in the syrup. Chill. (Or place 6 large, good-quality canned pear halves in a bowl with their syrup just to cover, and allow to stand with 1 teaspoon vanilla extract in the refrigerator for about 3 hours.)

To serve, prepare the Chocolate Sauce. Divide the ice cream among 6 dessert glasses. Place a pear half in each glass. Pour the hot Chocolate Sauce over each portion. Top with a crystallized violet and serve immediately.

Makes 6 servings.

BOMBE ANGERIENNE

5 egg yolks
¼ cup sugar
2 cups milk
1½ cups heavy cream
2 envelopes plain gelatin
¼ cup cold water
2 teaspoons vanilla extract
3 tablespoons orange liqueur

1 tablespoon brandy
About 30 packaged champagne
  biscuits (such as Lu brand)
5 egg whites
⅔ cup sugar
Bar-le-Duc currant preserves or
  good brand currant jelly

In a heavy saucepan off heat, beat the egg yolks well. Add ¼ cup sugar and beat well. Add the milk and 1 cup of the heavy cream gradually and mix well. Cook over low heat, stirring constantly, until the mixture coats a spoon, but do not allow it to boil. Remove from the heat. Meanwhile, soften the gelatin in the cold water. Stir into the hot custard until the gelatin has dissolved. Cool and refrigerate until the mixture thickens slightly. Whip the remaining ½ cup heavy cream until stiff. Add it to the custard along with the vanilla extract.

Combine the orange liqueur and brandy and brush the champagne biscuits on both sides with the mixture. Line the bottom and sides of a large charlotte mold or similarly shaped dish or mold with some of the brushed biscuits. Spoon a layer of custard into the mold, top with a layer of brushed biscuits, and continue layering until the mold is filled. Cover and chill until firm.

To serve, preheat the oven at 400°. Unmold onto an ovenproof serving plate. Beat the egg whites until stiff. Add ⅔ cup sugar, a tablespoon at a time, and continue beating until the mixture is thick and glossy. With a spatula, spread the meringue over the top and sides of the dessert. Pipe some meringue through a pastry bag fitted with a large star tip to make rosettes on the top and around the bottom of the bombe. Make a depression in each rosette on top of the dessert to be filled with preserves after baking. Bake for 4 minutes, or until lightly browned, watching carefully. Spoon the Bar-le-Duc currant preserves into the rosettes on the top of the dessert, or fill them with curant jelly that has been beaten with a fork. Serve immediately, cutting into wedge-shaped portions.

Makes 8 servings.

CHAPTER 14

The Puff Family

Whole pyramids of sweetmeats.
—*John Dryden,* Preface to Fables

For many of us, cream puffs evoke a wave of childhood nostalgia, when having such a dessert was tantamount to having a dream come true. Children and adults alike are beguiled by the cream puff, a seeming miracle of the kitchen. Actually this pastry, no more than a very thick white sauce enriched with eggs and baked to puffiness, is simple to make.

Made basically as they were generations ago, all cream puffs are made from one basic dough called *pâte à chou* (pronounced *pat-a-shoe*), or cream-puff pastry. Blended together first on the stove, the pastry billows out to two or three times its original size while baking, and forms firm yet tender shells that can be stuffed with any number of delicious fillings and/or be decorated with sifted confectioners' sugar or various sauces.

The puffs can be baked individually, or in groups to form a cake, or in sections to put together to form tiny Swans. The baked puffs can be stacked up after filling to form elaborate desserts, such as Croquembouche, a pyramid of caramel-covered puffs, or Profiteroles, a mountain of tiny chocolate-sauce-covered puffs.

For an altogether different kind of cream puff, the pastry can be fried, rather than baked, to make Beignets Soufflés, or cream-puff fritters. These can be sprinkled with sifted confectioners' sugar and served while still warm.

Even more impressive than the cream puff in the realm of puffy pastries is the most delicate of all pastries, puff pastry. This pastry is composed of dozens, if not hundreds, of layers of dough sandwiched between layers of butter, and is formed by rolling out and folding the dough repeatedly until many paper-thin layers have been built up. Puff pastry as we make it today was popularized over three hundred years ago by a pastry chef in France, and there's evidence that similar forms of flaky pastry were made in that country at least three hundred years earlier. Even the ancient Greeks had their version of the superb pastry.

A fascinating pastry to make, puff pastry requires time, care, your undivided attention while working with it, and a cold refrigerator for it to take rests in. The most important and easiest step is stopping in between each rolling and turning of the pastry in order to chill it thoroughly and allow it to rest. Since most of the time used in making puff pastry is waiting time, there's no need to plan on spending the whole day in the kitchen. If you should happen to leave the dough in the refrigerator longer than necessary, there's no need to worry, since over-chilling can only benefit the pastry.

Remember when working with puff pastry to keep everything—the kitchen, the utensils (chill them in the refrigerator), and yourself—as cool as possible. It probably wouldn't be a good idea to make your first puff pastry on a hot summer's day unless your kitchen is air-conditioned, but any other time is fine. When rolling out the pastry, take care not to let the butter break through, but if it does, mend the spot right away with a bit of dough in order to seal in the air. The pastry depends on air trapped between the layers to produce its puffiness.

One of the best features of this ultimate in doughs is that one batch makes enough for at least two different kinds of dessert, and any unused portion freezes beautifully for later use. Puff pastry is used to make cakes, small pastries such as Napoleons and Cream Horns, cookies such as Palm Leaves, tart, pie, and tartlet crusts and shells, and of course various cocktail and entrée items which we won't be able to cover here. The pastry is so light, tender, and delicious that it can almost be eaten alone, without adornment. A simple whipped cream filling is the best complement in many cases.

In addition to the recipes in this chapter, another puff pastry recipe in this book is:

Brie en Croûte

BASIC CREAM PUFFS

1 cup water	1 cup sifted flour
½ cup butter	4 eggs
⅛ teaspoon salt	

Preheat the oven at 400°. Place the water, butter, and salt in a small saucepan and bring slowly to a boil, allowing the butter to melt. Remove from the stove, and, with a wooden spoon, stir in the flour all at once. Return to stove, and cook, stirring, until the mixture leaves the sides of the pan and forms a heavy ball. Remove from the stove and beat in the eggs, 1 at a time, beating after each addition until the egg is completely blended in.

Drop the paste from a teaspoon onto an ungreased baking sheet, making mounds according to the size directed in the recipe being used. Bake until puffed and golden, about 20 to 25 minutes. Turn off the oven. Stab a hole in bottom of each puff and return them to the oven for 15 minutes to dry out centers. Cool the puffs on a wire rack and use them as directed in individual recipes.

FILLED CREAM PUFFS

Make BASIC CREAM PUFFS, making mounds 1½ inches in diameter on the baking sheet. When the puffs have cooled, slit them open. Use one of the following fillings:

Ice Cream

Fill with any flavor of ice cream. Put the cream puff back together. Sprinkle with sifted confectioners' sugar or serve with a sauce. Some possible flavor combinations are: pistachio ice cream with chocolate sauce, vanilla ice cream with strawberry sauce, coffee ice cream with English Toffee sauce, or mango ice cream with pineapple sauce.

Pastry Cream

Fill with PASTRY CREAM which has been flavored with an extract or liqueur or into which some fruit has been stirred. Some flavorings which can be added to the basic recipe are: 1 tablespoon rosewater, 1 tablespoon orange liqueur, 1 tablespoon raspberry liqueur or strawberry liqueur, or 1 ten-ounce package frozen sweetened strawberries or raspberries (thawed and drained). Replace the top of the cream puff and sprinkle with sifted confectioners' sugar.

Fill with whipped cream which has been sweetened with sugar and flavored with almond or vanilla extract. Replace the top of the cream puff and sprinkle with sifted confectioners' sugar.

CREAM PUFFS CEVENOLE

These cream puffs take their name from the beautiful Cévennes Mountains of France, one of the world's greatest chestnut-growing areas. Chestnut trees, once the loveliest and most common of American trees, have literally vanished from our land due to an uncontrollable blight. Now the bulk of our chestnuts are imported from Europe, particularly from France.

1 recipe BASIC CREAM PUFFS
1 cup heavy cream
½ cup sweetened chestnut spread
   (*crème de marrons*)
1 teaspoon kirsch (optional)

Sifted confectioners' sugar
CHOCOLATE SAUCE (homemade
   or bought good brand)
   (optional)

Prepare Basic Cream Puffs, making mounds 1½ inches in diameter on the baking sheet. When cool slit the cream puffs open on one side.

Beat the heavy cream until stiff. Fold in the chestnut spread until well blended. Fold in the kirsch if desired. Fill the cream puffs with the mixture, close, and sprinkle with sifted confectioners' sugar. If desired, serve with Chocolate Sauce.

Makes 16 to 18.

ECLAIRS

1 recipe BASIC CREAM PUFFS
¼ cup light corn syrup
3 tablespoons strong coffee
2 tablespoons plus 1½ teaspoons
   butter

6 ounces semisweet chocolate,
   broken up into very small
   pieces
PASTRY CREAM or sweetened
   whipped cream flavored with
   vanilla extract

Prepare and bake Basic Cream Puffs, forming the paste with a spoon on the baking sheet into finger-shaped pieces about 4 inches long. While the Éclairs are baking, prepare the following glaze.

Combine the light corn syrup, coffee, and butter in a saucepan. Cook, stirring, until the mixture begins to boil. Remove from the heat and add the broken up chocolate. Stir until the chocolate has completely melted. Set aside.

When the Éclairs have cooled, slit each one at the side and fill with Pastry Cream or whipped cream. Spread the chocolate glaze over the Éclairs with a knife or rubber spatula. Refrigerate them if they are not being served immediately. Remove the Éclairs to room temperature 30 minutes before serving.

Makes about 2 dozen.

PROFITEROLES WITH CHOCOLATE SAUCE

1 recipe BASIC CREAM PUFFS
1 egg, beaten
Vanilla ice cream
4 ounces semisweet chocolate,
  broken up
1 cup cold coffee

1 teaspoon cornstarch
2 egg yolks
½ cup cream
1 tablespoon butter
1 tablespoon brandy

Bake Basic Cream Puffs, making ¾-inch mounds on the baking sheet and brushing with beaten egg before baking. With a spoon, make the same number of small ice cream balls as you have puffs, using vanilla ice cream. Freeze the ice cream balls on a plate or flat plastic tray until serving time.

Melt the broken-up chocolate with ¾ cup of the cold coffee in the top of a double boiler set over hot water, stirring until the chocolate has completely melted. Dissolve the cornstarch in the remaining ¼ cup cold coffee and add to the chocolate mixture, stirring constantly. Beat the egg yolks lightly with the cream and add to the chocolate mixture along with the butter, stirring until the butter melts and the mixture thickens slightly and coats a metal spoon. Remove from the heat and stir in the brandy. Leave the top of the double boiler over hot water while assembling the dessert.

Slit the puffs in half, horizontally, and place a frozen ice cream ball in each. Press lightly to seal in the ice cream as much as possible.

Arrange the filled puffs in a shallow glass bowl or other serving dish, or place 3 puffs in each individual dessert glass or on dessert plates. Pour the hot chocolate sauce over the cream puffs and serve immediately.

Makes about 8 servings.

PARIS BREST

1 recipe BASIC CREAM PUFFS
1 egg, beaten
¼ cup thinly sliced almonds
Sifted confectioners' sugar
½ cup slivered blanched almonds

½ cup sugar
3 tablespoons water
⅛ teaspoon cream of tartar
1 recipe VANILLA BUTTER
   CREAM

Prepare the cream-puff paste. Preheat the oven at 450°. Lightly grease and flour a baking sheet. With an 8-inch cake pan, mark a circle on the baking sheet. Spoon the cream-puff paste into a ring or crown shape about 2 inches wide, using the circle as a guide for the outside edge. Smooth the paste with a rubber spatula. Brush with the beaten egg and sprinkle all over with the thinly sliced almonds. Bake for 10 to 15 minutes until the crown begins to puff. Lower the heat to 350° and continue baking 15 minutes longer. With a sharp-tined fork, pierce the sides of the crown near the bottom in several places to allow steam to escape, and bake for 10 to 15 minutes more. Cool on a wire rack. Dust with confectioners' sugar. With a sharp knife, slit the crown into two layers, horizontally.

Prepare a praline by spreading out the slivered blanched almonds on a baking sheet and toasting them in a moderate oven for 5 to 7 minutes until they are lightly browned. Watch carefully to see that the nuts do not scorch, and turn them over once during toasting. In a saucepan, combine the sugar, water, and cream of tartar. Heat, stirring constantly, until the mixture comes to a boil and the sugar has completely dissolved. Stir in the toasted almonds and cook over medium heat without stirring until the mixture is golden-brown in color. Pour the mixture out onto a piece of buttered aluminum foil and allow it to cool. Break up the praline and crush it with a rolling pin or with a mortar and pestle or in an electric blender or food processor until the mixture is reduced to a powder. Stir ¼ cup of the powder into the Vanilla Butter Cream and spread over the bottom layer of the crown, or, if desired, pipe the cream from a pastry bag fitted with a large star tip. Replace the top layer of the crown, and place the dessert on a serving dish.

Makes 8 servings.

SWANS

1 recipe BASIC CREAM PUFFS	1½ cups heavy cream
Fresh strawberries or canned	1 tablespoon sugar
sweet cherries or pineapple	1 teaspoon vanilla extract
bits, drained	

Preheat the oven at 400°. Prepare the cream-puff paste. Put one-fourth of the paste in a pastry bag fitted with a plain round tip, and on an ungreased baking sheet pipe out 24 sections, each resembling a swan's neck and head. These will look like question marks, small at the top and leaning heavily to the left at the bottom before tapering off to the right. When forming them, force more of the filling out at the top, so that the heads will be larger than the necks, and make the entire head and neck about 2½ to 3 inches long. Bake about 7 to 10 minutes and cool on a wire rack.

Using a larger plain round tip, pipe out on ungreased baking sheets the balance of the cream-puff paste in 3- to 3½-inch lengths to form bodies that taper at the ends to resemble tails. Bake about 15 to 20 minutes until puffed and golden. Cool on a wire rack. When cooled cut away about three-fourths of the top of the puffs in an oval shape. Cut each oval in half lengthwise, to form two wings. Remove any moist dough from the inside of each puff shell and insert a spoonful of strawberries, cherries, or pineapple.

Whip the heavy cream until stiff, and add the sugar and vanilla extract. Place the whipped cream in a pastry bag fitted with a large star tip, and pipe the whipped cream onto each swan in a layer about 1-inch thick. Place the neck on the front of each swan, pushing it into the whipped cream. Crisscross the wings over the swan's back.

Makes about 24.

GATEAU SAINT HONORE

For the base and trim:
1 recipe TART PASTRY
1 recipe BASIC CREAM PUFFS
1 egg, beaten
1 cup heavy cream
1 tablespoon sugar
1 teaspoon vanilla extract

For the caramel:
⅔ cup water
2 cups sugar
½ teaspoon cream of tartar

For the filling and garnishing:
5 egg yolks
¾ cup sugar
½ cup sifted flour
2 cups boiling milk
1 tablespoon butter
2 teaspoons vanilla extract
1 envelope plain gelatin
2 tablespoons cold water
5 egg whites
3 tablespoons sugar
Candied red cherries and green cherries

For the base and trim: Prepare the Tart Pastry and roll it out about ¼-inch thick on a floured board. Using a round 9-inch cake pan as a guide, cut a 9-inch circle from the pastry with a small, sharp knife. Drape the circle over the rolling pin and transfer it to an ungreased baking sheet. Refrigerate.

Preheat the oven at 400°. Prepare the Basic Cream Puff paste and place about two-thirds of the paste in a pastry bag fitted with a large plain tip. Remove the Tart Pastry circle from the refrigerator and pipe a cream-puff paste rim around the edge of the circle, about ¾-inch wide and about 1-inch high. Brush the rim with the beaten egg. Bake about 25 to 30 minutes until the rim is puffed and the entire pastry is browned. Remove from the oven and cool.

Spoon the remaining cream-puff paste onto an ungreased baking sheet in mounds about ¾ inches in diameter, and bake about 15 minutes until puffed and golden. Cool on a wire rack. Whip the heavy cream until stiff. Add the sugar and vanilla extract. Put some of the whipped cream in a pastry bag fitted with a plain tip, and pipe it into the centers of the cream puffs. Refrigerate the filled puffs as well as the remaining whipped cream.

For the caramel: Combine the water, sugar, and cream of tartar in a small, heavy saucepan. Bring to a boil stirring, and lower the heat to moderate. Continue cooking without stirring until the mixture is slightly thickened and amber in color. Remove the filled cream puffs from the refrigerator. With a fork, stab one puff at a time and dip each one quickly into the caramel. Reserving one dipped puff, arrange the others on top of the pastry rim, using the caramel to aid in holding the puffs in place. Use only forks, spoons, or tongs for this operation because your fingers can easily be burned by the caramel. Set the *gâteau* on a serving plate and refrigerate.

For the filling: Beat the egg yolks lightly with an electric beater. Gradually beat in ¾ cup of sugar, and continue beating for several minutes until the mixture forms a slowly dissolving ribbon when the beater is lifted. Beat in the flour. Gradually add the boiling milk, beating constantly. Transfer the mixture to a nonaluminum saucepan and cook over moderate heat, stirring constantly with a wire whisk. When the mixture boils, lower the heat and continue cooking several minutes longer, stirring vigorously with the whisk until the mixture becomes very thick. Make sure the whisk reaches all parts of the pan bottom and that the custard does not scorch. Remove from the heat and stir in the butter and vanilla extract, stirring until the butter has melted and is well blended.

Meanwhile, soften the gelatin in the cold water. Add to the custard and stir until the gelatin has completely dissolved. Transfer the mixture to a bowl. Beat the egg whites until stiff peaks form. Add 3 tablespoons sugar gradually, continuing to beat until the mixture is thick and glossy. Fold the egg whites into the custard mixture. Cover and chill for 30 minutes. Spoon the filling into the shell and smooth the top with a spatula. Chill well.

Garnishing: With the reserved whipped cream, pipe out rosettes or other decorations between the cream puffs. Pipe a large rosette in the center and set the reserved cream puff on it. Continue decorating with the whipped cream and candied red and green cherries.

Makes 10 to 12 servings.

CREAM PUFF FRITTERS

For the fritters:
1 recipe BASIC CREAM PUFFS
1 tablespoon rum
Oil or fat for frying
Sifted confectioners' sugar

For the custard sauce:
4 egg yolks
¼ cup sugar
1 teaspoon cornstarch
¾ cup milk
1 cup heavy cream
2 tablespoons rum

For the fritters: Prepare the Basic Cream Puff paste, adding the rum with the last egg added. In a deep fryer, heat the oil or fat to 360°. Drop the paste by tablespoons into the hot fat, and fry about 12 minutes until the fritters are golden-brown and puffed. If the fritters do not turn over during frying, turn them with a skimmer or slotted spoon so that the sides brown evenly. Drain on paper towels. Sprinkle with confectioners' sugar. Serve with a dessert bowl of the following sauce.

For the custard sauce (crème anglaise): Beat the egg yolks until thick. Gradually add the sugar, and continue beating until the mixture is thick and pale and forms a slowly dissolving ribbon when the beater is lifted. Add the cornstarch and beat again. Scald the milk and cream together in the top of a double boiler. Add to the egg yolk mixture very gradually, beating constantly. Turn the mixture into the top of a double boiler and cook over simmering water, stirring constantly, until the mixture coats a metal spoon. Remove from the heat and stir in the rum. Transfer to a serving bowl and serve immediately.

Makes about 8 servings.

Note: Any sauce not used can be stored in a covered glass jar in the refrigerator for use within a few days, and may be served cold.

BASIC PUFF PASTRY

2¾ cups unsifted flour	¼ cup corn oil
¾ cup unsifted cake flour	1 cup ice water
1½ teaspoons salt	3 sticks (1½ cups) sweet butter

In a bowl, mix together the flour, cake flour, and salt with a rubber spatula. Set aside ½ cup of this mixture. Stir the corn oil into the remaining flour mixture and mix well with the rubber spatula. Sprinkle the ice water over the flour and mix well with the spatula, pressing the mixture against the sides of the bowl to combine the mixture. Complete the mixing with the cupped fingers of one hand. Remove the dough to a board or a marble slab and quickly press it into a cushion-shaped ball. The texture will not be smooth. Sprinkle the ball lightly with flour, wrap it in waxed paper, and place it in a plastic bag. Refrigerate for 1 hour.

Unwrap the sticks of butter and place them together on a board. With a rolling pin, beat the butter from one end to the other until it has softened. With the heel of your hand, press the butter out, down, and away from you across the board. Continue smearing out the butter, scraping it up with a pastry scraper, and gradually working in the ½ cup of reserved flour mixture. Form the mass of butter and flour into a flat, rectangular cake, measuring about 11x7 inches.

Remove the pastry from the refrigerator, flour it lightly, place it on a board, and with floured hands push and pat it into a rectangle measuring about 18x8 inches. Using a pastry scraper to loosen the butter from the board, pick up the rectangle of butter and place it on two-thirds of the pastry, allowing a ½-inch border on three sides. The third of the pastry nearest the front of the board will have no butter on it. Fold the bottom third of the pastry up. Fold the top third of the pastry, which contains half the butter, down to cover the first half, just as you would fold a business letter. Give the pastry a quarter turn counterclockwise, so that the open side of the flap is to your right.

With a rolling pin, roll out the dough firmly and evenly to make a rectangle, again measuring about 18x8 inches. Fold the top edge of the pastry down, and the bottom edge of the pastry up, so that they almost meet in the center. Then fold the bottom half up again, so that the pastry is closed like the pages of a book. This rolling, folding, and turning is called a "turn." You may wish to make two depressions in the dough with the balls of your fingers to show that two turns have been made. (The dough may be frozen at this point.) Wrap the pastry in waxed paper, place it in a plastic bag, and refrigerate it on a plate or marble slab from 1 hour to overnight.

Unwrap the dough and flour it lightly. If it is quite hard, beat it firmly with a rolling pin, but make sure to maintain its rectangular shape. Roll it out into an 18x8-inch rectangle. Fold the bottom third of the pastry up. Fold the top third down to cover the first half, just as you did in the beginning. Give the pastry a quarter turn counterclockwise, so that the open side of the flap is to your right. This is called the "third turn." Roll it into a rectangle measuring 18x8-inches. Fold as before for the fourth turn. Make four depressions in the dough with the balls of your fingers. Wrap the dough in waxed paper, place it in a plastic bag, place the bag on a plate or marble slab and refrigerate from 2 hours to overnight. (The dough may be frozen at this point also.)

Roll out as directed in individual recipes.

THOUSAND LEAVES CAKE

½ recipe BASIC PUFF PASTRY
Sugar
Sweetened whipped cream

1 teaspoon vanilla extract or 1
tablespoon any fruit liqueur,
or 1 ten-ounce box frozen
strawberries, thawed and
drained
Sifted confectioners' sugar

Roll out the pastry ⅛-inch thick on a very lightly floured board. With a sharp knife, cut 3 rectangles measuring about 4x12-inches. Transfer to ungreased baking sheets. Chill for 30 minutes.

Preheat the oven at 450°. Remove the pastry from the refrigerator and prick all over with the tines of a fork. Sprinkle with sugar. Bake for 5 to 10 minutes until it is puffed and light brown in color. Reduce the oven temperature to 350° and continue baking 10 to 15 minutes longer until it is dry. Cool on a wire rack.

Flavor the whipped cream with the vanilla extract or fruit liqueur, or fold into it thawed and drained strawberries which have been forced through a sieve or put through an electric blender or food processor. Spread 2 pastry layers with this mixture and stack them up, with the remaining plain layer on top. Dust with confectioners' sugar. Set on a serving plate. To serve, slice the cake crosswise with a very sharp knife —ideally, one with a serrated blade.

Makes 6 servings.

NAPOLEONS

½ recipe BASIC PUFF PASTRY
5 egg yolks
¾ cup sugar
½ cup sifted flour
2 cups boiling milk
1 tablespoon butter
2 teaspoons vanilla extract
2 tablespoons light corn syrup

1 tablespoon plus 1½ teaspoons
strong coffee
1 tablespoon plus 1 teaspoon
butter
3 ounces semisweet chocolate,
broken into very small pieces
ROYAL ICING

Roll out the pastry thin enough to cut three 4x12-inch rectangles with a sharp knife. Transfer to ungreased baking sheets. Prick all over closely with the tines of a fork. Chill for 1 hour.

Preheat the oven at 450°. Bake the pastry for 5 to 10 minutes until it is puffed and light-brown in color. Reduce the oven temperature to 350° and continue baking 10 to 15 minutes longer until it is dry. Cool on a wire rack.

Prepare a custard filling by beating the egg yolks with an electric beater. Add the sugar gradually, and continue beating until the mixture forms a slowly dissolving ribbon when the beater is lifted. Beat in the flour. Gradually add the boiling milk, beating constantly. Transfer the mixture to a nonaluminum saucepan and cook over moderate heat, stirring constantly with a wire whisk. When the mixture boils, lower the heat and continue cooking several minutes longer, stirring vigorously with the wire whisk until the mixture becomes very thick. Make sure the whisk reaches all parts of the pan bottom and that the custard does not scorch. Remove from the heat and stir in the butter and vanilla extract. Pour the custard into a bowl and cool. Chill.

Spread one of the pastry rectangles with a layer of the custard filling about ¼-inch thick. Cut the second pastry rectangle into strips 2 inches wide. (You will have 6 strips, each measuring 2x4-inches.) Lay these strips on the custard-covered rectangle, and slice in between them evenly. Spread another layer of custard gently on the top of each Napoleon.

Prepare a chocolate glaze by combining the light corn syrup, coffee, and 1 tablespoon plus 1 teaspoon butter in a small saucepan. Cook, stirring, until the mixture begins to boil. Remove from the heat and add the broken-up chocolate. Stir until the chocolate has completely melted. Set aside.

Spread the Royal Icing on the third pastry rectangle. Put the chocolate glaze in a decorating tube fitted with a small plain tip, or put it in a paper cone with a small hole cut in the end. Squeeze out lines of chocolate about ¾ inch apart (like lines on a page) from the top to the bottom of the rectangle that is covered with Royal Icing. Draw the back of a knife blade straight through the chocolate lines from one end of the pastry to the other in the center. Then draw the knife blade in the opposite direction midway between the center line and the edge of the pastry on either side. This will pull the chocolate glaze into a design. Allow to set. Cut the glazed rectangle into 6 equal parts, as before, and set them on the partially assembled Napoleons. Chill 1 hour, and remove from the refrigerator 30 minutes before serving.

Makes 6 servings.

GATEAU PITHIVIERS

¼ cup butter
4 ounces almond paste
¼ cup sugar
1 egg yolk

1 tablespoon rum
1 recipe BASIC PUFF PASTRY
1 egg, lightly beaten

Cream the butter and work in the almond paste. Add the sugar gradually and beat until fluffy. Add the egg yolk and mix well. Add the rum and mix well. Cover and refrigerate for 1 hour. Place the mixture on a sheet of waxed paper or plastic wrap and form it into a flat circle with a diameter of 6½ inches. Wrap it all around with waxed paper or plastic wrap and refrigerate until you are ready to bake the *gâteau.*

Prepare the pastry and roll it out a little less than ¼-inch thick. Using a round 8-inch cake pan as a guide, cut two 8-inch circles out of the dough with a sharp knife. Drape 1 circle over the rolling pin and transfer it to a moistened baking sheet. Remove the almond mixture from the refrigerator, unwrap it, and set it on the circle on the baking sheet. Gently spread the almond mixture to within ¾ inch from the edge of the pastry. Moisten the edges of the pastry all around. Place the second pastry circle on top and press down firmly all around with your thumbs. Refrigerate for 45 minutes.

Preheat the oven at 450°. Brush the pastry with the lightly beaten egg. Allow the pastry to sit for 3 minutes. With a small, sharp knife, make curving lines radiating from the center of the pastry to the edge like a pinwheel, making about 18 lines. Make sure the knife point does not pierce all the way through the pastry. Make a small hole in the very center. Bake for 15 minutes. Reduce the heat to 375° and bake 25 to 30 minutes longer. Cover with aluminum foil if it begins to brown too much. Cool on a wire rack.

Makes 8 servings.

CREAM HORNS

½ recipe BASIC PUFF PASTRY
1 cup heavy cream
1 or 2 tablespoons sugar to taste

1 teaspoon vanilla extract or
1 tablespoon liqueur

Preheat the oven at 450°. Roll out the pastry ⅛-inch thick on a very lightly floured board. Cut into strips ¾-inch wide. Working with one strip at a time, moisten one long edge of the pastry with water. Place the tip of a cream horn mold under one end of the pastry, secure the end by pinching together with the fingers, and roll the pastry strip around the cream horn mold by turning the mold and allowing the pastry to overlap itself ⅛ to ¼ inch until the mold is covered. Press the pastry in at the end to seal it. Repeat the procedure until all Cream Horns are formed. Roll the Cream Horns in sugar on all sides except the bottom, or seam side. Set them on an ungreased baking sheet, seam side down, and place in the oven. Reduce the heat to 350° after 5 minutes. Bake 5 to 10 minutes longer, watching carefully to be sure that the horns do not burn. Remove the baking sheet from the oven, and the horns will slip away from the molds easily. Cool them on a wire rack.

Whip the heavy cream until stiff, and sweeten with sugar to taste. Add the vanilla extract or any preferred liqueur. Spoon the whipped cream into the cooled Cream Horns, or pipe it in with a pastry bag fitted with a large plain tip. If the Cream Horns are not served immediately, refrigerate them until serving time.

Makes about 1½ dozen.

PALM LEAVES

½ **recipe** BASIC PUFF PASTRY   **Sugar**

Roll out the pastry on a sugared board until it is ¼-inch thick and 10 inches wide. Sprinkle with sugar. Working with the long sides, roll each side halfway across the pastry until they meet at the center, forming a double roll. Press together slightly. Cut crosswise into ⅓-inch-thick slices and place the slices on greased baking sheets. Chill for 30 minutes.

Preheat the oven at 450°. Sprinkle the Palm Leaves with sugar, and bake them 5 to 10 minutes. Reduce the heat to 350°. Turn the Palm Leaves over and bake 10 minutes longer until golden. Cool on a wire rack.

Makes about 2 dozen.

CHAPTER 15

The Magic of Meringues

Trifles light as air . . .
—William Shakespeare, Othello

When meringues were first served to Queen Elizabeth I, she was so smitten with them that she kissed the cloth on which the little pastries sat, and named them "kisses." Marie Antoinette, equally charmed by meringues, is said to have gone into the royal kitchens at the Petit Trianon and whipped up luxuriously rich and fancy meringue cakes with her own well-manicured hands. Royalty and commoners alike have enjoyed these near-confections for centuries, and we probably owe the creation of today's most commonly used meringue mixture, Swiss meringue, to Gasparini, an early-eighteenth-century Swiss pastry chef.

Swiss meringue, or hard meringue, is the recipe used for Meringue Shells in this chapter, and it differs from soft meringue used on desserts such as lemon meringue pies in several ways. It contains a good deal more sugar, requires more beating, is much firmer in texture, is baked at a low temperature for a long time, and should never be allowed to brown. Swiss meringue can either be piped onto a baking sheet from a pastry bag or dropped onto the sheet and shaped with a spoon as it was done before the nineteenth-century invention of the pastry bag. Line the baking sheet you use with that irreplaceable twentieth-century invention, aluminum foil, sprinkle it all over with cornstarch before you form the meringues, and you'll find them easy to remove after baking. Meringues baked on paper-lined, waxed-paper-lined, or buttered and floured baking sheets all tend to stick.

Italian meringue. used as a frosting for cakes, topping for tarts, or base for sherbets, is made by adding hot sugar syrup to beaten egg whites, and requires no baking, since the egg whites are cooked when the boiling syrup is poured over them. You can brown Italian meringue lightly in the oven if you wish, but it isn't necessary. Another use for this meringue mixture is to fold it into whipped cream and use it as a filling for cream puffs, Napoleons, or other pastries that need firm, whipped-cream-type fillings; or you can freeze the mixture in a covered container and use it exactly as you would ice cream.

Whether you're making Italian, Swiss or other meringues, do use an electric beater if you can. If you use a wire whisk or rotary beater to beat the egg whites and add sugar to them, your arm can wear out in no time, and you can't stop to rest. Meringues, by the way, do not behave nicely in humid weather, so avoid making them on rainy or damp days if you would avoid disappointment.

In addition to the recipes in this chapter, other meringue recipes in this book are:

Angel Pie
Baked Alaska
Double Orange Meringue
Lemon Meringue Pie
Midnight Sun Baked Alaska

MERINGUE SHELLS

5 egg whites
¼ teaspoon cream of tartar
Pinch of salt
1 cup superfine sugar*

1 teaspoon vanilla extract or
  1 teaspoon rosewater
Cornstarch

Preheat the oven at 200°. Beat the egg whites with an electric beater until foamy. Add the cream of tartar and salt, and continue beating until soft peaks form. Add the sugar, a small spoonful at a time, beating after each addition, until the mixture is very thick and shiny. Add the vanilla extract or rosewater.

Line a baking sheet with aluminum foil, shiny side down. Sift a thin layer of cornstarch all over the foil. Using a round cookie cutter or drinking glass 3 to 3½ inches in diameter as a guide, mark circles on the cornstarch about 1½ inches apart. Fill a pastry bag fitted with a star tip with the meringue. Pipe the meringue onto the circles, filling in the

* VANILLA SUGAR may be used instead, in which case omit the vanilla extract.

round areas completely. Then build up a wall, 2 layers high, on the edge of each circle to make a nestlike form.

Bake 1½ to 2 hours, watching carefully toward the end of the baking time to be sure the meringues do not brown. Remove them from the baking sheet with a spatula peeling the foil from any meringue that sticks. Cool on a wire rack.

Makes 10 to 12.

Note: Meringue Shells may be made a day or two ahead, but they must be stored in an absolutely airtight tin box in a cool, dry place. They may be filled with fruit, ice cream, sherbet, water ice, frozen dessert, pastry cream, or any desired filling, and topped with a dessert sauce and/or a candied flower or other garnish if desired.

NUTTED MERINGUE SHELLS

5 egg whites
¼ teaspoon cream of tartar
Pinch of salt
1 cup superfine sugar

½ teaspoon almond extract
Pistachios, filberts, pecans, almonds, or Macadamia nuts, finely chopped

Preheat the oven at 200°. Beat the egg whites with an electric beater until foamy. Add the cream of tartar and salt and continue beating until soft peaks form. Add the sugar, a small spoonful at a time, beating after each addition until the mixture is thick and glossy. Add the almond extract and beat again.

Line a baking sheet with aluminum foil, shiny side down. With a spoon, form mounds about 3 inches in diameter (or any size desired), placing them about 1½ inches apart. Make a hollow in the center of each meringue to make nestlike forms. Sprinkle all over with the finely chopped nuts. Bake for 1½ to 2 hours until the meringues are firm. Remove the foil with the meringues to a wire rack and cool. When cool, peel the meringues from the foil.

Makes about 1 dozen.

MERINGUES GLACES

1 recipe MERINGUE SHELLS or
   NUTTED MERINGUE SHELLS
Ice cream

Sweetened whipped cream or a
dessert sauce

Make ice cream balls with a spoon or ice cream scoop, and freeze them on a tray until serving time. To serve, place an ice cream ball gently on each meringue shell. Decorate with sweetened whipped cream or a dessert sauce. Some attractive flavor combinations for shells, ice creams, and sauces (consult the index for recipes) follow.

Plain Meringue Shells

Strawberry Ice Cream and Strawberry Sauce
Ginger Ice Cream and Whipped Cream Topped with Crystallized Lilac
Melon Sherbet and Rum Sauce
Walnut Bisque and Chocolate Sauce
English Toffee Ice Cream and Whipped Cream dusted with Praline Powder
Fig Ice Cream and Whipped Cream topped with Crystallized Violet

Nutted Meringue Shells: Sprinkle shells before baking with finely chopped nuts

Almonds: Almond Ice Milk and Cassis Sauce
Pistachios: Pistachio Crème Glacé and Mocha Sauce
Hazelnuts: Coffee Ice Cream and Chocolate Sauce
Macadamia Nuts: Mango Ice Cream and Whipped Cream Topped with Crystallized Mint Leaf
Pecans: Pumpkin Parfait and Brandy Sauce

LIME CREAM MERINGUES

1 recipe NUTTED MERINGUE
   SHELLS
Macadamia nuts, chopped
2 egg yolks
3 tablespoons sugar

2 tablespoons lime juice
1 drop green pure vegetable
   coloring for food
1 cup heavy cream

Make the Nutted Meringue Shells, using the Macadamia nuts to sprinkle over the shells before baking.

Beat the egg yolks until thick in the top of a double boiler off heat. Add the sugar gradually, and continue beating until the mixture is thick and pale in color. Beat in the lime juice and food coloring. Place over hot water and cook, stirring, until the mixture thickens. Remove from the heat and cool for 10 minutes.

Whip the heavy cream until stiff. Stir about one-fourth of the whipped cream into the lime mixture. Then fold the balance of the whipped cream into the lime mixture. Chill well.

To serve, spoon into 8 of the Nutted Meringue Shells.

Makes 8 servings.

RASPBERRY CREAM MERINGUES

1 recipe MERINGUE SHELLS	¼ cup sugar
1 ten-ounce package frozen sweetened raspberries, thawed	Pinch of salt
	1 cup heavy cream
4 egg yolks	½ teaspoon vanilla extract

Puree the raspberries in an electric blender or food processor. Strain through a fine sieve to remove the seeds.

In the top of a double boiler off heat, beat the egg yolks well. Add the raspberry puree and beat thoroughly. Stir in the sugar and salt. Set over simmering water and cook over moderate heat, stirring, until the mixture thickens. Remove from the heat, cover, and cool to room temperature.

Whip the heavy cream until stiff, and add the vanilla extract. Fold into the raspberry mixture. Chill thoroughly, covered. Spoon into the Meringue Shells and serve.

Makes 10 to 12 servings.

MIROIRS

For the meringues:
5 egg whites
¼ teaspoon cream of tartar
Pinch of salt
1 cup superfine sugar
½ teaspoon almond extract
Almond paste

For the frosting:
1 cup plus 6 tablespoons sugar
¼ teaspoon cream of tartar
Pinch of salt
¾ cup water
2 cups sifted confectioners' sugar
  (approximately)
1 tablespoon rum

For the meringues: Preheat the oven at 200°. Beat the egg whites with an electric beater until foamy. Add the cream of tartar and salt, and continue beating until soft peaks form. Add the sugar, a spoonful at a time, beating after each addition, until the mixture is thick and glossy. Add the almond extract and beat again.

Line a baking sheet with aluminum foil, shiny side down. With a pastry bag fitted with a large plain tip, pipe small mounds about 1¾ inches in diameter onto the foil. With the tip of a spoon, make a small indentation in the top of each meringue. Insert a small piece of almond paste in each indentation. Bake for 1½ to 2 hours until the meringues are firm. Remove the foil containing the meringues to a wire rack and cool. Peel the meringues from the foil.

For the frosting: Combine the sugar, cream of tartar, salt, and water in a heavy saucepan. Cook over low heat, stirring, until the sugar has dissolved. Raise the heat, cover, and cook to the soft-ball stage, about 238°. Remove from the heat, uncover, and cool to 110°, or until you can place your hand comfortably on the bottom of the pan. Gradually beat in enough confectioners' sugar until the mixture is firm enough to pour, but not stiff. Stir in the rum. Place the meringues on a wire rack and set over a platter. Pour the frosting over them and allow it to drip onto the platter, where you can scoop it up and reuse it. Allow the frosting to set.

Makes about 3 dozen.

STRAWBERRY MERINGUE CAKE

2 cups strawberries
1½ tablespoons sugar
Double recipe MERINGUE
  SHELLS mixture

Cornstarch
2 cups heavy cream
1 tablespoon strawberry liqueur
  or raspberry liqueur

Reserving 3 whole strawberries for decorating the top of the cake, slice the balance and combine them with the sugar. Cover and refrigerate.

Preheat the oven at 200°. Prepare the meringue mixture. Line 2 baking sheets with aluminum foil, shiny side down. Sift a thin layer of cornstarch over the foil. Using a round 8-inch cake pan as a guide, mark four 8-inch circles on the baking sheets. With a spoon, fill in the circles with meringue, smoothing it with a rubber spatula. Bake for 1½ to 2 hours until the meringues are dry. Remove the meringues on the foil to a wire rack and cool. Peel them from the foil.

Whip the heavy cream until stiff, and fold in the liqueur. Set aside one-fourth of this mixture. Into the balance of the mixture, fold the chilled, sliced strawberry mixture. Place a meringue layer on a serving plate and cover it with one-third of the strawberry mixture. Repeat with the remaining layers. Spread the reserved whipped cream over the top layer. Decorate with the 3 reserved whole strawberries.

Makes 8 servings.

CHESTNUT MERINGUE CAKE

1 recipe MERINGUE SHELLS
  mixture
Cornstarch
1½ cups heavy cream
2 tablespoons sugar

½ cup sweetened chestnut spread
  (crème de marrons)
2 tablespoons rum
1 tablespoon sugar
Crystallized violets or other
  crystallized flowers

Preheat the oven at 200°. Prepare the meringue mixture. Line a baking sheet with aluminum foil, shiny side down. Sift a thin layer of cornstarch over the foil. Using a round 8-inch cake pan as a guide, mark an 8-inch circle on the baking sheet. Spoon some of the meringue mixture into the circle and smooth with a rubber spatula. Spoon the balance of the meringue around the circle to build up a rim about 2 inches high.

Bake for 1½ to 2 hours until the meringue is dry. Remove the meringue with the foil to a wire rack and allow it to cool. Peel off the foil and set the meringue on a serving plate.

Whip 1 cup of the heavy cream until stiff. Add 2 tablespoons sugar and beat again. Combine the chestnut spread with the rum. Fold the whipped cream into the chestnut mixture, one-half at a time, and spoon the mixture into the center of the meringue shell. Chill for several hours.

To serve, whip the remaining ½ cup heavy cream until stiff. Add 1 tablespoon sugar and beat again. Using a pastry bag fitted with a star tip, pipe out the whipped cream into rosettes on the meringue cake. Place a crystallized violet or other crystallized flower on each rosette.

Makes 8 servings.

MERINGUE BUTTER CREAM CAKE

For the layers:
Cornstarch
1 cup chopped almonds
¼ cup sugar
2 teaspoons cornstarch
5 egg whites
¼ teaspoon cream of tartar
Pinch of salt
¾ cup superfine sugar
½ teaspoon vanilla extract
½ teaspoon almond extract

For the filling:
2 ounces baking chocolate, chopped, or 2 ounces bittersweet chocolate, broken up
½ cup sugar
Generous pinch of cream of tartar
2 tablespoons water
2 egg yolks
½ cup butter
1½ teaspoons vanilla extract
Sifted confectioners' sugar

For the layers: Line a baking sheet with aluminum foil, shiny side down. Sift a thin layer of cornstarch over the foil. Using a round 8-inch cake pan as a guide, make two 8-inch circles on the baking sheet, 1 or 2 inches apart.

Preheat the oven at 250°. Blend the chopped almonds and ¼ cup sugar in an electric blender or food processor until the almonds are completely pulverized. Empty into a small bowl. Add 2 teaspoons cornstarch and mix with the fingertips, discarding any unground pieces of almond that may remain. Beat the egg whites with an electric beater until foamy. Add the cream of tartar and salt, and continue beating until soft peaks form. Add the superfine sugar, a small spoonful at a time, beating after each addition, until the mixture is thick and glossy. Fold in the vanilla extract and almond extract. Fold the pulverized almond mixture into the egg white mixture, about one-fourth at a time. Spoon half the mixture into a pastry bag fitted with a large plain tip. Pipe the meringue onto one circle on the baking sheet, starting at the outside of the circle and working your way circularly toward the center, using half the meringue. Repeat with the remaining meringue to make the second circle. Smooth out the ridges with a rubber spatula. Bake for 30 to 40 minutes until firm. Remove the foil and meringue to a wire rack and cool. Peel off the foil.

For the filling: Melt the chocolate in the top of a double boiler over hot water, stirring. Set it aside to cool. Combine the sugar, cream of tartar, and water in a small saucepan. Bring to a boil over medium heat, stirring constantly until the sugar has dissolved. Raise the heat and cook, without stirring, until the mixture spins a long thread (244° on a candy thermometer). Remove from the heat and set aside.

Beat the egg yolks with an electric beater until they are thick and pale in color. Beat in the sugar syrup gradually. Beat in the butter, 1 tablespoon at a time until it is well blended. Beat in the vanilla extract and the melted chocolate. Chill the mixture until it stiffens a little, and beat it with a wooden spoon. Chill it again until the mixture is of a spreading consistency.

To assemble: Place one meringue layer on a serving plate. Place the filling mixture in a pastry bag fitted with a large star tip. Pipe out a thick layer of filling to cover the entire meringue layer. Place the second meringue layer over the butter cream filling. Pipe an attractive design all around the cake between the two layers. Dust the top of the cake heavily with confectioners' sugar. Chill for several hours before serving.

Makes 6 servings.

FROZEN PORT MERINGUE WITH APRICOT SAUCE

For the mold:
1 cup heavy cream
⅓ cup sugar
2 tablespoons Port wine
6 meringue shells, broken into small pieces (about 4 cups)

For the sauce:
1 one-pound can peeled apricots, drained, reserving juice
⅓ cup sugar
Juice and grated zest of ½ lemon

For the mold: Whip the heavy cream until stiff. Add the sugar and mix well. Fold in the Port, 1 tablespoon at a time. Fold in the meringue pieces. Pour the mixture into a lightly oiled 4-cup plain mold. Cover with aluminum foil and freeze for 8 hours or overnight.

For the sauce: Drain the syrup from the apricots into a saucepan. Add the sugar and cook, stirring, until the sugar has dissolved. Boil the syrup down rapidly until thick. Cut the apricots into small dice, discarding the pits. Add them to the syrup along with the lemon juice and zest. Simmer for 5 minutes. Remove from the heat and allow to cool.

To serve, unmold the dessert onto a serving plate. Serve with the Apricot Sauce, spooning it over each portion.

Makes 6 servings.

SNOW EGGS

4 egg yolks
1¼ cups sugar
Pinch of salt

2½ cups milk
1 two-inch piece vanilla bean*
4 egg whites

Beat the egg yolks lightly. Add ¼ cup of the sugar and the salt, and beat again. Set the mixture aside. In a skillet, slowly heat the milk with the vanilla bean. Adjust the temperature so that the surface of the milk barely shimmers. Beat the egg whites until soft peaks form. Add ½ cup

---

* If the vanilla bean is unavailable, use 2 teaspoons vanilla extract, adding it at the point when the milk is combined with the egg yolk mixture.

of the sugar, 1 spoonful at a time, beating after each addition, until the mixture is thick and glossy.

Using 2 tablespoons, scoop out the meringue and form it as nearly as possible into egg shapes, dropping them into the milk to poach. Poach about 3 at a time, and allow them to poach for 2 to 2½ minutes, turning them once during the cooking time. Drain on paper towels and continue until all the meringue has been used.

Strain the milk through a fine strainer into the egg yolk mixture, mixing briskly all the while. Transfer the mixture to a saucepan and cook over medium heat, stirring constantly, until the mixture begins to thicken and coats a metal spoon. Pour it into a large, shallow serving bowl. Arrange the meringues on top and chill well.

To serve, melt the remaining ½ cup sugar in a heavy saucepan and allow it to become amber in color. With a fork, drizzle it over the meringue eggs and serve immediately.

Makes 6 servings.

CHAPTER 16

The Tart Family

The Queen of Hearts
She made some tarts,
All on a summer's day.

—*nursery rhyme*

Looking over old Roman menus reveals that tarts and pies have been made for over two thousand years. The apricot pastries were probably made of flour, eggs, lard (which had better keeping qualities than butter), and honey, and they were usually filled with peculiar concoctions of meat or birds. During the Middle Ages, just as the nursery rhyme says, "four-and-twenty blackbirds" *were* baked in pies. Creations of this sort were made with singing or chattering birds, and the ones made with mag(pies) are thought to have given the name "pies" to this family of desserts. Actually the pies were not baked with the birds in them, but live birds were massed under the pastry after baking so that when the pie was cut open the flock would fly out to surprise unsuspecting guests.

Some dessert tarts, not unlike those we make today, were made during medieval times, and one such recipe for custard tarts seems to have undergone only minor changes during the passage of six centuries, the original version having contained the undessertlike flavoring of saffron. Most tarts and pies made today are for dessert, and there are many different kinds of pastries and fillings to choose from.

While closely related, tarts and pies are somewhat different in structure. A tart can be round, or even triangular, but it is always open-faced and freestanding—that is, it is removed from its baking pan and served with all of its sides showing. Since it must rely on itself to stand without crumbling or breaking, a tart is generally shallow and baked in a straight-sided flan ring or tart pan rather than in a pie pan, as the latter would tend to let the tart crack and fall at the sides due to the unsupported excess width of its top when removed from the pan. The best and most beautiful of all tarts are, undoubtedly, fruit tarts, sometimes made with a cream or custard base, filled with attractively arranged berries or sliced fruit, and painted with a glittering fruit glaze.

Small tarts made as individual servings are called tartlets and are miniature forms of the tart. "Flan" is another name for tart and has no relationship to the Spanish flan, which is a baked custard. The rings in which tarts, flans, and tartlets are baked are called flan rings. They come in many shapes, including squares and triangles, and look somewhat like embroidery hoops.

Pies, distinctly American desserts dating to colonial and pioneer days, are baked in sloping-sided pie pans with wide rims or lips for making attractive borders. Whether made from pastry dough or cookie crumbs, with or without top crusts, or with latticework pastry topping, pies rank high on the list of American dessert favorites. Fillings run the gamut from fruit to custard to nut fillings and frothy chiffonlike mixtures held together by gelatin.

Also a member of the pie family is the deep-dish pie, which has no crust on the bottom but lots of fruit filling and a crust over the top. Cobblers, which are included in Chapter 6, are akin to the deep-dish pie.

The most important part of any pie or tart is, of course, the pastry that makes up its shell or crust. A few things to keep in mind about making pastry are to try to handle the pastry as lightly and as little as you can; use as little water as you can; get as much air into the pastry as you can; flour the pastry board enough to prevent sticking but not to excess; and when rolling out pastry, roll lightly from the center of the dough in all directions, lifting the rolling pin near the edges to keep them from cracking or getting too thin. Of course, no rules about pastry making will ever do as much good as actually making pastry and learning from your own experience how to do it with the most ease.

If you plan to bake in a flan ring, the first step is to set the ring on a baking sheet which acts as the bottom of the pan. Place the pastry over the ring, allowing it to settle down into the ring and lifting it slightly and lowering it again to let it sink against the sides of the ring and into the corners. Press it against the ring with your fingers and trim off the excess pastry. After baking, lift off the ring and slide the tart onto a rack or serving plate.

If you want to bake an empty or "blind," tart shell or pie shell arrange the pastry for baking, cover it with a piece of waxed paper, and fill the hollow space with dried beans or rice. Bake the shell until set, and the weight of the beans or rice will keep the pastry from puffing up and getting out of shape. This will take about eight to ten minutes for pie or tart shells, a minute or two less for tartlet shells. Remove the waxed paper and beans or rice and return the shell to the oven to finish baking. The beans or rice can be saved and used repeatedly in this way.

One of the nicest parts of having any of the tart family for dessert is that you can do most of the work ahead by making the pastry, arranging it in the pan, wrapping it in plastic wrap and freezing it as is, or baking it first if you wish. Then it can be ready to use at a moment's notice. Frozen unbaked tart shells can be put directly into the oven without thawing.

There are recipes in this chapter for a good variety of pastry doughs, including sweet pastry, cookielike pastry, old-fashioned pie pastry, and pastries enriched by cream cheese, nuts, or other ingredients. Puff pastry, which makes excellent tart or tartlet shells, can be found in Chapter 14, "The Puff Family."

In addition to the recipes in this chapter, other tart and pie recipes in this book are:

Brie en Croûte
Chocolate Cream Pie
Cream Cheese Tarts
Honey Cheese Pie
Lemon Meringue Pie
Pecan Pie
Portuguese Egg Yolk Cream Tarts
Puff Pastry
Shoofly Pie

TART PASTRY

1 cup flour
1 tablespoon sugar
Pinch of salt
4 tablespoons butter, well chilled

2 tablespoons vegetable shortening, well chilled
¼ cup or less ice water

Combine the flour, sugar, and salt. Add the well-chilled butter, cut into tiny pieces, and well-chilled vegetable shortening, and cut in with a pastry blender or two knives. Sprinkle enough ice water over the mixture, tossing it lightly and quickly with a fork, so that it holds together. Form the mixture into a ball and wrap it in plastic wrap. Chill for 1 to 2 hours or longer. When you are ready to use the dough, preheat the oven at 425°. Roll out the dough and use it to line a tart pan or pie pan.

If the pie shell is to be baked alone ("blind"), prick it all over with the tines of a fork. Set a smaller pie pan or tart pan or a piece of waxed paper or lightweight aluminum foil on top, and fill with beans or rice. Bake for 10 minutes. Remove the lining and bake for another 2 to 5 minutes.

If it is to be filled before baking, follow the instructions in individual recipes.

Makes 1 tart shell or pie shell. The recipe may be doubled.

SWEET TART PASTRY

2 cups flour
6 tablespoons sugar
⅛ teaspoon baking powder
4 tablespoons butter, well chilled

3 tablespoons vegetable shortening, well chilled
1 egg
1 teaspoon water
½ teaspoon vanilla extract

Put the flour, sugar, baking powder, well-chilled butter, and well-chilled vegetable shortening together in a bowl, and toss and rub the ingredients together quickly with the fingers until the mixture resembles rolled oats. Beat the egg with the water and vanilla extract. Add to the flour mixture and combine quickly with a fork. Form the pastry into a ball. Place it on a pastry board and with the heel of the hand quickly press the pastry, bit by bit, down and away from you in long smears. Scrape it up with a pastry scraper and divide it into 2 balls. Wrap the balls in plastic wrap and chill for 3 hours or longer.

Use the pastry as directed in individual recipes, or preheat the oven at 400°. Roll out the pastry and mold it into 2 removable-bottom tart pans or quiche pans. Weight the pastry shells with dry beans or rice in waxed paper or light aluminum foil and bake them for 8 or 9 minutes. Remove the weights and prick the bottom crusts with the tines of a fork. Return the shells to the oven for 2 or 3 minutes if they are to be baked further with a filling, or for 7 to 10 minutes, or until lightly browned, if the crusts are to be finished before filling. Remove the shells from the pans and slip them onto wire racks to cool.

Makes 2 tart shells.

BUTTER PASTRY

1 tablespoon tarragon vinegar
2 tablespoons water
1¼ cups flour

½ teaspoon salt
¼ teaspoon baking powder
½ cup butter, well chilled

In a cup, combine the tarragon vinegar and water. Cover and refrigerate until well chilled. Sift the flour, salt, and baking powder together into a bowl. Cut the well-chilled butter into small pieces into the flour mixture. Cut it in with a pastry blender until the mixture resembles coarse meal. Sprinkle the vinegar water over the flour mixture and toss lightly with a fork until combined. Form into a ball and wrap in plastic wrap. Chill well.

Use the pastry as directed in individual recipes, or preheat the oven at 400°. Roll out the pastry and use it to line a tart shell or pie plate. Weight the pastry with dry beans or rice in waxed paper or light aluminum foil, and bake for about 10 minutes. Remove the weight and prick the bottom crust all over with the tines of a fork. Return to the oven until it is lightly browned.

Makes 1 tart shell.

Note: This pastry is the tiniest bit tangy and is very good with fruit fillings.

CREAM CHEESE PASTRY

8 ounces sweet butter
8 ounces cream cheese

2 cups flour

Cream the butter and cream cheese together with an electric beater until the mixture is well blended and creamy. Add the flour and mix with a wooden spoon until all flour has been absorbed, finishing the mixing with the hands if necessary. Form the pastry into a ball. Wrap it in plastic wrap and refrigerate it for 8 hours or overnight. Remove the pastry from the refrigerator 30 minutes before you are ready to work with it.

Use as directed in individual recipes, or preheat the oven at 450°. Roll the pastry out thinly on a lightly floured board and arrange it in tart or pie pan(s). If it is to be baked empty ("blind"), freeze it for

10 minutes before baking. Bake for 5 minutes, then reduce the oven temperature to 400°. Continue baking for 5 to 10 minutes longer. Watch it carefully during the baking time, and quickly break any air bubbles with a fork as they form.

Makes two tart shells or pie shells, or one 9-inch, 2-crust pie.

OLD-FASHIONED PASTRY

¼ pound lard
1½ cups flour
Pinch of salt

3 or 4 tablespoons ice water
Milk

Put the lard, flour, and salt in a bowl, and cut in the lard with a pastry blender or 2 knives until the mixture is quite fine. Add the ice water and work it in quickly with a fork. Divide the dough in half, and roll out each half on a floured board to form 2 pie shells or a top crust and a bottom crust.

After filling the pie, brush the top with some milk, and bake it in a 400° oven, or as directed in the individual recipe. If baking the pastry "blind," bake it, weighted with dry beans or rice in waxed paper, for about 10 minutes. Remove the weight and bake until it is lightly browned.

Makes one 2-crust pie or two pie shells. The recipe can be doubled, tripled, or quadrupled.

WALNUT OR PECAN PIE SHELL

1 cup pecans or walnuts
1 rounded tablespoon sugar

¼ teaspoon salt
1 tablespoon (or more) butter

Preheat the oven at 400°. Blend the nuts and sugar in an electric blender or food processor until the nuts have been completely ground. Butter an 8-inch pie plate, using at least 1 tablespoon butter. Sprinkle in the nut mixture, distributing it evenly, and press it firmly into the butter. Bake for about 6 minutes. Cool on a wire rack.

Makes one 8-inch shell.

PUMPKIN CHEESE PIE

1 recipe SWEET TART PASTRY,
   unbaked
2 eggs
Pinch of salt
⅔ cup sugar
1 teaspoon cinnamon
½ teaspoon nutmeg
¼ teaspoon ground ginger

Pinch of cloves
1 pound ricotta cheese
1½ cups canned pumpkin or
   thick, mashed, cooked
   pumpkin
2 tablespoons rum
Beaten egg

Divide the Sweet Tart Pastry dough in half, and chill. Roll out two-thirds of the pastry and line a 9-inch pie pan, leaving about 1 inch of dough all around. Roll out the remaining dough, and cut it into strips about ½-inch wide.

Preheat the oven at 450°. Beat 2 eggs lightly and stir in the salt, sugar, cinnamon, nutmeg, ginger, and cloves. Add the ricotta, pumpkin, and rum, and mix well. Pour into the pie shell. Arrange the pastry strips over the pie, starting from the center, to form a lattice top, crisscrossing the strips as you work toward the sides. Turn the bottom pastry up over the ends of the lattice strips and pinch together. Flute the edges deeply. Bake for 10 minutes, then reduce the oven temperature to 325°. Brush the latticework with the beaten egg and continue baking for about 45 minutes longer, or until a knife inserted in the center comes out clean. Cool and chill.

Makes 6 servings.

ALMOND CREAM PIE

1 nine-inch baked pie shell, made
   with CREAM CHEESE PASTRY
8 ounces almond paste
2 cups milk
4 egg yolks
1 tablespoon plain gelatin

2 tablespoons cold water
½ teaspoon almond extract
1½ cups heavy cream
Toasted blanched slivered
   almonds

Crumble the almond paste into a saucepan. Add the milk and combine. Cook, stirring constantly, over low heat until the mixture is smooth and slightly thickened. Beat the egg yolks in the top of a double

---

boiler off heat and gradually add the almond mixture. Place over boiling water and cook, stirring, until the mixture coats a metal spoon. Soften the gelatin in the cold water and stir it into the almond mixture, stirring until the gelatin has dissolved. Remove from the heat and add the almond extract. Cool.

Whip 1 cup of the heavy cream until stiff. Fold into the almond mixture. Turn into the baked pie shell and chill for several hours. To serve, whip the remaining ½ cup heavy cream until stiff. Make a border of whipped cream about 1½ inches wide around the edge of the pie. Stud the cream with toasted blanched slivered almonds.

Makes 6 servings.

RAISIN RUM PIE

1 nine-inch unbaked pie shell,
   made with TART PASTRY
2 cups raisins
¾ cup water
¼ cup rum
½ cup butter
½ cup brown sugar, firmly
   packed
1 tablespoon flour

2 egg yolks, slightly beaten
¾ cup chopped pecans
1 teaspoon grated zest of lemon
   peel
2 teaspoons grated zest of orange
   peel
2 egg whites
Whipped cream (optional)
1 tablespoon rum (optional)

Bring the raisins, water, and ¼ cup rum to a boil in a saucepan and simmer until the raisins have puffed slightly, about 10 minutes. Remove from the heat and add the butter, stirring until it has melted. Add the brown sugar, flour, egg yolks, chopped pecans, lemon zest, and orange zest, and mix well. Allow to stand for 10 minutes.

Preheat the oven at 325°. Beat the egg whites until stiff, and fold them into the raisin mixture. Spoon into the pie shell. With a rubber spatula, mound the raisins toward the center of the pie. Bake for about 45 to 55 minutes, or until a knife inserted in the center comes out clean. Serve warm or chilled, with whipped cream flavored with 1 tablespoon rum if desired.

Makes 6 servings.

GOOSEBERRY HONEY PIE

1 recipe unbaked **BUTTER**
  PASTRY
3½ cups gooseberries
¾ cup honey
¼ teaspoon cinnamon

Pinch of nutmeg
Pinch of cloves
Pinch of salt
2 tablespoons arrowroot
2 tablespoons butter

Line a 9-inch pie pan with Butter Pastry. Remove the stem and tail ends from the gooseberries. Combine the honey, cinnamon, nutmeg, cloves, and salt in a saucepan. Stir in the gooseberries and simmer for about 5 minutes. Remove from the heat and cool slightly. Stir in the arrowroot.

Preheat the oven at 400°. Turn the gooseberry filling into the pie shell. Dot with butter. Roll out the top crust and place over the pie. Trim and flute the edges. Cut vents in the top crust. Bake for about 30 minutes.

Makes 6 to 8 servings.

MULBERRY RHUBARB PIE

1 recipe unbaked
  OLD-FASHIONED PASTRY
2 cups mulberries
1 cup finely sliced rhubarb

½ cup sugar
¼ cup flour
2 tablespoons butter

Line a 9-inch pie pan with Old-fashioned Pastry. Combine the mulberries and sliced rhubarb. Combine the sugar and flour and sprinkle about one-third of the mixture into the pie shell. Arrange the mulberries and rhubarb in the pie shell. Sprinkle with the balance of the sugar-flour mixture. Dot with butter.

Preheat the oven at 425°. Roll out the top crust and place over the pie. Trim and flute the edges. Cut vents in the top crust. Bake for 40 to 50 minutes.

Makes 6 servings.

MOCHA ANGEL PIE

3 egg whites
Pinch of cream of tartar
Pinch of salt
¾ cup sugar
1 teaspoon vanilla extract
2 ounces baking chocolate
1½ cups strong coffee

⅓ cup sugar
½ cup light cream or 6
  tablespoons heavy cream and
  2 tablespoons milk
⅓ cup instant or quick-mixing
  flour
3 egg yolks

Preheat the oven at 275°. Beat the egg whites until foamy. Add the cream of tartar and salt, and beat until soft peaks form. Add ¾ cup sugar, a little at a time, until the mixture is thick and glossy. Fold in the vanilla extract. Butter a 9-inch pie pan and spoon in the meringue, banking the sides thickly and higher than the pan sides, using a rubber spatula or a large spoon. Bake for 45 to 55 minutes. Remove from the oven and cool on a wire rack.

Put the baking chocolate and coffee in the top of a double boiler, set over hot water, and heat, stirring, until the chocolate has melted. Stir in ⅓ cup sugar. Combine the cream and instant flour, making sure no lumps remain. Stir into the chocolate mixture and cook, stirring for about 15 minutes, until the mixture is thick and smooth. Beat the egg yolks and stir a little of the chocolate mixture into them. Then stir the egg yolks into the chocolate mixture and combine quickly and well to prevent the eggs from curdling. Heat for 1 or 2 minutes, stirring constantly. Remove from the heat and cool the mixture, covered, to prevent a skin from forming, about 20 minutes. Pour into the meringue shell and cover the chocolate filling with plastic wrap. Chill well. Remove the plastic wrap before serving.

Makes 6 servings.

FROZEN NESSELRODE PIE

1 nine-inch baked pie shell, made
  with SWEET TART PASTRY
¼ cup Marsala wine
¼ cup candied orange peel, diced
¼ cup candied red cherries,
  quartered
¼ cup candied chestnuts
  (*marrons glacés*) or chestnuts
  in syrup (*marrons au sirop*),
  drained, cut in small pieces
1¾ cups milk
½ cup sugar
¼ cup cornstarch

Pinch of salt
4 egg yolks
¼ cup cold milk
1 teaspoon vanilla extract
1 cup chestnut spread (*crème de
  marrons*)
1 cup heavy cream
1 tablespoon sugar
1 tablespoon maraschino liqueur
  or orange liqueur
Pieces of *marrons glacés* or
  marrons au sirop, drained
  (optional)

Combine the Marsala wine, candied orange peel, candied red cherries, and candied chestnuts, and set aside. Heat 1¾ cups milk until hot but not boiling. Combine ½ cup sugar, the cornstarch, and the salt in the top of a double boiler off heat. Add the heated milk gradually, using a wire whisk if necessary to blend the ingredients smoothly. Place over direct heat and cook, stirring, until the mixture becomes very thick. Remove from the heat. Combine the egg yolks and cold milk. Add a little of the custard mixture to the egg yolks. Then add the egg yolk mixture to the custard. Place over hot water and cook, stirring, until the mixture becomes very thick. Remove from the heat. Stir in the vanilla extract.

Place the chestnut spread in a bowl and add the custard gradually, stirring until smooth. Whip the heavy cream until stiff and add 1 tablespoon sugar and the maraschino liqueur or orange liqueur. Add the macerated fruits and Marsala wine to the chestnut mixture. Fold the whipped cream into the chestnut mixture. Spoon into the baked pie shell as much of the chestnut mixture as will fit. Place the pie in the freezer, along with the balance of the chestnut mixture in the bowl. Freeze for about 1½ hours until partially frozen. With a wooden spoon, working quickly, loosen and slightly soften the chestnut mixture in the bowl. Heap it on top of the pie and freeze until firm. Cover with plastic wrap until serving time. If desired, decorate the pie with pieces of *marrons glacés* or *marrons au sirop*, drained.

Makes 8 servings.

GRASSHOPPER PIE

Vegetable shortening
1¼ cups finely crushed chocolate
   wafers
¼ cup sugar
3 tablespoons melted butter
1 envelope plain gelatin
2 tablespoons cold milk
¼ cup boiling milk

1 egg yolk
2 tablespoons sugar
¼ cup white crème de cacao
¼ cup green crème de menthe
1 cup heavy cream
CHOCOLATE TRIANGLES or
   grated chocolate (optional)

Preheat the oven at 450°. Grease a 9-inch pie pan heavily with vegetable shortening. Combine the finely crushed chocolate wafers with the ¼ cup sugar. Add the melted butter and mix well. Press the mixture firmly into the bottom and sides of the pie plate. Bake for 3 minutes. Cool.

Soften the gelatin in the cold milk. Add the boiling milk and stir until the gelatin has dissolved. Beat the egg yolk lightly. Add 2 tablespoons sugar and mix well. Add the gelatin mixture and mix well. Stir in the crème de cacao and crème de menthe. Refrigerate until the mixture thickens slightly, about 15 minutes, watching carefully to be sure that it does not become really thick. Whip the heavy cream until stiff. Fold into the gelatin mixture and pour into the pie shell. Chill for 3 hours or longer. If desired, decorate the pie with Chocolate Triangles or grated chocolate.

Makes 6 servings.

NORMANDY APPLE TART

Apple pies, which we think of as an American invention, were being made in distant lands as far back as the days of the Vikings. When these marauders overran Europe they took along their Scandinavian know-how for apple cooking, and today, in scattered places on the Continent where apples are abundant, one finds recipes for apple tarts under various names whose origins can be traced to the old Norsemen. One such recipe is from Normandy, a major apple-producing area for hundreds of years, whose coasts were invaded by the Vikings as early as the ninth century. This recipe is for an apple tart with an open top, as contrasted with the American apple pie, which traditionally has both a top and a bottom crust.

1½ cups flour	3 cups peeled, cored, and sliced
2 tablespoons sugar	firm apples
Pinch of salt	¼ cup flour
½ cup butter	⅓ cup sugar
3 egg yolks	¼ teaspoon nutmeg
1 tablespoon water	⅔ cup heavy cream

Preheat the oven at 375°. Sift 1½ cups flour with 2 tablespoons sugar and a pinch of salt. Cut in the butter and work until the mixture is in crumbs the size of peas. Add the egg yolks and water, blending and kneading until the mixture is smooth. Pat the dough into a 9-inch pie pan and flute the edges to stand up all around.

Combine the peeled, cored, and sliced apples with ¼ cup flour, ⅓ cup cugar, and the nutmeg, tossing to coat the apple slices well. Arrange the apple mixture in the pie shell. Bake for 10 minutes. Pour in the heavy cream and continue baking 30 minutes longer, or until the pastry is golden and the apples are just tender. Cool and serve.

Makes 6 to 8 servings.

BRANDIED PEACH TART

1 nine-inch baked tart shell,	Brandied peaches, drained
made with BUTTER PASTRY	1 cup peach or apricot jam
1 recipe PASTRY CREAM,	
substituting 1 tablespoon	
peach brandy for 2 teaspoons	
vanilla extract	

Spread a ½-inch layer of Pastry Cream in the baked, cooled tart shell. Arrange a layer of brandied peaches, rounded side up, over the Pastry Cream. Melt the peach or apricot jam in a small saucepan, stirring, and put it through a sieve. Brush over the peaches. Chill.

Makes 6 servings.

GINGER PEAR TART

1 nine-inch baked tart shell,
   made with BUTTER PASTRY
1 recipe PASTRY CREAM,
   reducing vanilla extract to 1
   teaspoon and, at the same
   time, adding 3 tablespoons
   finely chopped preserved
   ginger and 2 tablespoons syrup
   from the jar of preserved ginger

2 cups water
1¼ cups sugar
1 one-inch piece vanilla bean
About 9 fresh pears
Syrup from jar of preserved
   ginger in syrup

Combine the water, sugar, and vanilla bean in a saucepan and bring to a boil, stirring to dissolve the sugar. Simmer for 5 minutes. Meanwhile, peel, halve, and core the pears. Place them in the saucepan with the syrup and simmer gently until just tender, poaching as many pears as can fit in the pan at one time, and turning the pears once as they cook. Remove them from the syrup and cool.

Spread a ½-inch-thick layer of Pastry Cream in the baked, cooled tart shell. Arrange a layer of poached pear halves over the Pastry Cream. Chill. Just before serving, brush the pear halves with syrup from the jar of preserved ginger in syrup.

Makes 6 servings.

STRAWBERRY TART
WITH KIRSCH

1 nine-inch baked tart shell,
   made with SWEET TART
   PASTRY
2 pints strawberries
½ cup sugar

4½ teaspoons cornstarch
5 teaspoons kirsch
Sweetened whipped cream
Thinly sliced almonds

Sort the strawberries according to size, making 1 pint of large berries and 1 pint of small. Cut the large strawberries in half lengthwise and place them in a bowl with ¼ cup of the sugar. Cut the smaller strawberries into slices and place them in another bowl with the remaining ¼ cup sugar. Allow the berries to stand for 15 minutes and drain the juice into a measuring cup. Add water, if necessary, to measure 1 cup of juice. Transfer the juice to a small saucepan and stir in the cornstarch until no lumps remain. Place over medium heat and cook, stirring, until the mixture thickens and becomes clear. Remove from the heat and stir in 3 teaspoons of the kirsch. Allow the mixture to cool slightly, or set the pan in a bowl of ice cubes and stir until slightly cooled.

Arrange the sliced strawberries in the bottom of the baked, cooled tart shell. Arrange the halved strawberries, rounded side up, over them. Pour the cornstarch mixture evenly and thinly over the fruit until each berry has been covered. Refrigerate for 1 or 2 hours. To serve, stir the remaining 2 teaspoons of kirsch into the sweetened whipped cream, and spoon a border of whipped cream around the tart. Scatter the thinly sliced almonds over the whipped cream.

Makes 6 servings.

GREEN PLUM TART

1 nine-inch unbaked tart shell, made with BUTTER PASTRY
4 or 4½ cups fresh green or yellow plums, sliced and pitted
¼ cup honey
1 tablespoon lemon juice

2 tablespoons butter
1 teaspoon grated zest of lemon peel
⅛ teaspoon nutmeg
1 cup lemon marmalade or greengage plum jam

Combine 2 cups of sliced plums, the honey, and the lemon juice in a saucepan. Bring to a boil and simmer until the plums are soft. Put the mixture through a coarse sieve or food mill and return it to the saucepan. Add the butter, lemon zest, and nutmeg, and simmer until the mixture is quite thick, stirring occasionally.

Preheat the oven at 400°. Line the tart shell with waxed paper and fill it with dry beans or rice. Bake for 5 minutes. Remove the waxed paper and beans. Spread the plum mixture in the tart shell and return to the oven. Bake about 20 minutes longer. Cool.

Arrange the balance of the sliced plums attractively over the plum puree in the tart shell. Melt the lemon marmalade or greengage plum jam in a small saucepan, stirring. Put it through a sieve and brush it over the plums.

Makes 6 servings.

BAKEWELL TART

Bakewell Tarts, with jam lining and lemon filling, are named after the English town of Bakewell, where they originated.

1 nine-inch unbaked tart shell, made with OLD-FASHIONED PASTRY
Seedless raspberry jam or strawberry jam
½ cup butter
2 egg yolks
½ cup sugar
Pinch of salt
1 teaspoon grated zest of lemon peel
3 tablespoons lemon juice
2 egg whites

Prick the bottom of the unbaked tart shell all over with the tines of a fork. Spread a ½-inch layer of seedless raspberry or strawberry jam over the pastry. Refrigerate.

Preheat the oven at 350°. Melt the butter and set it aside to cool. Beat the egg yolks until very thick. Add the sugar gradually, and continue beating until the mixture is pale and thick and forms a slowly dissolving ribbon when the beater is lifted. Beat in the cooled butter gradually. Add the salt, lemon zest, and lemon juice, and beat again. Beat the egg whites until stiff, and fold them into the egg yolk mixture. Pour into the pastry shell over the jam. Bake for 25 to 30 minutes, or until the filling is set. Serve warm or cold.

Makes 6 servings.

QUICK TARTLET FILLINGS

Bake SWEET TART PASTRY in individual 4-inch tartlet pans. Cool and fill with any of the following.

Whipped Cream and Fruit Filling

Brush the baked tartlet shells with apricot, seedless raspberry, or strawberry jam. Whip 1 cup heavy cream until stiff and add 1 or 2 tablespoons sugar to taste. Fold in 2 cups of any one of the following fruits: blueberries, sliced bananas, sliced apricots, strawberries, raspberries, sliced peaches or nectarines, or mandarin oranges. Spoon into the tartlets over the jam and serve immediately.

Cream Cheese and Fruit Filling

Combine 2 cups sliced strawberries, bananas, apricots, peaches, or nectarines in a bowl with 2 tablespoons sugar, and chill for 30 minutes. Soften an 8-ounce package of cream cheese, and beat in enough milk or cream to make the cream cheese spreadable. Add 1 tablespoon sugar. Spoon the cream cheese mixture into the baked tartlet shells, and spread it out with a rubber spatula. Spoon in the sugared fruit and serve immediately.

Ice Cream Filling

Soften any flavor of ice cream and spoon it into baked tartlet shells. Decorate with a crystallized flower or any appropriate decoration and serve immediately, or freeze the dessert until serving time.

Ice Cream and Chocolate Sauce Filling

Soften coffee, pistachio, or vanilla ice cream, and spoon it into baked tartlet shells. Spoon CHOCOLATE SAUCE over the ice cream and serve immediately.

Custard and Whipped Cream–Liqueur Filling

Spoon any flavor leftover custard into baked tartlet shells. Top with sweetened whipped cream flavored with 1 tablespoon of an appropriately flavored liqueur, such as orange liqueur or strawberry liqueur with vanilla custard, or chocolate mint liqueur with chocolate custard.

GLAZED FRESH FRUIT TARTLETS

8 four-inch baked tartlet shells,
  made with TART PASTRY
¾ cup cold water and ¼ cup
  raspberry syrup (if making
  tarts with red fruit), or 1 cup
  apricot nectar (if making tarts
  with light-colored fruit)
4½ teaspoons cornstarch
1 cup heavy cream, 1 tablespoon
  sugar, and 1 teaspoon vanilla
  extract, or 1 recipe PASTRY
  CREAM

Any one of the following fruits;
  whole or halved strawberries,
  whole raspberries, dark
  cherries (fresh or canned, pits
  removed), freestone peach
  halves (fresh and poached, or
  canned), pear halves (fresh and
  poached, or canned), seedless
  grapes (halved), or pineapple
  chunks, (fresh or canned)

Combine the cold water and raspberry syrup with the cornstarch, or combine the apricot nectar with the cornstarch, stirring until no lumps remain. Cook over medium heat, stirring, until the mixture thickens and becomes clear. Remove from the heat and allow to cool slightly.

Whip the heavy cream until stiff, and add the sugar and vanilla extract. Spoon into the baked, cooled tartlet shells, filling them halfway, or spoon the Pastry Cream into the tartlet shells, filling them halfway. Arrange the fruit, rounded side up, attractively over the cream filling. Pour the cornstarch mixture thinly and evenly over the fruit. Refrigerate for 1 hour.

Makes 8 servings.

PECAN EGGNOG TARTLETS

8 four-inch baked tartlet shells,
  made with double recipe
  PECAN PIE SHELL
1 cup light cream
3 egg yolks
¼ cup sugar
¼ teaspoon nutmeg
Pinch of salt

1 envelope plain gelatin
¼ cup sherry
3 egg whites
2 tablespoons sugar
Pecan halves
Sweetened whipped cream
1 tablespoon rum

Scald the light cream and allow it to cool. Beat the egg yolks in the top of a double boiler off heat. Add ¼ cup sugar, the nutmeg, and the salt, and beat again. Add the cooled cream and combine well. Set over hot water and cook, stirring, until the mixture thickens slightly and coats a metal spoon. Remove from the heat. Soften the gelatin in the Sherry. Add to the egg yolk mixture and stir until the gelatin has dissolved. Set the top of the double boiler in a bowl of ice cubes.

Beat the egg whites until soft peaks form. Beat in 2 tablespoons sugar, 1 tablespoon at a time, and continue beating until the mixture is thick and glossy. Fold the egg whites into the egg yolk mixture. Pour as much of the filling into the tartlet shells as they will hold. Refrigerate. When the filling begins to set, about 15 to 20 minutes, bank the remaining filling over the set filling in the shells. Chill for several hours. To serve, decorate with the pecan halves and serve with the sweetened whipped cream (which has been flavored with the rum).

Makes 8 servings.

COUNTRY CURRANT TARTLETS

4 four-inch or 6 three-inch
   unbaked tartlet shells, made
   with TART PASTRY
¾ cup currants
Water
¼ cup butter

¼ cup orange marmalade
1 egg, lightly beaten
⅓ cup flaked coconut
1 tablespoon brown sugar
1 teaspoon vanilla extract

Refrigerate the unbaked tartlet shells. Preheat the oven at 350°. Place the currants in saucepan and cover with water. Bring to a boil, reduce heat, and simmer for 5 minutes. Drain. Add the butter to the currants and stir until it has melted. Add the orange marmalade, lightly beaten egg, coconut, brown sugar, and vanilla extract and combine well. Spoon into the chilled shells. Bake for about 30 minutes.

Makes 4 to 6 servings.

DEEP-DISH NECTARINE PIE

1 cup sugar
Pinch of salt
¼ cup cornstarch
6 cups peeled, sliced nectarines
½ teaspoon almond extract

3 tablespoons butter
¼ recipe OLD-FASHIONED
  PASTRY
Beaten egg
Heavy cream (optional)

Preheat the oven at 450°. Combine the sugar, salt, and cornstarch. Toss with the nectarine slices. Place in a well-buttered 1½-quart baking dish 2 to 3 inches deep. Sprinkle the almond extract over the fruit, and dot it with the butter. Roll out the Old-fashioned Pastry to fit the top of the baking dish. Place the pastry over the nectarines and trim the crust 1 inch larger than the baking dish. Turn the crust under and pinch and flute the edges. Make 2 or 3 slashes in the top of the crust. Bake for 10 minutes, then reduce the oven temperature to 350°. Brush the top of the pastry with beaten egg, and bake about 25 minutes longer. Serve hot or cold, with heavy cream if desired.

Makes 8 servings.

DEEP-DISH MANGO PIE

¼ cup Macadamia nuts
¼ cup sugar
2 tablespoons cornstarch
5 cups peeled, sliced mangos
½ cup canned sweetened coconut
  cream (such as Siboney or
  Coco Lopez)

1 teaspoon lemon juice
½ recipe CREAM CHEESE
  PASTRY
Beaten egg

Preheat the oven at 450°. Blend the Macadamia nuts, sugar, and cornstarch in an electric blender or food processor until the nuts are pulverized. Turn the mixture into a bowl and add the mango slices, tossing well. Add the coconut cream and lemon juice, and toss again. Turn into a buttered 1-quart soufflé dish. Roll out the Cream Cheese Pastry to fit the top of the soufflé dish. Place the pastry over the mango slices and trim the crust 1 inch larger than the soufflé dish. Turn the crust under and pinch and flute the edges. Make 2 or 3 slashes in the top of the crust. Brush with the beaten egg and bake for about 30 minutes.

Makes 6 servings.

DEEP-DISH BLUEBERRY PIE

½ recipe CREAM CHEESE
  PASTRY, refrigerated
5 cups blueberries
3 tablespoons flour

1 cup currant jelly
Beaten egg
Sweetened whipped cream, or
  lemon water ice or sherbet

Preheat the oven at 400°. Toss the blueberries with the flour. Spoon in the currant jelly and toss again. Turn the mixture into a buttered round 9-inch baking pan, 1½ inches deep. Roll out the pastry thinly to fit the top of the baking dish. Place the pastry over the blueberries and trim the crust 1 inch larger than the baking dish. Turn the crust under and pinch and flute the edges. Make 2 or 3 slashes in the top of the crust. Brush with the beaten egg. Bake for about 30 minutes.

Serve hot with sweetened whipped cream, or cold with lemon water ice or sherbet.

Makes 6 servings.

CHAPTER 17

Omelets for Dessert

*Yet, who can help loving the land
that has taught us
Six hundred and eighty-five ways
to dress eggs?*
—*Thomas Moore,* The Fudge
Family in Paris

Marcus Gabius Apicius, a Roman who lived in the first century A.D., was not only the alleged author of the world's first cookbook but also the creator of what may have been the world's first omelet. He cooked eggs with honey, added a dash of pepper, and called the combination *ovemele,* or "egg-honey," which is probably the origin of our present-day word *omelet.* The Romans, who ate just about everything in sight, didn't stop at hens' eggs in the preparation of their food, but included eggs of ducks, geese, partridges, pigeons, pheasants, peacocks, and ostriches. Even as late as the nineteenth century, Europeans were still using combinations as exotic as ostrich and flamingo eggs for their omelets, and a recipe for one of these oddities, called Arabian Omelet, appears in Alexandre Dumas's *Grand Dictionnaire de Cuisine.*

Today's omelets are generally made only with hens' eggs—and the very freshest ones, at that. This is one of the necessities for producing a really good omelet. Another is using the right pan. It's best to have an omelet pan made of iron, steel, or thick aluminum, and to use it for nothing but omelets. It should be fairly shallow, have gently sloping sides so it will be easy to roll out the omelet after cooking, and it should be about nine or ten inches in diameter (measured across the top) for the kind of three- and four-egg omelets you will want to make for desserts and most entrées. Omelets of this size can be served to two or three people for dessert, and you need only make another omelet to serve from four to six. It's a much better idea to make several omelets than to try to make one giant omelet and be caught up in an ocean of eggs.

If you're starting out with a brand-new omelet pan, it will need to be cured before you use it. If the manufacturer fails to include instructions for this, you can follow these directions. For iron or steel pans (not stainless steel) wash the pan in soapy water, rinse, and dry it. Place the pan on the stove, fill it with milk, and heat, but do not allow the milk to boil. Turn off the heat and allow to cool for several hours or overnight. Pour out the milk, rinse the pan with water, and dry it with a paper towel. Coat the pan with cooking oil and wipe off the excess with a paper towel. The pan is now ready to be used. In no case wash the pan again, and remove any food particles that stick in the pan by rubbing with salt and a paper towel. Keep the pan lightly coated with oil between uses to prevent rusting.

For heavy, cast-aluminum pans, polish the pan with a steel-wool soap pad, rinse, and dry. Put a tablespoonful of oil in the bottom of the pan and heat it very slowly on the stove. Sprinkle in a little salt and rub the pan all over with the oil-and-salt mixture. Thereafter, care for the pan in the same way as the iron or steel pan.

Omelets are a good dessert choice after light lunches or dinners, especially when such meals are scant on proteins. The classic dessert omelet mixture is just about the same as for entrée omelets, with sugar added. Other types of omelets that are particularly nice for dessert are the mousseline omelet, which has the yolks and whites beaten separately before combining, sometimes with extra yolks or cream added, and the omelet soufflé, which has extra whites added, is baked in the oven in a shallow oval pan, and is more of a soufflé than a true omelet. All three kinds of dessert omelets are included in this chapter.

The egg's bland flavor lends itself to almost any kind of flavoring, and a dessert omelet can be made with almost anything you have on hand in the kitchen—chocolate, preserves, dessert sauces, fruits (whether fresh, brandied, or candied), crumbled macaroons, nuts, and so on. Liqueurs of all kinds can be added, or, for more spectacular desserts, the omelets can be flamed with warmed rum or brandy. If you prepare the filling for an omelet ahead of time, you will need only a few minutes to make the omelet and assemble it at serving time. Omelets, of course, can't be made ahead and must be served hot, directly from the stove or oven.

Making a good omelet takes some practice but is one of the most rewarding, quickest, and most useful things you can learn to do in the kitchen. To make a classic omelet, remove the eggs from the refrigerator at least an hour before you plan to use them. Beat them very lightly with a fork, not an eggbeater, to just mix the yolks and whites together—not more than about thirty seconds. If any other ingredients are called for, stir them in quickly.

Heat the omelet pan over a brisk flame, and melt a generous tablespoon of butter until the bubbles subside, making sure the butter doesn't brown at all. Pour in the eggs. When bubbles form on the surface of the eggs, alternately stir them with a fork to incorporate air into them and shake the pan to keep the omelet loose so it won't stick. Do this until the eggs are just about set. Then allow them to stand for a few seconds. (If you plan to fill the omelet, do it at this point. Spoon the filling onto the side of the omelet opposite the handle.) Then grasp the handle with your left hand, palm side up, and, with a fork in your right hand, start rolling the omelet from the handle side of the pan across to the opposite side, at the same time raising the handle side of the pan until it is almost vertical. If the omelet is not done enough to your liking, hold the pan in this position for a few seconds more. Roll the omelet out onto a waiting heated plate and serve it at once. The entire operation should not take more than a minute or two.

A good omelet should be light in texture, golden in color (not browned), and when cut into the center, should still be slightly creamy.

To flame an omelet, heat brandy or rum slightly, pour it over the omelet, and set it aflame. Spoon the flaming liquor over the omelet until the flames die out.

FRESH STRAWBERRY OMELET

1 cup sliced fresh strawberries
3 tablespoons sugar
2 tablespoons orange liqueur
4 eggs
1 tablespoon tepid water

1 tablespoon sugar
Pinch of salt
1½ tablespoons butter
Sugar

Combine the strawberries, 3 tablespoons sugar, and the orange liqueur, and allow to stand for 30 minutes. Preheat the broiler. Beat the eggs well with a fork, and add the water, 1 tablespoon sugar, and the salt, stirring to combine.

Heat the omelet pan and melt the butter until it is bubbly. Pour in the eggs and make the omelet by stirring with a fork and shaking the pan as outlined in the chapter introduction. When the omelet is finished, place the sliced, drained strawberries (reserve the liquid) across the center of the omelet and, with the aid of a broad spatula, fold it in half. Slip it onto an ovenproof serving plate. Pour the reserved strawberry liquid around the omelet. Sprinkle the omelet with a little sugar and place it under a very hot broiler for a few seconds to glaze, watching carefully to make sure the omelet does not get too dark.

Makes 3 servings. To make 6 servings, make 2 omelets and glaze them together.

VARIATION:

Fresh Strawberry Omelet Mousseline

1 cup sliced strawberries, prepared as above with 3 tablespoons sugar and 2 tablespoons orange liqueur	**3 tablespoons sugar**
	1 tablespoon heavy cream
	3 egg whites
	2½ tablespoons butter
4 egg yolks	**Sugar**

Preheat the broiler. Beat the egg yolks until thick. Beat in 3 tablespoons sugar, 1 tablespoon at a time, and continue beating until the mixture is thick and pale and forms a slowly dissolving ribbon when the beater is lifted. Beat in the heavy cream. Beat the egg whites until stiff, and fold them into the egg yolk mixture. While beating the egg whites, heat the omelet pan and melt the butter until it is bubbly. Add the egg mixture, and cook, stirring with a spoon and bringing the outside portions toward the center. When the omelet is cooked but still creamy, arrange the drained strawberries on one-half of it. With the aid of a wide spatula, fold the omelet in half and slip it onto an ovenproof serving plate. Pour the reserved strawberry liquid around the omelet. Sprinkle the omelet with a little sugar, and glaze as above.

Makes 4 servings.

FLAMING RUM OMELET

4 egg yolks	**4 egg whites**
¼ cup sugar	**2 tablespoons sweet butter**
Pinch of cinnamon	**¼ cup brown sugar**
Pinch of nutmeg	**¼ cup rum**

Beat the egg yolks until thick. Beat in the sugar, cinnamon, and nutmeg, and continue beating until the mixture is very thick. Beat the egg whites until stiff. Fold into the egg yolk mixture. Heat the omelet pan over low to medium heat, and melt the butter until it is bubbly. Add the eggs and cook slowly without disturbing them until they have set and the bottom of the omelet is browned. Fold the omelet in half and turn it out onto a serving plate. Sprinkle the brown sugar over the top. Warm the rum and pour it over the brown sugar. Ignite the rum immediately and spoon it over the omelet until the flames die. Serve the omelet on heated dessert plates.

Makes 4 generous servings.

Rum Soufflé Omelet

A soufflé omelet is similar to a soufflé, but it takes less time to cook because it is baked in a shallow dish, and it has a creamier consistency.

4 egg yolks	**2 tablespoons rum**
¼ cup sugar	**6 egg whites**
Pinch of cinnamon	**Sugar**
Pinch of nutmeg	**RUM SAUCE (optional)**

Preheat the oven at 300°. Beat the egg yolks until thick, and add the sugar gradually, continuing to beat until the mixture is thick and pale and forms a slowly dissolving ribbon when the beater is lifted. Add the cinnamon, nutmeg, and rum. Beat the egg whites until stiff, and gently fold them into the egg yolk mixture. Turn the egg mixture into a shallow oval baking dish which has been buttered and sugared, and mound it toward the center with a rubber spatula. Bake for 10 minutes. Make a lengthwise slit about ½-inch deep in the center mounded section, and spread it open. Sprinkle a little sugar over the top of the omelet, raise the oven temperature to 500°, and cook about 5 minutes longer until the top is glazed. Serve, if desired, with Rum Sauce.

Makes 6 servings.

CHOCOLATE OMELET

1 ounce semisweet chocolate	**Sugar**
2 tablespoons heavy cream	**1 small glassful brandy or rum**
4 teaspoons sugar	**1 small glassful chocolate liqueur**
3 eggs, beaten	**Heavy cream**
1 tablespoon butter	**CHOCOLATE SAUCE (optional)**

Melt the chocolate with the heavy cream and 4 teaspoons sugar in a small saucepan over medium-low heat, stirring constantly until the mixture is smooth. Stir into the beaten eggs. Heat the omelet pan, and melt the butter until it is bubbly. Pour in the egg mixture and make the omelet by stirring with a fork and shaking the pan as outlined in the chapter introduction. When the omelet is finished, fold it in half with the aid of a wide spatula, and slip it onto a serving plate. Sprinkle a little sugar over the top of the omelet. Warm the brandy or rum a little, and pour it over the omelet. Ignite immediately. Spoon rum or brandy over omelet until flames die. Pour the chocolate liqueur and a little heavy cream over the omelet. Serve, if desired, with Chocolate Sauce.

Makes 2 servings. To make 4 servings, make 2 omelets, and when both are prepared, place them on the same serving plate and ignite them at the same time.

VARIATION:

Chocolate Omelet Mousseline

1 ounce semisweet chocolate prepared as above with 2 tablespoons heavy cream and 4 teaspoons sugar
3 egg yolks
2 tablespoons sugar
2 egg whites

2 tablespoons butter
Sugar
1 small glassful rum or brandy
1 small glassful chocolate liqueur
Heavy cream
CHOCOLATE SAUCE (optional)

Prepare the chocolate mixture and allow it to cool slightly. Beat the egg yolks until thick, and add 2 tablespoons sugar, 1 tablespoonful at a time, beating until the mixture is thick and pale and forms a slowly dissolving ribbon when the beater is lifted. Stir in the chocolate mixture and mix until smooth and evenly blended. Beat the egg whites until stiff, and fold them into the chocolate mixture. While beating the egg whites, heat the omelet pan and melt the butter until it is bubbly. Pour in the egg mixture, and cook, stirring with a spoon and bringing the outside portions toward the center. When the omelet is cooked but still creamy, fold it in half with the aid of a broad spatula, and slip it onto a serving plate. Sprinkle with a little sugar and finish as above.

Makes 3 servings. To make 6 servings, make 2 omelets, and when both are prepared, place them on the same serving plate and ignite them at the same time.

AMARETTI OMELET

Ameretti *is the name for almond macaroons it Italy, where the famous cookie was first made. It's believed that the lady who owned the local pastry shop near Marengo dreamed up the recipe for Napoleon, after the famous battle in that area, as a very special dessert for his victory celebration dinner. Evidently today's version has been sweetened up a bit from the original* amaretti, *which means "little bitter ones." The following omelet combines the haunting flavor of sweet almonds in the macaroons with raspberry jam.*

3 large or 4 medium eggs	2 tablespoons sweet butter
1 tablespoon tepid water	¼ cup well-crushed almond
1 tablespoon sugar	macaroons
Pinch of salt	3 tablespoons seedless raspberry jam

Beat the eggs well with a fork, and add the water, sugar, and salt, stirring to combine them. Melt the butter in an omelet pan. Sprinkle in the crushed macaroons, and toss until they are heated. Add the egg mixture and make the omelet by lifting the sides of the omelet with a fork and bringing them toward the center, allowing the uncooked egg to run underneath. When the omelet is finished, spread the jam down the center. Fold the omelet in half and slip it onto a serving plate.

Makes 2 or 3 servings.

BRANDIED PEACH OMELET

1 large or 2 small brandied peaches, drained	Pinch of salt
3 large or 4 medium eggs	1½ tablespoons sweet butter
1 tablespoon tepid water	Sugar
1 tablespoon sugar	3 tablespoons brandy

Cut the peaches into small pieces. Beat the eggs with a fork, and add the water, 1 tablespoon sugar, and the salt, stirring to combine them. Heat an omelet pan and melt the butter until it is bubbly. Pour in the egg mixture and make the omelet by stirring with a fork and shaking the pan as outlined in the chapter introduction. When the omelet is half-finished, add the brandied peach pieces. Continue cooking until the omelet is just set. Roll or fold the omelet and turn it out onto a serving plate. Sprinkle a little sugar over the top. Warm the brandy a little and pour it over the omelet. Ignite immediately and spoon the brandy over the omelet until the flames die.

Makes 3 servings. To make 6 servings, make 2 omelets and flame them together.

VARIATION:

Use any brandied fruit, such as brandied pears or pitted black cherries, or any fruits in liqueur, in place of the brandied peaches.

CHESTNUT APPLE OMELET (OMELETTE AUX MARRONS ET POMMES)

3 chestnuts in syrup (*marrons au sirop*), drained, or 3 whole candied chestnuts (*marrons glacés*)
1 small apple
1½ tablespoons sweet butter

3 large or 4 medium eggs
1 tablespoon tepid water
1 tablespoon sugar
Pinch of salt
Sugar or 1 small glassful brandy (preferably Armagnac)

Preheat the broiler (see the second paragraph). Break the chestnuts into small pieces. Peel and core the apple and cut it into thin slices. Heat an omelet pan and melt the butter until it is bubbly. Add the apple slices and brown them very lightly. Meanwhile, beat the eggs well with a fork and add the water, 1 tablespoon sugar, and the salt, stirring to combine them. Pour the mixture over the apple slices. Make the omelet by stirring with a fork and shaking the pan as outlined in the chapter introduction. When the omelet is half-finished, sprinkle the broken-up chestnuts over the top. Continue cooking until the omelet just sets. Fold it in half and slip it onto an ovenproof serving plate.

Either sprinkle the top of the omelet with a little sugar and place it under the broiler for a few seconds to glaze, or pour warmed brandy over the omelet, ignite immediately, and spoon the brandy over the omelet until the flames die.

Makes 3 servings. To make 6 servings, make 2 omelets, and glaze or flame them together.

CHAPTER 18

Soufflés

Wasn't that a dainty dish
To set before a king?
—Tom Thumb's Pretty Songbook

There's no longer any need to stand in awe of the soufflé. Its reputation for being unpredictable probably started in the days when soufflés had to be baked in wood- or coal-burning stoves, which *were* unpredictable. It was difficult, if not impossible, to regulate oven temperatures properly, and soufflés were at the mercy of the whims of the fuel. Nowadays, with good gas and electric ovens equipped with reliable thermostats to maintain even oven temperatures, there's little reason to turn out anything but a good soufflé.

Not only is a soufflé beautiful, but it is a show in itself and one of the most economical of desserts. It can be made in an almost limitless variety of flavors. Egg whites beaten to frothy lightness make a soufflé the airy baked delicacy that it is, and it's this ingredient that requires your attention to achieve good results.

As in all desserts that contain beaten egg whites, it's important when making a soufflé to bring the eggs out of the refrigerator and leave them at room temperature for at least an hour before using them. Always break each egg separately and allow the white to drain into a small bowl or custard cup. Then, if the egg is perfect, the yolk and white can each be added to the master bowls of yolks and whites. This prevents a less-than-perfect egg from spoiling a whole bowlful of eggs, or a broken yolk from getting into the egg whites. Broken-yolked eggs can simply be set aside for another use.

Egg whites will not beat high and easily if there is a speck of yolk in them, if the bowl and whisk or beater are not spotlessly clean and dry, if there is any trace of grease on any utensils used, or if you use a plastic bowl. For best results in egg white beating, add salt to the egg whites and beat them until foamy. Then add a quarter teaspoon of cream of tartar and continue to beat until the whites form soft peaks. They should still be shiny and the tips should just bend over when you lift the beater out of the bowl and hold it upside down. Overbeating or underbeating will not produce a high soufflé. A tablespoon or so of sugar is generally beaten in at this point, and the whites are beaten until they form sharp, stiff peaks when the beater is raised. Beating some sugar into the whites helps to stabilize them and keep air trapped for puffing in the oven.

Using a whisk, beater, or electric beater is a matter of personal choice, and each method has its devotees. The whisk used with a copper bowl probably produces the highest-rising egg whites, but this is a subject for debate. Incidentally, if you do use a copper bowl, it won't be necessary to use cream of tartar, since the chemical reaction between the egg whites and the copper will produce the same effect.

In general, a dessert soufflé is made with a custard or similar base into which the yolks are blended and the whites folded. A good idea is to stir a little of the beaten egg whites into the base mixture to lighten it before folding the remaining egg whites in. Then fold the egg whites in gently, making sure not to overfold. Don't worry if you can still see a few foamy streaks of egg white after you've turned the mixture into the soufflé dish. A soufflé should be made in a soufflé dish or any straight-sided porcelain or other ovenproof dish with high sides.

To prepare a soufflé dish for baking dessert soufflés (and this should be done before you start preparing the soufflé itself), first butter it well, then dust it with a coating of superfine sugar. Not only will this give the crust a nice texture, but it will add to its flavor as well. If it seems appropriate to the recipe you're making, you can use finely ground nuts or cookie crumbs in place of the sugar.

It is seldom necessary to put a collar on a soufflé dish for a hot soufflé, but when making a cold soufflé it's a must. A cold soufflé—which is not baked in the first place—should nevertheless look like a baked soufflé when finished, so the soufflé mixture must be poured into the soufflé dish above the level of the top. To form a collar, cut a strip of aluminum foil long enough to go around the dish with about two inches overlap. Fold the strip in half lengthwise, and then again in half lengthwise. Oil one side of the strip lightly and dust with sugar. Wrap the collar around the soufflé dish, oiled side in, allowing it to extend about two inches above the edge of the soufflé dish. Pin the overlapping ends securely, and tie a string around the dish to secure the collar well.

When making a hot soufflé, always preheat the oven well. The initial penetration of the proper heat into the soufflé is an important step in making it rise. Don't open the oven door unnecessarily during the baking. When you think the soufflé is done, open the oven door, but don't move the soufflé dish or pull out the shelf. Rather, put your hand in the oven and touch the top of the soufflé with one finger. If it springs back, it's done. Rush it to the table and serve it right away. As everyone has probably heard, soufflés should never wait for people, but if necessary, people can wait for soufflés. This is a good rule to follow if a soufflé is to be at its best. However, if it happens that the soufflé absolutely has to wait for the people, it can often be held in the oven with the heat turned off and the door left closed for fifteen minutes or so.

The best way to serve a soufflé is to use two forks or spoons held back to back, and, using little downward motions, spread the soufflé apart with the two utensils and scoop some out to serve. Include some of the top, bottom, sides, and center in each serving.

In addition to the recipes in this chapter, other soufflé recipes in this book are:

Chocolate Grand Marnier Soufflé
Chocolate Soufflé

FRESH BLUEBERRY SOUFFLE (HOT)

For the soufflé:
1 pint blueberries
1 tablespoon lemon juice
1 slice zest of lemon peel
1 cup sugar
3 tablespoons water
¼ teaspoon almond extract
6 egg whites
¼ teaspoon cream of tartar
Pinch of salt

For the sauce:
¼ cup sugar
1 tablespoon cornstarch
Pinch of salt
1 tablespoon lemon juice
¾ cup hot water
1 cup blueberries
1 tablespoon butter
1 tablespoon brandy, kirsch, or rum

For the soufflé: Blend the blueberries, lemon juice, and zest of lemon peel in an electric blender or food processor until pureed. Combine the sugar and water in a small saucepan. Bring it to a boil, cover, and cook to the soft ball stage, about 238°. Combine the syrup with the pureed blueberries. Put the mixture through a fine sieve. Add the almond extract. Refrigerate or set in a bowl of ice and stir until cooled.

Preheat the oven at 400°. Beat the egg whites until foamy, and add the cream of tartar and salt. Continue beating until stiff peaks form. Fold the egg whites into the cooled puree with a rubber spatula, and turn the mixture into a buttered 1-quart soufflé dish. Bake for 20 to 25 minutes until nicely browned.

For the sauce: Meanwhile, combine the sugar, cornstarch, and salt in a saucepan. Stir in the lemon juice and hot water, and cook, stirring, until the mixture thickens. Add the blueberries, bring to a boil, and cook for 1 minute. Remove from the heat and stir in the butter until it has melted. Add the brandy, kirsch, or rum. Serve the soufflé directly from the oven with the warm sauce spooned over each serving.

Makes 6 or more servings.

ALMOND CREME SOUFFLE (HOT)

¼ cup butter	¼ cup blanched almonds
¼ cup flour	4 tablespoons sugar
1 cup scalded milk	6 egg whites
½ teaspoon almond extract	Sweetened whipped cream
½ teaspoon vanilla extract	Thinly sliced unblanched
5 egg yolks	almonds

Preheat the oven at 375°. Melt the butter in a saucepan. Add the flour and combine with a wire whisk. Add the scalded milk and cook, stirring with the whisk, until the mixture thickens. Remove from the heat. Beat in the almond and vanilla extracts with the whisk. Beat the egg yolks and add them to the milk mixture gradually, beating with the whisk. Blend the blanched almonds with 2 tablespoons of the sugar in an electric blender or food processor until they are pulverized. Add to the milk mixture and stir until completely smooth.

Beat the egg whites until soft peaks form. Add the remaining 2 tablespoons of sugar, 1 tablespoonful at a time, and beat until the mixture is thick and glossy. Fold the egg whites into the almond mixture gently but thoroughly. Turn the mixture into a buttered and sugared 1½-quart soufflé dish and bake for 40 minutes. To serve, spoon a dollop of sweetened whipped cream on each serving, and strew with thinly sliced unblanched almonds.

Makes 6 servings.

WINTER APRICOT SOUFFLE (HOT)

½ cup dried apricots
Water
3 tablespoons butter
3 tablespoons flour
¾ cup scalded milk

2 tablespoons lemon juice
¼ cup sugar
2 tablespoons honey
3 egg yolks, beaten
4 egg whites

Place the apricots in a saucepan with enough water to cover generously. Bring to a boil and simmer, uncovered, for 30 minutes. Remove from the heat, drain, and put the apricots through a food mill, electric blender, or food processor until pureed.

Preheat the oven at 375°. Melt the butter in a saucepan. Add the flour and blend with the wire whisk. Cook, stirring with the whisk, until the mixture bubbles. Add the scalded milk and cook, stirring with the whisk, until the mixture thickens. Remove from the heat and add the lemon juice, sugar, apricot puree, and honey, mixing well to combine. Add the beaten egg yolks. Beat the egg whites until stiff and fold into the apricot mixture. Turn into a buttered and sugared 1-quart soufflé dish and bake for 30 minutes.

Makes 4 servings.

GINGER SOUFFLE (HOT)

3 tablespoons butter
3 tablespoons flour
¼ teaspoon ground ginger
1 cup scalded milk
¼ cup sugar

1 tablespoon syrup from
   preserved ginger in syrup
⅓ cup finely chopped preserved
   ginger, drained
4 egg yolks, beaten
5 egg whites

Preheat the oven at 375°. In a saucepan, melt the butter and add the flour and ground ginger, stirring with a wire whisk until the mixture bubbles. Add the scalded milk, stirring constantly with the whisk, and cook until the mixture thickens. Remove from the heat and stir in the sugar and the syrup from the preserved ginger in syrup. Allow the mixture to cool. Stir in the finely chopped preserved ginger. Add the beaten egg yolks, stirring constantly. Beat the egg whites until stiff, and fold them into the ginger mixture. Turn the mixture into a buttered and sugared 1½-quart soufflé dish, and bake for 40 to 45 minutes.

Makes 6 servings.

MARRONS SOUFFLE (HOT)

1 cup chestnut spread (*crème de marrons*)	Pinch of nutmeg
	1 teaspoon vanilla extract
1 cup milk	4 egg yolks
¼ cup sugar	4 egg whites
3 tablespoons butter	2 tablespoons sugar
2 tablespoons flour	VANILLA SAUCE (optional)
Pinch of salt	

Preheat the oven at 400°. Place the chestnut spread in a saucepan and stir until smooth. Add the milk gradually and cook over medium heat, stirring, until the mixture just reaches the boiling point. Remove from the heat and stir in ¼ cup sugar. In another saucepan, melt the butter and stir in the flour. Cook, stirring with a wire whisk, until the mixture begins to bubble. Add the chestnut mixture gradually, stirring constantly, and cook until the mixture thickens. Stir in the salt and nutmeg. Remove from the heat. Add the vanilla extract. Set the saucepan in a bowl of ice cubes and stir occasionally for a few minutes until the mixture cools slightly. Beat the egg yolks and add them to the chestnut mixture, stirring constantly, allowing the saucepan to remain in the bowl of ice cubes.

Beat the egg whites until soft peaks form. Beat in 2 tablespoons sugar, 1 tablespoonful at a time, and continue beating until the mixture is thick and glossy. Fold the egg whites into the chestnut mixture. Turn into a buttered and sugared 1½-quart soufflé dish and bake for 15 minutes. Reduce the oven temperature to 375° and bake for another 30 minutes. If desired, serve with Vanilla Sauce.

Makes 6 servings.

ORANGE MARMALADE SOUFFLE (HOT)

1 seedless orange	4 egg yolks
1 cup milk	¼ cup orange marmalade
¼ cup sugar	(preferably Seville orange
⅓ cup sifted flour	marmalade)
Pinch of salt	4 egg whites

With a vegetable peeler, remove the zest of orange peel from the orange. Place it in a small saucepan and cover with boiling water. Boil it for 3 minutes and drain it on paper towels. Cut it into narrow shreds and set it aside.

Preheat the oven at 350°. Scald the milk. Combine the sugar, flour, and salt in a saucepan, and add the scalded milk gradually, stirring constantly. Cook over medium heat, stirring, until the mixture thickens. Simmer for 2 minutes. Beat the egg yolks and blend in some of the hot milk mixture. Then add the egg yolk mixture to the hot milk mixture, stirring constantly, and simmer for another minute. Remove from the heat and allow to cool. Add the shredded orange peel and orange marmalade. Beat the egg whites until stiff, and fold them into the marmalade mixture. Turn the mixture into a buttered and sugared 1½-quart soufflé dish and bake for about 40 minutes until it is lightly browned.

Makes 6 servings.

STRAWBERRY SOUFFLE WITH NUT SAUCE (HOT)

1 cup finely chopped fresh strawberries, firmly packed	5 egg yolks
	5 egg whites
7 tablespoons sugar	Sifted confectioners' sugar
3 tablespoons butter	(optional) and/or 1 cup heavy
3 tablespoons flour	cream, 3 tablespoons orgeat
1 cup half-and-half (milk and cream mixture)	syrup or almond syrup, 2
	tablespoons finely chopped
Pinch of salt	blanched almonds (all optional)
2 teaspoons orange liqueur	

Combine the strawberries and 2 tablespoons of the sugar, and set aside. Preheat the oven at 375°. Melt the butter in a saucepan, and stir in the flour with a wire whisk. Cook until the mixture bubbles, and then add the half-and-half, stirring constantly. Cook until the mixture thickens, stirring, then remove from the heat. Add 3 tablespoons of the sugar and a pinch of salt. Stir in the orange liqueur. Beat the egg yolks lightly and add them to the half-and-half mixture, stirring constantly. Add the strawberries (which have been drained). Beat the egg whites until soft peaks form. Beat in the remaining 2 tablespoons of the sugar, 1 tablespoonful at a time, and beat until the mixture is stiff and glossy. Fold the egg whites into the soufflé mixture with a rubber spatula. Pour into a buttered and sugared 1½-quart soufflé dish and bake for about 25 minutes. If desired, sprinkle the top with confectioners' sugar and/or serve with a nut sauce made by combining the heavy cream, orgeat or almond syrup, and finely chopped blanched almonds.

Makes 6 servings.

COFFEE LIQUEUR SOUFFLE (COLD)

1 envelope plain gelatin
2 tablespoons cold strong coffee
⅓ cup hot strong coffee
⅔ cup sugar
Pinch of salt
3 egg yolks
1 teaspoon vanilla extract

2 teaspoons coffee liqueur
3 egg whites
1 cup heavy cream
Whipped cream (optional)
Liquid-center candy coffee
    beans (optional)

Soften the gelatin in the cold coffee in the top of a double boiler off heat. Add the hot coffee, ⅓ cup of the sugar, and a pinch of salt, and set over simmering water. Stir until the gelatin and sugar have dissolved. Beat the egg yolks, and with a wire whisk beat a little of the coffee mixture into the eggs. Quickly beat the egg mixture into the coffee mixture with the whisk, and cook, stirring constantly, until the mixture is very foamy and slightly thickened. Remove from the heat and stir in the vanilla extract and coffee liqueur. Set the top of the double boiler in a bowl of ice cubes and stir until the mixture is cool, making certain it does not begin to set.

Beat the egg whites until soft peaks form. Gradually beat in the remaining ⅓ cup sugar and continue beating until the mixture is stiff and glossy. Whip the heavy cream until stiff, and fold it into the beaten egg whites. Fold the cooled coffee mixture into the egg white mixture. Pour into a 1-quart soufflé dish which has been lightly oiled and has an oiled waxed paper or aluminum foil collar tied around it to stand up 1 inch all around the rim. Chill until set. Remove the collar before serving. If desired, decorate with whipped cream and liquid-center candy coffee beans.

Makes 6 servings.

LEMON SOUFFLE WITH RASPBERRY SAUCE (COLD)

1 envelope plain gelatin	¾ cup sugar
2 tablespoons cold water	4 egg whites
½ cup lemon juice	1 cup heavy cream
1 tablespoon grated zest of lemon peel	1 ten-ounce box frozen raspberries, thawed
4 egg yolks	1½ tablespoons kirsch

In a small saucepan, soften the gelatin in the cold water. Add the lemon juice, and heat, stirring, until the gelatin has dissolved. Remove from the heat. Add the grated lemon zest. Beat the egg yolks until thick, and add ¼ cup of the sugar gradually, beating constantly. Continue beating until the mixture is thick and pale and forms a slowly dissolving ribbon when the beater is lifted. Beat in the lemon juice mixture. Beat the egg whites until soft peaks form. Add ¼ cup of the sugar gradually, and continue beating until the mixture is thick and glossy. Fold a little of the egg yolk mixture into the egg whites. Then fold the egg whites into the egg yolk mixture. Whip the heavy cream until stiff. Fold into the egg-lemon mixture. Fasten a waxed paper collar around a 1-quart soufflé dish so that it stands 1 inch above the rim. Pour the mixture into the soufflé dish and chill for several hours until firm.

Meanwhile, puree the raspberries in an electric blender or food processor. Put the puree through a fine sieve to remove the seeds. Add the remaining ¼ cup sugar and the kirsch. Spoon over the soufflé when serving.

Makes 8 servings.

PINEAPPLE SOUFFLE WITH STRAWBERRY SAUCE (COLD)

4 egg yolks
1 one-pound, four-ounce can
   unsweetened crushed pineapple
2 tablespoons lemon juice
2 envelopes plain gelatin
1 teaspoon vanilla extract

4 egg whites
3 tablespoons sugar
1 cup heavy cream
1 tablespoon orange liqueur
STRAWBERRY SAUCE

Beat the egg yolks and combine in a saucepan with the crushed pineapple and its liquid, the lemon juice, and the gelatin. Allow to sit a few minutes while the gelatin softens. Cook over medium heat for several minutes, stirring, until the gelatin has dissolved and the mixture comes just to the boiling point. Remove from the heat, stir in the vanilla extract, and set the saucepan in a bowl of ice cubes. Stir until the mixture begins to thicken slightly. Remove the pan from the ice cubes.

Beat the egg whites until soft peaks form. Add the sugar, 1 tablespoonful at a time, and beat until the mixture is thick and glossy. Fold the pineapple mixture into the egg whites, half at a time, folding gently but thoroughly. Whip the heavy cream until stiff. Add the orange liqueur and combine well. Fold the whipped cream into the pineapple mixture. Turn into a 1-quart soufflé dish which has been fastened with a waxed paper collar standing 1 inch above the rim. Chill for several hours until firm. Remove the collar and serve the soufflé with Strawberry Sauce spooned on each serving.

Makes 8 servings.

CHAPTER 19

Old-fashioned Favorites

Old things are always in good repute.
—Tacitus, from the Latin

No matter how elegant some desserts may be, they can't always replace the simple, down-to-earth ones that have been made and loved for generations. Many of these longtime favorites can be traced straight back to the days when the colonies were first settled, and easy-to-obtain staples such as molasses, flour, and eggs, as well as native fruits, nuts, berries, and even corn and pumpkins, were utilized to launch a whole family of American desserts.

Colonists planted apple orchards by the score, and the fruit provided not only cider and applejack to warm the hearts of the rugged settlers, but apple sauce, apple butter, apple jelly, baked apples, and myriads of tarts, pies, cobblers, and pandowdies as well. Apple pies were so well liked in the New England colonies that they were even eaten for breakfast.

Pecan Pie became a favorite in the Old South, where the nuts grew in profusion. Gingerbread, although an Old World specialty, was adopted by the colonists and became a standard and typical Colonial dessert. No sugar was needed to make it, and nearly everyone could afford to buy molasses, its principal flavoring ingredient. Molasses-based recipes were generally held in high favor, with Shoofly Pie and Indian Pudding ranking among the top choices. America's native corn was used in making Indian Pudding, too, and the dessert became so well known both here and abroad that well-to-do Europeans found it fashionable to import the ingredients for its making from America.

All these old-time desserts have a singular charm and warmth that is difficult to equal. A Bread and Butter Pudding, a Jelly Roll, a plain Rice Pudding, or a Lemon Meringue Pie, can be grand in its simplicity. Try any one of these desserts, all included in this chapter, or a batch of nut-laden brownies or some rich vanilla ice cream for an old, yet ever new, delicious dessert. In addition to the recipes in this chapter, other old-fashioned favorites in this book are:

Bourbon Brownies
Chocolate Ice Cream
Vanilla Ice Cream

STRAWBERRY SHORTCAKE

For the filling:
1½ cups strawberries, crushed
2 tablespoons sugar
1 tablespoon orange liqueur,
   strawberry brandy, or
   strawberry liqueur

½ teaspoon salt
Generous pinch of nutmeg
½ cup butter
1 egg
⅔ cup milk or cream
Softened butter

For the cake:
2 cups flour
1 tablespoon sugar
3 teaspoons baking powder

For the top:
1 cup heavy cream
1 tablespoon sugar
1½ cups whole strawberries

For the filling: Combine the crushed strawberries, sugar, and liqueur, and set aside to macerate.

For the cake: Preheat the oven at 450°. Sift the flour, sugar, baking powder, salt, and nutmeg together into a bowl. Cut in the butter with a pastry blender until the mixture resembles coarse meal. Beat the egg with the milk or cream and stir into the flour mixture. Make sure the ingredients are well combined, but do not overmix. Turn into a buttered and floured round 9-inch cake pan. With floured fingers, pat the dough out smoothly so that it reaches all sides of the pan, and pat the top evenly. Bake for about 15 minutes. Cool slightly on a wire rack. With a long, sharp knife, split the cake horizontally into two layers. Spread some softened butter on the bottom layer.

For the top and finishing: Whip the heavy cream until stiff, and sweeten it with the sugar. To serve, spread the crushed berry mixture over the bottom layer. Place the top layer over the crushed berries. Arrange the whipped cream and whole berries over the top of the cake, allowing the whipped cream to fall over the sides of the cake. Serve immediately while the cake is still warm.

Makes 6 servings.

Note: If you prefer, you may serve the cake with the heavy cream poured over the cake, instead of whipping it.

LEMON MERINGUE PIE

Of all the fruits, lemons are probably the cook's best friend. They make themselves available on a twelve-month basis by producing fruit nonstop all year long. Not only do they supply an unmatched piquant flavor, but they also provide a healthy portion of vitamin C. Both rind and juice are used to make this tangy, all-time-favorite pie. When you remove rind from lemons, use just the thinnest shaving from the outside, and avoid all the white area, which can produce a bitter taste in your cooking. The following is a particularly good dessert choice following a seafood dinner.

1 nine-inch baked pie shell,
    made with TART PASTRY

For the filling:
¾ cup sugar
⅓ cup cornstarch
Generous pinch of salt
1¾ cups water
6 egg yolks
2 tablespoons grated zest of
    lemon peel

2 tablespoons softened butter
⅓ cup lemon juice

For the meringue:
4 egg whites
1 teaspoon cream of tartar
Pinch of salt
½ cup sugar

For the filling: Combine the sugar, cornstarch, and salt in a non-aluminum saucepan. Add the water and combine well. Cook over medium heat, stirring, until the mixture thickens and boils. Lower the heat and simmer, stirring, for several minutes more. Remove from the heat and beat in the egg yolks, 1 at a time, with a wire whisk, making sure not to include any egg white, and combining well after each addition. Stir in the lemon zest. Return the mixture to the stove, and cook over low heat, stirring, until the mixture is quite thick. If necessary, beat out any lumps with the wire whisk. Remove from the heat and beat in the softened butter and lemon juice, a spoonful at a time. Cover, cool to room temperature, and pour into the baked pie shell.

For the meringue: Preheat the oven at 325°. Beat the egg whites until foamy. Add the cream of tartar and salt, and beat until soft peaks form. Add the sugar gradually, and beat until stiff peaks form. Spoon the meringue onto the filling, making it high in the center and swirling it with a spatula in an attractive pattern. Make certain all the filling is covered with meringue and that no air holes remain next to the piecrust. Bake for 15 to 20 minutes until the meringue is nicely browned. Cool on a rack at room temperature (not in the refrigerator) for 1 or 2 hours before serving.

Makes 6 to 8 servings.

RICE PUDDING

½ cup long-grain rice
1 teaspoon salt
Boiling water
½ cup raisins or sultanas
4 eggs
½ cup brown sugar, firmly
 packed
1 teaspoon vanilla extract

3 cups scalded milk
1 tablespoon butter
1 teaspoon grated zest of lemon
 peel
⅛ teaspoon nutmeg
Plain or whipped cream
 (optional)

Combine the rice and salt in a heavy, straight-sided saucepan, and add enough boiling water to cover the rice by 1 inch. Cover and bring to a boil. Lower the heat and simmer without lifting the lid for about 20 minutes until the rice is tender and the water has been absorbed. Meanwhile, cover the raisins or sultanas with boiling water and allow to sit.

Preheat the oven at 325°. Beat the eggs. Add the brown sugar and vanilla extract, and mix well. Add the scalded milk and butter, and stir until the butter has melted. Stir in the grated lemon zest and nutmeg. Add the rice and drained raisins (which have been patted dry with paper towels). Pour into a buttered 1½-quart baking dish, and bake for 50 to 60 minutes, or until set, stirring once during the baking time. Serve hot or cold, with plain or whipped cream if desired.

Makes 6 servings.

SHOOFLY PIE

Whether this pie was so named because it was so attractive to flies that they had to be shooed away when it was made, or whether it is a corruption of the French name for cauliflower (chou-fleur), which the baked pie resembles slightly in appearance, it is, nonetheless, a good, sweet, gooey treat. (The first explanation seems more likely, since the pie is a specialty of the Pennsylvania Dutch people, whose mother tongue is German, not French.)

1 deep, high-rimmed, 9-inch
  unbaked pie shell, made with
  ½ recipe OLD-FASHIONED
  PASTRY
1 cup flour
⅔ cup brown sugar
¼ teaspoon cinnamon

4 tablespoons butter
½ cup boiling water
½ cup dark unsulphured
  molasses
½ teaspoon baking soda
Whipped cream (optional)

Preheat the oven at 450°. Combine the flour, brown sugar, and cinnamon, and cut in the butter with a pastry blender or with the fingers until the mixture is crumbly. Combine the boiling water, molasses, and baking soda, mixing quickly with a spoon until foamy. Pour into the pie shell. Sprinkle with the crumbled mixture and press it down slightly into the molasses. Bake for 10 minutes. Reduce the oven temperature to 350°, and bake for 35 to 40 minutes longer until the pie is firm. If desired, serve with whipped cream.

Makes 6 servings.

APPLE PANDOWDY

6 or 7 cups pared, cored, and
  sliced tart apples
⅓ cup sugar
½ teaspoon cinnamon
¼ teaspoon nutmeg
Pinch of cloves
Pinch of salt
¼ cup butter
⅓ cup dark unsulphured
  molasses

1 cup flour
2 teaspoons baking powder
½ teaspoon salt
1 teaspoon sugar
3 tablespoons butter
¼ cup milk
1 egg, lightly beaten
Cream

Toss together the apple slices, ⅓ cup sugar, cinnamon, nutmeg, cloves, and salt, and arrange in a deep, 1½-quart baking dish or casserole. (There should be enough apple slices to come to the top of the baking dish.) Melt ¼ cup butter and combine with the molasses. Pour over the apples. Sift the flour, baking powder, ½ teaspoon salt, and 1 teaspoon sugar into a bowl. Add 3 tablespoons butter, cut into small pieces, and work it in with a pastry blender or with the fingers until the mixture resembles fine meal. Add the milk and lightly beaten egg, and combine well. Turn the dough out on a floured board, knead it gently for a minute, and roll or pat it out to fit the top of the baking dish. Transfer the dough to the top of the baking dish and trim the edges if necessary. Put 1 or 2 gashes in the top to allow steam to escape. Bake for about 45 minutes until the apples are tender and the biscuit dough is browned. Cool slightly and serve with cream while still warm.

Makes 6 to 8 servings.

JELLY ROLL

4 egg yolks
¾ cup sugar
1 teaspoon vanilla extract
¾ cup sifted cake flour
¾ teaspoon baking powder

Pinch of salt
4 egg whites
Sifted confectioners' sugar
¾ cup currant jelly

Preheat the oven at 375°. Beat the egg yolks, gradually add ½ cup of the sugar, and beat well. Add the vanilla extract. Sift together the cake flour, baking powder, and salt, and add gradually to the egg yolk mixture. Beat the egg whites until soft peaks form. Add the remaining ¼ cup sugar gradually, and beat until the mixture is shiny. Fold into the batter, half at a time, folding gently but thoroughly until well blended. Butter an 11x13½-inch jelly roll pan, line it with waxed paper, and butter the waxed paper. Turn the batter into the pan, and spread it out evenly with a rubber spatula. Bake for 10 to 13 minutes until the cake is lightly browned and springs back when touched gently.

Remove the cake from the oven, and with a sharp knife quickly trim off the outside edges. Turn the cake right side down on a dish towel well sprinkled with confectioners' sugar. Peel off the waxed paper. Roll the cake up with the aid of the towel, and set it on a wire rack to cool. When it is cool, unroll the cake and spread it thinly with the currant jelly. Roll it up again and place it seam side down on a serving plate or board.

Makes 8 servings.

VARIATION:

Lemon Jelly Roll

Spread the cake with lemon curd instead of currant jelly.

INDIAN PUDDING

½ cup cornmeal (preferably
   stone-ground)
4 cups milk
¼ cup butter
½ cup sugar
½ cup dark unsulfured molasses
1 egg

½ teaspoon salt
½ teaspoon ground ginger
Pinch of nutmeg
Pinch of cinnamon
Vanilla ice cream or unsweetened
   whipped cream (optional)

Preheat the oven at 300°. Combine the cornmeal and ½ cup of the milk. Scald 3 cups of the milk and add the cornmeal mixture, mixing well. Cook, stirring, until the mixture is fairly thick, about 15 minutes. Remove from the heat. Stir in the butter and stir until it has melted. Add the sugar and stir until it has dissolved. Add the molasses and stir until it is well blended, making certain there are no lumps. Beat the egg lightly and stir a little of the cornmeal mixture into it. Then add the egg to the cornmeal mixture. Add the salt, ginger, nutmeg, and cinnamon, and mix well. Pour into a buttered 1½-quart casserole. Very gently pour the remaining ½ cup of milk over the top of the pudding and place it in the oven without jiggling. Bake for 1½ hours. Cool it slightly before serving, or serve it chilled. Serve, if desired, with vanilla ice cream or unsweetened whipped cream.

Makes 6 servings.

EASY APPLE STRUDEL

1 package phyllo pastry (if
  frozen, thaw, but do not
  expose to air)
3 medium-sized tart apples,
  peeled, cored, and thinly sliced
½ cup sugar

¼ cup chopped walnuts or
  almonds
¼ cup sultanas (optional)
1 teaspoon cinnamon
1 teaspoon grated zest of lemon
  peel
Melted butter
Dry fine bread crumbs

Toss the apple slices, sugar, nuts, sultanas, cinnamon, and lemon zest together. Preheat the oven at 400°. Line a baking sheet with aluminum foil and butter the foil.

Place a damp dish towel on the working surface. Open the phyllo pastry and lay 1 sheet on the damp towel. Brush with the melted butter and sprinkle with the dry fine bread crumbs. Repeat with another sheet of pastry on top of the first sheet. Spoon the apple filling onto the pastry along the long edge of pastry nearest you, making a row about 3 inches wide. With the aid of the dish towel, roll up the pastry into a roll and transfer it to the baking sheet, seam side down. Brush the outside of the pastry with melted butter and tuck in the ends to prevent the filling from leaking. Bake for 20 minutes, reduce the oven temperature to 350°, and bake for another 15 minutes, or until nicely browned.

Remove the strudel from the oven and, with the aid of the aluminum foil, transfer it to a board to cool. While it is still warm, cut it into serving portions about 2 inches long. Serve warm or cold.

Makes 6 servings.

GINGERBREAD WITH HONEYSCOTCH SAUCE

For the gingerbread:
¼ cup vegetable shortening
¼ cup sugar
½ cup dark unsulphured molasses
½ teaspoon baking soda
1¼ cups flour
1 teaspoon baking powder
½ teaspoon cinnamon
2½ teaspoons ground ginger
¼ teaspoon cloves

¼ teaspoon salt
¾ cup boiling water
¼ teaspoon baking soda
1 egg, lightly beaten

For the sauce:
¼ cup sugar
¾ cup honey
¼ cup butter
⅔ cup heavy cream
Pinch of salt

For the gingerbread: Preheat the oven at 325°. Cream the shortening, add the sugar, and mix well. Add the molasses (which has been combined with ¼ teaspoon baking soda). Sift together the flour, baking powder, cinnamon, ginger, cloves, and salt, and add to the molasses mixture alternately with the boiling water (which has been combined with ¼ teaspoon baking soda). Stir in the lightly beaten egg, and pour the batter into a greased and floured 9-inch-square baking pan. Bake for 20 to 25 minutes, or until a cake tester inserted in the center comes out clean. Cool on a wire rack. Cut into 9 squares.

For the sauce: Place the sugar, honey, butter, ⅓ cup heavy cream, and salt in saucepan, and cook over moderate heat, stirring, until the mixture reaches the soft-ball stage, about 238°. Add another ⅓ cup heavy cream, and cook for about 3 minutes more. Serve hot or cold over the gingerbread.
Makes 9 servings.

PECAN PIE LINCOLN

1 nine-inch unbaked pie shell,
   made with OLD-FASHIONED
   PASTRY
2 cups brown sugar
3 eggs

½ teaspoon vanilla extract
¼ cup milk
¼ cup butter, melted
¾ cup pecan halves
Slightly whipped cream (optional)

Preheat the oven at 350°. Combine the brown sugar, eggs, vanilla extract, milk, and melted butter. Pour into the unbaked pie shell. Arrange the pecan halves on top. Bake for about 45 minutes. Cool. If desired, serve with slightly whipped cream.

Makes 6 servings.

BREAD AND BUTTER PUDDING

¼ cup sultanas
Boiling water
¼ cup candied orange peel
¼ cup candied lemon peel
French bread
Butter
1¾ cups milk

½ cup heavy cream
⅓ cup sugar
1 teaspoon vanilla extract
1 teaspoon grated zest of lemon peel
2 eggs plus 2 egg yolks
Sugar
APRICOT SAUCE (optional)

Soak the sultanas in the boiling water to cover for 10 minutes. Drain and pat dry with paper towels. Butter a shallow baking dish. Sprinkle the candied orange peel, candied lemon peel, and sultanas into the baking dish. Cut enough French bread into ¼- to ½-inch-thick slices to make a single layer in the baking dish. Butter the bread slices well, and arrange them, buttered side up, over the fruits.

Preheat the oven at 375°. Scald the milk and heavy cream in a saucepan. Remove from the heat and add the ⅓ cup sugar, stirring until it has dissolved. Add the vanilla extract and grated lemon zest. Beat the eggs and egg yolks, and add the milk mixture to them gradually, stirring constantly. Pour over the bread in the baking dish. Set the baking dish in a pan of hot water, then set the pan in the oven. Bake for about 45 minutes, or until the pudding has set. Sprinkle a little sugar over the top, and place under the broiler for a few seconds to glaze. Cool to room temperature. If desired, serve with Apricot sauce.

Makes 6 servings.

CHAPTER 20

National Specialties

It is very nice to think
The world is full of meat and drink.

—*Robert Louis Stevenson,*
   "A Thought"

Every country has its dessert favorite, some dating back hundreds, if not thousands, of years. At the time of Emperor Justinian, people in Turkey were rolling out tissue-paper-thin pastry made with the finest flour to produce Baklava very much like that made in Greece, Turkey, and many other parts of the world today. Ancient Scots baked Short-bread of fine oats, and still specialize in a modern version made with wheat and/or rice flour.

Generally, desserts have evolved in each nation according to the nature of the native ingredients—and sometimes the kind of cooking methods available. Scandinavian countries, for instance, specialize in desserts featuring red berries, which grow there in ample supply; Italians utilize their never-ending supply of ricotta to produce any number of sweet cheese dessert mixtures; and people in North Africa and the Middle East convert their staple couscous into a dessert dish by making it with fruit mixtures instead of preparing the typical entrée chicken or lamb versions. In China, as in many Oriental countries, ovens are not always standard equipment in the home. Steaming takes the place of baking, and little sweet steamed cakes are one of the dessert classics.

It would be nice to include a dessert recipe from every country in this chapter, but the list of nations is, regrettably, far too long, and the number of good desserts made in a particular country equally formidable —the dessert specialties of France alone could fill a volume, as could the baked delights of even a single city like Vienna. The recipes in this chapter, then, are a good representation of international dessert favorites that are appealing to make in their own right and genuine in character for serving with ethnic meals. In addition to the recipes in this chapter, another national specialty in this book is:

Irish Coffee

GREEK BAKLAVA

1 one-pound package phyllo
   pastry (if frozen, thaw, but do
   not expose to air)
¾ pound (or more) butter
1 pound finely chopped walnut
   meats or pistachios
1 teaspoon cinnamon

½ teaspoon allspice
1 cup honey
1 cup light corn syrup
1 cinnamon stick
Strips of zest of peel from 1
   orange
Strips of zest of peel from 1
   lemon

Preheat the oven at 350°. Melt the butter, and brush a baking pan measuring about 11x14x2 inches with the melted butter. Lay in 1 sheet of the phyllo pastry. Brush it with melted butter. Repeat until 10 layers of phyllo have been used.

Combine the chopped nuts, cinnamon, and allspice, and sprinkle the phyllo with one-third of the mixture. Lay 1 sheet of the phyllo over the nuts, brush with butter, and repeat one more time. Sprinkle on another third of the nut mixture, and repeat with 2 more sheets of phyllo. Sprinkle on the remaining nut mixture, and furnish with 10 more layers of the phyllo, each brushed with melted butter. With a very sharp knife or razor blade, cut through the layers, about halfway down and 2 inches apart, forming a diamond pattern in the pastry. Bake for about 1 hour.

Meanwhile, combine the honey, corn syrup, cinnamon stick, and strips of zest of orange and lemon peel in a small saucepan. Bring to a boil, lower the heat, and simmer for 5 minutes. Remove the cinnamon stick and orange and lemon peels. Cool.

When the pastry has finished baking, remove it from the oven and pour the syrup over the top, allowing it to run down into the cuts in the pastry. When cool, cut apart completely.

Makes about 5 dozen pieces.

ITALIAN CANNOLI

To make this Sicilian dessert specialty, you'll need metal cannoli tubes, which are 6 to 8 inches in length and about 1 inch in diameter. They can be bought in cookware or hardware stores, particularly in shopping areas that specialize in Italian products.

For the shells:
1⅓ cups flour
1½ tablespoons shortening
½ teaspoon sugar
Pinch of salt
¼ cup (or more) white wine
1 egg white, slightly beaten
Fat or oil for frying

For the filling:
1 pound ricotta cheese
½ cup superfine sugar
¼ teaspoon cinnamon

1 tablespoon grated semisweet
  or bittersweet chocolate
½ teaspoon vanilla extract
2 tablespoons finely chopped
  candied orange peel
1 tablespoon chocolate liqueur
  or coffee liqueur
Chopped pistachios
Pieces of candied cherries
  (optional)
Sifted confectioners' sugar

For the shells: Mix together the flour, shortening, sugar, and salt. Add enough white wine to make a fairly stiff dough. Form into a ball, wrap in plastic wrap, and allow to stand at room temperature for 1 hour. Roll the dough out thinly, and cut it into 3-inch rounds. Roll the rounds out into ovals. Roll an oval around each cannoli tube, brush with the slightly beaten egg white where the edges overlap, and press with the fingers to seal.

In a deep fryer, heat the fat or oil to 370°. Fry the tubes, 1 or 2 at a time, until the Cannoli are golden-brown, turning, if necessary, with tongs. Drain on paper towels. Cool slightly and remove the shells carefully from the tubes, holding the tubes with a pot holder. When all the Cannoli have been made and thoroughly cooled, fill with the following filling.

For the filling: Combine the ricotta and sugar. Add the cinnamon, grated chocolate, vanilla extract, candied orange peel, and liqueur, and combine thoroughly. Chill well. Pipe into the cooled Cannoli shells with a pastry bag fitted with a large plain tip. Smooth the ends with a knife, and sprinkle with the chopped pistachios. Decorate with pieces of candied cherries if desired. Sift confectioners' sugar over all.

Makes about 1½ dozen.

ENGLISH TRIFLE

Probably anyone who has ever made trifle has settled on his or her own favorite combination of flavors and ingredients to put in it. There are literally hundreds of versions of this delightful dessert, and you can give free rein to your own ideas in making it. Basically, trifle is a conglomerate of rich custard, sponge cake pieces drenched in brandy, spoonfuls of fruits or preserves, dollops of whipped cream, and handfuls of almonds or candied fruits as decorations. This version includes tiny macaroons, brandied cherries, and a dusting of nutmeg. Other ideas for trifle include using Sherry, Port, or Madeira wines or a fruit liqueur in place of, or in addition to, the brandy. If you don't want to limit yourself to sponge cake, then use some LADYFINGERS (preferably some you've made yourself) to make a decorative border all around the edge. Macaroons can be used either for trimming or in the body of the trifle. Let apricot preserves substitute for strawberry or raspberry, or use currant jelly or two kinds of preserves. Instead of preserves, you might want to use fresh fruit in season—strawberries, raspberries, or peaches, perhaps soaked in a bit of kirsch. You can gauge the color of your trifle as you see fit—it can be a delicately colored one, or a racy one with bits of bright, sparkling gelatin dessert scattered through it.

For the custard:
5 egg yolks
¾ cup sugar
½ cup sifted flour
2 cups boiling milk
1 tablespoon butter
2 teaspoons vanilla extract

For the cake and assembling:
2 eight-inch layers SPONGE CAKE (homemade, or good-quality bakery sponge cake)

Brandy
Strawberry, raspberry, or cherry preserves
Blanched slivered almonds
Brandied cherries
Almond macaroons
1 cup heavy cream
1 tablespoon sugar
½ teaspoon vanilla extract
Freshly grated nutmeg

For the custard: Beat the egg yolks lightly with an electric beater. Gradually beat in the sugar, and continue beating until the mixture is thick and pale and forms a slowly dissolving ribbon when the beater is lifted. Beat in the flour. Gradually add the boiling milk, beating constantly. Transfer the mixture to a nonaluminum saucepan, and cook over moderate heat, stirring constantly, using a wire whisk. When the mixture boils, lower the heat and continue cooking for several minutes longer, stirring vigorously with the wire whisk until the mixture becomes very thick. Make sure the whisk reaches all parts of the pan's bottom and that the custard does not scorch. Remove from the heat, and add the butter and vanilla extract, stirring until the butter has melted. Pour the custard into a bowl and cover the top with plastic wrap—right on the surface of the custard—to prevent a skin from forming. Cool and chill.

For the cake and assembling: Cut the cake into slices. Line the bottom of a large, fairly shallow glass dish or bowl with the cake slices. Sprinkle a jigger or so of brandy over the cake. Spoon some of the custard over the cake. Place ½ tablespoonful of preserves here and there. Scatter the cake with blanched slivered almonds and a few brandied cherries, and nestle almond macaroons, whole or broken, here and there. Repeat the layers until the bowl is filled and the arrangement suits you. Beat the heavy cream until stiff, and flavor it with the sugar and vanilla extract. Swirl the whipped cream over the entire top of the dessert, building it into a slight pyramid. Dust lightly with freshly grated nutmeg.

Makes 12 servings.

PORTUGUESE EGG YOLK CREAM TARTS

10 unbaked tartlet shells about
   3 inches in diameter, made
   with TART PASTRY
5 egg yolks

⅓ cup sugar
Pinch of salt
1 cup heavy cream
Cinnamon

Preheat the oven at 400°. Beat the egg yolks lightly. Add the sugar and salt, and continue beating until the mixture is thick. Add the heavy cream gradually, and mix well. Spoon the mixture into the tartlet shells, filling them nearly to the top. Sprinkle with cinnamon. Bake for 20 minutes. Cool on wire racks. When the tartlets are cool enough to handle, slip them out of their pans.

Makes 10 three-inch tarts.

AUSTRIAN LINZER TORTE

1½ cups sifted flour
½ teaspoon cinnamon
⅛ teaspoon ground cloves
Pinch of salt
1 cup butter
1 cup unblanched almonds

½ cup sugar
2 egg yolks
1 teaspoon grated zest of lemon
   peel
1 cup raspberry jam
1 egg white, slightly beaten
Sifted confectioners' sugar

Sift together the flour, cinnamon, cloves, and salt. Cream the butter with an electric beater until it is very fluffy. Blend the almonds and sugar in an electric blender or food processor until the nuts are pulverized. Add to the butter and mix well. Add the egg yolks, 1 at a time, beating well after each addition. Add the lemon zest and flour mixture, and combine well. Place about three-quarters of the mixture in a 9-inch spring-form pan, and, with a rubber spatula, spread the mixture over the bottom and about 1 inch up the sides. Chill the filled pan and the balance of the dough for at least 2 hours.

Preheat the oven at 325°. Spread the raspberry jam on the dough in the pan. Sprinkle some flour on a board or waxed paper, and, with the palms open and using the remaining dough, roll ropes of dough. Place the ropes over the raspberry jam in a crisscross pattern. It is not necessary to weave the ropes, just lay them down and pinch them together where necessary. Brush the latticework with the slightly beaten egg white. Bake for 50 to 60 minutes. Cool on a wire rack. Remove the outside rim of spring-form pan. Fill in any empty spaces with more raspberry jam. To serve, sift confectioners' sugar over the top and cut into wedges.

Makes 8 servings.

SCOTTISH SHORTBREAD

1 cup butter
½ cup sugar
2 cups white flour

½ cup rice flour
Pinch of salt

Preheat the oven at 350°. Cream the butter. Add the sugar gradually, and cream well. Sift together the white flour, rice flour, and salt, and

---

add to the butter mixture, mixing well. Press the dough into 2 ungreased 9-inch pie pans. Prick all over lightly with the tines of a fork. Poke through the dough once or twice with the point of a sharp knife to make air holes. With the back of a knife, divide the dough lightly into 8 wedges. Bake for about 30 minutes. Test for doneness by cutting a small corner from one piece of the Shortbread. When it is done all the way through, remove it from the oven. Cut the marked wedges with a sharp knife immediately, but do not remove the Shortbread from the pan. After 15 minutes, remove the Shortbread from the pan and allow it to finish cooling on a wire rack.

If desired, brew coffee to serve with the Shortbread, adding a 1-inch piece of vanilla bean to the coffeepot.

Makes 8 wedges.

SPANISH CHULAS

2 eggs, separated
¼ cup sugar
¼ teaspoon baking powder
¼ teaspoon cinnamon
½ teaspoon grated zest of lemon peel

¼ cup (or more) fine dry bread crumbs
Cooking oil
2 cups milk
3 tablespoons sugar
2 slivers zest of lemon rind
¼ teaspoon cinnamon

Separate the eggs and beat the egg whites until they form peaks. Beat the egg yolks well, add them to the egg whites, and mix well. Add ¼ cup sugar, the baking powder, ¼ teaspoon cinnamon, and the grated zest of lemon peel, and combine well. Add enough fine dry breadcrumbs to make a fairly thick batter. Heat about ½-inch of cooking oil in a skillet or frying pan until it is hot but not smoking. Drop the batter by tablespoonsful into the hot oil, making a few at a time. Fry the Chulas until golden-brown, turning them once during the frying time. Drain them on paper towels.

Heat the milk in a saucepan with the 3 tablespoons sugar, 2 slivers of zest of lemon rind, and ¼ teaspoon cinnamon. When the boiling point is reached, remove from the heat. Place 2 or 3 Chulas in each sherbet glass, and pour some of the milk mixture over them. Serve them warm or cold.

Makes 4 or more servings.

BELGIAN WAFFLES

Belgian Waffles became well-known in the United States when they were served at the New York World's Fair in 1964–65. Eaten with the fingers by hundreds of people daily, they became the most popular food at the fair. Served on plates and eaten with forks as in this recipe, they make a neater, but still nostalgic, dessert.

1 quart strawberries, cut in half
  lengthwise
2 cups heavy cream
2 tablespoons superfine or
  confectioners' sugar
½ teaspoon vanilla extract
1¼ cups sifted cake flour
2 teaspoons baking powder

¼ cup sugar
Generous pinch of salt
4 egg yolks
1½ cups milk
1 teaspoon vanilla extract
½ cup melted butter
4 egg whites
Sifted confectioners' sugar

Cut the strawberries in half lengthwise, and refrigerate. Whip the heavy cream until it holds its shape. Add the superfine or confectioners' sugar and ½ teaspoon vanilla extract, and whip until stiff. Refrigerate. Preheat a waffle iron. Sift together the cake flour, baking powder, sugar, and salt. Beat the egg yolks lightly, and add the milk, 1 teaspoon vanilla extract, and the melted butter. Stir in the sifted dry ingredients. Beat the egg whites until they are stiff, and fold them into the batter. Bake the waffles on the lightly oiled waffle iron at the medium setting, or according to the manufacturer's directions.

Dust the baked waffles with sifted confectioners' sugar, and place them on individual serving plates. Pipe the whipped cream onto the waffles through a pastry bag fitted with a large star tip, or spoon it on attractively. Strew some of the strawberries over each serving.

Makes 12 servings.

GERMAN BLACK FOREST CAKE

For the cake:
⅔ cup flour
¼ cup cornstarch
3 tablespoons cocoa
½ teaspoon baking powder
¼ teaspoon cinnamon
Pinch of cloves
½ cup blanched slivered almonds
¼ cup sugar
4 egg yolks
1 teaspoon lemon juice
2 tablespoons water
6 tablespoons sugar
4 egg whites

For the filling:
¼ cup sugar
½ cup water
2½ cups pitted fresh cherries
    plus whole, stemmed cherries
    for decoration
1 tablespoon arrowroot
2 tablespoons kirsch
1 recipe VANILLA BUTTER
    CREAM

For the finishing:
1½ cups heavy cream
1½ tablespoons sugar
1 tablespoon kirsch
Shaved bitter chocolate
CHOCOLATE TRIANGLES
Sifted confectioners' sugar

For the cake: Preheat the oven at 350°. Sift together the flour, cornstarch, cocoa, baking powder, cinnamon, and cloves. Blend the blanched slivered almonds with ¼ cup sugar in an electric blender or food processor until they are pulverized. Beat the egg yolks with the lemon juice and water. Add 3 tablespoons of the sugar, and beat until the mixture is thick and pale in color. Stir in the almond mixture. Sift the flour mixture over the batter, and fold it in, gently but thoroughly. Beat the egg whites until soft peaks form. Add the remaining 3 tablespoons sugar, 1 tablespoonful at a time, and beat until the mixture is stiff and glossy. Fold the egg whites into the batter. Pour into a well-buttered and floured 9-inch spring-form pan. Drop the pan once on the table to remove any air bubbles. Bake for about 30 minutes, or until a cake tester inserted in the center comes out clean. Cool slightly on a wire rack, remove the rim of the spring-form pan, and allow the cake to cool completely. Split the cake into 2 layers by cutting horizontally through it with a long, sharp knife.

For the filling: Combine the sugar and ¼ cup of the water in a saucepan. Bring to a boil, stirring. Add the pitted cherries, and simmer gently for 1 or 2 minutes. Remove the cherries. Combine the arrowroot with the remaining ¼ cup of water. Add to the syrup and cook, stirring, until it is thickened and clear. Remove from the heat and add the kirsch. Add the cherries and toss gently to coat them evenly. Set aside to cool.

Place one of the cake layers on a serving plate. Fill a pastry bag fitted with a large star tip with the Vanilla Butter Cream. Pipe a rim of butter cream to stand about 1 inch high all around the layer. Spoon the cooled cherry filling into the center. Set the second layer over the cherries and butter cream.

For finishing: Whip the heavy cream until stiff. Add the sugar and kirsch. Cover the top and sides of the cake with the whipped cream, using some to pipe rosettes around the top edge of the cake. Place a stemmed cherry in the center of each rosette. Press the shaved chocolate around the sides of cake into the whipped cream. Decorate the top of the cake inside the rosette border with Chocolate Triangles or shaved chocolate. Sift confectioners' sugar over the chocolate in the center of the cake.

Makes 8 to 10 servings.

Note: You may substitute canned pitted sour cherries (drained, and with the liquid reserved) for the fresh cherries in this recipe. In this case, substitute the cherry liquid for the water in preparing the cherry filling, and decorate the top of the cake with stemmed maraschino cherries.

SWEDISH PANCAKES WITH LINGONBERRIES

2 egg yolks
1 cup milk
¾ cup instant or quick-mixing
    flour
2 tablespoons sugar

¼ teaspoon salt
1 teaspoon baking powder
2 egg whites
1 jar or can lingonberries in
    syrup*

Beat the egg yolks well. Add the milk. Combine and add the flour, sugar, salt, and baking powder, stirring until no lumps remain. Beat the egg whites until stiff, and fold them into the batter. Heat a pancake griddle or Swedish plattar pan and butter well. Pour out small pancakes

* Lingonberries can be bought in specialty food stores or fancy groceries and are usually imported from Sweden.

and turn them over when they are brown at the sides and bubbly in the center. Continue cooking pancakes until the batter is used, buttering the pan as necessary. Serve about 5 pancakes per person, and spoon the lingonberries in syrup on each portion.

Makes 4 servings (about 20 pancakes).

NORWEGIAN FRUIT SOUP

1 pound (about 3 cups) dried
    mixed apples, pears, peaches,
    and apricots (no prunes)
Cold water
1 cinnamon stick
½ cup sugar
	1 cup orange juice
	1 tablespoon lemon juice
	2 tablespoons cornstarch
	¼ cup cold water
	3 thin slices orange

Place the dried fruit in a bowl, cover with cold water, and allow to stand for 6 hours or overnight. Measure the water and add or discard enough to make 5 cups. Place the water and fruit in a saucepan with the cinnamon stick, and bring to a boil. Simmer until all the fruit is tender. Discard the cinnamon stick. Puree the contents of the saucepan in an electric blender, food processor, or food mill. Return the mixture to the saucepan, and add the sugar, orange juice, and lemon juice. Mix the cornstarch with ¼ cup cold water, and stir into the soup. Bring to a boil and simmer for several minutes until the mixture is well heated and slightly thickened. Spoon into soup bowls and serve immediately, or cool, refrigerate, and serve the soup cold. Cut the orange slices in half, and garnish each serving with half a slice.

Makes 6 servings.

DANISH RED FRUIT MOLD
WITH CHERRY HEERING

1 one-pound can pitted tart red
    cherries
1 cup red currant jelly
¼ cup sugar
2 ten-ounce packages frozen
    raspberries, thawed
	½ cup cornstarch
	¼ cup cold water
	3 tablespoons Cherry Heering
	1 teaspoon lemon juice
	½ cup heavy cream
	2 teaspoons sugar

Combine the cherries (with their liquid), the red currant jelly, and ¼ cup sugar in a saucepan and bring to a boil, stirring until the sugar and jelly have dissolved. Remove from the heat and puree the mixture in an electric blender or food processor, along with the thawed raspberries and their liquid. Put the mixture through a sieve. Return it to the saucepan.

Combine the cornstarch and ¼ cup cold water. Add to the saucepan, and cook over medium heat, stirring constantly, until the mixture thickens and clears somewhat. Remove from the heat and stir in 2 tablespoons Cherry Heering and the lemon juice. Allow to cool slightly, then pour the mixture into a glass serving bowl. Cover and chill until firm. To serve, whip the heavy cream until stiff. Add 2 teaspoons sugar and the remaining 1 tablespoon Cherry Heering. Spoon onto the dessert.

Makes 8 servings.

RUSSIAN PASKA

The Russians like to serve this dessert with kulich, a sweet, fruit-studded, coffee cake–type cake. You may serve it with a similar type of cake, but it really isn't necessary. The Paska stands alone.

1½ pounds cottage cheese	½ cup candied citrus peel
1 cup sweet butter	½ cup sultanas or white raisins
1½ cups superfine sugar	½ cup slivered blanched almonds
3 egg yolks	Candied fruits, petite jelly eggs
2 teaspoons vanilla extract	(such as Maillard's), or
2 cups heavy cream	crystallized flowers

Wrap the cottage cheese in a clean piece of linen or muslin and flatten it out to make a rather flat cake. Place it between 2 boards or 2 flat, heavy baking pans with a weight on top. Refrigerate for 8 hours or overnight to remove excess water. Put the cottage cheese through a food ricer 7 times.

Cream the butter until soft. Add 1 cup of the superfine sugar and cream well. Beat the egg yolks thoroughly. Add the remaining ½ cup superfine sugar gradually and continue beating until the mixture is thick and pale and forms a slowly dissolving ribbon when the beater is lifted. Add the egg yolk mixture to the butter mixture along with the vanilla extract, and mix well. Add the sieved cottage cheese and combine thoroughly.

Whip the heavy cream until stiff, and fold it well but gently into the above mixture, about one-third at a time. Fold in the candied citrus peel, sultanas or white raisins, and slivered blanched almonds.

Line a clean clay flower pot (which must have a drainage hole at the bottom) with moistened cheesecloth. Make the cheesecloth as smooth as possible to avoid any ridges. Spoon the mixture into the cheesecloth-lined pot, and fold the edges of the cheesecloth over the top. Put a plate that just fits into the pot on top of the cheesecloth. There should be enough room for the plate to press down on the cheese without becoming wedged. Place a heavy weight on the plate, and set the pot in the refrigerator on a soup plate or dinner plate with a saucer in between to catch any drainage from the bottom of the pot. Allow it to sit for 1 or 2 days before serving.

To serve, peel back the cheesecloth from the top, unmold the dessert onto a serving plate, and carefully peel off the cheesecloth. With candied fruits or petite jelly eggs (since this dessert is traditionally served at Eastertime), mark the initials "XB" (which stands for "Christ is risen") on the side of the Paska, or decorate it in any way you wish with candied fruits or crystallized flowers. Serve on dessert plates and eat with a fork.

Makes 15 or more servings.

ALGERIAN COUSCOUS WITH FRUIT

1 cup couscous	½ cup combined raisins and
2 cups milk	currants
Pinch of salt	⅓ cup apricot jam
2 tablespoons butter	Blanched slivered almonds
¼ cup sugar	Heavy cream

Place the couscous in a fine strainer and rinse under cold running water, fluffing the grains with the fingers. Allow to stand for 5 minutes. Meanwhile, bring the milk to a boil in a saucepan. Rinse the couscous again under cold running water, fluffing. Add the salt and butter to the boiling milk, and stir until the butter has melted. Sprinkle in the couscous and cook, stirring, for several minutes until most of the milk has been absorbed. Remove from the heat and stir in the sugar, raisins, and currants. Cover and allow to stand off the heat for 15 minutes.

Stir in the apricot jam. Spoon the dessert into serving dishes. Strew some slivered blanched almonds over the top, and pour some heavy cream over each serving.

Makes 4 to 5 servings.

MEXICAN ROYAL EGGS

2 tablespoons raisins	½ cup water
¼ cup Sherry	1 cinnamon stick
5 egg yolks	2 whole cloves
1 cup sugar	3 tablespoons pine nuts

Preheat the oven at 350°. Combine the raisins and Sherry, and set aside. Beat the egg yolks until they are very thick and form a slowly dissolving ribbon when the beater is lifted. Pour the egg yolks into a buttered shallow baking pan about 9 inches square. Set the baking pan in a larger pan and pour hot water all around. Bake for 30 to 35 minutes, or until the eggs have set. Remove from the oven and allow to cool slightly.

Meanwhile, combine the sugar, water, cinnamon stick, and cloves in a saucepan. Bring to a boil, stirring, and simmer for 5 minutes. Remove from the heat and discard the spices. Add the raisin-Sherry mixture and the pine nuts.

Cut the egg yolks into squares, and remove them from the pan with a spatula. Place the squares on a flat serving dish. Pour the hot syrup over them. Allow them to cool before serving.

Makes 6 servings.

WEST INDIAN LIME CREAM

For the mold:
3 egg yolks
¼ cup sugar
1 cup canned sweetened coconut
   cream
1 cup milk
2 envelopes plain gelatin
2 tablespoons cold water
2 tablespoons rum
3 egg whites
2 tablespoons sugar
1 cup heavy cream

For the sauce:
¼ cup sugar
1 tablespoon cornstarch
1 cup cold water
Pinch of salt
3 tablespoons butter, cut into
   small pieces
2 tablespoons lime juice
1 drop green pure vegetable
   food coloring
Thin slices of lime dipped in
   superfine sugar

For the mold: Beat the egg yolks until thick and add ¼ cup sugar gradually, continuing to beat until the mixture is thick and pale and forms a slowly dissolving ribbon when the beater is lifted. Transfer the mixture to a saucepan and add the sweetened coconut cream and milk gradually. Cook over medium heat, stirring, until the mixture thickens slightly. Soften the gelatin in the cold water combined with the rum. Stir into the egg mixture and stir until the gelatin has dissolved. Remove from the heat. Set the saucepan in a bowl of ice cubes and stir until cool. Place the saucepan in freezer and freeze until the mixture begins to set slightly.

Beat the egg whites until soft peaks form. Add 2 tablespoons sugar, 1 tablespoonful at a time, and continue beating until the mixture is thick and glossy. Fold a little of the egg yolk mixture into the egg whites. Then fold the egg whites into the egg yolk mixture. Whip the heavy cream until stiff. Fold a little of the egg mixture into the whipped cream. Then fold the whipped cream into the egg mixture. Pour into a lightly oiled 6-cup mold and cover with plastic wrap. Chill until firm.

For the sauce: Combine the sugar, cornstarch, and cold water in a saucepan. Bring to a boil, stirring, and cook until the mixture thickens. Remove from the heat and stir in the salt and pieces of butter. Stir in the lime juice and food coloring. Cool. To serve, unmold the dessert on a serving dish. Stir the sauce with a wire whisk to make it smooth, and pour it over the dessert. Decorate with thin slices of lime which have been dipped in superfine sugar.

Makes 8 servings.

CHINESE STEAMED CAKE

3 egg whites
⅔ cup sugar
3 egg yolks
1 teaspoon vanilla extract

⅔ cup flour
¼ teaspoon baking powder
3 tablespoons finely chopped
   crystallized ginger

Beat the egg whites until soft peaks form. Add the sugar gradually and continue beating until the mixture is stiff and glossy. Beat the egg yolks with the vanilla extract and fold into the egg whites. Sift the flour and baking powder together over the batter and fold in gently. Fold in the chopped crystallized ginger. Pour the mixture into a well-buttered, round, 1-quart baking dish about 7 inches in diameter. Set on a rack in a large pot with 1 inch of boiling water in the bottom. Place a lid on the pot, and allow the water to simmer, steaming the cake, for about 25 minutes. Test with a cake tester in the center, and when the cake is done, invert it on a wire rack to cool.

Makes 6 servings.

INDONESIAN COCONUT DESSERT

2 tablespoons butter
⅓ cup sugar
¼ cup sifted flour
1 teaspoon cinnamon
Pinch of salt
6 egg yolks

1½ cups canned sweetened
   coconut cream
6 egg whites
¼ cup sugar
2 tablespoons grated coconut

Preheat the oven at 350°. Cream the butter. Add ⅓ cup sugar gradually, beating constantly. Sift the flour, cinnamon, and salt together and add to the butter-syrup mixture, beating well. Add the egg yolks, 1 at a time, beating well after each addition. Add the sweetened coconut cream and mix well. Beat the egg whites until soft peaks form. Add ¼ cup sugar gradually, and continue beating until the mixture is thick and glossy. Fold into the first mixture. Pour into a buttered 1½-quart baking dish and sprinkle with grated coconut. Set the baking dish in a pan of hot water, which should reach a level halfway up the side of the baking dish. Bake for about 45 minutes until the top half sets. The bottom half will be moist. Cool and chill.

Makes 6 servings.

INDIAN VERMICELLI DESSERT

½ cup butter
4 ounces fine Indian vermicelli*
1½ cups milk
2 tablespoons brown sugar
Pinch of saffron
Pinch of cinnamon

¼ teaspoon ground cardamom
1 teaspoon rosewater (optional)
3 or 4 tablespoons blanched
  slivered almonds or chopped
  pistachios

Melt the butter in a heavy saucepan over a medium flame. Add the vermicelli and stir until all the strands are coated with butter and are separated and slightly wilted. Add the milk and stir, lowering the flame, until the vermicelli is soft and creamy. Remove from the heat. (The entire operation takes only a few minutes.) Add the brown sugar and stir well. Add the saffron, cinnamon, and cardamom, and combine. Arrange the mixture in a serving bowl and sprinkle with rosewater, if desired, and strew with blanched slivered almonds or chopped pistachios. Serve the dessert at room temperature or chilled.

Makes 6 servings.

* A threadlike vermicelli made of rice. It may be bought in specialty food shops or Indian markets.

CHAPTER 21

Superfast Desserts

Quickly enough if done well enough.
—Cato, from the Latin

It seems as though Americans have been in a hurry to get dessert made since the first settlers landed on our Eastern shores centuries ago. Old recipe collections from colonial times show that such dishes as "hurry-up gingerbread" and "ten-minute cake" are not unique to the twentieth century.

Packaged dessert mixes are lined up on grocers' shelves by the score, promising to get you in and out of the kitchen in almost no time. Baked goods, frozen and fresh, can be bought at every supermarket across the nation. Yet most of these desserts seem to lack something in either quality, flavor, natural goodness, or appearance, and many have a distinctly chemical taste or mass-produced look.

One can bypass these products with no regrets, to have, instead, a decidedly superior and equally fast dessert. Only an ingredient or two such as some fruit, a good ice cream, or a bit of leftover homemade pound cake, can form the basis of a quick dessert with genuine character. With a little planning, you can have the fixings for special yet fast desserts always at your fingertips. Utilizing your freezer, taking a trip to your wine and liquor store, and visiting specialty food shops can all help you accomplish this.

Your freezer is your best friend for supplying you with instant desserts. Anytime you make crêpes, cream puffs, pie shells or tartlet shells, make enough to put some in your freezer. Store them in plastic containers to keep them from being crushed. Crêpes, cream puffs, and shells can be filled with fresh, frozen, or canned fruit, custard, or ice cream. Other shells that are good for quick serving are meringue shells, bought or homemade, which can be kept in a tin box or in the freezer; chocolate cups, bought or homemade, which can be kept in a cool place; or sponge shells, either a very good bought brand or homemade, which can be kept in the freezer. When you bake cookies that are especially nice, freeze enough of them, too, to serve with one or two future desserts.

Visit your local wine and liquor store and buy a bottle or two of liqueur to keep on hand just for your desserts. Liqueurs can make a plain dessert seem special, and since you'll need to use only a spoonful or two at a time, two bottles will last a long time. An orange-flavored liqueur such as curaçao or Grand Marnier is nice, and another flavor to choose might be chocolate (crème de cacao), or coffee (Kahlua or Tia Maria), or a fruit-flavored brandy or liqueur such as strawberry, raspberry, cherry (kirsch), or black currant (crème de cassis). Liqueurs can be used to sweeten and flavor whipped cream for toppings or fillings, added to cut-up fruits before serving, poured over frozen desserts, and used to flavor creams, custards, and puddings.

Drop into gourmet shops or specialty food stores and markets whenever you have the opportunity, and build up a little collection of special dessert ingredients. A package of crystallized violets or mint leaves, a jar of chestnuts (marrons) in vanilla syrup, a bottle of sliced ginger in syrup, a jar or can of unusual fruit, a box of meringue shells, a tin of gaufrettes (fan-shaped ice cream wafers), a jar of distinctive dessert sauce, some imported honey, some canned nuts, candied fruits, a special preserve or jam such as Bar-le-Duc currants or wild strawberries—all will keep on your pantry shelf almost indefinitely and be ready to use at any time. These niceties make the difference between a dessert that will be remembered and another that will simply be acceptable.

One of the fastest yet most impressive speedy desserts you can make is the coupe. Coupes are composed of one or more flavors of ice cream, sherbet, or ice, often with a sprinkling of fruit, sometimes with sweetened, flavored whipped cream, and usually with a garnish of nuts or fruit or confection of some sort. Brandied fruits, candied flowers, and exotic nuts like pistachios or Macadamias all dress up these desserts beautifully. Served in silver or glass cups, or coupes, these desserts can be made in endless combinations of flavors—all great fun to invent. Six excellent coupes are included in this chapter to use as starting points for your own combinations. The Coupe Jacques, by the way, is the granddaddy of all coupes and might be considered as a model for others. Since coupes are fairly light desserts, they're equally nice at lunchtime or after a heavy dinner. In fact, it's difficult to think of a meal where they wouldn't be appropriate.

Fruits lend themselves to quick preparation and are among the most satisfying of all desserts. Especially quick fruit recipes are included in this chapter, as is a list of fast fruit desserts in other parts of this book.

Don't overlook cheese, or cheese and fruit together, as the fastest of all desserts (see Chapter 11). The only thing you will need to remember ahead of time is to remove the cheeses from the refrigerator several hours before serving, so that they will be at their best at dessert time.

Dessert sauces can provide interesting flavor and texture contrasts to the foods you use them with. Many hot dessert sauces (see Chapter 3) are fast to make and can dress up almost anything. Serve, for instance, butterscotch sauce over simple- made-the-day-before custard, apricot sauce over toasted angel food cake, chocolate sauce over coffee-ice-cream-filled crêpes, vanilla custard sauce over drained, chilled, poached peaches. Sauces which are served cold can be kept on hand in your pantry or freezer. Almost any flavor of sauce can be spread on crêpes before rolling them up, Blueberry sauce would be nice over lemon sherbet and fluffy orange sauce would be good over strawberries.

At informal gatherings you can make dessert so fast that you really don't make it at all. Let your guests make their own desserts. Put out the fixings for ice cream sundaes and two or three different kinds of ice cream or ices turned out onto serving plates. Do this in the same spirit that you'd serve a fondue, with everyone doing his own food in his own way. Or serve waffles (your own which you've made previously, frozen, thawed, and heated up in the toaster) with an assortment of sauces, and let everyone choose his or her own favorite.

These and other quick dessert ideas included in this chapter, as well as the following recipes in other parts of this book, will please you and your guests far more than anything you might buy already made on hurry-up days.

Banana Cream Crêpes
Bananas à la Crème
Blueberries in Cream
Brandied Grapefruit
Cheeses for Dessert
Cheeses and Fruit for Dessert
Chocolate Fondue
Coeur à la Crème with Strawberries
Coffee Ring
Coupe Vanderbilt
Double Mocha
Flaming Rum Omelet
Gold Brick Sundae

Honey Parfait
Irish Coffee
Orange Coffee Cream
Persimmons in Cream
Raspberries with Liqueur
Rum Bananas with Kumquats
Strawberry Mincemeat Crêpes
Vanilla Ice Cream Converts to . . .
Zabaglione

MARRONS IN SYRUP OVER VANILLA ICE CREAM

1 eleven-ounce jar chestnuts in syrup (*marrons au sirop*)

2 tablespoons brandy
1 quart vanilla ice cream

Combine the chestnuts and their syrup with the brandy, and allow the mixture to sit at room temperature for 1 hour. Drain and break up coarsely all but 6 of the best-looking chestnuts. Distribute the broken-up chestnuts evenly in dessert glasses. Spoon the ice cream over the chestnuts. Top each glass with 1 whole reserved chestnut. Pour the syrup over all.

Makes 6 servings.

CHINESE GOOSEBERRY CUP

2 fourteen-ounce jars or cans Chinese gooseberries
¼ cup drained ginger in syrup, finely chopped
2 tablespoons syrup from ginger in syrup

6 tablespoons heavy cream
6 tablespoons canned sweetened coconut cream

Place the gooseberries with 6 tablespoons of their liquid in a glass or china bowl. Add the finely chopped ginger and the ginger syrup Refrigerate for 1 or 2 hours. Spoon into dessert glasses. Combine the heavy cream and sweetened coconut cream and pour over the gooseberries.

Makes 6 servings.

SHERBET CREME DE MENTHE

1 pint raspberry sherbet* **6 tablespoons crème de menthe**

Spoon the sherbet into dessert glasses. Pour 2 tablespoons crème de menthe over each serving.

Makes 3 servings. The recipe may be doubled.

* This dessert may also be made with orange, strawberry, or lemon sherbet.

CHINESE TREAT

**1 twenty-ounce can seedless
 lichees in syrup
1 eleven-ounce can mandarin
 orange segments**

1 small can pineapple chunks
CHINESE ALMOND COOKIES
 **(homemade or bought)
 (optional)**

Drain the lichees and mandarin orange segments, and combine with the undrained pineapple chunks. Chill well. Divide into dessert glasses. If desired, serve with Chinese Almond Cookies.

Makes 8 servings.

BLUEBERRIES
IN KAHLUA CREAM

**1 pint blueberries
½ cup heavy cream**

**1 tablespoon sugar
¼ cup Kahlua**

Chill the blueberries, and divide them among 4 dessert glasses. Combine the heavy cream, sugar, and Kahlua, and pour over the berries.

Makes 4 servings.

BRANDIED FRUIT CUP

6 large scoops vanilla ice cream
or APRICOT HONEY ICE
CREAM

12 to 18 spoonfuls mixed
brandied fruits, or 12 brandied
pear halves, or 12 brandied
peach halves
Whipped cream

Place a large scoop of ice cream in each dessert glass. Spoon 2 or 3 spoonfuls of mixed brandied fruits or 2 brandied pear or peach halves around each serving. Top with a dollop of whipped cream.

Makes 6 servings.

QUICK-AS-A-WINK
STRAWBERRY SOUFFLE

1 sixteen-ounce jar strawberry*
jelly (not preserves)
5 egg whites
Pinch of cream of tartar

LADYFINGERS (homemade, or
good bakery ladyfingers)
(optional)

Preheat the oven at 325°. Beat the strawberry jelly with a wire whisk or spoon until it is free of lumps. Beat the egg whites until foamy. Add the cream of tartar, and beat until stiff. Fold the egg whites into the jelly with a rubber spatula, and turn into a buttered 1½-quart soufflé dish. Bake for 15 minutes, or until the top is lightly browned. Serve immediately, preferably with Ladyfingers or some simple, not-too-sweet cookies.

Makes 6 servings.

* Any distinctive flavor of jelly, such as blueberry or beach plum, may be used instead.

ICED FRUIT IN GINGER WINE

1 jar or package frozen assorted
mixed fruits, peaches, whole
strawberries, or cherries

Ginger wine (such as Stone's
Ginger Wine), chilled

Defrost the frozen fruit until it is nearly thawed but still contains some ice crystals. Drain and divide the fruit among 4 wide dessert glasses. Fill the glasses halfway with ginger wine and serve immediately.
Makes 4 servings.

MINTED APRICOTS

1 cup heavy cream
2 tablespoons white crème de menthe

24 to 30 canned apricot halves, drained and chilled
Crystallized or fresh mint leaves

Whip the heavy cream until stiff, and fold in the crème de menthe. Arrange 4 or 5 apricot halves, drained, in each of 6 dessert glasses. Spoon the whipped cream over the apricots. Decorate with a mint leaf on each glass.
Makes 6 servings.

MANDARIN ORANGES IN LIME

1 small can crushed pineapple
1 can mandarin orange segments

1 pint lime sherbet or water ice.*

Chill the pineapple and mandarin orange segments well. Drain. Soften the sherbet and quickly work the fruit mixture into it. Spoon into 4 dessert glasses and serve immediately.
Makes 4 servings.

* This dessert may also be made with orange or lemon sherbet or water ice.

BABAS WITH ICE CREAM

1 jar petite babas au rhum

Vanilla ice cream

Divide the babas into dessert glasses, allowing 3 per portion. Top each with a small scoop of vanilla ice cream.

GINGERED HONEYDEW

1 small honeydew, well chilled
1 tablespoon preserved ginger in
syrup, drained (reserving the
syrup) and finely sliced

2 tablespoons syrup from
preserved ginger in syrup

Remove the seeds and peel the shell from the honeydew. Cut the meat into enough bite-sized pieces to make 3 cups. Toss with the sliced preserved ginger and syrup. Spoon into 4 dessert glasses.
Makes 4 servings.

BLACKBERRIES IN PORT CREAM

1 tablespoon superfine sugar
¼ cup Port wine

½ cup heavy cream
1 pint blackberries

Combine the sugar, Port, and heavy cream. Divide the berries into dessert glasses. Pour the port cream over the berries.
Makes 4 servings.

TOASTED CAKE GLACE

1 POUND CAKE (homemade, or
good-quality bought pound
cake) or any good-quality
simple cake containing fruit,
seeds, or nuts

Any flavor ice cream, slightly
softened

Cut the cake into ½-inch-thick slices, allowing 1 slice per serving. Lay the slices on a baking sheet and toast under the broiler. Turn and toast the other side. Place a slice of cake on each individual dessert plate and top with a large spoonful of slightly softened ice cream. Serve immediately.

FRUITED SPONGE SHELL

1 good-quality bought sponge cake shell (such as Bahlsen's)	2 tablespoons superfine sugar 2 tablespoons orange liqueur
2 cups heavy cream	4 chilled peaches or nectarines

Set the sponge cake shell on a serving dish. Whip the heavy cream until stiff and add the sugar and orange liqueur. Peel and slice enough peaches or nectarines to measure 3½ to 4 cups. Arrange 2 cups of sliced fruit in the cake shell. Spoon the whipped cream over the top. Arrange the balance of the fruit slices over the whipped cream. Serve immediately.

Makes 6 servings.

VARIATIONS:

Strawberry Sponge Shell

Substitute fresh strawberries for the peaches, and substitute strawberry or raspberry liqueur for the orange liqueur. (Blueberries, apricots, or other fruits may be used instead, or a combination of 2 fruits.)

Fruited Ice Cream Sponge Shell

Fill the cake shell with 1 pint softened vanilla ice cream. Freeze until firm. Top with whipped cream and 2 cups of chilled, sliced fruit, and serve immediately.

PETIT SUISSE
WITH GUAVA SHELLS

1 can guava shells	3 or 4 Petit Suisse

Chill the guava shells, drain them, and arrange 2 or 3 pieces in each dessert glass. Remove the wrappings from the Petit Suisse and place 1 piece of cheese over the fruit in each dish.

Makes 3 or 4 servings.

FILLED CHOCOLATE CUPS

CHOCOLATE CUPS (homemade
  or bought)
Large scoop of ice cream, such
  as vanilla, coffee, or pistachio,
  or large scoop of mousse or

frozen cream, such as banana,
violet, orange liqueur, and
so on
Crystallized flowers or mint
leaves

Arrange the Chocolate Cups, 1 per serving, on individual dessert plates. Make ice cream or frozen dessert balls, and transfer them gently into the Chocolate Cups. Don't attempt to push against the Chocolate Cups with an ice cream scoop, or you may break them. Top each with a crystallized flower or mint leaf and serve immediately.

FILLED MERINGUE SHELLS

MERINGUE SHELLS (homemade
  or bought)
Ice cream
Whipped cream

Crystallized flowers or
appropriate flavor of candied
fruit

Place a Meringue Shell on each individual serving plate. Make ice cream balls and transfer them gently into the Meringue Shells. Do not attempt to push against the Meringue Shells with an ice cream scoop, or you may break them. Decorate the top of each ice cream ball with whipped cream piped through a pastry bag fitted with a star tip. Top with a crystallized flower or small piece of candied fruit.

The Meringue Shells may also be filled with any fresh fruit, sliced if necessary, and sweetened if desired. Serve with or without whipped cream.

SNEAKY CHOCOLATE MOUSSE

Good-quality frozen chocolate
  mousse (such as Gourmaid),
  allowing ¼ cup per serving

Crystallized violets or lilacs

Thaw the mousse sufficiently to spoon it out. Transfer to *pots au crème* cups. Place a crystallized violet or lilac on each and serve immediately, or freeze until 30 minutes before serving and then transfer to the refrigerator.

SNEAKY PETITS FOURS

Good-quality bought pastel and
  chocolate petits fours

1 seven-ounce package glazed
  chestnuts (*marrons glacés*)

Arrange the petits fours on a serving plate with the candied chestnuts, which come wrapped in gold foil and look very festive with the frosted petits fours. Add any other small cookies or confections you think appropriate.

COUPE DE PARMA

Napoleon is said to have loved Parma, Italy, where violets grow in abundance. This coupe is trimmed with crystallized violets, probably the most beautiful edible dessert decoration there is. Crystallized violets, or candied violets, can be purchased at gourmet food shops or in specialty food departments, and one box lasts a very long time without spoiling or fading.

1 cup pineapple chunks, fresh
  or canned, unsweetened
  (drained)
1 tablespoon brandy

1 pint orange sherbet or orange
  water ice
Whipped cream
3 crystallized violets

Pour the brandy over the pineapple chunks in a glass or china bowl. Cover and chill for 1 hour or longer. Divide the fruit among 3 dessert glasses. Arrange a large scoop of sherbet or water ice on top of the pineapple in each glass. Top with a dollop of whipped cream and a crystallized violet.

Makes 3 servings.

COUPE SULTANE

1 pint pistachio ice cream　　　　**Chopped pistachios**
3 large, chilled peach halves

Place a large scoop of ice cream in each of 3 dessert glasses. Arrange a peach half, hollow side down, over the ice cream. Top with chopped pistachios.

Makes 3 servings.

COUPE AUX ROSES VANILLE

½ cup firmly packed red rose　　　**1 tablespoon rosewater**
petals* and 1 tablespoon　　　　　**½ cup heavy cream**
confectioners' sugar, or 2　　　　　**½ teaspoon vanilla extract**
tablespoons rose petal jam　　　　**2 teaspoon sugar**
1 pint vanilla ice cream　　　　　　**3 crystallized rose petals**

Pound the rose petals in a mortar and pestle with the confectioners' sugar until they are thoroughly broken down. Soften the ice cream and mix in the rose petal mixture or the rose petal jam along with the rose-water. Pack into a plastic container, cover it tightly, and freeze until firm.

Whip the heavy cream until stiff, and add the vanilla extract and sugar. Divide the ice cream among 3 dessert glasses. Spoon on the whipped cream and top with a crystallized rose petal.

Makes 3 servings.

Note: This dessert is especially pretty served with a plate of TUILES or bought fan wafers (*gaufrettes*).

* Use only rose petals that you know do not have any chemicals or insecticides on them. Roses that are too open to be sold but that are still fresh and good can sometimes be bought from a florist at very low cost, but make sure about the chemicals before you buy at any cost.

COUPE JACQUES

1½ cups fresh raspberries,
  halved strawberries, or pitted,
  halved sweet cherries
1 tablespoon sugar
2 tablespoons kirsch

1 pint lemon water ice or sherbet
1 pint strawberry ice cream
Almond halves
Candied cherries (optional)

Combine the fruit, sugar, and kirsch in a small bowl. Cover and allow to macerate for 1 hour or longer. Place a scoop each of lemon water ice or sherbet and strawberry ice cream side by side in 6 dessert glasses wide enough to hold them. Spoon a few tablespoonsful of the macerated fruit into the space between the ice and the ice cream. Decorate the dessert with almond halves and, if desired, candied cherries.

Makes 6 servings.

GUAVA PINEAPPLE COUPE

¾ cup guava jelly
1 cup drained, crushed pineapple

1 quart lime, lemon, or pineapple
  sherbet or vanilla ice cream

Melt the guava jelly in a saucepan, and stir in the crushed pineapple. Remove from the heat and allow to cool. Spoon into tall sherbet glasses in alternate layers with sherbet or ice cream, ending with the guava-pineapple mixture.

Makes 6 to 8 servings.

COFFEE CHESTNUT COUPE

1 cup chestnuts in syrup
  (*marron au sirop*), drained
  (reserving syrup)
2 or 3 tablespoons coffee liqueur

1 pint vanilla ice cream
1 pint coffee ice cream
Whipped cream (optional)
2 tablespoons syrup from
  chestnuts in syrup

Break the chestnuts up into small pieces and combine them in a bowl with the coffee liqueur. Place a scoop each of vanilla ice cream and coffee ice cream side by side in 6 dessert glasses wide enough to hold them. Spoon a few tablespoonsful of the chestnut mixture into the space between the ice cream scoops. If desired, top with whipped cream which has been combined with the syrup from the chestnuts in syrup.

Makes 6 servings.

CHAPTER 22

VIP Desserts for Very Impressive Presentation

A wilderness of sweets.

—*John Milton,* Paradise Lost

Here are the show-offs, the dazzlers, the spectacular, the elaborate, the most beautiful among desserts. Choose them for special occasions, holidays, or just for the fun of making them to share with an appreciative audience.

Impressive desserts are by no means a twentieth-century innovation. In the early nineteenth century, some desserts were so dazzling as to be outrageous. Pastries, custards, and confectionery were stacked up, molded, sculpted, and chiseled according to involved patterns more like architecture than food to simulate buildings, people, animals, birds, trees, and just about anything else the cook dreamed up. These arrangements, known as set pieces, were presented as tableaux to be looked at, admired, and sometimes cheered, but almost never eaten. Solomon's Temple, a specialty of the day, was made of three shades of flummery (a sort of pudding): pale brown for the building stones, and pink and white for the turrets and trimmings. The edifice was adorned with flower sprays and rock candy, and was often whisked away to be saved for another showing as soon as it had been paraded around the room.

Ostentatious desserts seem to have given way to quite charming ones in early America. Virginia housewives with infinite patience made "hen's nests" for special occasions. Shredded lemon and orange peel, cooked and sugared to resemble straw, was strewn over a jelly base in a serving dish to form a nest. Into the nest went blancmange eggs which had been molded in blown-out eggshells, carefully peeled off.

Most of the impressiveness of present-day special desserts, as in the past, comes from the amount of time spent in their creation, or the ingenuity of their concept. While there are some recipes in this collection that call for expensive ingredients like brandied fruits or champagne, most utilize everyday ingredients treated in interesting ways. Croquembouche is nothing more than simple cream puffs piled up in a unique fashion, and Mont Blanc is just a hill of chestnut puree pushed through a ricer.

In addition to the recipes in this chapter, other Very Impressive Presentation desserts in this book are:

Beehive Cake
Brie en Croûte
Candied Oranges in White Wine Jelly
Gâteau Saint Honoré
Glazed Chestnut Cake with Black Currant Sauce
Meringue Butter Cream Cake
Midnight Sun Baked Alaska
Paris Brest
Strawberry Orange Flambé
The Versatile Bombe
Treasure Chest Torte
Spotted Dog (trimmed with holly and flamed with brandy)

COUPE VANDERBILT

1 cup chopped fresh strawberries **1 pint orange water ice or sherbet**
2 tablespoons orange liqueur **Chilled Champagne**

Combine the chopped strawberries and orange liqueur. Cover and chill for 1 hour. Divide the water ice or sherbet among 4 dessert glasses. Spoon the strawberry mixture on top. Pour enough chilled champagne into each glass to nearly fill it. Serve immediately.

Makes 4 servings.

CROQUEMBOUCHE

For the base:
½ recipe PUFF PASTRY

For the cream puffs:
1 recipe BASIC CREAM PUFFS
1 egg beaten
1 teaspoon water
1 recipe PASTRY CREAM, chilled

For the caramel
and to assemble:
⅔ cup water
2 cups sugar
½ teaspoon cream of tartar

For the base: Roll out the puff pastry ¼-inch thick. With a sharp knife, cut a circle 8 inches in diameter in the pastry, transfer the circle to a baking sheet, and chill for 30 minutes. Freeze the balance of the pastry for another use. (The Croquembouche can be made without this base by building directly on the serving plate, but it is easier to build and looks better if you do make the base.) Preheat the oven at 450°. Remove the pastry circle from the refrigerator and prick all over with the tines of a fork. Bake for 5 to 10 minutes until it is puffed and light brown. Reduce the oven temperature to 350° and continue baking for 10 to 15 minutes until it is dry. Cool on a wire rack.

For the cream puffs: Make the cream-puff dough and make mounds a scant 1 inch in diameter on a baking sheet. Brush with a mixture of beaten egg and water. Bake according to directions and cool on a wire rack. Fill the cooled cream puffs with the pastry cream, using a pastry bag fitted with a large plain tip and forcing the cream through holes in the bottoms of the puffs.

For the caramel and to assemble: Place the puff pastry base on a serving plate. Select an appropriately shaped dish or mold to use as a guide in building a pyramid atop the pastry base, or use a croquembouche cone. Set it on the puff pastry base.

Combine the water, sugar, and cream of tartar in a heavy saucepan. Bring to a boil, stirring, and lower the heat to moderate. Continue to cook without stirring until the mixture is thickened and amber in color. Pierce a filled cream puff with a fork and dip it into the syrup. Place on the base to start forming the first layer of puffs around the mold. Continue dipping the puffs 1 at a time, and place them next to each other, touching, until the first ring is formed. Build the second layer on the first, placing puffs between the puffs of the row below, and so on, each row smaller than the one before, until you have built a pyramid, ending with one cream puff on top. Any extra syrup can be poured over the entire pyramid, but do not overcoat.

Do not allow the pyramid to stand too long before serving. Ideally the mold should be removed and the free-standing pyramid of cream puffs set on the base, but this is difficult to do and not absolutely necessary. Serve 3 or 4 cream puffs per portion.

Makes 10 or more portions.

MONT BLANC

Mont Blanc recreates in the most spectacular gastronomic manner the snow-covered peak of the most impressive mountain of the Alps. The "mountain" is a lightly packed drift of chestnut puree covered by a billow of whipped cream "snow."

1 fifteen-ounce can chestnut puree
   (*purée de marrons au*
   naturel)
⅔ cup sugar
¼ cup water
2 tablespoons softened butter

2 teaspoons vanilla extract
1 cup heavy cream
2 tablespoons sugar
1 tablespoon brandy or rum
Coarsely shaved chocolate

Stir the chestnut puree until it is smooth. Combine ⅔ cup sugar and the water in a saucepan and bring to a boil, stirring, until the sugar has dissolved. Cover and boil until the soft-ball stage is reached, about 238°, removing the cover every few minutes to test. Stir the syrup into the chestnut puree and mix well. Add the softened butter and vanilla extract and combine well. Chill for 3 hours.

Force the puree through a pastry bag fitted with a plain tip ⅛ to 3/16 inch in diameter, or through a cookie press with a disk containing a number of plain holes of the same size, into a ring mold 6 or 7 inches in diameter. Allow the puree to fall carelessly into the mold, and do not press it down, but let it pile up loosely. It should look like thick, cooked spaghetti. Unmold onto a serving plate. Chill for several hours or overnight, covered loosely with plastic wrap.

To serve, whip the heavy cream until stiff. Add 2 tablespoons sugar and the brandy or rum. Pile the flavored whipped cream up in the center of the chestnut ring. Sprinkle the whipped cream with coarsely shaved chocolate.

Makes 6 to 8 servings.

BRANDIED FRUITS IN CHAMPAGNE AND ORANGE JELLY

1 cup brandied fruits, drained
   and dried well
2 envelopes plain gelatin
¾ cup orange juice
½ cup boiling water

10 ice cubes
1 cup Champagne
1 cup heavy cream
1 tablespoon orange liqueur

Arrange the brandied fruits attractively in the bottom of a lightly oiled 4-cup mold. Soften the gelatin in ¼ cup of the orange juice. Add the boiling water and stir until the gelatin has dissolved. Add the remaining ½ cup of the orange juice, the ice cubes, and the Champagne, and stir until the mixture begins to thicken slightly. Remove the ice cubes. Spoon enough of the mixture over the fruit in the mold to make a layer about ½-inch deep. Freeze for several minutes until the fruit is firmly set in the jelly. Pour the remaining gelatin gently over the back of a spoon into the mold. Cover and chill for several hours. Unmold on a serving plate and serve with heavy cream (which has been whipped until stiff, and flavored with the orange liqueur).

Makes 4 servings.

BUCHE DE NOEL

For the cake:
3 eggs
1 cup sugar
5 tablespoons water
1 teaspoon vanilla extract
1 cup sifted cake flour
1 teaspoon baking powder
¼ teaspoon salt
Granulated sugar

For the filling:
½ cup sweet butter
2 fifteen-ounce cans chestnut
  puree (*purée de marrons au
  naturel*)
4 ounces semisweet chocolate,
  broken up
2 tablespoons milk

1 tablespoon instant espresso
  coffee powder
1 teaspoon vanilla extract
1 cup sifted confectioners' sugar

For the meringue mushrooms:
1 egg white
Pinch of cream of tartar
¼ cup sugar
Cornstarch
1 tablespoon butter
Sifted confectioners' sugar

For assembling:
1 recipe CHOCOLATE BUTTER
  CREAM FROSTING
½ cup chopped pistachios
Confectioners' sugar

For the cake: Preheat the oven at 375°. Beat the eggs until thick. Add the sugar gradually, and continue beating until the mixture is thick and pale and forms a slowly dissolving ribbon when the beater is lifted. Beat in water and vanilla extract. Sift the cake flour, baking powder, and salt together, and sift again over the batter. Fold in gently but thoroughly. Heavily butter a jelly roll pan measuring about 10½x14 inches, and line it with waxed paper. Butter the waxed paper heavily. Spread the batter evenly in the pan and bake for 12 to 15 minutes. Turn out onto a clean dish towel covered with granulated sugar. Peel off the waxed paper and trim off the edges of the cake all around. Starting at the long side, roll up the cake, using the towel to aid in the process. Place on a wire rack to cool.

For the filling: Cream the butter. Add the chestnut puree gradually. Place the chocolate, milk, instant espresso coffee powder, and vanilla extract in the top of a double boiler. Set over hot water and heat, stirring, until the chocolate has completely melted and is smooth. Remove from the heat and add the confectioners' sugar, stirring until it has dissolved. Add to the chestnut mixture and mix until it is well blended. Place in a plastic wrap and chill until firm. Shape the mixture, still in the plastic wrap, into a long roll the same length as the cake, and refrigerate until ready to use.

For the meringue mushrooms: Preheat the oven at 200°. Beat the egg white until foamy. Add the cream of tartar, and beat until soft peaks form. Add the sugar gradually and continue beating until stiff peaks form. Line a baking sheet with aluminum foil and sprinkle all over with sifted cornstarch. Place the meringue in a pastry bag fitted with a large plain tip. Pipe out small ¾-inch mounds for mushroom caps, and smooth the tops if necessary with a spatula. Holding the bag vertically, pipe out meringue for stems, pulling the bag straight up. Make an equal number of caps and stems. Bake about 1 hour until thoroughly dry. Cool and remove from the baking sheet. Cream the butter and add enough sifted confectioners' sugar to make a stiff frosting. Make a little hollow in the underside of the meringue caps and put a bit of the frosting in each. Insert the pointed ends of the stems into the frosting.

For assembling: Unroll the cake and place the roll of chilled chestnut filling on it. Roll it up. Place the cake on a long wooden board or serving platter, seam side down. Spread the Chocolate Butter Cream all over the cake, marking it to resemble the bark on a tree. Pat chopped pistachios into the ends. Place the meringue mushrooms here and there on and around the log. Sift confectioners' sugar over the log and meringue mushrooms to resemble freshly fallen snow.

Makes about 16 servings.

BOMBE ROTHSCHILD

1 recipe MERINGUE SHELLS
  mixture
1 quart VANILLA ICE CREAM
  (homemade or bought)
½ cup preserved or candied
  assorted fruits
2 tablespoons orange liqueur

1 pint CHOCOLATE ICE CREAM
  (homemade or bought)
1 cup heavy cream
2 teaspoons orange liqueur
Crystallized flowers
CHOCOLATE SAUCE

Before making, please read the general directions for THE VERSATILE BOMBE. Make this meringue mixture, shaping half the meringues in finger-shaped pieces, and the remaining half in small mounds. Bake as directed, and cool.

Soften the vanilla ice cream and, with it, line a 1½-quart mold, leaving the center hollow. Freeze until firm. Meanwhile, combine the preserved or candied assorted fruits with 2 tablespoons orange liqueur and allow to stand. When the vanilla ice cream is firm, soften the chocolate ice cream and quickly mix in the fruits and liqueur. Fill the mold with the mixture and cover with a lid or aluminum foil. Freeze until very firm. Dip the mold into hot water, dry, and unmold onto a serving plate. Arrange a row of round meringues around the bottom of the mold. Then arrange the finger-shaped meringues in a column above them. Decorate the top of the mold with the remaining round meringues. Freeze until serving time.

To serve, whip the heavy cream until stiff. Add 2 teaspoons orange liqueur. Pipe through a pastry bag fitted with a fluted tip to cover spaces where the ice cream shows through and to create an attractive design wherever needed. Decorate with crystallized flowers. Cut into wedge shapes and serve with Chocolate Sauce, either heated or cold.

Makes 8 to 10 servings.

PEARS SCHOUVALOFF

1 eight-inch-diameter baked BASIC SPONGE CAKE	Pinch of salt ¼ teaspoon cream of tartar
Apricot jam	6 tablespoons sugar
8 to 12 canned or poached pear halves, drained	½ teaspoon vanilla extract Currant jelly
3 egg whites	

Preheat the oven at 275°. Place the baked and cooled sponge layer on a baking sheet. Spread it thickly with apricot jam. Arrange the pear halves over the apricot jam, with the narrow ends pointing toward the center. Beat the egg whites until foamy. Add the salt and cream of tartar, and continue beating until soft peaks form. Add the sugar, 1 tablespoonful at a time, and continue beating until the mixture is thick and glossy. Beat in the vanilla extract. Spread two-thirds of the mixture over the top and sides of the cake. Put the balance in a pastry bag fitted with a large star tip, and pipe across the top in a latticework pattern. Bake for 20 to 25 minutes until the meringue is lightly colored. Remove from the oven and cool.

To serve, transfer to a serving plate. Place a tiny bit of apricot jam in every other square formed by the latticework design, and place a tiny bit of currant jelly in the remaining squares, forming an alternating pattern of color.

Makes 6 servings.

CHAPTER 23

Coffee-Time Treats

Now for the muffin and toast,
Now for the gay Sally Lunn!
—*Sir William Gilbert*, The Sorcerer

There are a number of theories on how the Kugelhopf, king of all sweet yeast cakes, came to be. Some give credit to Carême, the famous nineteenth-century French chef, not so much for its creation, since the recipe was said to have been handed to Carême, as for his making it the well-known baking masterpiece that it is. Other people say that trend-setting Marie Antoinette brought the Kugelhopf into popularity, along with other dessert treats made from risen dough, and still others say it was conceived in Vienna where it was a coffeehouse favorite. Another theory is that the Kugelhopf was first made in Poland by King Stanislaus some two hundred years before its appearance in Paris.

That the Kugelhopf rates all this theorizing becomes evident with its first sampling. Perhaps too grand to be classed as a coffee-time cake, it is nevertheless a comparatively plain yet completely sophisticated member of the cake family, equally at home at the most elegant table and the coziest kaffeeklatsch. It is the precursor of the other famous yeast cakes—namely, the savarin and the babas—which are variations on the original theme, and is probably also the inspiration for most all of the other yeast coffee cakes we like so well.

Scones, which are sweet, biscuitlike cakes made without yeast, were widely eaten at teatime in Victorian days, and are just as nice for that occasion today. Recipes for Scones, quick-as-lightning Blitzkuchen, and other quick coffee cakes are included in this chapter.

Whether you choose to make a coffee cake with or without yeast, any one of these cakes is a truly versatile dessert that can be served at any hour and for any occasion, beginning with breakfast and going straight through after-theater gatherings and midnight snacks.

In addition to the recipes in this chapter, other coffeetime treats in this book are:

Scottish Shortbread
Swedish Pancakes with Lingonberries

YOGURT COFFEE CAKE

1½ cups whole wheat flour
½ teaspoon baking soda
1 teaspoon cream of tartar
½ teaspoon salt
2 eggs, beaten
¼ cup melted butter, cooled
½ cup plain yogurt

⅓ cup turbinado sugar
¼ cup chopped walnuts
¼ cup sultanas or light raisins
2 tablespoons turbinado sugar
1 tablespoon wheat germ
¼ teaspoon cinnamon
2 tablespoons melted butter

Preheat the oven at 425°. Sift the flour, baking soda, cream of tartar, and salt into a bowl. Add the beaten eggs, ¼ cup melted butter, and the yogurt, and mix lightly. Add ⅓ cup turbinado sugar, the walnuts, and the raisins, and mix lightly. Turn into a greased round 9-inch baking pan. Sprinkle 2 tablespoons turbinado sugar, the wheat germ, and the cinnamon over the top. Drizzle 2 tablespoons melted butter over the top. Bake for 20 minutes, or until a cake tester inserted in the center comes out clean. Serve while warm if possible.

Makes 6 servings.

FUNNY CAKE

It's a Funny Cake because it's partly a pie and partly a cake, and the chocolate mixture poured over it forms a crust as well as mixing in with the cake part.

For the sauce:
1 square baking chocolate
½ cup water
⅔ cup sugar
¼ cup butter
1 teaspoon vanilla extract

For the pie:
1 nine-inch unbaked pie shell, made with OLD-FASHIONED PASTRY
1½ cups flour

1 teaspoon baking powder
½ teaspoon salt
¾ cup sugar
¼ cup lard or vegetable shortening
½ cup milk
1 teaspoon vanilla extract
1 egg
⅓ cup chopped walnuts or pecans

For the sauce: Melt the chocolate in the water in a saucepan over low heat, stirring. Add the sugar, stirring constantly, and bring to a boil. Remove from the heat, and add the butter and vanilla extract. Set aside.

For the pie: Preheat the oven at 350°. Sift the flour, baking powder, salt, and sugar together into a bowl. Add the lard or vegetable shortening, milk, and vanilla extract, and mix until all the flour is dampened. Beat well, preferably with an electric beater. Add the egg and beat again. Pour into a pastry-lined pie pan. Pour the chocolate sauce very gently over the top. Sprinkle with the chopped nuts. Bake for 45 minutes, or until a cake tester inserted in the center comes out clean. Serve warm.
Makes 5 or 6 servings.

SCONES

2 cups flour
¼ cup butter, cut into small pieces
1 teaspoon salt
2 tablespoons sugar

5 teaspoons baking powder
2 eggs
⅓ cup milk
¼ cup currants (optional)

Preheat the oven at 350°. Place the flour in a bowl and add the butter, cut up into small pieces. With the fingers, work in the butter until the mixture is crumbly. Add the salt, sugar, baking powder, eggs, and milk, and mix well. Add the currants if desired. Turn the dough out onto a floured board and roll it out ¾-inch thick. With a biscuit cutter or round cookie cutter, cut circles about 2½ inches in diameter. Arrange them on a greased baking sheet and bake for 12 to 15 minutes. Serve hot, split and buttered, or with heavy cream whipped until almost like butter.

Makes about 1½ dozen.

POPPY-SEED HORSESHOE

Poppy-Seed Horseshoe, which can also be shaped into a straight roll instead of a curved one if you prefer, is often made by Czechoslovakians, who call it koláče, *for holidays and special occasions. It can also be made with equally delicious prune or walnut filling.*

For the dough:
2 cups milk
½ cup butter
1 package active dry yeast
1 cup warm water (110° to 115°)
¾ cup sugar
9 cups flour
2 teaspoons salt

1 egg plus 2 egg yolks
Beaten egg for brushing over
  pastry

For the filling:
½ pound ground poppy seeds
¾ cup milk
½ cup sugar
3 tablespoons honey

For the dough: Heat the milk and butter in a saucepan until the butter has melted. Cool to lukewarm. In a large, warmed bowl, dissolve the yeast in the warm water with 1 teaspoon of the sugar. Allow to stand in a warm place for about 5 minutes until the mixture begins to foam. Stir in the milk-and-butter mixture. Sift the balance of the sugar, the flour, and the salt together and add, mixing well. Beat the egg and egg yolks lightly and add to the dough, mixing well. Place in a greased bowl, cover with plastic wrap, and set in a warm place to rise for 2 hours.

For the filling: Prepare the filling while the dough is rising. Combine the poppy seeds, milk, and sugar in a saucepan. Cook over low heat for 15 minutes, stirring constantly. Remove from the heat and add the honey. Cool.

Punch down the dough. Knead it lightly. Divide it into 3 parts. Roll each part out separately on a floured board. Spread with one-third of the filling and roll up as for a jelly roll. Cover lightly and allow to rise on the board for 45 minutes. Preheat the oven at 350°. Transfer the pastry to baking sheets, and shape it into horseshoe forms. Brush all over with beaten egg. Bake for about 40 minutes, or until nicely browned.

Makes 3 horseshoes.

VARIATIONS:

Use either of the following alternate fillings:

Prune Filling

Spread the dough with 1 jar lekvar (prune butter) straight from the jar.

Nut Filling

Combine in a bowl in the following order: 1 pound walnuts (ground), ½ cup sugar, ¼ teaspoon cinnamon, 2 tablespoons flour, ¼ cup milk, and 3 tablespoons honey. Spread on the dough.

KUGELHOPF

½ cup currants	Grated zest of 1 lemon
3 tablespoons kirsch	4 cups instant or quick-mixing
1 package active dry yeast	flour
¼ cup warm water (110° to 115°)	2 eggs
½ cup plus 1 teaspoon sugar	Whole or thinly sliced blanched almonds (optional)
1½ cups milk	Sifted vanilla confectioners'
1 cup butter, cut into pieces	sugar or plain confectioners'
1 teaspoon salt	sugar

Soak the currants in the kirsch for 1 hour or longer. Dissolve the yeast in the warm water with 1 teaspoon sugar and let it stand in a warm place for about 5 minutes until it begins to foam. Meanwhile, scald the milk. Remove it from the heat and add the butter, cut into

* Vanilla confectioners' sugar is made by storing a cut piece of vanilla bean in a jar of confectioners' sugar.

pieces, stirring until the butter has melted. Add ½ cup sugar, the salt, and the grated lemon zest. Stir in the yeast mixture. Add 2 cups of instant flour and the eggs, 1 at a time. Beat by hand or with an electric beater for 5 minutes. Add the remaining cups of instant flour and combine well. Stir in the currants (which have been drained and patted dry with paper towels). Turn the mixture into a greased bowl, cover with plastic wrap, and allow to stand in a place until doubled in bulk.

Heavily butter two 8- or 8½-inch Kugelhopf molds or similar tall ring molds. If desired, sprinkle the bottoms of the molds with whole or thinly sliced blanched almonds. Punch down the dough, divide it in half, and arrange the halves evenly in the pans. Cover and allow to rise in a warm place until the dough has almost reached the tops of the pans. Meanwhile, preheat the oven at 400°. Bake for 10 to 15 minutes until the dough begins to rise and starts to brown. Reduce the oven temperature to 350°, and continue baking for about 30 minutes longer until the cakes are nicely browned and slightly shrunken from the sides of the pans.

Allow them to cool slightly in the pans, invert the pans on a wire rack and remove the cakes. When cool, sift vanilla confectioners' sugar or plain confectioners' sugar over them.

Makes 2.

POFFERTJES

This is a Dutch treat one can buy in Holland at stalls at fairs, circuses, and along the canals where skaters race in the wintertime. It's served with butter and confectioners' sugar and accompanied by steaming cups of hot chocolate. To make Poffertjes, you will need either a Dutch Poffertjes pan or a Swedish plattar pan. These are wide, flat pans with a number of round cup-shaped depressions into which the batter is poured to bake on top of the stove.

4 eggs
1 cup milk
1½ cups flour
1 teaspoon baking powder
2 tablespoons melted butter
1 teaspoon salt
3 tablespoons brandy

1 cup beer, club soda, or
   ginger ale
⅔ cup raisins and/or currants
Melted butter
Confectioners' sugar
Pats of butter

Separate the eggs and beat the yolks and whites separately. Add the milk, flour, and baking powder to the yolks. Stir in the 2 tablespoons melted butter and the salt. Add the brandy and the beer, club soda, or ginger ale. Stir in the raisins and/or currants. Fold in the beaten egg whites. Pour a little melted butter in each depression of the poffertjes pan and fill about half full with the batter. Place over medium heat and allow to bake several minutes until the edges are dry, lowering the heat if necessary. Turn each Poffertje over with an icepick or knitting needle and allow it to brown on the other side. Serve about 5 Poffertjes to each person with confectioners' sugar and pats of butter.

Makes about 3 dozen.

BEIGNET KNOTS

1½ teaspoons active dry yeast
2 tablespoons warm water
   (110° to 115°)
4 cups flour
¼ cup sugar
Pinch of salt

½ cup butter, cut into pieces
4 eggs
2 tablespoons rum
Grated zest of 2 lemons
Vegetable oil
½ cup VANILLA SUGAR

Dissolve the yeast in the warm water. Combine the flour, sugar, and salt in a bowl. Cut the butter into pieces and add to the flour mixture along with the eggs, rum, grated lemon zest, and yeast mixture. Work the mixture with the hands until all ingredients are well blended. Knead on a board until smooth. Wrap in plastic wrap and refrigerate for several hours.

Roll the dough out on a lightly floured board. With a knife or pastry wheel, cut it into strips about 8 inches long and ¾-inch wide. Form each strip into a loosely tied knot and allow to sit at room temperature for 15 to 30 minutes. Heat 2 inches of vegetable oil to 350° in a heavy, high-sided saucepan. Deep-fry the knots, several at a time, by lowering them into the oil with a wide spatula and allowing them to fry on each side for about 2 minutes. Drain on paper towels. Shake in a paper bag with vanilla sugar and serve warm or hot if possible.

Makes about 6 dozen.

BLITZKUCHEN

¼ cup butter
½ cup sugar
1 egg
Grated zest of 1 lemon
1½ cups sifted cake flour
¼ teaspoon salt
¼ teaspoon nutmeg

1½ teaspoons baking powder
½ cup milk
2 tablespoons melted butter
½ cup brown sugar
1 tablespoon flour
¼ teaspoon cinnamon
½ cup chopped pecans

Preheat the oven at 375°. Cream the butter and add the sugar gradually. Add the egg and grated lemon zest, and mix well. Sift together the cake flour, salt, nutmeg, and baking powder, and add to the butter-egg mixture alternately with the milk. Pour about two-thirds of the batter into a greased 8-inch-square baking pan. Mix together the melted butter, brown sugar, flour, cinnamon, and pecans, and sprinkle over the batter in the pan. Pour the remaining batter over the top. Bake for about 35 minutes, or until a cake tester inserted in the center comes out clean. Cool and cut into squares, or serve while still warm.

Makes 9 servings.

CAN CAKE

3 cups buttermilk biscuit mix
  (such as Bisquick)
¾ cup brown sugar, firmly
  packed
¼ cup whole wheat flour
1 egg
½ cup milk

2 teaspoons instant espresso
  coffee powder
1 cup mashed bananas (about 2
  bananas)
¾ cup chopped dates
¾ cup chopped nuts

Preheat the oven at 350°. Combine the buttermilk biscuit mix, brown sugar, and whole wheat flour in a bowl. Beat the egg and combine with the milk. Dissolve the instant espresso coffee powder in the egg mixture and add to dry ingredients along with the mashed bananas. Add the dates and nuts, and mix well. Spoon into 3 clean cans, about 3¼ inches in diameter by 4½ inches deep, which have been well buttered. Bake for about 45 minutes, or until a cake tester inserted in the center comes out clean. Remove the cakes from the cans by running a table knife around the rims. Cool on a wire rack.

To serve, slice into circles and serve plain or toasted.

Makes 3 cakes.

CARDAMOM COFFEE BRAID

1 package active dry yeast
¼ cup warm water (110° to 115°)
¾ cup plus 1 teaspoon sugar
½ cup milk
3½ to 4 cups flour
4 eggs

1 teaspoon salt
¾ teaspoon ground cardamom
¾ cup butter, well softened
Superfine sugar
Finely chopped walnuts (optional)

Dissolve the yeast in the warm water with 1 teaspoon sugar, and allow to stand in a warm place for about 5 minutes until it begins to foam. Heat the milk until lukewarm. Transfer the milk to a bowl and add 1 cup of the flour and the yeast mixture. Combine ¾ cup sugar and 3 eggs, and add to the dough, mixing well. Add the salt and ground cardamom, and mix again. Add the remaining flour and the butter gradually, and blend the dough until it is pliable and does not stick to the hands. Place the dough in a greased bowl, cover with plastic wrap, and allow to stand in a warm place until doubled in bulk.

Punch down the dough, turn it out onto a board and divide it into 2 equal parts. Cut each half into 3 equal parts. Roll each of the 6 pieces of dough into a ropelike shape about 14 inches long. Join 3 ropes at one end and braid to form a bread about 14 inches long. Pinch the ends together. Repeat with the remaining 3 rolls. Set on a greased baking sheet, cover with plastic wrap, and allow to rise until again doubled in bulk. Meanwhile, preheat the oven at 350°. Beat 1 egg and brush it over the dough. Sprinkle with superfine sugar and, if desired, finely chopped walnuts. Bake for 30 minutes. Cool on a wire rack.

Makes 2 loaves.

WHOLE WHEAT DOUGHNUTS

2 eggs
1 teaspoon salt
½ teaspoon cinnamon
¼ teaspoon nutmeg
1 cup brown sugar

1 teaspoon baking soda
⅔ cup sour cream
4 cups whole wheat flour
Vegetable oil
¾ cup superfine sugar
1½ teaspoons cinnamon

Beat the eggs lightly, and add the salt, ½ teaspoon cinnamon, nutmeg, and brown sugar, combining well. Mix the baking soda with the sour cream and add to the egg mixture. Add the whole wheat flour and mix well. Refrigerate for 30 minutes or longer.

Roll out the dough ⅓- to ½-inch thick, and cut out doughnuts with a doughnut cutter. Set the doughnuts and doughnut holes on waxed paper until all the dough has been rolled out. Let them stand for 15 minutes. Heat 2 or 3 inches of vegetable oil in a deep, heavy saucepan to 350° to 375°. Slide the doughnuts into the hot oil, 2 or 3 at a time, with a wide spatula, and fry 3½ to 4 minutes, turning the doughnuts over to brown evenly. Remove with a long, two-tined fork, and drain on paper towels. Adjust the heat to maintain an even temperature while frying the doughnuts. When all have been made, combine the superfine sugar with 1½ teaspoons cinnamon in a paper bag. Shake the doughnuts, 6 at a time, in the bag until all have been coated.

Makes about 1½ dozen.

BEEHIVE CAKE

1 package active dry yeast
¼ cup warm water (110° to
    115°)
⅓ cup sugar
6 tablespoons melted butter
½ teaspoon salt
1 cup milk, scalded and cooled
    to lukewarm

2 eggs
1 cup yellow cornmeal
3 or 3½ cups flour
Melted butter
¾ cup honey
3 tablespoons water
Candy bees or other decorative
    bees (optional)

Dissolve the yeast in the warm water with 1 teaspoon of the sugar and allow to stand in a warm place for about 5 minutes until it begins to foam. Combine the melted butter with the balance of the sugar and the salt. Add the scalded milk and eggs, and beat well. Stir in the cornmeal and the yeast mixture. Add enough of the flour to make a soft dough. Turn out on a floured board and knead until smooth, about 10 minutes. Place in a greased bowl, cover with plastic wrap, and allow to stand in a warm place until doubled in bulk, about 1 hour.

Punch down the dough and divide it into 8 pieces of graduated size. Form the pieces into rope shapes, and form the rope shapes into 8 rings ranging from 3 inches to 10 inches in diameter. Place the rings on greased baking sheets, brush with melted butter, and allow to stand in a warm place, covered, until almost doubled in bulk, about 45 minutes. Meanwhile, preheat the oven at 350°. Bake the rings for about 25 to 30 minutes, or until browned and firm. Meanwhile, heat the honey and water just to the boiling point in a saucepan. Remove from the heat and set aside. Remove the rings from the baking sheets, brush with melted butter, then with the honey mixture. Cool on wire racks.

Set the largest ring on a serving plate. Stack the other rings on it, one on top of the other, ending with the smallest at the top, to resemble a beehive in appearance. Pour the remaining honey mixture over all. If desired, decorate with candy bees or other decorative bees. Serve from the top layer down, slicing layers as necessary.

Makes about 15 servings.

CHAPTER 24

Cookies and Small Cakes

They are very good to eat with tea,
And fit for lord or clown.
—old London street cry

Cookies served along with desserts are always welcome and are almost indispensable with creams, custards, fruits, and frozen desserts.

When served as adjuncts to desserts, cookies should be dainty and delicate, unlike the heartier types such as oatmeal hermits or gingerbread men. Dessert cookies should be very special cookies—small in size, generally light in texture, yet rich and unusual in shape or flavor. Called biscuits in England and petits fours secs in France, cookies can be made days or even weeks before you want to serve them, so you can make them up to keep on hand for any occasion that arises.

Perfect for serving at teas and receptions or as light desserts, particularly at lunchtime, are small cakes. These include Madeleines, Frosted Petits Fours, and Ladyfingers, which also double as liners for molded desserts. To complete a tray of little cakes or petits fours, add a few cookies such as Almond Macaroons, Chocolate Leaves, or Cat Tongues, and for added charm include some Petits Strawberries, all in this chapter. In addition to the recipes in this chapter, another cookie recipe in this book is:

Palm Leaves

CAT TONGUES

Cat Tongues are very thin, crisp cookies shaped like little Ladyfingers or "cat tongues."

¼ cup butter
½ cup sugar
1 teaspoon vanilla extract

2 egg whites
¼ cup sifted flour

Preheat the oven at 450°. Cream the butter until fluffy. Add the sugar gradually, beating well. Add the vanilla extract. Beat in the egg whites, 1 at a time, beating well after each addition. Sift the flour over the surface of the dough, and fold it in carefully. Place the dough in a pastry bag fitted with a plain tip that will allow the dough to come out no longer than the diameter of a pencil. Pipe out strips about 3 inches long on well-buttered and floured baking sheets. Bake 4 to 5 minutes until the cookie edges have browned slightly. Remove from the cookie sheets and cool on paper towels.

Makes about 5 dozen.

TUILES

The French word tuile *means "tile," and the cookies are thought to resemble roof tiles in France.*

1 cup butter
1¾ cups sugar
5 eggs

1 teaspoon vanilla extract
2 cups sifted cake flour

Preheat the oven at 375°. Cream the butter and add the sugar gradually, creaming well after each addition. Add the eggs, 1 at a time, mixing well after each addition. Add the vanilla extract. Add the cake flour and mix well. Drop by spoonfuls well apart in mounds the size of a quarter on greased baking sheets, and bake for about 8 minutes. Do not bake too many at one time. Remove the cookies, one at a time, from the baking sheet, and mold into half circles (resembling curved roof tiles) over a rolling pin. If the cookies harden before you can shape them, put them back in the oven for a minute to soften.

Makes 5 to 6 dozen.

VARIATION:

Almond Tuiles

Scatter very thinly sliced almonds over the cookies before baking.

SAND COOKIES

A grainy, "sandy" texture gives these cookies their name. They are also called Sables *("sand" in French).*

1¼ cups sifted flour
Pinch of salt
¼ cup sugar

½ cup butter, cut into small
   pieces
1 teaspoon vanilla extract
2 egg yolks

Place the flour on a work table and make a hole in the center. Into the hole put the salt, sugar, butter (which has been cut into small pieces), vanilla extract, and egg yolks. With the fingers, work the center ingredients together as quickly as possible. Draw in the flour and mix well but quickly. Form into a ball, place in waxed paper or plastic wrap, and chill for 30 minutes.

Preheat the oven at 325°. Roll the dough out on a floured board to a thickness of about ¼ inch. Cut the cookies out with a round, scalloped cookie cutter, and bake them on a greased baking sheet for about 15 minutes. Cool on a wire rack.

Makes 2 to 3 dozen, depending on the size of the cookie cutter.

BRANDY WAFERS

1¼ cups sifted cake flour
¼ teaspoon salt
⅔ cup sugar
1 tablespoon ground ginger

½ cup molasses
½ cup butter
3 tablespoons brandy

Preheat the oven at 300°. Sift together the cake flour, salt, sugar, and ground ginger. Heat the molasses to the boiling point in a small saucepan. Remove from the heat. Add the butter and stir until it has melted. Transfer the molasses mixture to a bowl and add the sifted dry ingredients gradually, stirring constantly. Mix in the brandy. Drop by half teaspoonsful onto greased baking sheets, allowing 6 to 8 cookies per sheet. Bake 1 sheet at a time for 8 to 10 minutes. Remove from the oven and allow to cool for 1 minute. Remove the cookies with a spatula or pancake turner and immediately wrap them around the handle of a large, thick-handled wooden spoon, or any similar thick wooden handle. Slide the cookies off the handle to cool.

Makes 50 to 60.

ALMOND MACAROONS

1 cup almond paste
3 egg whites, slightly beaten
1 cup sugar

½ cup sifted flour
Pinch of salt
Sugar

Preheat the oven at 300°. Work the almond paste in a bowl until nicely softened. Add the slightly beaten egg whites and blend thoroughly. Add 1 cup sugar and blend well. Add the flour and salt and blend well. Line a baking sheet with aluminum foil. Drop the dough by teaspoonsful onto the aluminum foil, or force it through a pastry bag fitted with a plain large tip into shallow mounds about 1 inch in diameter. Sprinkle lightly with sugar and bake for about 20 minutes. Remove from the foil and cool on a wire rack.

Makes about 2½ dozen.

LACE COOKIES

½ cup butter
½ cup sugar
¾ cup ground filberts or
hazelnuts

1 tablespoon flour
2 tablespoons heavy cream
Pinch of salt

Preheat the oven at 350°. Put the butter, sugar, ground nuts, flour, heavy cream, and salt together in a saucepan, and cook over low heat, stirring, until the butter has melted. Drop by scant teaspoonsful onto ungreased baking sheets, putting 6 cookies on a sheet. Bake for 5 to 7 minutes, or until the cookies are pale brown. Remove the baking sheets from the oven and allow to stand for 1 minute until the cookies are firm. Remove from the baking sheets and cool on a wire rack.

Makes about 4 dozen.

MADELEINES

Tea and Madeleines served to Marcel Proust one day by his mother during his adult years brought back recollections of similar occasions in his childhood and a flood of memories of that era that inspired the writing of his famous cyclic novel, Remembrances of Things Past. *Try Madeleines with tea yourself for an inspired dessert or dessert accompaniment.*

1 cup sugar
2 cups sifted cake flour
4 eggs
Pinch of salt

1 teaspoon grated zest of lemon
   peel
1 cup melted butter
Confectioners' sugar

Preheat the oven at 350°. Combine the sugar, cake flour, eggs, salt, and grated lemon zest. Add the cooled melted butter and mix well. Butter and flour Madeleine tins and fill each shell two-thirds full. Bake for 15 to 20 minutes, or until a cake tester inserted through the thickest part comes out clean. Cool on a wire rack. Dust with sifted confectioners' sugar.

Makes about 2½ dozen.

RUM BALLS

1 cup crushed vanilla wafers
1 cup confectioners' sugar
1½ cups finely chopped pecans

2 tablespoons cocoa
2 tablespoons light corn syrup
¼ cup rum
Superfine sugar

Mix together the crushed vanilla wafers, confectioners' sugar, finely chopped pecans, cocoa, corn syrup, and rum, combining well. Form into

---

balls about 1 inch in diameter. Roll the balls in the superfine sugar. (These cookies remain unbaked.)

Makes about 3 dozen.

SPECULAAS

Speculaas *means "mirrors" and the cookies are so named because they "reflect" the designs of Speculaas molds. There are generally three or four rectangular shaped forms of windmills, animals, or human figures carved into each mold. Speculaas molds can be bought in specialty cookware shops or in stores that sell Dutch cookware or giftware. An alternate method to make the shapes is to use cookie cutters.*

¾ cup butter	1½ teaspoons nutmeg
½ cup sugar	1½ teaspoons cinnamon
½ cup dark brown sugar, firmly packed	1½ teaspoons coriander
Grated zest of 1 lemon	¾ teaspoon cloves
2¼ cups flour	¼ teaspoon white pepper
1 teaspoon baking soda	1 teaspoon salt
	1 or 2 tablespoons milk

Preheat the oven at 350°. Cream the butter. Add the sugar and dark brown sugar gradually and mix well. Add the grated lemon zest. Sift together the flour, baking soda, nutmeg, cinnamon, coriander, cloves, white pepper, and salt, and add gradually, mixing well. Add 1 or 2 tablespoons milk and knead well to form a smooth dough. Roll out by either of the following methods: (1) Roll out on a floured board ¼-inch thick and press a Speculaas mold into the dough. Cut around the forms with a sharp knife and transfer to greased baking sheets. (2) Roll out the dough about ⅛-inch thick and cut out with cookie cutters, preferably those in a rectangular shape. Place on greased baking sheets. Bake the cookies 8 to 12 minutes, depending on their thickness.

Makes about 3 dozen.

VARIATION:

Almond Speculaas

Scatter thinly sliced almonds over the cookies before baking.

CHINESE ALMOND COOKIES

For a pleasing ending to an Oriental dinner, serve CHINESE ALMOND COOKIES *with* CHINESE GOOSEBERRY CUP *or* CHINESE TREAT.

2½ cups flour
¼ teaspoon salt
1 teaspoon baking powder
1 cup sugar
1 cup lard or vegetable
    shortening
1 egg, lightly beaten

1 teaspoon almond extract
1 tablespoon cold water
48 whole blanched almonds
    (more or less)
1 egg yolk mixed with 1
    tablespoon water

Sift together the flour, salt, baking powder, and sugar. Cut in the lard or vegetable shortening with a pastry blender. Beat the egg lightly and combine with the almond extract. Add to the flour mixture and toss together. Add the cold water and mix quickly to form a firm dough. Push into a ball, wrap in plastic wrap, and chill for 1 hour.

Preheat the oven at 350°. Shape the dough into 1-inch balls and place on greased baking sheets. Flatten the balls with the palm of the hand. Press a whole blanched almond into the center of each cookie. Brush the top of each cookie with the egg yolk–water mixture. Bake for about 12 minutes.

Makes about 4 dozen.

LADYFINGERS

3 egg yolks
½ cup sugar
1 teaspoon vanilla extract
3 egg whites
Pinch of salt

Pinch of cream of tartar
1 tablespoon sugar
⅔ cup sifted cake flour
Sifted confectioners' sugar

Preheat the oven at 300°. Beat the egg yolks until thick. Add ½ cup sugar gradually, along with the vanilla extract, and beat until the mixture is thick and pale and forms a slowly dissolving ribbon when the beater is lifted. Beat the egg whites until foamy. Add the salt and cream of

---

tartar, and continue beating until soft peaks form. Add 1 tablespoon sugar and beat until stiff peaks form. Fold the egg white mixture and sifted cake flour into the egg yolk mixture, about a third of each at a time, taking care not to overfold. Place the mixture in a pastry bag fitted with a large plain top, and pipe it in thick strips about 4 inches long onto a buttered and floured baking sheet. Sprinkle heavily with sifted confectioners' sugar. Bake for about 20 minutes. Cool on a wire rack.

Makes about 2 dozen.

SHREWSBURY CAKES

1 cup butter	**2 cups flour**
¾ cup sugar	**Pinch of salt**
1 egg	**2 tablespoons caraway seeds**

In a mixing bowl, cream the butter until soft and add the sugar gradually. Add the egg and mix well. Sift the flour with the salt and add to the butter mixture gradually, mixing well. Add the caraway seeds, cover the bowl, and chill 1 hour.

Preheat the oven at 350°. Roll the dough out thinly on a well-floured board and cut the cookie shapes with a round cookie cutter about 2 inches in diameter. Place on a greased baking sheet and bake for 3 minutes. Prick all over with the tines of a fork and bake 5 or 6 minutes longer. Cool on a wire rack.

Makes about 6 dozen.

CHOCOLATE LEAVES

4½ tablespoons butter	**6 tablespoons blanched almonds**
4½ tablespoons sugar	**1 teaspoon brandy**
1 egg	**5 ounces dark sweet chocolate**
¾ cup plus 2 tablespoons	**(such as Eagle sweet**
sifted cake flour	**chocolate), broken up**

Preheat the oven at 350°. Cream the butter and add the sugar gradually, beating well. Beat in the egg. Add the cake flour and combine well. Blend the almonds in an electric blender or food processor until they are pulverized. Add to the dough. Add the brandy and mix well. On a buttered and floured baking sheet, spread the dough through a leaf stencil* with a rubber spatula, holding the stencil down flat and making sure the entire leaf is spread to the same thickness. Repeat until the sheet has been filled. Bake for 7 to 10 minutes, or until the cookies are lightly browned at the edges. Remove them from the baking sheet immediately and cool them on a wire rack.

Melt the chocolate in the top of a double boiler over hot water, stirring. Turn all the cookies over to the wrong side and place a small spoonful of melted chocolate on each. Spread the chocolate with a knife to cover the surface evenly. With the point of a sharp knife, mark veins on the leaves. Allow to set at room temperature for several hours or overnight.

Makes about 33 four-inch leaves.

* Leaf stencils are available at specialty cookware and hardware stores.

FROSTED PETITS FOURS

1 recipe GENOISE baked in
square or rectangular pans
(cake should be ¾-inch to
1-inch high when baked)

For the filling:
1 recipe VANILLA BUTTER
CREAM FROSTING, flavored
with vanilla, almond, or other
extract, or with kirsch, coffee,
ground nuts, or other
flavoring
And/or CHOCOLATE BUTTER
CREAM FROSTING
And/or apricot jam, seedless
raspberry jam, or other flavor
jam or marmalade

For the frosting:
2¾ cups sugar
¼ teaspoon cream of tartar

Pinch of salt
1½ cups water
4 to 6 cups sifted confectioners'
sugar
½ teaspoon almond or vanilla
extract or 1 tablespoon rum
Pure vegetable food coloring
(optional)

For the decorative frosting:
1 egg white
2 or more cups sifted
confectioners' sugar
Pure vegetable food coloring

For garnishing (optional):
Crystallized flowers, and/or bits
of candied fruits, and/or bits
of nuts, and/or tiny
chocolate drops, and so on

For the filling: Cut Génoise into squares, rectangles, triangles, circles, or other shapes about 1½ inches wide. Leave some cakes unfilled if desired, and split others in half horizontally and spread with butter cream frosting or jam as desired. Put together, sandwich fashion, and chill for 1 hour.

For the frosting: In a heavy saucepan, combine the sugar, cream of tartar, salt, and water, and cook over low heat, stirring, until the sugar has dissolved. Raise the heat, cover, and cook over medium heat until the soft-ball stage is reached, about 238°, testing the temperature every minute or two. Remove from the heat, uncover, and cool to 110°, or until you can place your hand comfortably on the pan bottom. Gradually beat enough sifted confectioners' sugar in to have a mixture fairly heavy but still thin enough to pour. Stir in the almond or vanilla extract or rum. If desired, tint portions of the frosting with 1 or 2 drops of food coloring in separate bowls.

Place the petits fours on a wire rack set over a plate or platter, and pour the frosting over the cakes, allowing it to cover the tops and sides completely. Scoop up the frosting from the plate and replace it in the pan to use again. If the frosting becomes too thick, add a little hot water, or place the pan over hot water while working with it. If it is too thin, add more sifted confectioners' sugar until it is the proper consistency. Let the cakes dry on a wire rack for 1 hour or longer until completely dry.

For the decorative frosting: Beat enough sifted confectioners' sugar into the egg white, using an electric beater, to make a stiff frosting. Divide it into small bowls or cups and color with food coloring as desired. Pipe onto the dried petits fours, forming various designs, flowers, leaves, and so on. If desired, top with any of the suggested garnishings.

Makes about 6 dozen.

DELICES WITH JAM

½ cup buter
½ cup ground almonds
⅓ cup sugar

1 cup flour, sifted
Strawberry or apricot jam

Cream the butter until soft. Add the ground almonds and mix well. Add the sugar and mix well. Add the flour and mix well. Cover and chill for 30 minutes or longer.

Preheat the oven at 350°. Roll out the dough about ⅛ inch thick on a floured board, and cut out the cookies with a round, scalloped cookie cutter about 1½ to 2 inches in diameter. Cut a small hole out of the centers of half the cookies, using a tiny round truffle cutter, thimble, or other small, round object. Bake the cookies on a greased baking sheet for about 7 minutes, or until they are very lightly browned. Cool on a wire rack.

Spread the solid cookies on the wrong side (the side that touched the baking sheet) with jam, and cover with the cookies with the holes on top, right side up, sandwich fashion.

Makes about 2½ dozen.

PETITS STRAWBERRIES

¼ cup butter
1 cup sifted confectioners'
  sugar
1 teaspoon cream
1 or 2 drops green pure
  vegetable food coloring
½ pound pitted, chopped dates
1 cup flaked coconut

½ cup sugar
¼ cup butter
1 egg, slightly beaten
1 cup finely chopped walnuts
½ cup crisp rice cereal
Grated zest of 1 lemon
1 teaspoon vanilla extract
Red granulated sugar

Cream ¼ cup butter until soft. Add the confectioners' sugar gradually, mixing well. Combine the cream and food coloring, and add to the butter-sugar mixture, mixing well. Place in a cake decorator fitted with a broad tip for forming leaves. Set aside.

Combine the dates, coconut, ½ cup sugar, ¼ cup butter, and slightly beaten egg in a saucepan, and cook over moderate heat, stirring, until the mixture bubbles. Remove from the heat and cool for 10 to 15 minutes. Add the walnuts, rice cereal, grated lemon zest, and vanilla extract, and blend well. With the fingers form the mixture into shapes like strawberries and roll them in the red granulated sugar. With the cake decorator, pipe on green icing to form hulls on the wide end of each "berry."

Makes about 4 dozen.

Cookies and Small Cakes

PETITS CORNETS

2 egg whites
Pinch of salt
¼ cup sugar
½ teaspoon vanilla extract
3 tablespoons flour
2 tablespoons finely ground
  almonds

3½ tablespoons (or more)
  melted and cooled butter*
Sweet, semisweet, or bittersweet
  chocolate (optional)

Preheat the oven at 425°. Beat the egg whites with the salt until stiff. Gradually add the sugar and beat well. Add the vanilla extract. Sift the flour over the egg white mixture and sprinkle the ground almonds over the flour. Fold the flour and almonds into the egg white mixture until well blended. Fold in the melted butter. Drop the mixture by heaping teaspoonful onto a buttered and floured baking sheet.* (Do not bake more than 6 cookies at a time.) With the back of a teaspoon, spread the cookies out as thinly as possible on the baking sheet before putting it into the oven. Bake for about 4 minutes, or until the cookies are lightly browned around the edges. Remove the baking sheet from the oven and remove the cookies from the baking sheet, 1 at a time, shaping each one into a cone or cornucopia shape before proceeding with the next cookie. Place on a wire rack, seam side down, to cool. If desired, melt the chocolate and dip the broad end of the cooled cookies into the chocolate. Allow to harden before serving or storing.

Makes 1½ to 2 dozen.

* It's best to bake a test cookie before proceeding with the rest of the baking. If the test cookie breaks when you try to form it into a cone, add a little more melted butter to the dough.

CHAPTER 25

Dessert Wines

There, with the wine before you,
you will tell of many things.
—*Ovid, from the Latin*

PART I: WINES WITH DESSERT

SAUTERNES

Sauternes is probably the most versatile, and at the same time one of the most magnificent, of dessert wines. It shares, with Hungary's Tokay and Germany's *Auslese, Beerenauslese,* and *Trockenbeerenauslese,* the similar and distinct features that make these sweet white wines the most outstanding in the world. Although wines can be made sweet by adding sugar, the best sweet wines are those whose sugar content has become concentrated in a natural way and whose fermentation has been halted before all the sugar has been converted into alcohol. All the wines mentioned above are made from late-picked, overripe, and sometimes dried grapes which have been attacked by a mold that penetrates the grape skins and draws off water, leaving behind a juice high in natural sugars. This action is called *la pourriture noble,* or "noble rot," in France, and the resultant wines are extremely smooth and sweet, sometimes almost unctuous in texture, high in alcoholic content, and consequently distinctly dessert wines. Sauternes are richly sweet in flavor and lightly golden in color, turning to ever-deepening mellow amber as they age.

Sauternes is made from a blend of Sémillon and Sauvignon Blanc grapes, the former having sweetness but lacking the liveliness, acidity, and fruit contributed by the latter. The wine comes from the Sauternes district, within the Bordeaux region of France, made up of the five communes of Sauternes, Barsac, Bommes, Preignac, and Fargues. Among these, Barsac alone is allowed to show its name separately on the label, as well as the name Sauternes, and it differs slightly from the other Sauternes in that it is more delicate and less luscious than other Sauternes, possibly because the soil of Barsac tends to be chalkier and the land less hilly than the rest of the Sauternes area. Sauternes comes from nowhere in the world but the Sauternes area of France, although you will find wines that call themselves sauternes or sauterne, but that in no way resemble and should not be confused with true Sauternes. California sauterne (always spelled without the final *s*), for example, is a medium-dry table wine that would be disastrous served as a dessert wine.

Any dry wine, in fact, is out of place at the end of a meal, since it tends to taste sour when served with sweet foods. Regardless of the course in question, wine should complement the food with which it is served, and each should accentuate the qualities of the other. Thus, wine should be sweet at dessert when the food is also sweet, and since dessert is eaten not to satisfy hunger but as a sweet finishing touch to satisfy the palate, the wine served with it should have character. Consider it a luxury if you like, for it probably is, but do buy a good wine to accompany your dessert.

While the most renowned of all Sauternes, and the only *Premier* GRAND CRU ("first great growth"), Château d'Yquem is unfortunately priced out of reach for most of us, with a truly great old bottle selling for perhaps seventy-five dollars, there are, happily, eleven other *premiers crus* ("first growths"), many of which are within the range of the affordable. A few of these that you might look for are Château Rieussec, Château Sudiuraut, Château LaTour Blanche, Château Rayne- Vigneau, and Château Coutet (Barsac) and Château Climens (Barsac), where good bottles can be found within the five- to seven-dollar range. *Seconds Crus* ("second growths") and many "minor growths" are priced lower and can be excellent choices.

Since Sauternes should be served in small quantities because of its richness, and sipped and savored thoughtfully with the dessert that it complements, one glass is all that would ordinarily be served. Considering this, one bottle is enough to serve eight persons, and a half bottle sufficient for four. Don't open a full-size bottle for two to four persons, since for a number of reasons, like any good wine, Sauternes really should be drunk the day it's opened. Some of these reasons are that exposure to air may introduce improper and unwanted bacteria, fermentation may begin again and spoil the wine, and if the wine is at maturity, it will lose life, or if past maturity, it may lose its taste altogether.

All dessert wines, including Sauternes, should be chilled, but not over-chilled, at an ideal temperature 55°F. or slightly below. The best way to achieve this temperature is to refrigerate the bottle for an hour to an hour and a half before serving it. If it is refrigerated, say, overnight or even longer, allow it to stand at room temperature for fifteen to forty-five minutes before serving, the time depending on how long it has been refrigerated and the temperature of the room in which you place it.

Sauternes goes beautifully with a wide variety of desserts, including custards, creams, soufflés, mousses, pastries, meringues, rice desserts, cheese desserts, desserts containing almonds or other nuts, cakes, small cakes and cookies, fruit desserts, and fresh fruit. Some specific desserts from this book that would make admirable companions to Sauternes are Apple Charlotte, Meringue Butter Cream Cake, Blueberries Limousin, Cream Cheese Tarts, Thousand Leaves Cake, Vanilla Pots de Crème, Pound Cake Pudding, Peaches Cardinal, Amaretti Omelet, Quick-as-a-Wink Strawberry Soufflé, Hazelnut Cream Cake, Figs with Raspberry Cream, Crêpes Melba, Portuguese Egg Yolk Cream Tarts, Apricots Condé, and Bread and Butter Pudding.

There are, understandably, some desserts that do not go well with Sauternes either because they are too cold and deaden the taste buds or because their flavors are tangy or otherwise too pronounced and would probably make both themselves and the wine taste unpleasant. For this reason, if you're serving Sauternes, avoid serving desserts containing discernible spice flavors; fresh citrus fruits; cranberry or rhubarb desserts; maple- or mint-flavored desserts; fritters or fried pastries; ice cream and frozen desserts; desserts containing more than a token amount of rum, brandy, or fortified wine; desserts flavored by most liqueurs; and desserts based completely on wine, such as Strawberries in Beaujolais.

These do's and don't's can really be applied not only to Sauternes but to all the dessert wines discussed below, with exceptions as noted along the way. While a mildly flavored chocolate dessert would not be amiss with a dessert wine, it probably would be best to avoid a heavily chocolated dessert such as chocolate cake with chocolate frosting or a chocolate dessert with chocolate sauce, which would tend to put off the taste of the wine. Liquid desserts, such as fruit soups, would not greatly benefit from being served with wine from the standpoint of similarity of texture, and drink-desserts, such as Irish Coffee, would obviously always be served alone.

OTHER FRENCH DESSERT WINES

While they are not, strictly speaking, dessert wines, there are a few other wines from France that can properly be served with desserts.

Choosing them involves some amount of risk or experimentation, but for those who want to deviate from the safe course of Sauternes, one might try:

Vouvray. Most of the Vouvrays available in the United States are lightly sweet wines, and some, produced in years when the sun has been especially strong or the harvesting late, fall in the category of dessert wines with longer lives than those of other Vouvrays. Since prices are modest and the odds are strongly in favor of your getting a sweet wine, it would be interesting to try your luck, taking the precaution of sampling the wine yourself at dessert time before serving it to company, or buying two bottles and having one first at a family gathering where mistakes are not embarrassing.

Vin de Paille. The name translates to "straw wine," apparently for two reasons. This sweet wine is not only straw-colored, but the grapes used in making it, at least before more efficient means were devised, were dried on straw mats before being pressed. Vin de Paille comes from the Jura region of France, and "straw wines" are also made in other countries, such as Italy and Germany, the latter calling its version Strohwein.

Cadillac. This is a sweet wine from the town of the same name in the Premières Côtes de Bordeaux district and, while not the Cadillac of dessert wines, is a nice, acceptable one whose purchase will put no strain on your wallet.

CHAMPAGNE

Champagne is certainly the most festive of wines and a gala accompaniment to dessert at special dinners. While one usually thinks of champagne as flowing freely and endlessly at parties and the like, it isn't the case when it is served with dessert. The budget is spared, for one bottle of champagne does nicely for eight people, since a glass per person is sufficient with a course as specialized as dessert. Another difference in serving champagne with dessert, as opposed to other times, is that one wants to serve a sweet champagne rather than a dry one. Although the sweetest, *doux*, is not available in this country, *demi-sec* (which means "semidry" or "semisweet," depending on how you look at it) is the next sweetest and can be bought or ordered from certain wine dealers. Failing this, buy *sec*, but never *extra sec* or *brut*, lest you spoil your dessert course with their out-of-place dryness.

The champagne referred to here is all from France, where the only true Champagne is made. Domestic "champagne" is simply a sparkling white wine, and while some of it is acceptable and some isn't, it is nevertheless a different wine from Champagne. An alternative to sweet

French champagne worth noting is Italy's Asti Spumante, a white sparkling wine, which, depending on the brand, can be slightly sweet to very sweet, and is good with desserts and fruit. Champagne can be served with any of the dessert types mentioned above under Sauternes, and would also be nice with desserts flavored by certain liqueurs such as orange, almond, raspberry, or strawberry.

TOKAY

Grapevines have been growing for so many centuries in the volcanic soil of the Tokaj-Hegyalja district in northeastern Hungary that no one is certain how long they've really grown there. But of one thing, everyone is certain. The most famous wine of Hungary, sweet Tokay (Tokaj), comes from the town of that name and ranks as one of the world's best dessert wines. Tokay Szamorodni is the most common and least expensive of the Tokays. Although in some years it tends to be dry, the Szamorodni shipped to the United States is labeled either sweet or dry, so there is no danger of ending up with the wrong kind. Sweet might also be designated as *edes* on the label, but don't buy *Edes Furmint*, which is a semidry wine not suitable for dessert.

More expensive, sweeter, richer, and a considerably better wine than Szamorodni, as well as more suitable and well-recognized as a superior dessert wine, is Tokay Aszu. Coppery-golden in color, Tokay Aszu is partially produced by the action of *la pourriture noble*, as previously discussed in regard to Sauternes. The difference with Tokay Aszu is that certain fixed proportions of honey-sweet juices from overripe dried grapes are added to casks of juices from normally ripened grapes, making a blend from the two sources. The number of containers of dried grapes added to a cask are represented by the word *puttonyos* or *puttonos*, with a number before it, and if you look at a bottle of Tokay Aszu, you will see 3 *puttonyos*, or whatever the quantity might be, printed on the label. This figure is sometimes represented by pictures of little baskets of grapes, with 3 baskets if it contains 3 *puttonyos*, and so on. The higher the number, which is never above 5, the sweeter, finer, richer, and inevitably, more expensive the wine will be.

An interesting feature of Tokay Aszu is its bottle size. It is always found in slightly stubby bottles that contain about a half liter or perhaps a little more. It is never found in a full-sized bottle, which is probably all to the good, since there is enough in one bottle to serve six persons at dessert time, and the wine is not inexpensive. Have it with any desserts, following the suggestions outlined under Sauternes above, but do not think of substituting an American Tokay, which is made from a different grape, by a different method, bears no resemblance to true

Tokay, and is nothing more than an undistinguished sweet wine. Since the spelling on a Tokay bottle will, of course, be in Hungarian, look for it as *Tokaji Aszu,* which means "Aszu of Tokay." *Aszu,* incidentally, refers to the method of making or grading the wine and not to the name of the grapes from which it is made. It's worth noting that since Hungary's vineyards are state-controlled, with the government the sole exporter, little is known about vintages or the size of the casks to which the *puttonyos* are added, and one must therefore buy with this in mind.

GERMAN SWEET WHITE WINES

There are several categories of fine German white wines from which to choose a dessert wine. These categories, *Spätlese, Auslese, Beerenauslese,* and *Trockenbeerenauslese,* indicate that there has been some kind of special selection of grape to make up the particular wine. They are usually estate-bottled, showing the vineyard and village name on the label, but the categories do not refer to, nor is the use of them restricted to, any certain district or grape variety. The wines can be from the Rhine, Moselle, Palatinate, Franconia, or elsewhere, but what they have in common is some certain grapes selection which makes them distinguished, naturally sweet dessert wines.

Trockenbeerenauslese is the sweetest, rarest, and richest of all. It is made from grapes that have been touched by the same mould—in Germany called *Edelfäule*—which creates the finest of Sauternes, dried on the vine, and individually picked, grape by grape, to make the most luxurious of dessert wines. The combined facts that the vineyards must be gone through as many as six times to hand-select the special dried grapes at their point of perfect overripeness, that in this state of extreme raisinlike dryness each grape yields only about a drop of juice, that labor costs are what they are, and that very little of this is produced some years and none at all in other years—all make the price exorbitant. A raid on all the piggy banks in the house would never raise enough to buy a bottle of this deep golden treasure, but the thought of tasting it provides a reason for dreaming of rich old uncles leaving one funds for such a purchase.

Not so expensive, but still dear, is *Beerenauslese,* made from individually selected (but not dried) overripe grapes that produce a less sweet wine with a wealth of bouquet, fruit, and flavor that would make a dessert course unforgettable.

Auslese is made from the ripest selected bunches of grapes (not individually selected grapes), some perhaps affected by the *Edelfäule.* Entirely affordable, this lovely dessert wine is full and fruity, although less sweet than *Beerenauslese.*

A rung down the ladder of sweetness is *Spätlese*, a ripe and full-bodied, superior, naturally sweet wine whose name translates to "late-picked." This means that after the main harvest is over, the grapes for *Spätlese* are gathered.

Although not in the same "family" as the above, a *Kabinett* ("cabinet"), which is a superior grade of natural German white wine, in some years has a delicate sweetness and can be used as a dessert wine. Ask your wine dealer to help you with a selection, but by all means taste the wine before you serve it for dessert. The best approach to the subject of German sweet wines, actually, is to begin with the least expensive and work your way up to the more costly and rare. The general guidelines for desserts to serve with Sauternes apply here also. Some of the less sweet German wines would be nice served with some of the less-sweet cakes in this book, such as Kugelhopf or Poppy-Seed Horseshoe.

DESSERT WINES FROM THE UNITED STATES

California produces some Late Harvest Zinfandel, which may be either sweet or dry, with a sweet one making a suitable dessert wine. A good white Catawba or a good Niagara from New York State can also find a place at the table with dessert. The adventurous may care to explore these and other possibilities for domestic wines to serve with dessert.

PART II: WINES AFTER DINNER (FORTIFIED WINES)

Dinner has ended, the coffee cups have been removed, possibly you and your guests have moved to the living room and, if the season suggests it, are relaxing before a crackling fire. What better time to bring out some heartwarming fortified wine as an after-dinner drink? Fortified wines are those to which brandy or other spirits have been added, raising the alcoholic content much above that of ordinary wines. Consequently, they should be served in small quantities and sipped in a leisurely manner. Their very nature suggests the accompaniment of a bowl of nuts, some fruit for those who would like it, and perhaps a dessert cheese or two. It is pure joy to select one of the following fortified wines to serve at such a time.

FROM PORTUGAL

Port. This is a grand old wine in terms of history, and sometimes in terms of bottle. The Portuguese were making Port much as they do today in the middle of the fifteenth century, and there are those who don't consider drinking Port unless it is of a certain vintage some fifty or more years old. Port is one of the most heavily fortified wines, with a good 20 percent of its makeup being brandy. For this reason, it benefits from being served in an ordinary tulip-shaped wineglass, where it has room to breathe, rather than in a constricting Port glass. Serve it, like all fortified wines discussed here, at room temperature.

The kind of Port you serve depends on your taste and your pocketbook, with Ruby Port being the fruitiest, youngest, and least expensive member of the family. Its color is exactly what its name implies. Tawny Port, which is perhaps the most popular, has spent more time in the oak, becoming softer and more mature, and perhaps tending toward a lighter color as it throws a sediment. There is Crusted Port, whose sediment makes a "crust" on the inner surface of the bottle, and this wine is more expensive than Tawny Port. Vintage Port is made from selected lots of wines in very good years, bottled young, and aged in the bottle for at least fifteen years. It is the most expensive of the Ports.

There are also some port-type wines made in the United States, which must by law carry the place of origin as part of their name on the label, such as California port. It would not be an easy task to find a decent bottle, however, and one would be far safer in selecting a true Port.

Madeira. Another fortified sweet wine comes from the Portuguese island of Madeira in the Atlantic. Most types of Madeira are named after the grape from which they are made, and acquire some of their flavor from being stored in special rooms at high temperatures for several months. The best-known Madeiras are Malmsey and Bual. Malmsey is a generous wine with considerable body, and ranks as the sweetest of the Madeiras. Bual, golden, full, and with a distinctive bouquet, is a little less sweet than Malmsey. People who live on Madiera serve these wines with cakes and pastries as well as with fruit, and this idea may also appeal to you. Or you may prefer it as an afternoon "tea" rather than after-dinner practice, and stick with the general rule of nuts, fruit, and cheese with fortified wines.

FROM SPAIN

Sherry. Sunny Spain's most inspired contribution to the world of wine is her incomparable Sherry. While the dry Sherries make excellent aperitifs, the sweeter ones make great dessert wines. The sweet *Olorosos* and Cream Sherries are fuller, darker, deeper, and richer than the dry types, and can be served with nuts, fruit (some people swear by the combination of Sherry with melon) and perhaps a simple cookie or biscuit. There are also those who like their Sherry with pastry. Some kinds of Sherry that you might want to look for are Harvey's Bristol Cream, Pedro Domecq's Celebration Cream, Duff Gordon's Cream Sherry, and Gonzales Byoss' Nectar. Few California producers make a Sherry by the proper, complicated, time-honored *solera* method used in Spain, but Louis M. Martini and Almadén are two that do, and you may want to taste some of their sherries. Serve your Sherry, like Port, in a small quantity in a standard wineglass. Sherry glasses aren't necessary.

Málaga. Spain also produces a sweet, dark-golden fortified wine in the Málaga district on the Mediterranean, and it is available in the United States. Serve it with the accompaniments already mentioned, but don't confuse it with California Malaga, which is made from table grapes instead of wine grapes, and bears no resemblance to true Málaga.

FROM FRANCE

Banyuls. Sometimes available in this country, Banyuls is a sweet, russet-brown fortified wine that is made from late-picked grapes gathered on the steep, sunny hillsides around Banyuls, in the southeast corner of France where the Pyrenees sweep to the sea near the Spanish border. Banyuls has been compared to a light Tawny Port and ranks as one of the best sweet fortified wines of France.

Muscat de Frontignan. Muscat de Frontignan, one of the best wines made from Muscat grapes, is a very sweet, generous wine that goes nicely with nuts and fruit, especially figs and grapes. A lesser-known wine from the same area is Muscat de Miravel. There is no connection between these wines and domestic wines made from poor-quality grapes that bear similar names, such as California muscatel, but are worlds apart in quality, flavor, and character. However, California's Beaulieu Vineyards makes a very lively light-bodied-to-medium Muscat wine that is nice and very inexpensive, and Christian Brothers produces a Château la Salle which can be used with dessert.

FROM ITALY

Marsala. Marsala is perhaps best known to Americans as one of the ingredients of Zabaglione or Veal Marsala. It is, however, Italy's most eminent dessert wine, but since it can be either sweet or dry, look at the label to be sure you get a sweet Marsala when you buy. The rich, golden-brown nutlike wine, which comes from Sicily, was developed in the eighteenth century by some English families who were looking for an alternative to Port and Sherry, which were too expensive for them.

The world today benefits from their efforts by having another distinctive fortified wine from which to choose.

Malvasia di Lipari. Malvasia di Lipari is not a fortified wine, but it is sweet, quite dark brown, and a lovely wine that is not too expensive and good with many desserts, including pastries and cakes as well as fruits. It is not readily available, but you may come upon some. It is made, incidentally, from the same grape that produces Portugal's Malmsey Madeira.

Miscellaneous. There are any number of sweet, unfortified wines from Italy that are sometimes available and of interest: Giro and Monica, both sweet red wines from Sardinia, and Nasco, a delicate, golden sweet wine from the same island; Cartizzi, a sparkling sweet wine from Liguria; Greco de Gerace, a golden sweet wine from Calabria; Pollio, a blended sweet wine from Syracuse; Zucco, a sweet white wine from Sicily; and Moscato wines from various regions.

FROM THE UNITED STATES

California's own grape, the Zinfandel, is used to make a number of wines, not the least of which is a fruity young table wine often thought of as California's answer to Beaujolais, but it is also used to make an excellent sweet dessert wine called Zinfandel Essence. (One is made by Ridge Vineyards.) Zinfandel Essence has a high alcoholic content, takes a long time to develop, and can even sometimes resemble a vintage port.

PART III: WINES WITH DESSERT CHEESES

There can be no hard-and-fast rules about which wines are correct to have with dessert cheeses, because so many factors are involved. This is a mixed blessing, because although you can't neatly categorize what goes with what to use as a guide, you can experiment to your heart's content. Some of the factors to consider are: (1) Sequence of course. You may decide to have cheese after the dessert course, in place of the dessert course, before coffee, or after coffee. (2) Personal preferences as to which types of wine go best with which cheeses. Two experts will seldom agree, so, generally speaking, the choice is yours. (3) Length of time during which you will be drinking wine during the course of the evening and the number of wines that will be served. (4) Length of time between courses.

The following are hypothetical examples of the possibilities of serving wine with dessert cheese, taking the above factors into consideration. But first, a quick summing up of the dessert cheeses discussed in Chapter 11. They include the soft-ripening cheeses like Brie and Camembert, the semisoft cheeses like Port Salut and Italian Fontina, the milder goat cheeses, the blue cheeses, and the fresh cheese like Petit Suisse and Gervais.

Any of the sweet dessert wines (not fortified wines) would be good to have with dessert cheeses if you are serving them as your final course before coffee, or if you are serving them after a dessert that did not include an accompanying wine.

If you have two or more wines throughout dinner, which is not too often the case in recent years, there should be a progression of wines from young to old, light to full, white to red, and drier to sweeter. This progression ends with the main course, so that while you will certainly have a sweet wine with dessert, if there is a proper time span to allow palates to clear, there's no reason why you couldn't serve a medium-dry wine with your cheese course.

If you served only one wine with dinner and wanted to serve the same wine with your cheese course, you could do so.

If you're going to be drinking wine after dinner with cheeses and through the evening, possibly the only rule would be that you should stay away from full-dry wines. Half-dry wines would work well at such times, and the best of the German half-dry wines would be compatible with any dessert cheese.

When you have a cheese course and wish to serve fruit, too, don't serve a dry wine, but a semisweet or sweet wine.

Cheeses served after coffee are probably best mated with Port, Sherry, or one of the other fortified wines. Certainly the classic combination of Port with Stilton can never be faulted. If you do serve this time-honored twosome, though, don't follow the offensive custom of soaking the cheese in the Port, because you'll not only destroy the flavor of the cheese but also create something very unpleasant to look at.

Cognac, like fortified wines, is appropriate to serve with cheese after dinner. And, of course, nuts can always be served along with the wine and cheese.

In summing up both this subject and the entire chapter, my final thought is that wine with food being the debatable subject that it is, you may not agree with all I've written. You may find, too, through considered tasting of dessert wines, that you'll make your own discoveries and form opinions of good wine-and-dessert combinations different from my own. This will be a step forward, since my purpose here is only to offer some guidelines with the hope you'll start on your own rewarding

---

adventure of having wines with desserts. Start on your explorations with inexpensive wines, have them as often as you can, but, most of all, enjoy yourself.

METRIC MEASURE CONVERSION TABLE
(Approximations)

When You Know (U.S.)	Multiply by	To Find (Metric)
WEIGHT		
ounces	28	grams
pounds	0.45	kilograms
VOLUME		
teaspoons	5	milliliters
tablespoons	15	milliliters
fluid ounces	30	milliliters
cups	0.24	liters
pints	0.47	liters
quarts	0.95	liters
TEMPERATURE		
degrees Fahrenheit	subtract 32° and multiply the remainder by 5/9 or .556	degrees Celsius or Centigrade

Index

Molded Purple Plums in Claret, 97
Orange Slices in Red Wine, 83
Peaches in Red Wine, 85
Pears in Port, 90
Prunes in Port with Gervais, 192
Prune Whip with Port, 140
Sherried Watermelon, 80
Strawberries Beaujolais, 104

Wines
  Dessert
    American, 359
    with cheese, suggested combinations of, 362–63
    chilling of, 355
    French, 353–56
    German Sweet White, 358, 359
    Hungarian, 357, 358
    types of desserts to serve with, 355
  Fortified
    American, 361, 362
    French, 361
    Italian, 361, 362
    Portuguese, 360
    Spanish, 360, 361

Winter Apricot Soufflé (Hot), 274
Winter Fruit Compote, 105

Yogurt Coffee Cake, 331

Zabaglione, 130
  in history, 4
  Sauce, 130

Also available from
STEIN AND DAY

The Great Year-Round Turkey Cookbook
    by Anita Borghese

The Complete Pork Cook Book
    by Louise Schoon and Corrinne Hardesty

The Complete International Salad Book
    by Kay Shaw Nelson

*The Complete International One-Dish Meal
Cookbook*
    by Kay Shaw Nelson

The International Jewish Cookbook
    by Nina Froud

The Eating Rich Cookbook
    by Leonard Louis Levinson

Food in History
    by Reay Tannahill

Ask your bookseller!